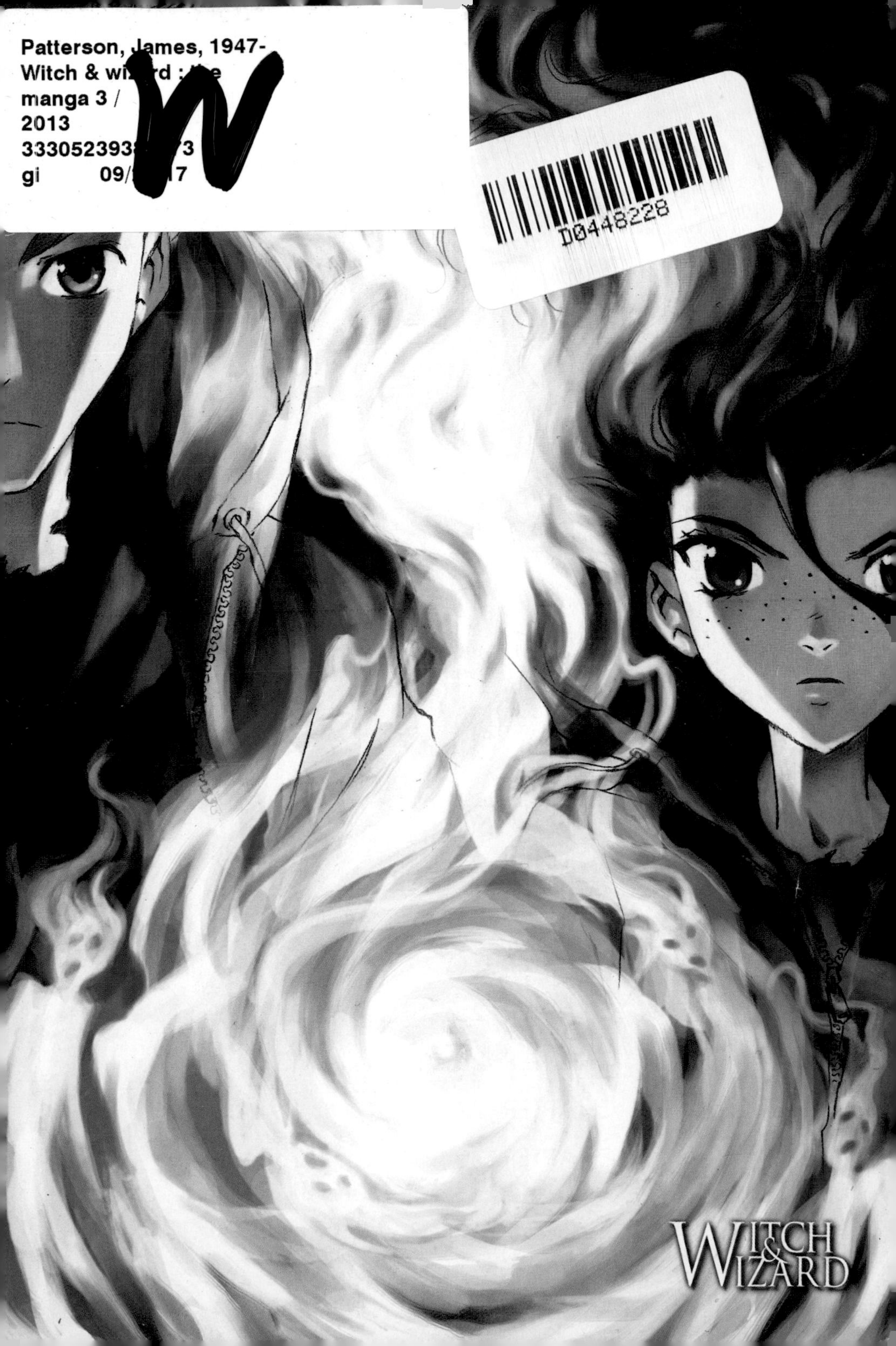
WITCH & WIZARD

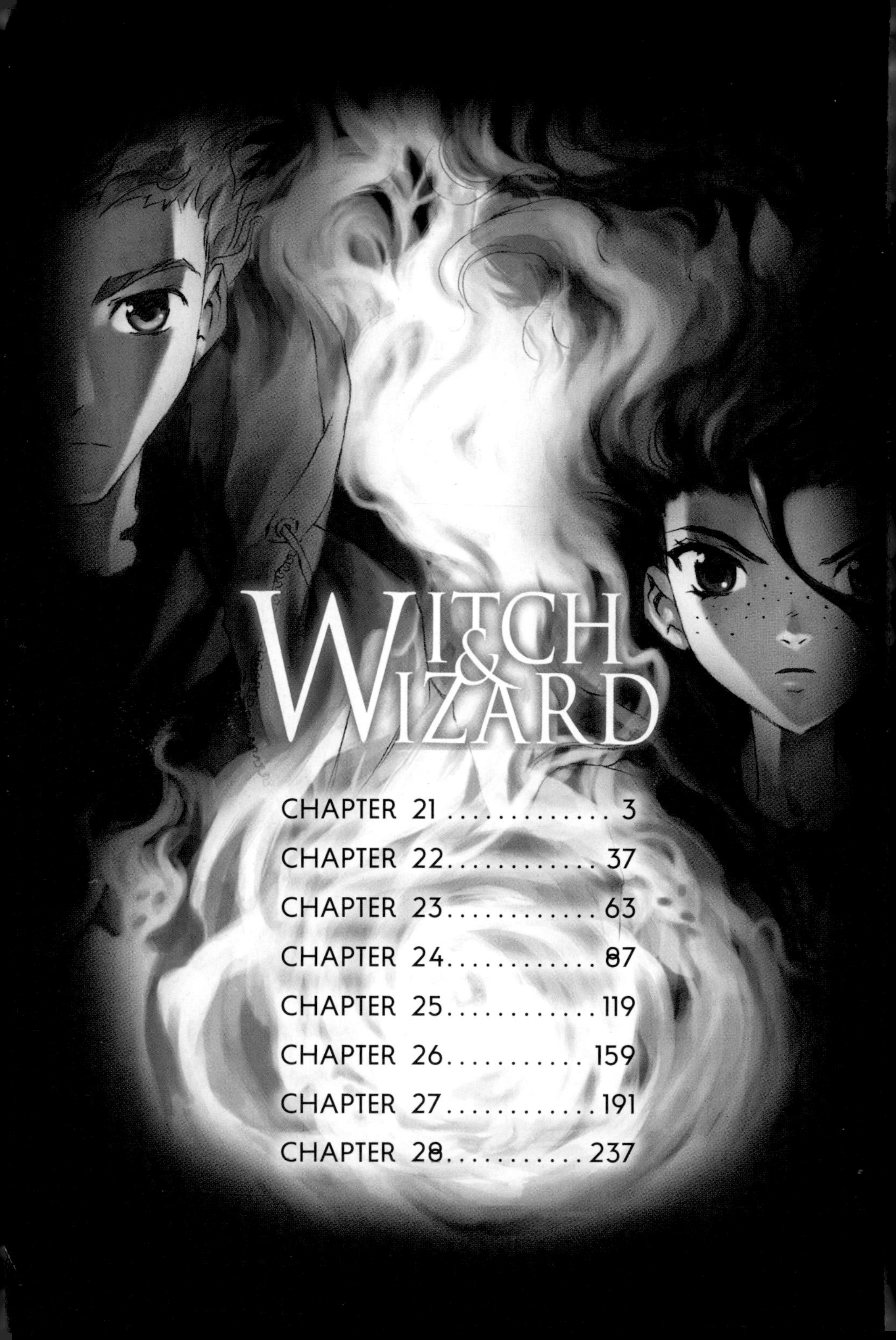

WITCH & WIZARD

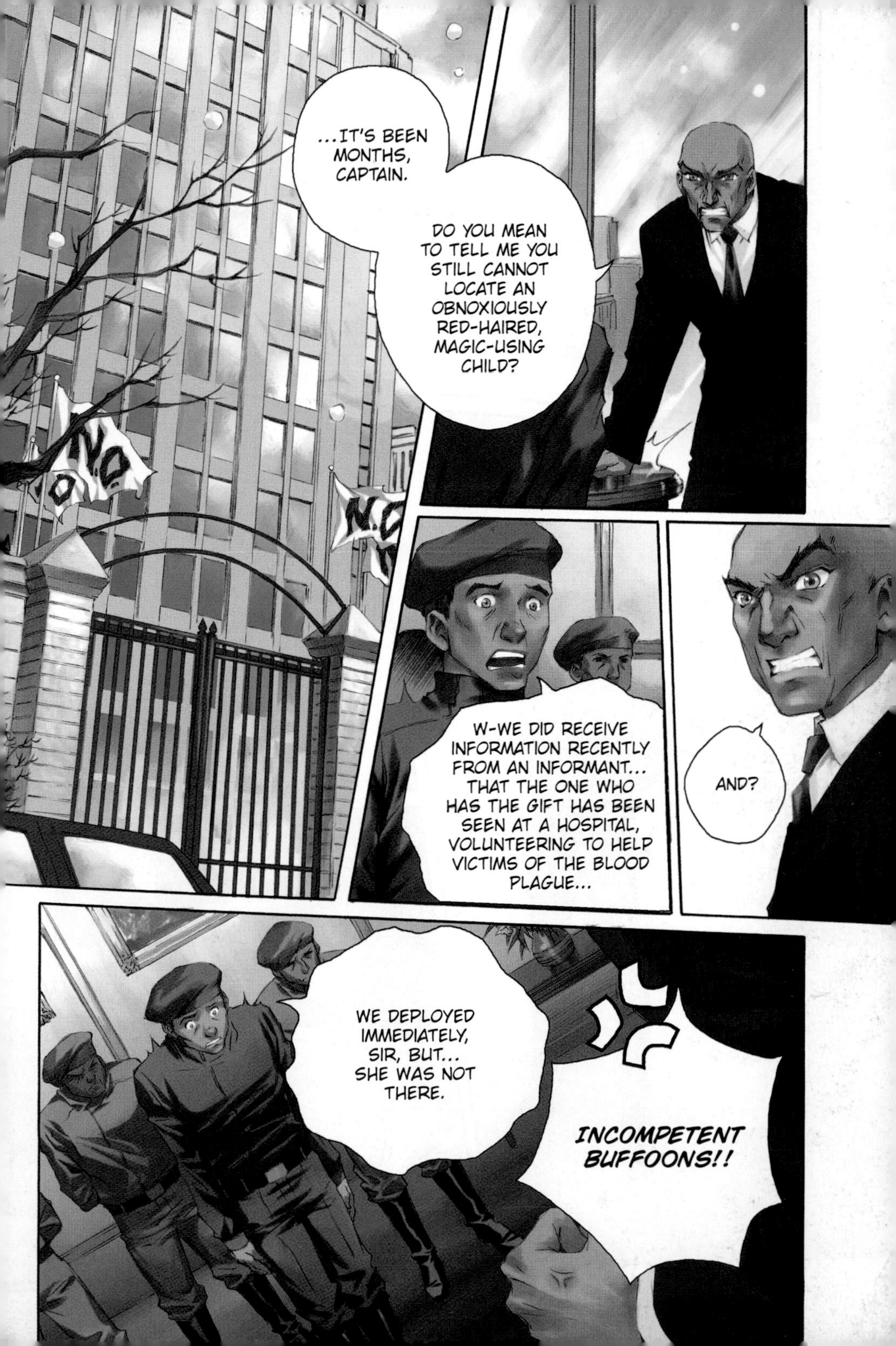
...IT'S BEEN MONTHS, CAPTAIN.
DO YOU MEAN TO TELL ME YOU STILL CANNOT LOCATE AN OBNOXIOUSLY RED-HAIRED, MAGIC-USING CHILD?
W-WE DID RECEIVE INFORMATION RECENTLY FROM AN INFORMANT... THAT THE ONE WHO HAS THE GIFT HAS BEEN SEEN AT A HOSPITAL, VOLUNTEERING TO HELP VICTIMS OF THE BLOOD PLAGUE...
AND?
WE DEPLOYED IMMEDIATELY, SIR, BUT... SHE WAS NOT THERE.
INCOMPETENT BUFFOONS!!

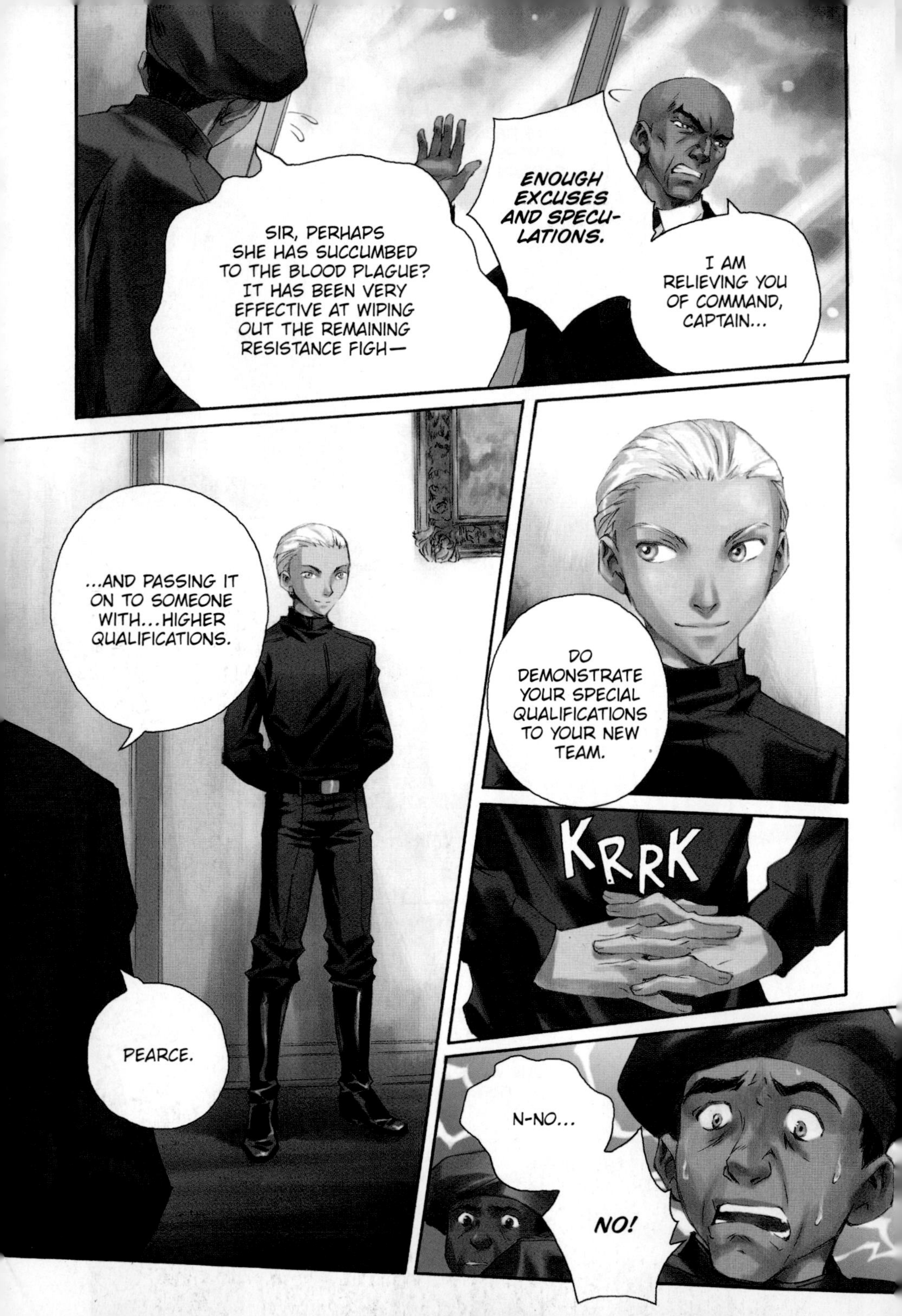
SIR, PERHAPS SHE HAS SUCCUMBED TO THE BLOOD PLAGUE? IT HAS BEEN VERY EFFECTIVE AT WIPING OUT THE REMAINING RESISTANCE FIGH—
ENOUGH EXCUSES AND SPECU-LATIONS.
I AM RELIEVING YOU OF COMMAND, CAPTAIN...
...AND PASSING IT ON TO SOMEONE WITH...HIGHER QUALIFICATIONS.
PEARCE.
DO DEMONSTRATE YOUR SPECIAL QUALIFICATIONS TO YOUR NEW TEAM.
KRRK
N-NO...
NO!

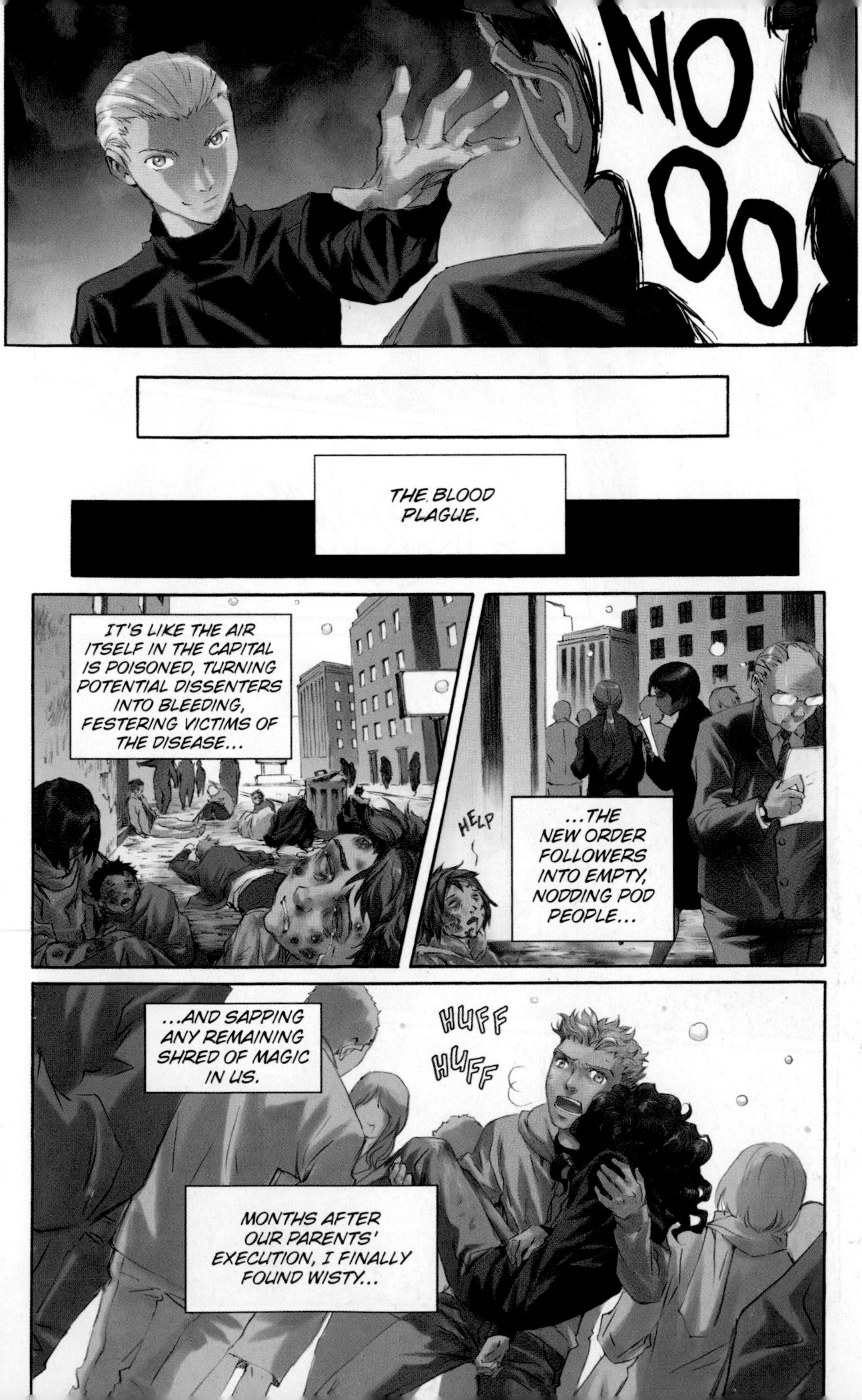
NOOOO
THE BLOOD PLAGUE.
IT'S LIKE THE AIR ITSELF IN THE CAPITAL IS POISONED, TURNING POTENTIAL DISSENTERS INTO BLEEDING, FESTERING VICTIMS OF THE DISEASE...
HELP
...THE NEW ORDER FOLLOWERS INTO EMPTY, NODDING POD PEOPLE...
...AND SAPPING ANY REMAINING SHRED OF MAGIC IN US.
HUFF
HUFF
MONTHS AFTER OUR PARENTS' EXECUTION, I FINALLY FOUND WISTY...

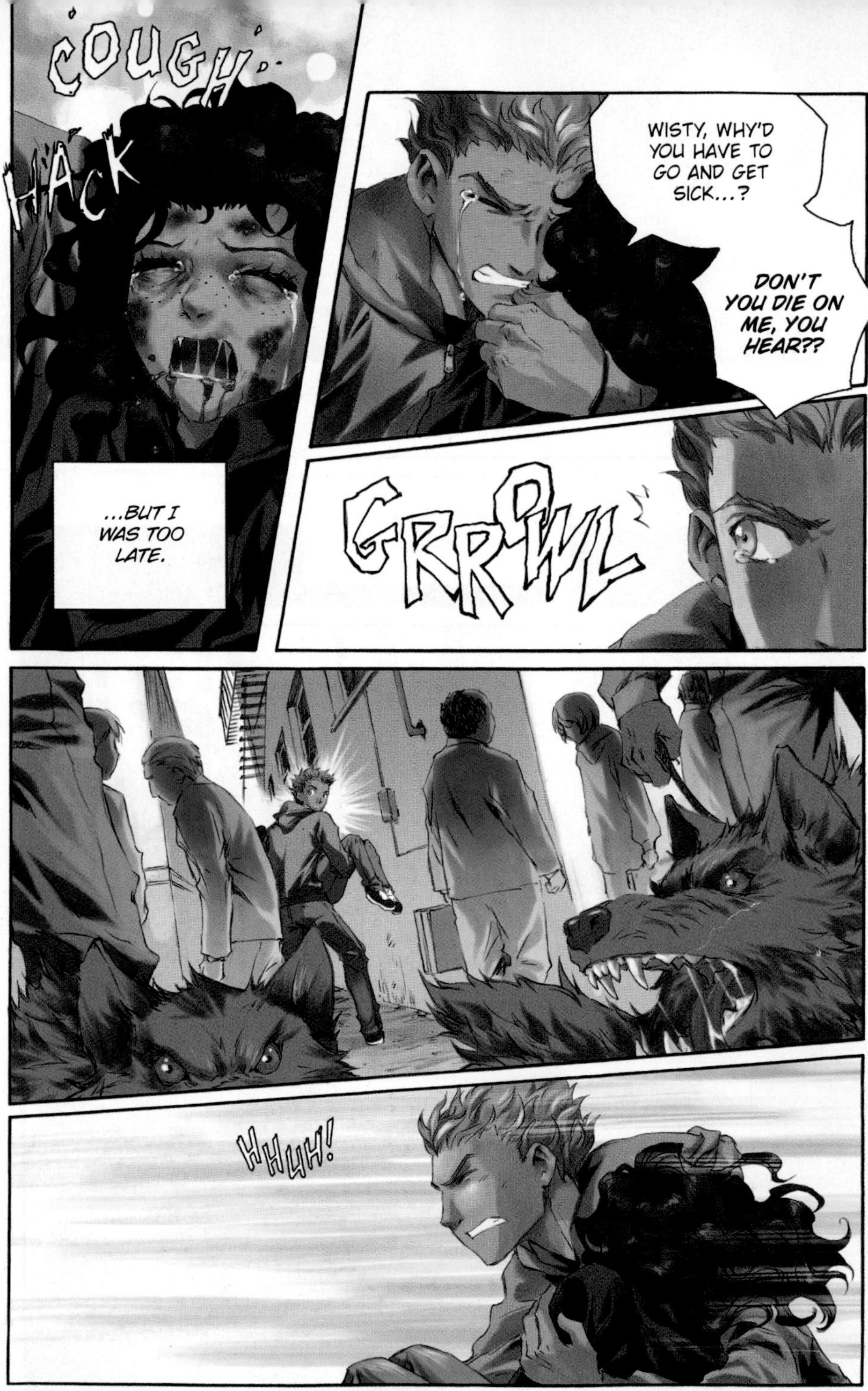
COUGH
HACK
WISTY, WHY'D YOU HAVE TO GO AND GET SICK...?
DON'T YOU DIE ON ME, YOU HEAR??
...BUT I WAS TOO LATE.
GRROWL
HHUH!

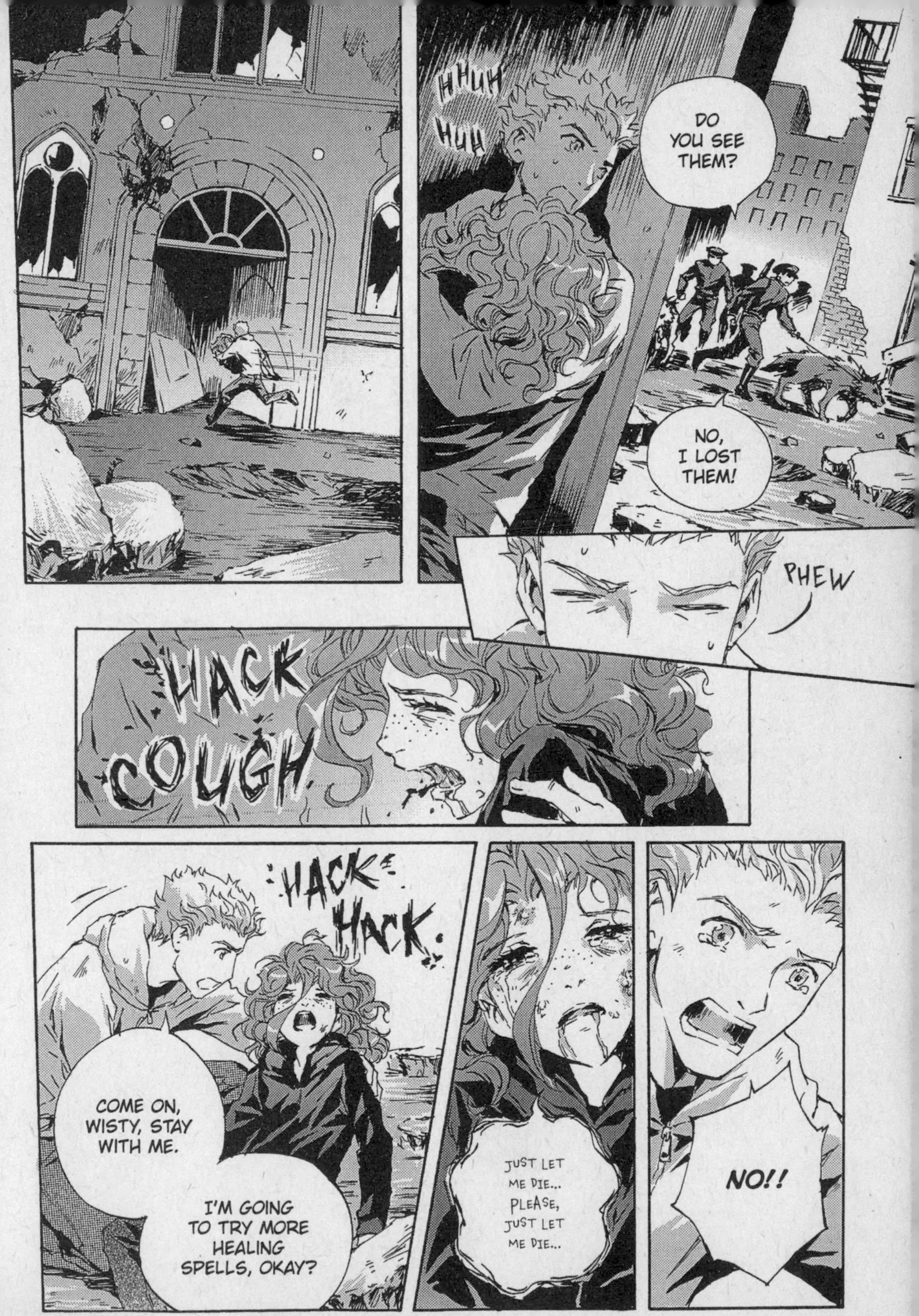
HHUH
HUH
DO YOU SEE THEM?
NO, I LOST THEM!
PHEW
HACK
COUGH
HACK
HACK
COME ON, WISTY, STAY WITH ME.
I'M GOING TO TRY MORE HEALING SPELLS, OKAY?
JUST LET ME DIE... PLEASE, JUST LET ME DIE...
NO!!

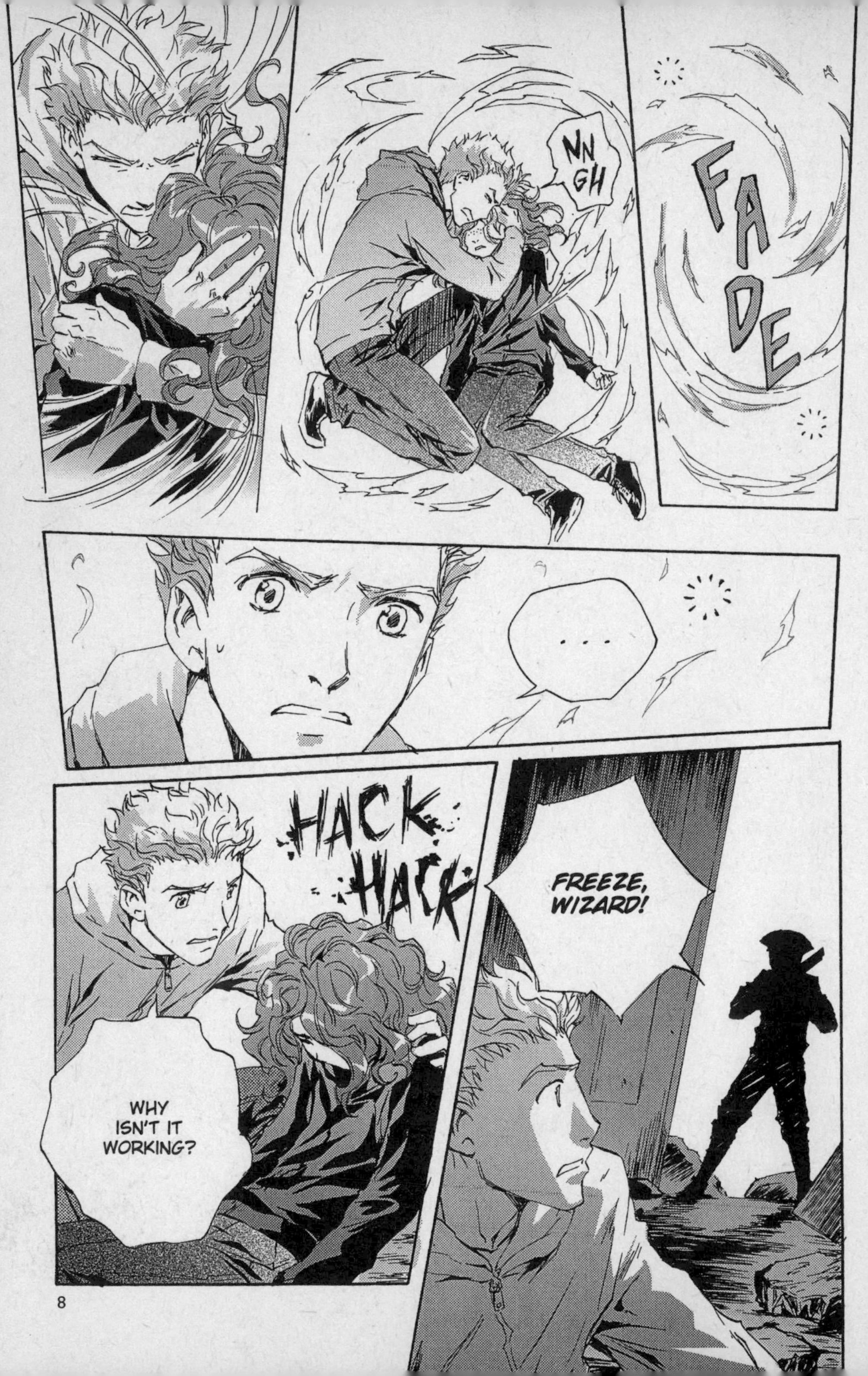
NNGH
FADE
...
HACK HACK
WHY ISN'T IT WORKING?
FREEZE, WIZARD!

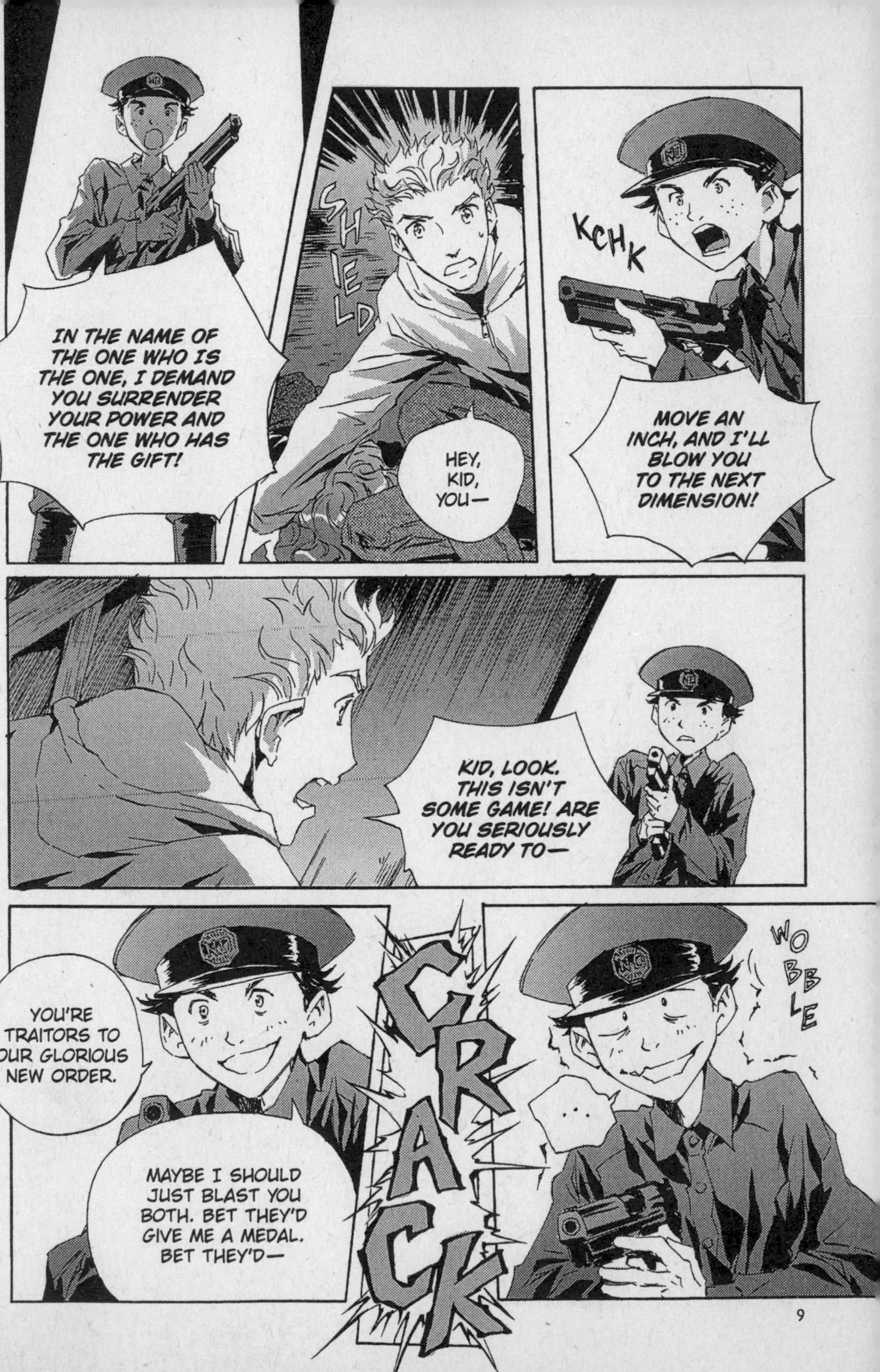
IN THE NAME OF THE ONE WHO IS THE ONE, I DEMAND YOU SURRENDER YOUR POWER AND THE ONE WHO HAS THE GIFT!
SHIELD
HEY, KID, YOU—
KCHK
MOVE AN INCH, AND I'LL BLOW YOU TO THE NEXT DIMENSION!
KID, LOOK. THIS ISN'T SOME GAME! ARE YOU SERIOUSLY READY TO—
YOU'RE TRAITORS TO OUR GLORIOUS NEW ORDER.
MAYBE I SHOULD JUST BLAST YOU BOTH. BET THEY'D GIVE ME A MEDAL. BET THEY'D—
CRACK
...
WOBBLE

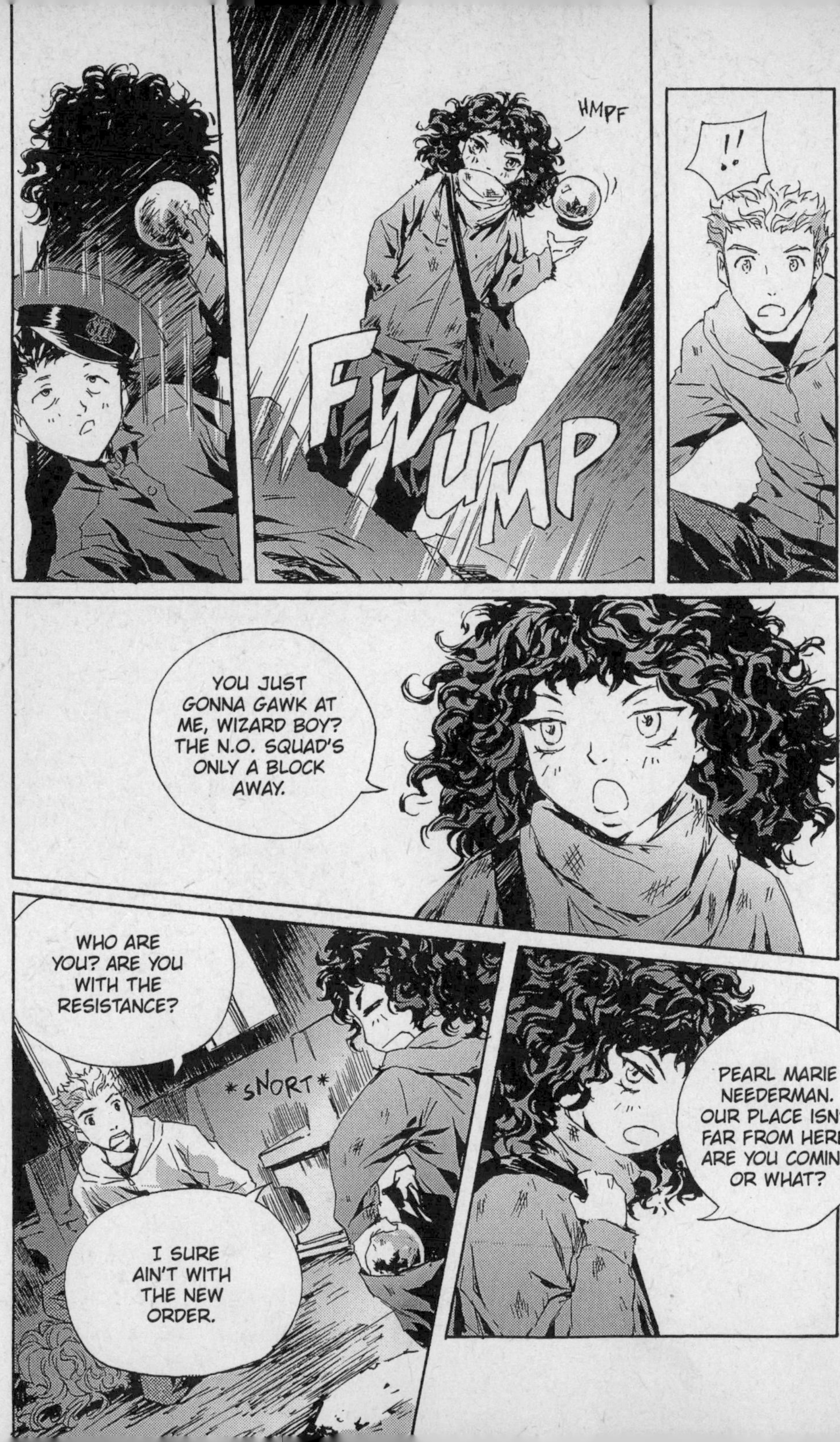
HMPF
!!
FWUMP
YOU JUST GONNA GAWK AT ME, WIZARD BOY? THE N.O. SQUAD'S ONLY A BLOCK AWAY.
WHO ARE YOU? ARE YOU WITH THE RESISTANCE?
SNORT
I SURE AIN'T WITH THE NEW ORDER.
PEARL MARIE NEEDERMAN. OUR PLACE ISN'T FAR FROM HERE. ARE YOU COMING OR WHAT?

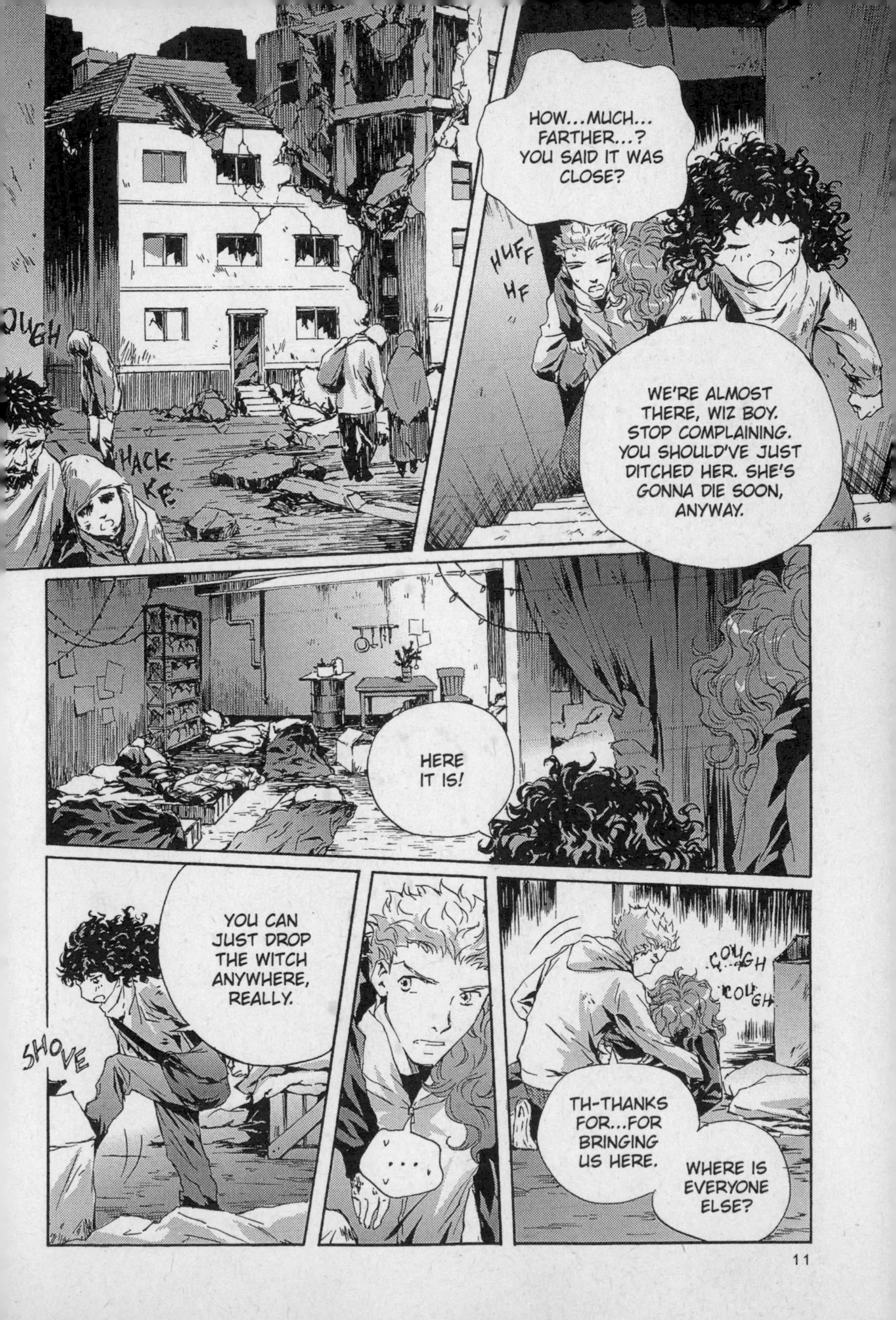
OUGH
HACK
KF
HOW...MUCH... FARTHER...? YOU SAID IT WAS CLOSE?
HUFF
HF
WE'RE ALMOST THERE, WIZ BOY. STOP COMPLAINING. YOU SHOULD'VE JUST DITCHED HER. SHE'S GONNA DIE SOON, ANYWAY.
HERE IT IS!
YOU CAN JUST DROP THE WITCH ANYWHERE, REALLY.
SHOVE
...
COUGH
COUGH
TH-THANKS FOR...FOR BRINGING US HERE.
WHERE IS EVERYONE ELSE?

OUT SCAVENGING NECESSITIES.

FINDING THINGS TO HELP US SURVIVE. YOU KNOW, IMPORTANT STUFF—NOT LIKE YOU, WAVING YOUR HANDS AROUND LIKE SOME HOCUS-POCUS IS GONNA HAPPEN.

LOOK, NEVER MIND. THIS WAS A BAD IDEA. WE'RE JUST GONNA GO.

NO, STAY!

...

I MEAN... EVERYONE WILL BE HOME SOON.

AND, AND... I WANT TO SHOW YOU SOMETHING.

WHAT I'VE BEEN COLLECTING ALL DAY! THEY GAVE ME THE BIGGEST JOB OF ANYONE.

SHOW ME WHAT?

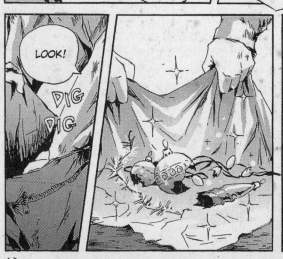

LOOK!

DIG DIG

AREN'T THEY BEAUTIFUL? THEY'RE FOR THE HOLIDAY.

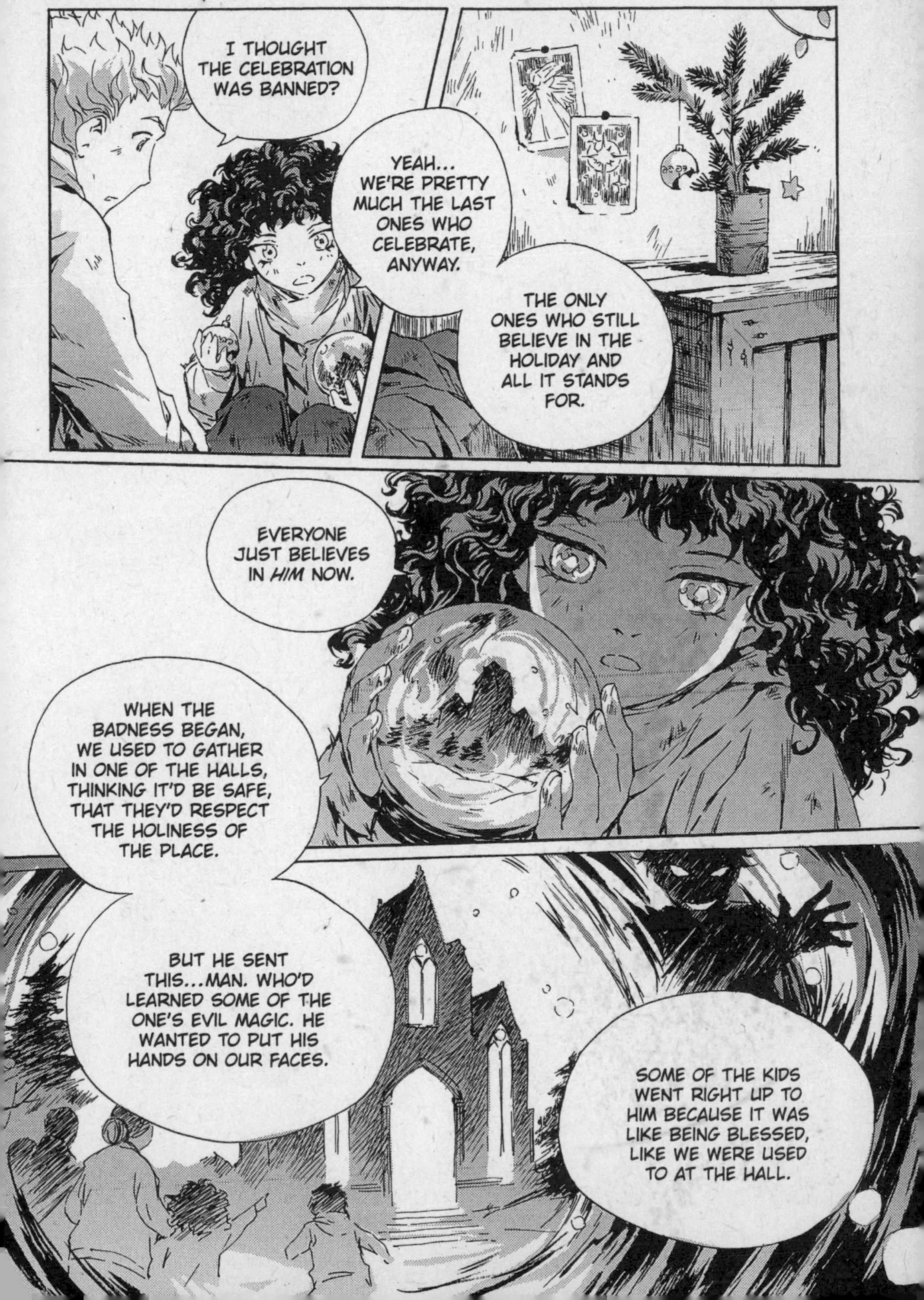
I THOUGHT THE CELEBRATION WAS BANNED?
YEAH... WE'RE PRETTY MUCH THE LAST ONES WHO CELEBRATE, ANYWAY.
THE ONLY ONES WHO STILL BELIEVE IN THE HOLIDAY AND ALL IT STANDS FOR.
EVERYONE JUST BELIEVES IN *HIM* NOW.
WHEN THE BADNESS BEGAN, WE USED TO GATHER IN ONE OF THE HALLS, THINKING IT'D BE SAFE, THAT THEY'D RESPECT THE HOLINESS OF THE PLACE.
BUT HE SENT THIS...MAN. WHO'D LEARNED SOME OF THE ONE'S EVIL MAGIC. HE WANTED TO PUT HIS HANDS ON OUR FACES.
SOME OF THE KIDS WENT RIGHT UP TO HIM BECAUSE IT WAS LIKE BEING BLESSED, LIKE WE WERE USED TO AT THE HALL.

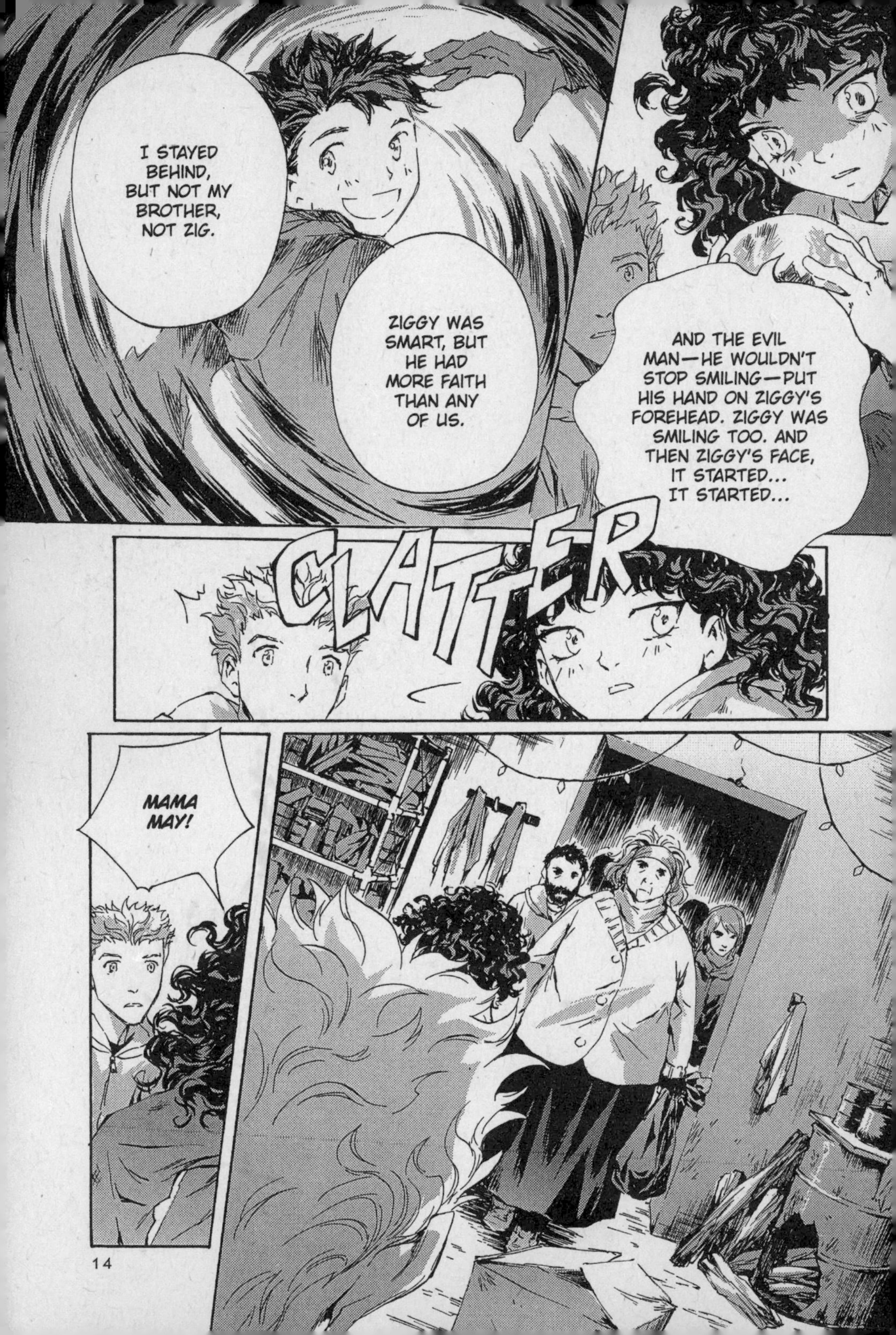
I STAYED BEHIND, BUT NOT MY BROTHER, NOT ZIG.
ZIGGY WAS SMART, BUT HE HAD MORE FAITH THAN ANY OF US.
AND THE EVIL MAN—HE WOULDN'T STOP SMILING—PUT HIS HAND ON ZIGGY'S FOREHEAD. ZIGGY WAS SMILING TOO. AND THEN ZIGGY'S FACE, IT STARTED... IT STARTED...
CLATTER
MAMA MAY!

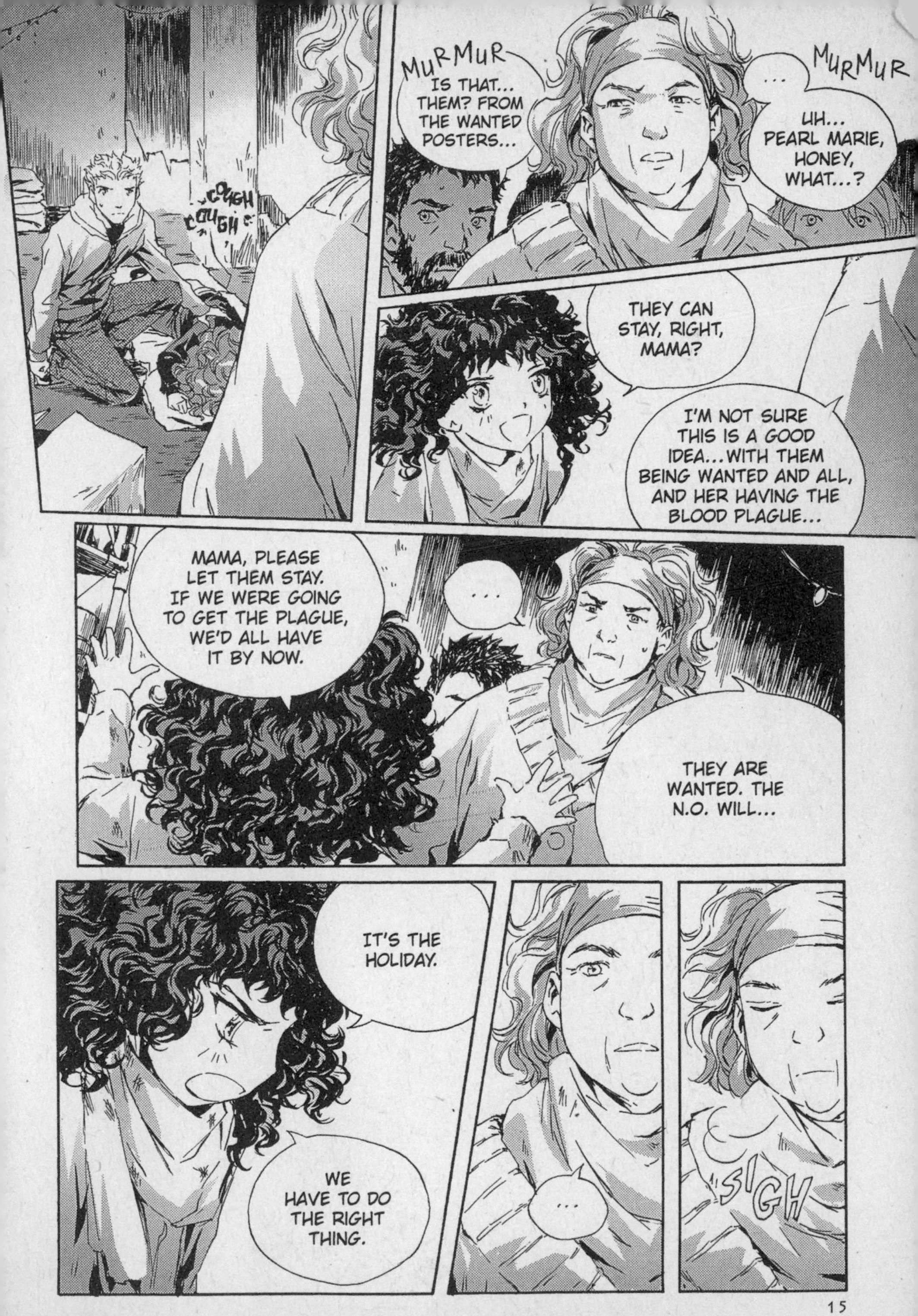
COUGH COUGH
MURMUR
IS THAT... THEM? FROM THE WANTED POSTERS...
...
MURMUR
UH... PEARL MARIE, HONEY, WHAT...?
THEY CAN STAY, RIGHT, MAMA?
I'M NOT SURE THIS IS A GOOD IDEA...WITH THEM BEING WANTED AND ALL, AND HER HAVING THE BLOOD PLAGUE...
MAMA, PLEASE LET THEM STAY. IF WE WERE GOING TO GET THE PLAGUE, WE'D ALL HAVE IT BY NOW.
...
THEY ARE WANTED. THE N.O. WILL...
IT'S THE HOLIDAY.
WE HAVE TO DO THE RIGHT THING.
...
SIGH

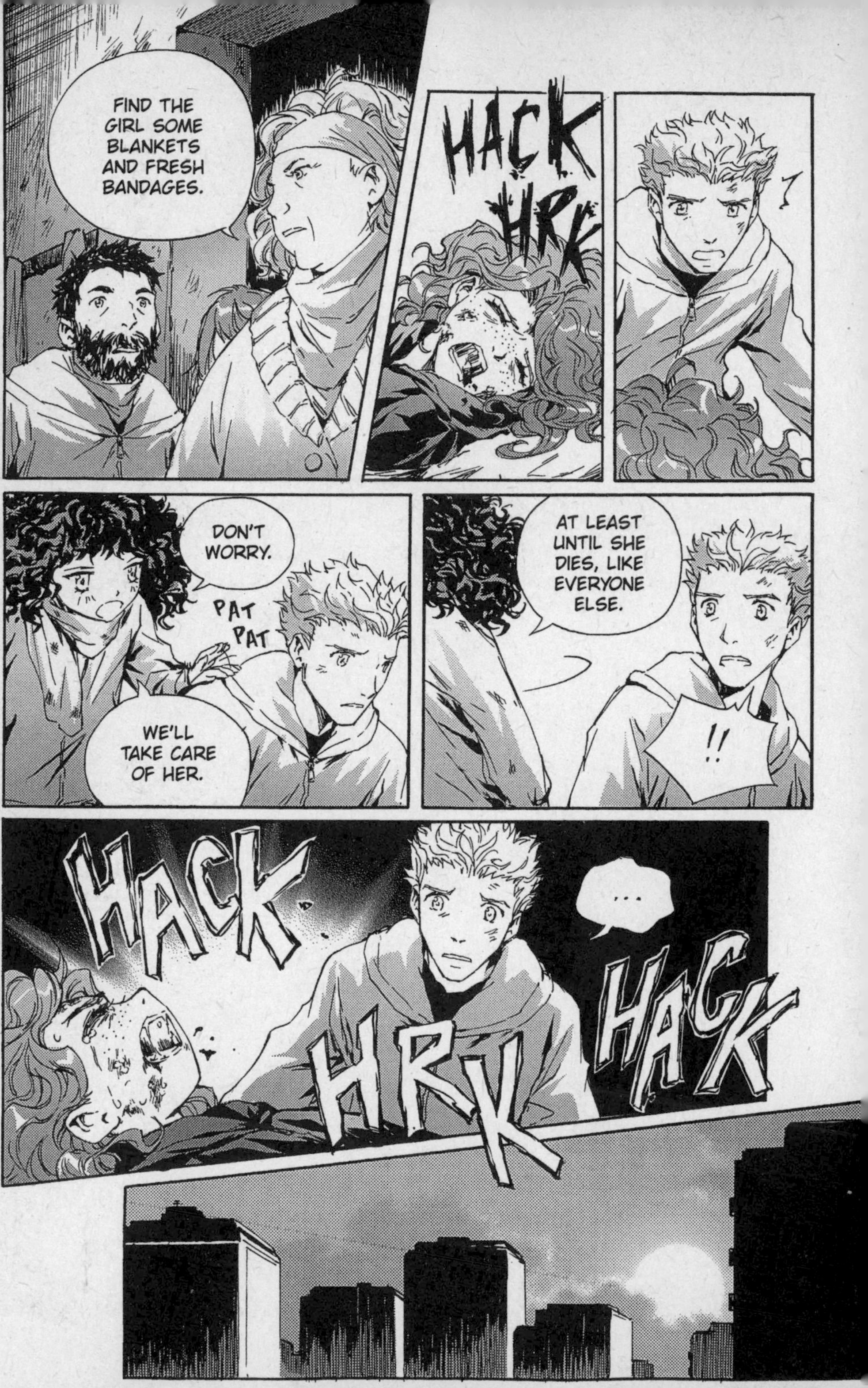
FIND THE GIRL SOME BLANKETS AND FRESH BANDAGES.
HACK HRK
?
DON'T WORRY.
PAT PAT
WE'LL TAKE CARE OF HER.
AT LEAST UNTIL SHE DIES, LIKE EVERYONE ELSE.
!!
HACK
...
HACK HACK
HRK

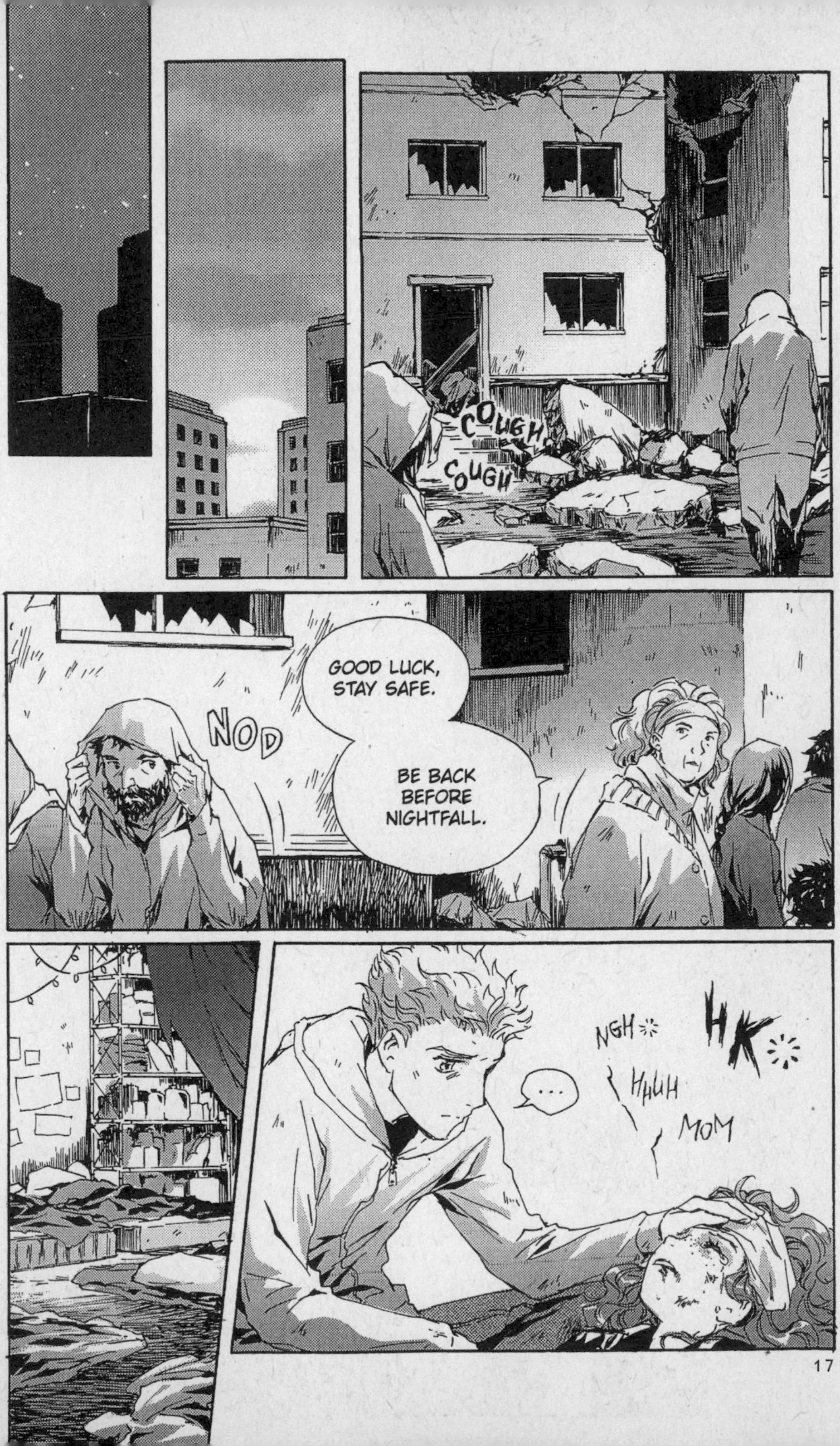
COUGH
COUGH
NOD
GOOD LUCK, STAY SAFE.
BE BACK BEFORE NIGHTFALL.
...
NGH
HK
HHUH
MOM

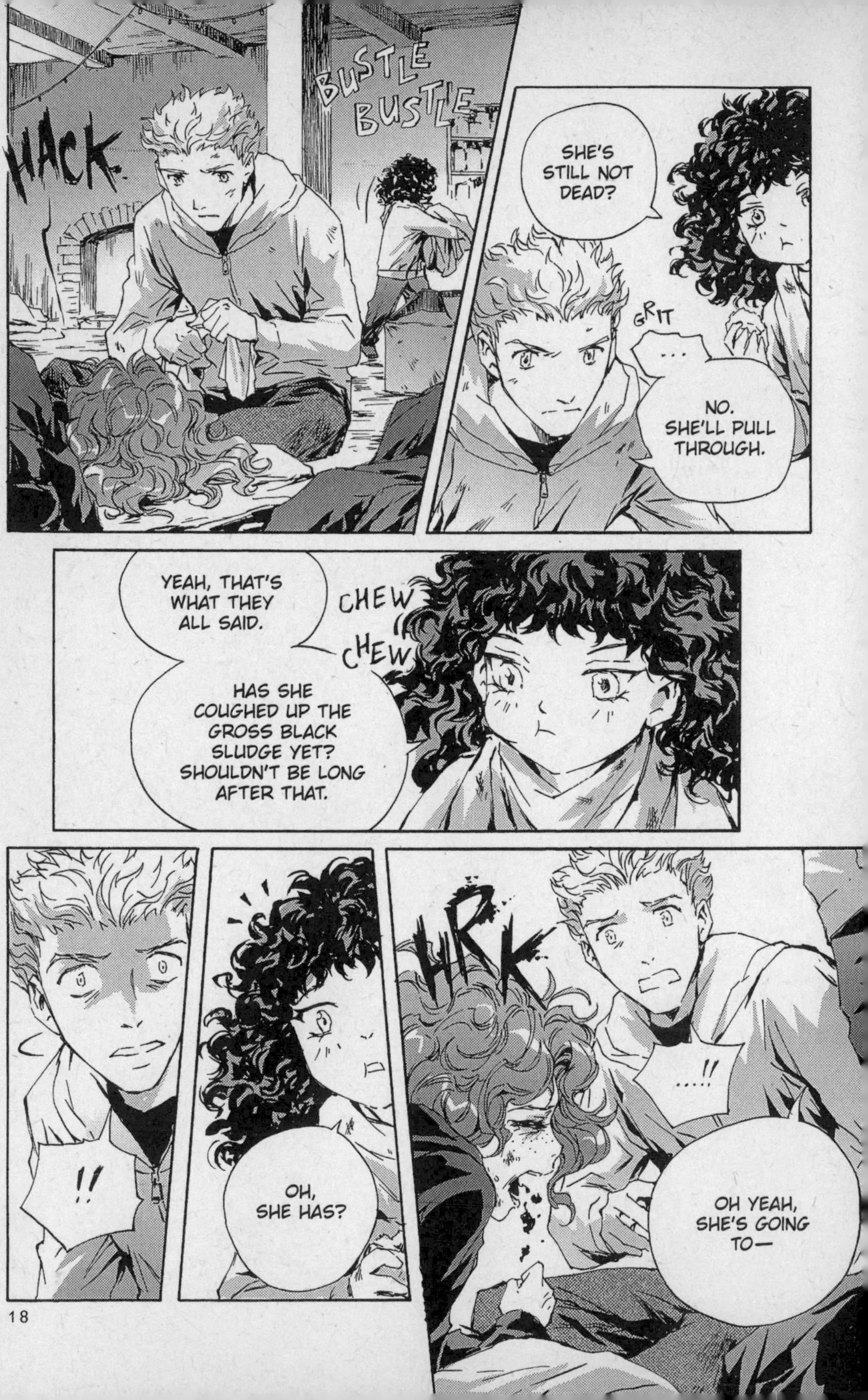
HACK
BUSTLE
BUSTLE
SHE'S STILL NOT DEAD?
GRIT
...
NO. SHE'LL PULL THROUGH.
YEAH, THAT'S WHAT THEY ALL SAID.
CHEW
CHEW
HAS SHE COUGHED UP THE GROSS BLACK SLUDGE YET? SHOULDN'T BE LONG AFTER THAT.
!!
OH, SHE HAS?
HRK
....!!
OH YEAH, SHE'S GOING TO—

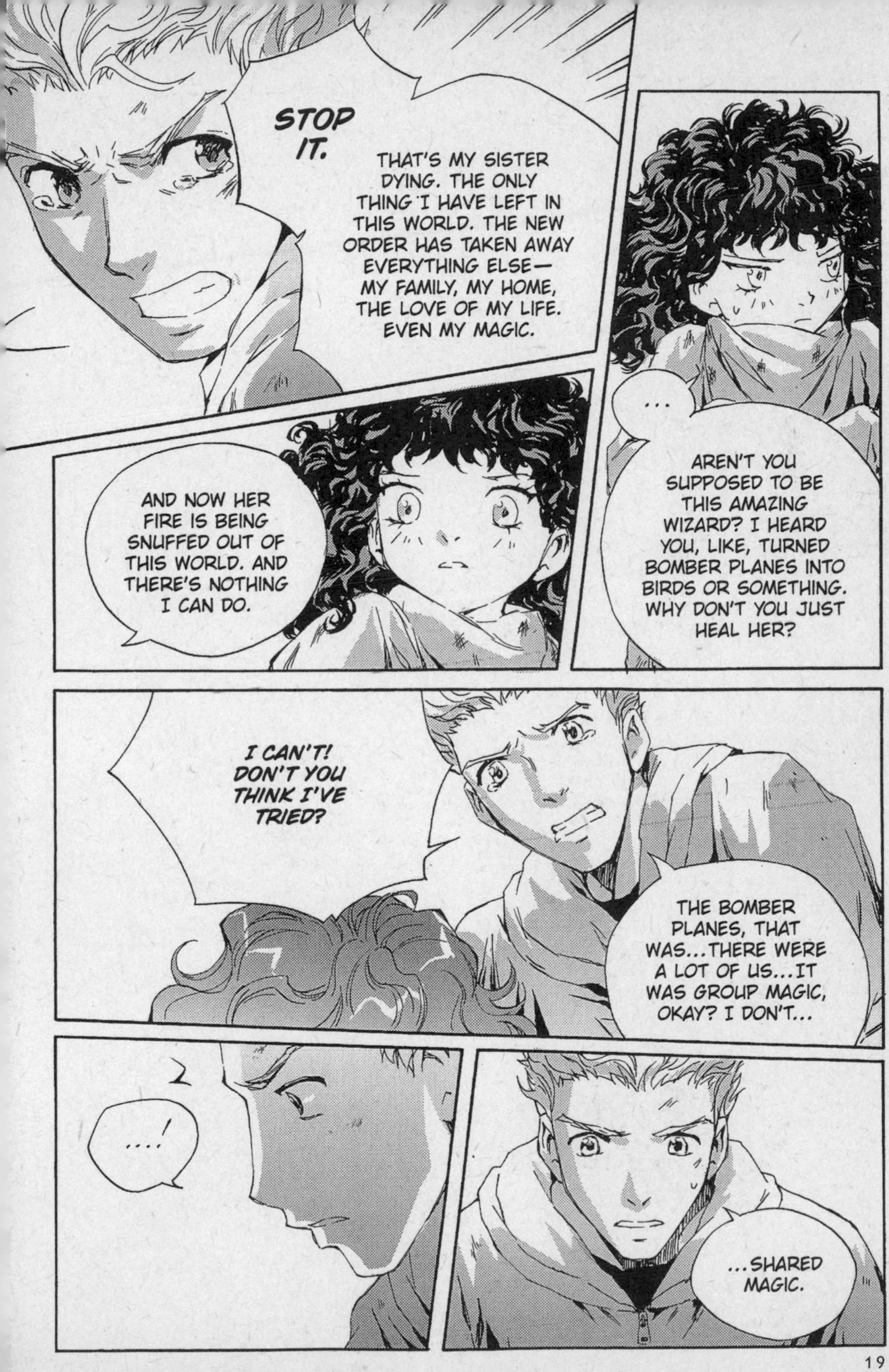
STOP IT.
THAT'S MY SISTER DYING. THE ONLY THING I HAVE LEFT IN THIS WORLD. THE NEW ORDER HAS TAKEN AWAY EVERYTHING ELSE— MY FAMILY, MY HOME, THE LOVE OF MY LIFE. EVEN MY MAGIC.
AND NOW HER FIRE IS BEING SNUFFED OUT OF THIS WORLD. AND THERE'S NOTHING I CAN DO.
...
AREN'T YOU SUPPOSED TO BE THIS AMAZING WIZARD? I HEARD YOU, LIKE, TURNED BOMBER PLANES INTO BIRDS OR SOMETHING. WHY DON'T YOU JUST HEAL HER?
I CAN'T! DON'T YOU THINK I'VE TRIED?
THE BOMBER PLANES, THAT WAS...THERE WERE A LOT OF US...IT WAS GROUP MAGIC, OKAY? I DON'T...
....!
...SHARED MAGIC.

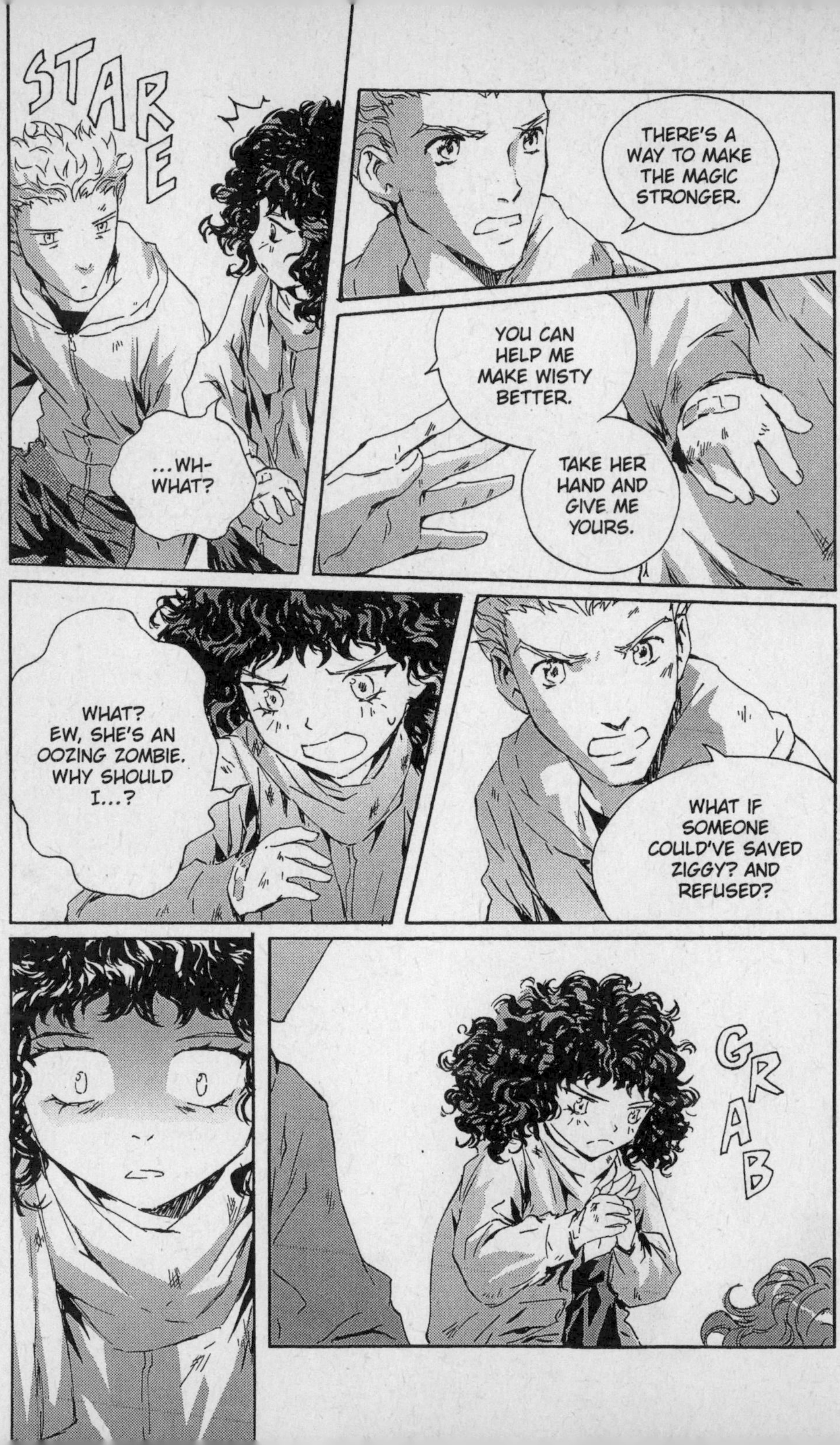
STARE
...WH-WHAT?
THERE'S A WAY TO MAKE THE MAGIC STRONGER.
YOU CAN HELP ME MAKE WISTY BETTER.
TAKE HER HAND AND GIVE ME YOURS.
WHAT? EW, SHE'S AN OOZING ZOMBIE. WHY SHOULD I...?
WHAT IF SOMEONE COULD'VE SAVED ZIGGY? AND REFUSED?
GRAB

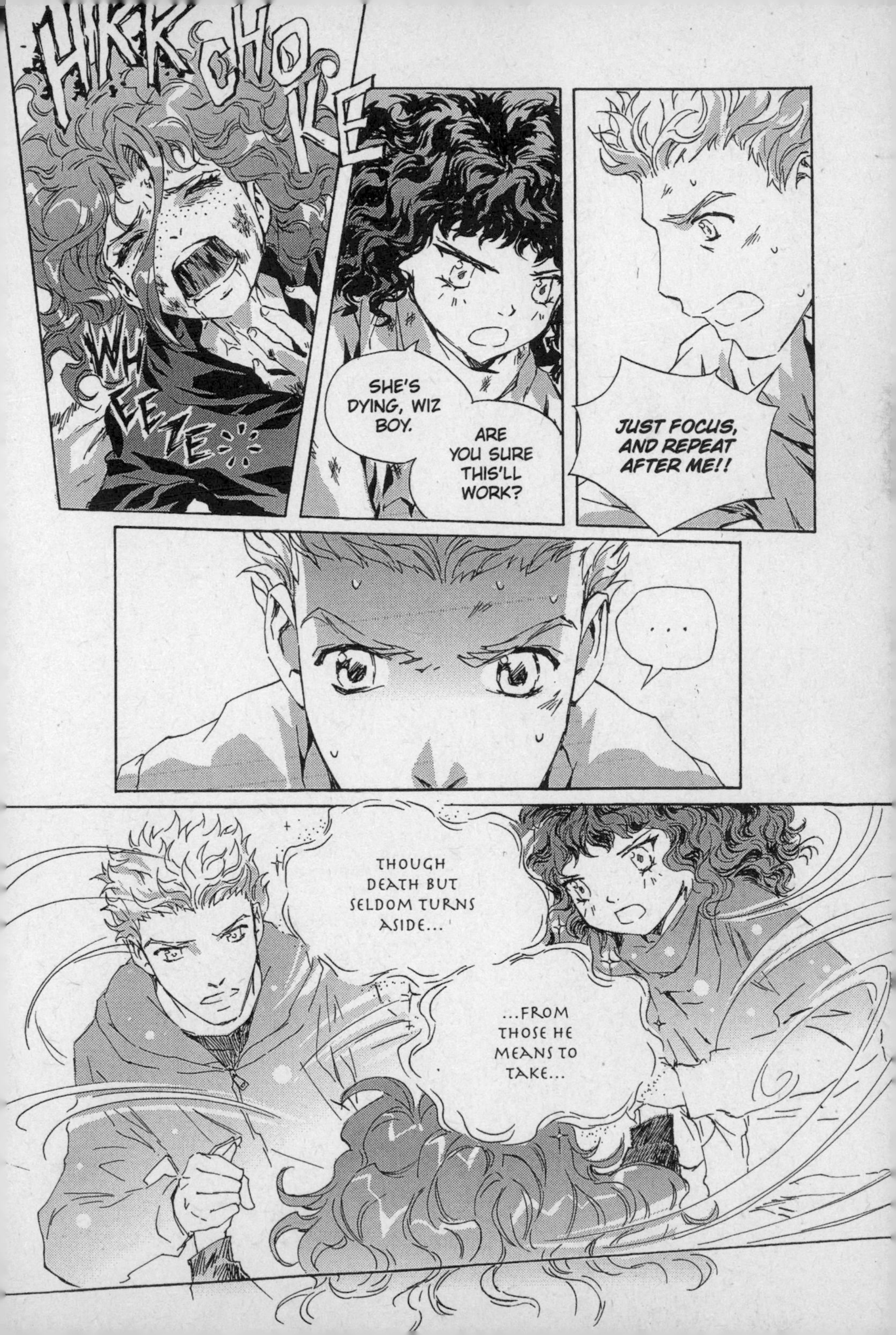

HIKK CHOKE
WHEEZE
SHE'S DYING, WIZ BOY.
ARE YOU SURE THIS'LL WORK?
JUST FOCUS, AND REPEAT AFTER ME!!
...
THOUGH DEATH BUT SELDOM TURNS ASIDE...
...FROM THOSE HE MEANS TO TAKE...

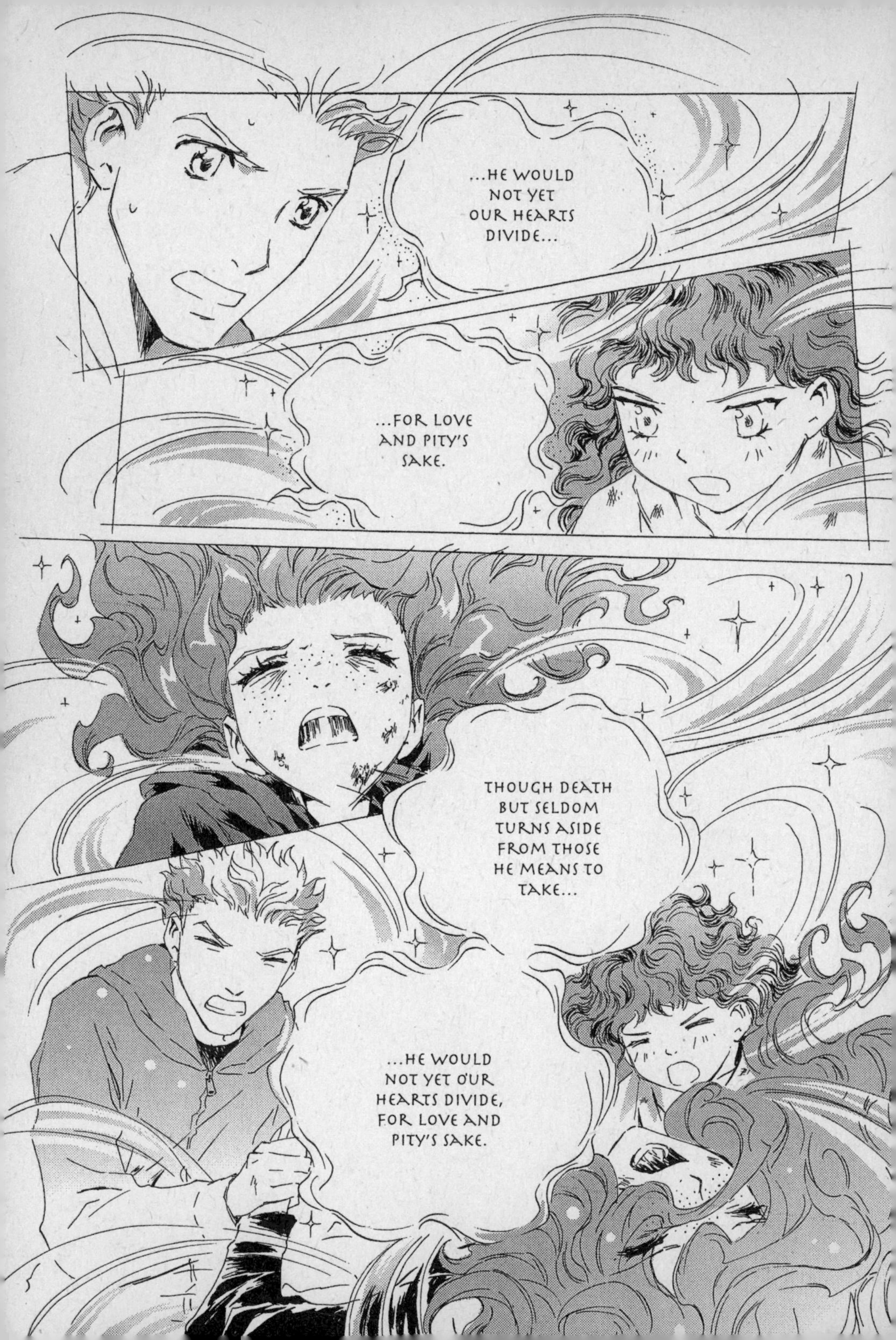
...HE WOULD NOT YET OUR HEARTS DIVIDE...
...FOR LOVE AND PITY'S SAKE.
THOUGH DEATH BUT SELDOM TURNS ASIDE FROM THOSE HE MEANS TO TAKE...
...HE WOULD NOT YET OUR HEARTS DIVIDE, FOR LOVE AND PITY'S SAKE.

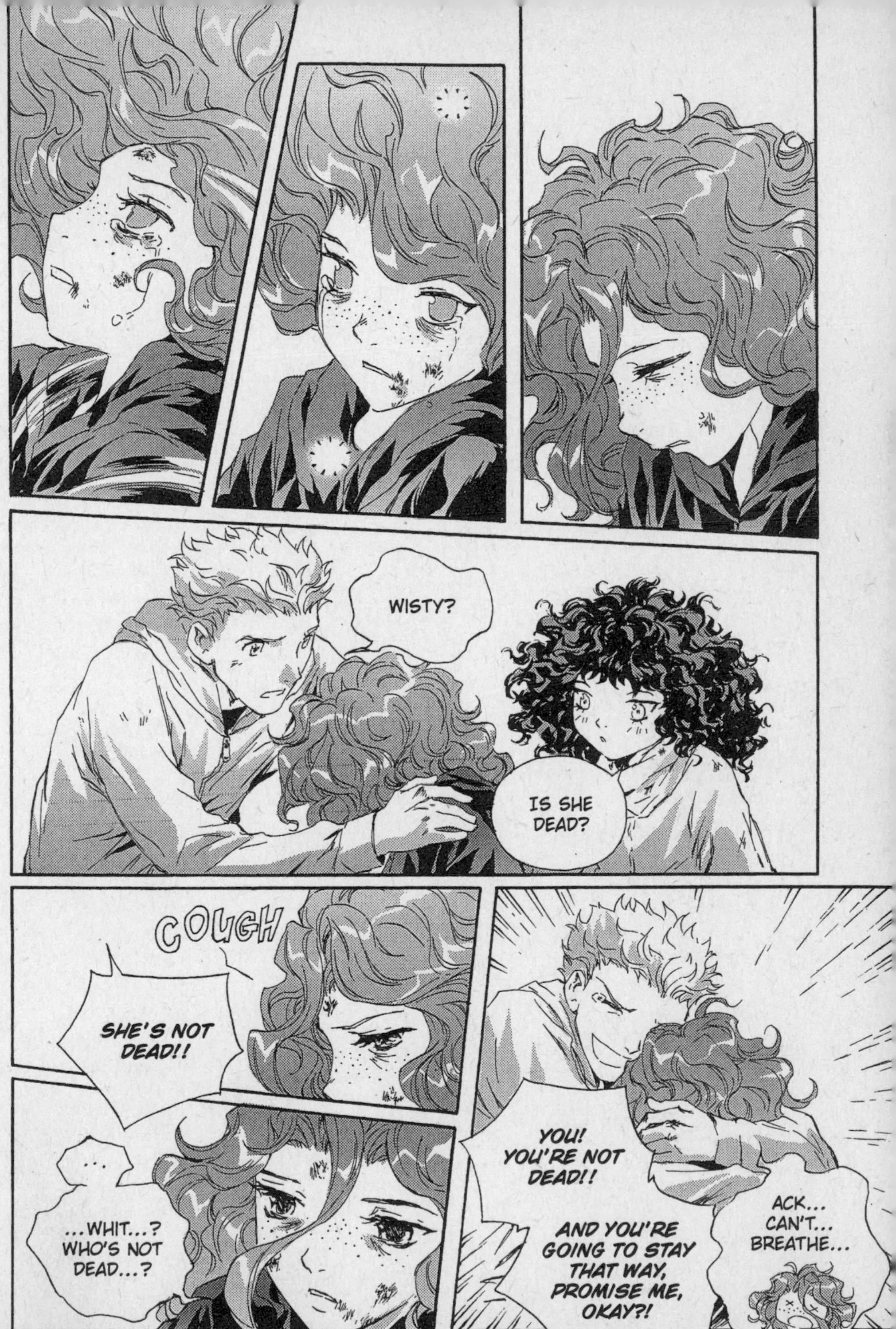
WISTY?
IS SHE DEAD?
COUGH
SHE'S NOT DEAD!!
YOU! YOU'RE NOT DEAD!!
AND YOU'RE GOING TO STAY THAT WAY, PROMISE ME, OKAY?!
ACK... CAN'T... BREATHE...
...
...WHIT...? WHO'S NOT DEAD...?

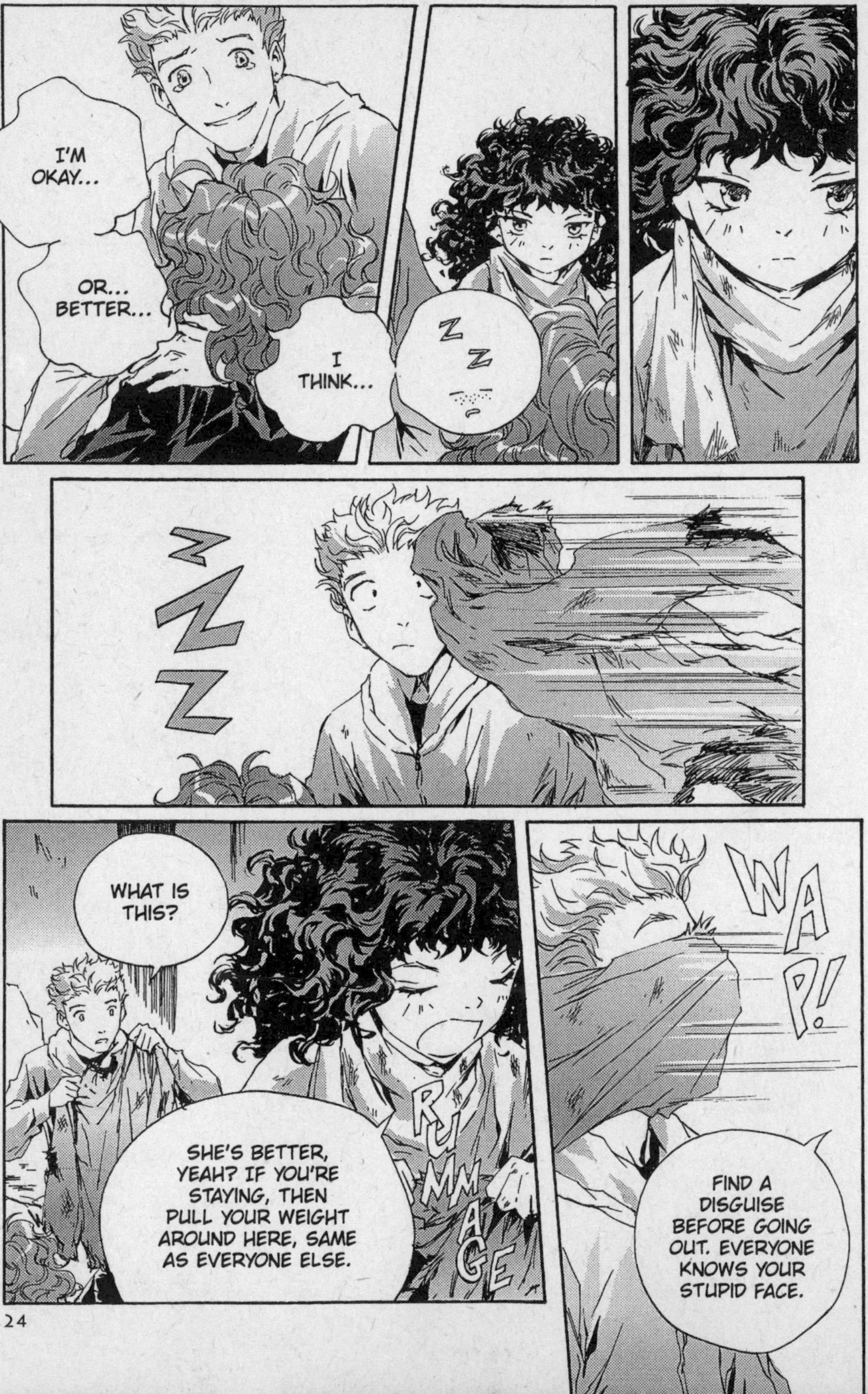
I'M OKAY...
OR... BETTER...
I THINK...
Z Z
ZZZ
WHAT IS THIS?
SHE'S BETTER, YEAH? IF YOU'RE STAYING, THEN PULL YOUR WEIGHT AROUND HERE, SAME AS EVERYONE ELSE.
RUMMAGE
WAP!
FIND A DISGUISE BEFORE GOING OUT. EVERYONE KNOWS YOUR STUPID FACE.

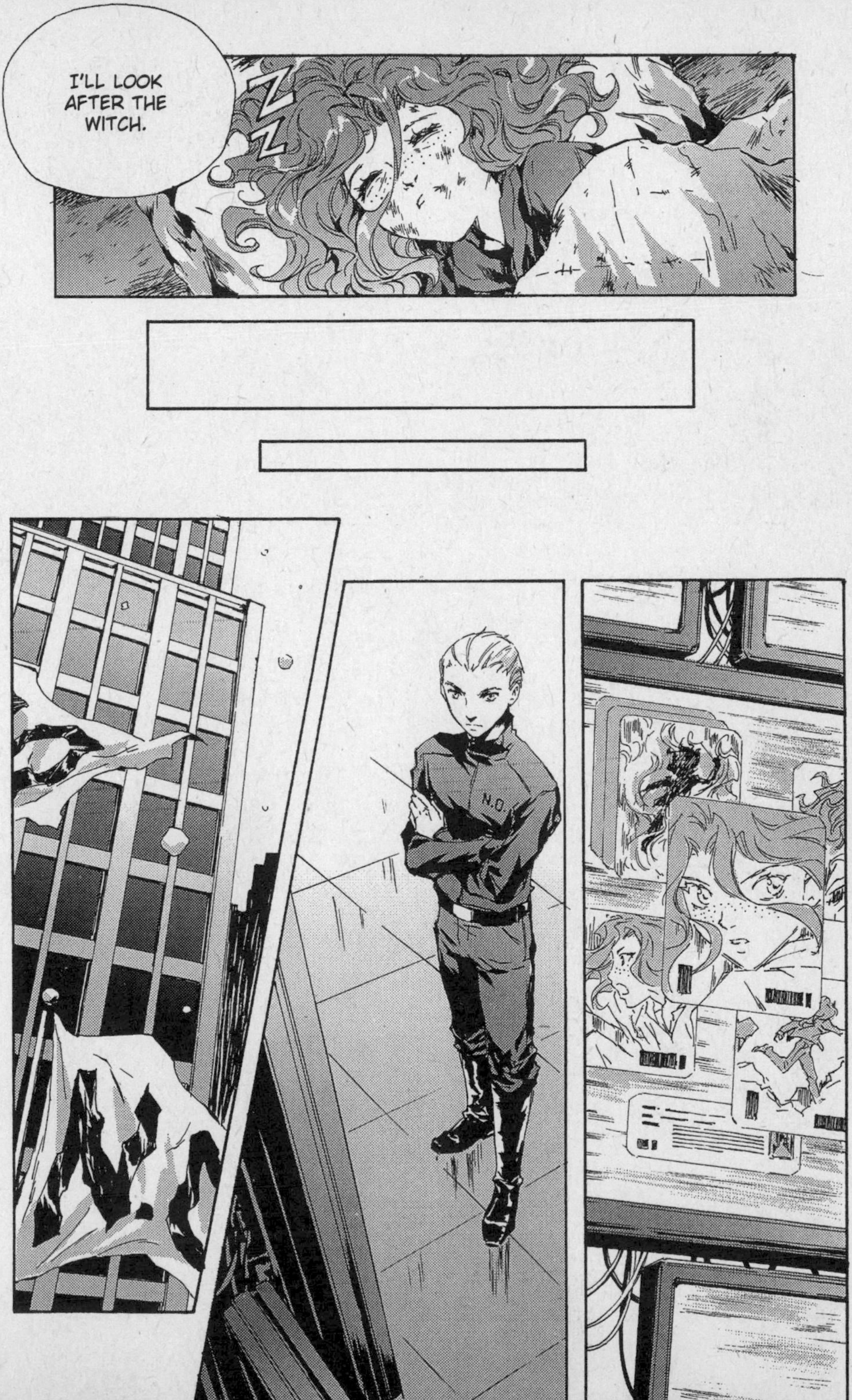
I'LL LOOK AFTER THE WITCH.

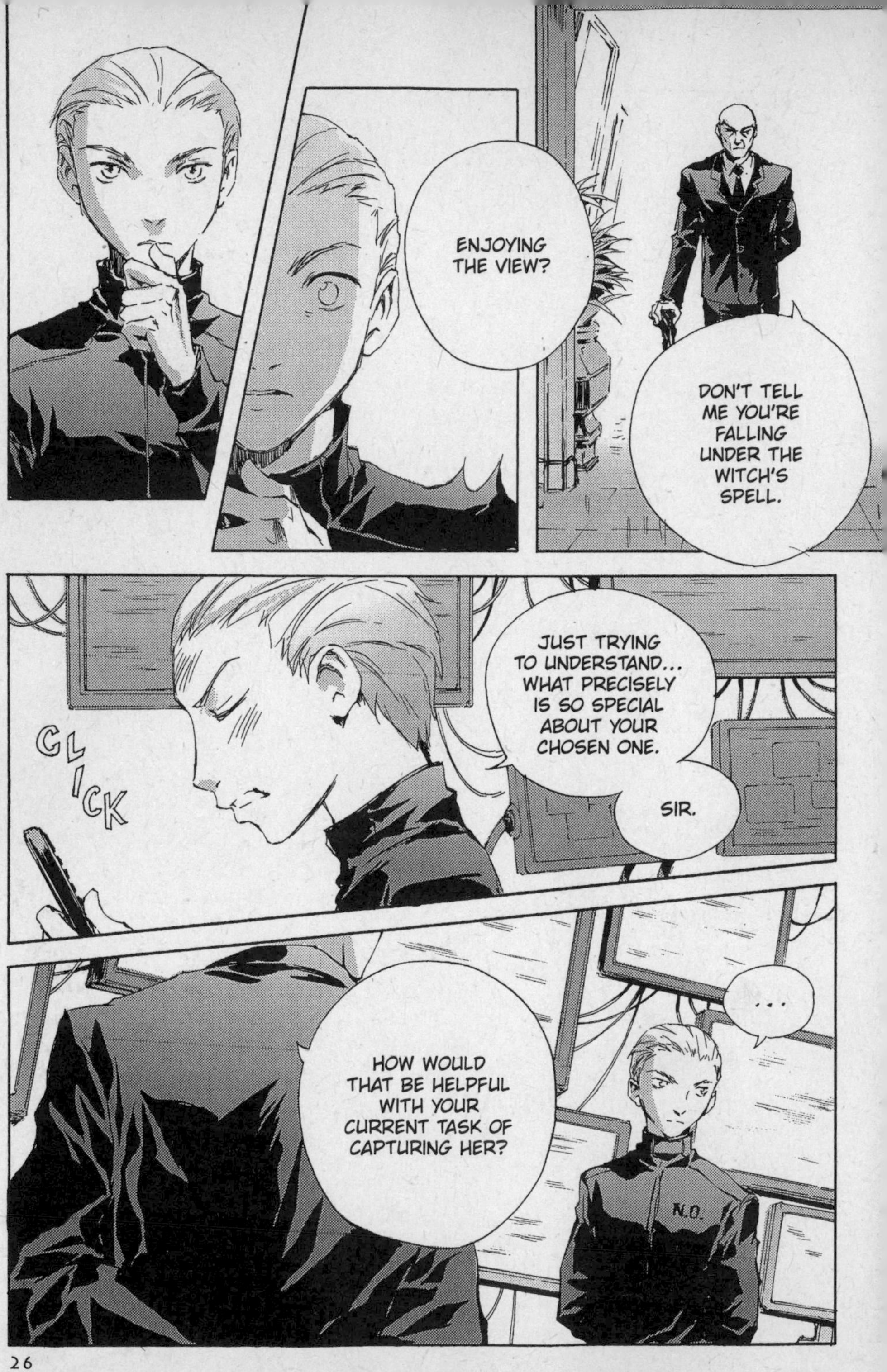
ENJOYING THE VIEW?
DON'T TELL ME YOU'RE FALLING UNDER THE WITCH'S SPELL.
CLICK
JUST TRYING TO UNDERSTAND... WHAT PRECISELY IS SO SPECIAL ABOUT YOUR CHOSEN ONE.
SIR.
HOW WOULD THAT BE HELPFUL WITH YOUR CURRENT TASK OF CAPTURING HER?
...
N.O.

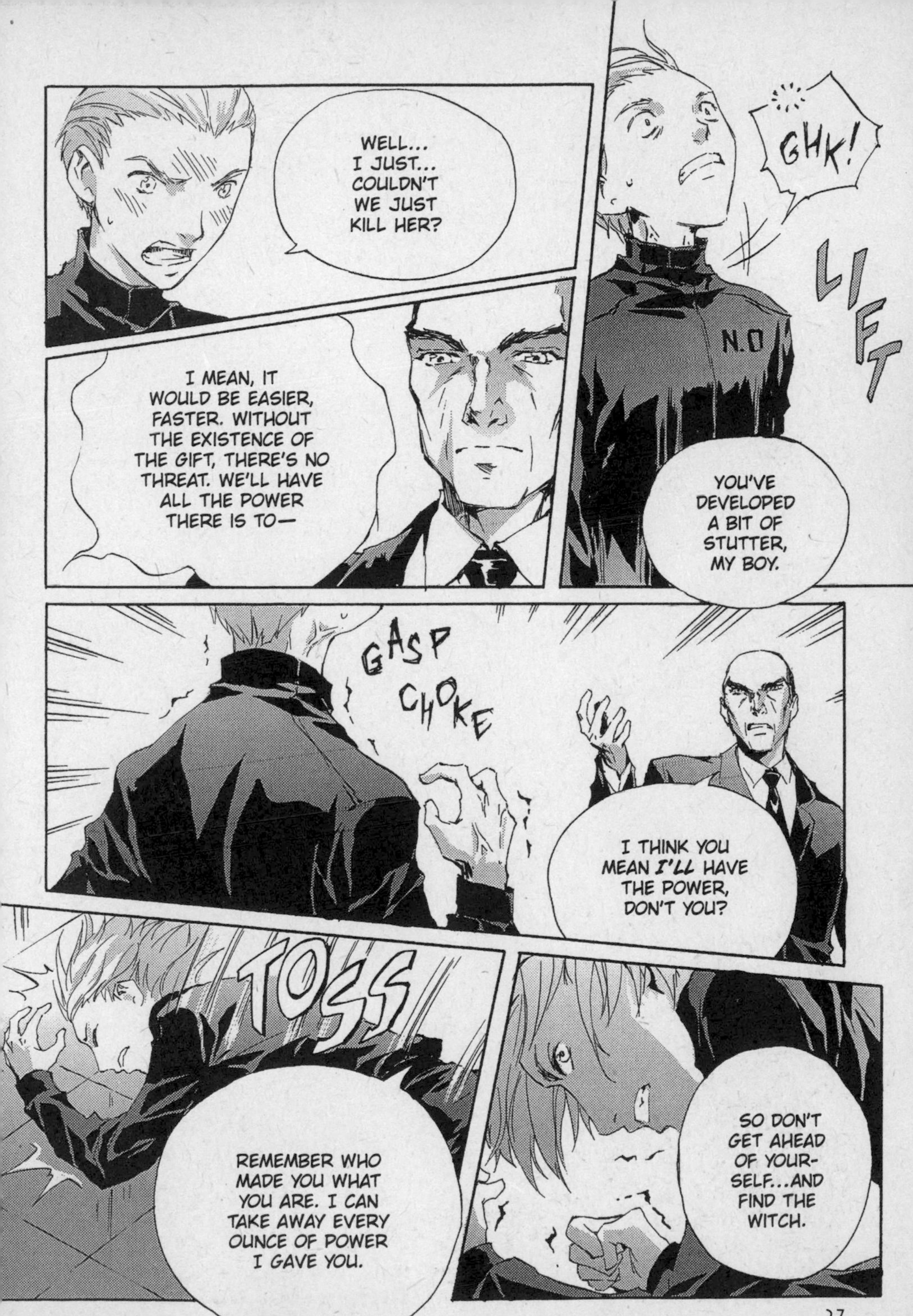
WELL... I JUST... COULDN'T WE JUST KILL HER?
I MEAN, IT WOULD BE EASIER, FASTER. WITHOUT THE EXISTENCE OF THE GIFT, THERE'S NO THREAT. WE'LL HAVE ALL THE POWER THERE IS TO—
GHK!
LIFT
N.O
YOU'VE DEVELOPED A BIT OF STUTTER, MY BOY.
GASP
CHOKE
I THINK YOU MEAN *I'LL* HAVE THE POWER, DON'T YOU?
TOSS
REMEMBER WHO MADE YOU WHAT YOU ARE. I CAN TAKE AWAY EVERY OUNCE OF POWER I GAVE YOU.
SO DON'T GET AHEAD OF YOUR-SELF...AND FIND THE WITCH.

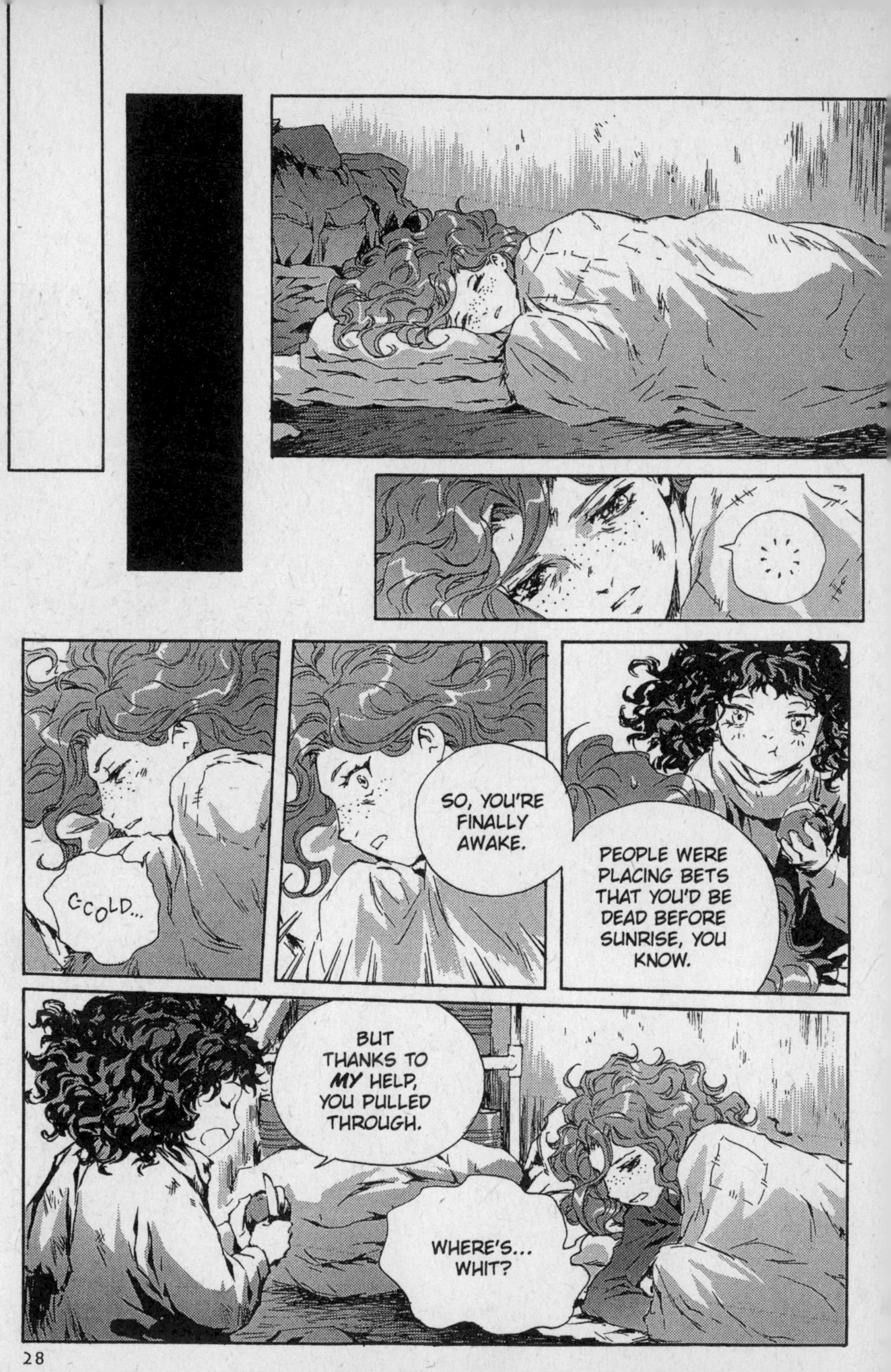
...
C-COLD...
SO, YOU'RE FINALLY AWAKE.
PEOPLE WERE PLACING BETS THAT YOU'D BE DEAD BEFORE SUNRISE, YOU KNOW.
BUT THANKS TO MY HELP, YOU PULLED THROUGH.
WHERE'S... WHIT?

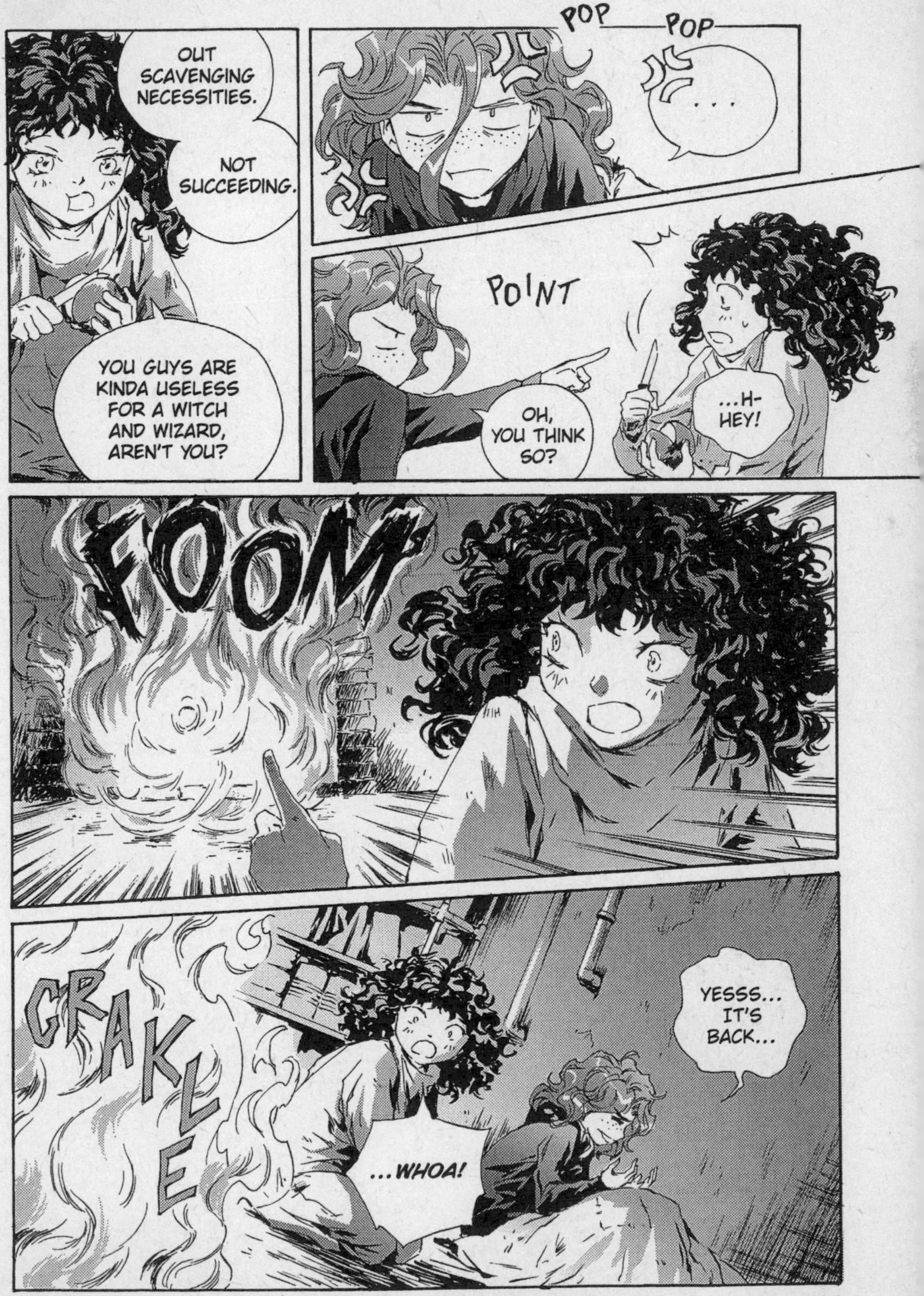
OUT SCAVENGING NECESSITIES.
NOT SUCCEEDING.
YOU GUYS ARE KINDA USELESS FOR A WITCH AND WIZARD, AREN'T YOU?
POP
POP
...
POINT
OH, YOU THINK SO?
...H-HEY!
FOOM
CRAKLE
YESSS... IT'S BACK...
...WHOA!

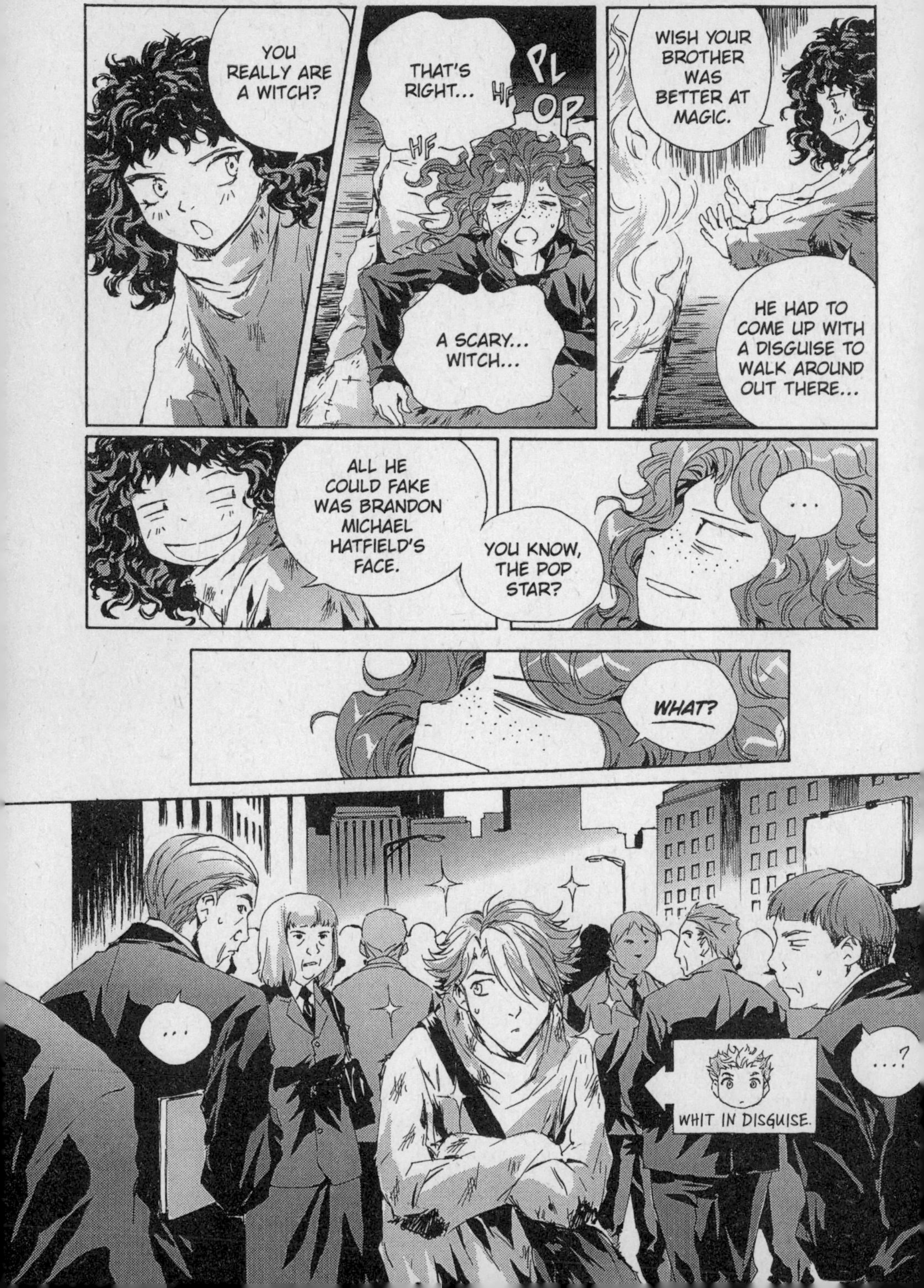
YOU REALLY ARE A WITCH?
THAT'S RIGHT... HF HF
PLOP
A SCARY... WITCH...
WISH YOUR BROTHER WAS BETTER AT MAGIC.
HE HAD TO COME UP WITH A DISGUISE TO WALK AROUND OUT THERE...
ALL HE COULD FAKE WAS BRANDON MICHAEL HATFIELD'S FACE.
YOU KNOW, THE POP STAR?
...
WHAT?
...
WHIT IN DISGUISE.
...?

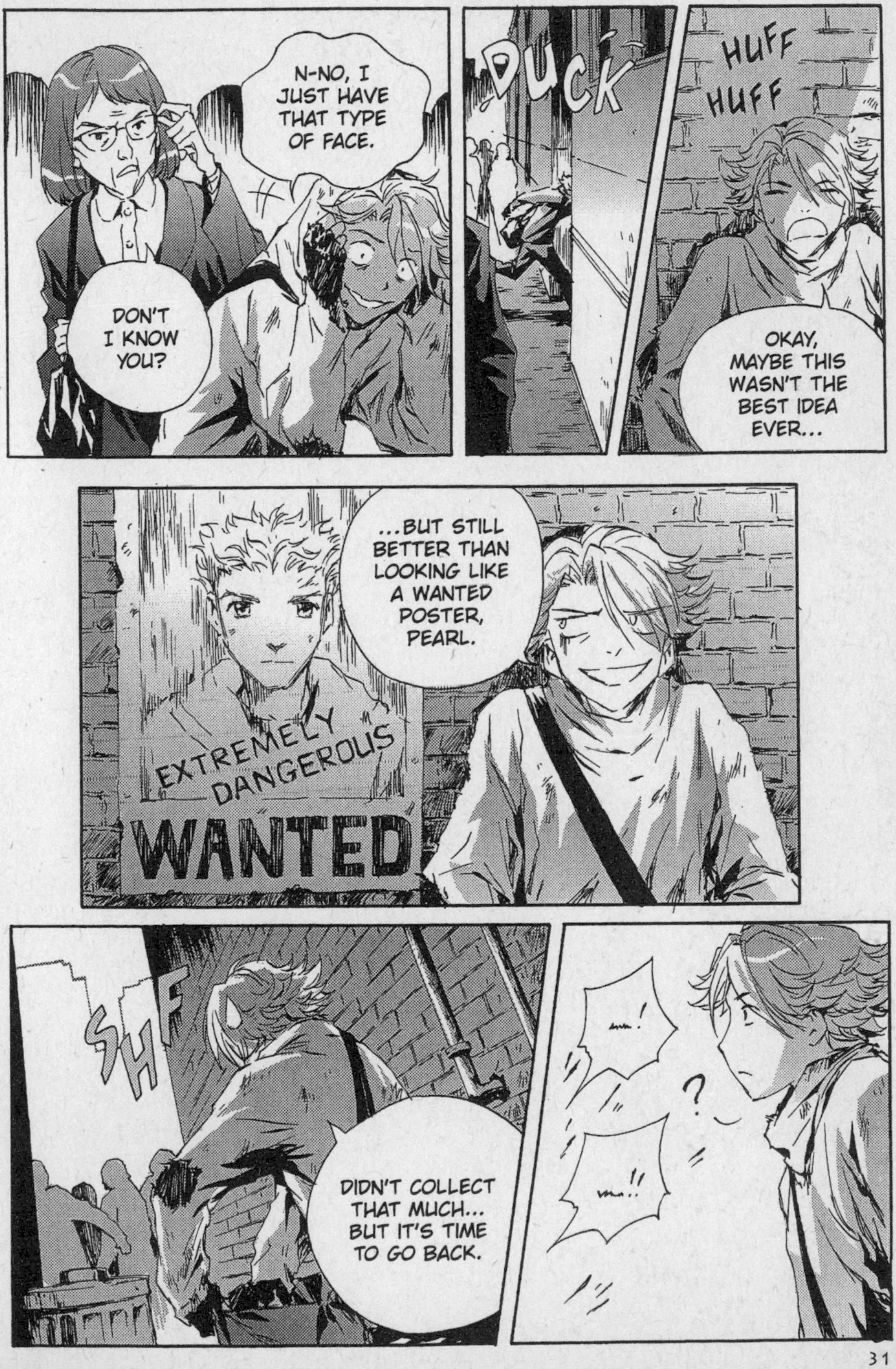
DON'T I KNOW YOU?
N-NO, I JUST HAVE THAT TYPE OF FACE.
DUCK
HUFF HUFF
OKAY, MAYBE THIS WASN'T THE BEST IDEA EVER...
...BUT STILL BETTER THAN LOOKING LIKE A WANTED POSTER, PEARL.
EXTREMELY DANGEROUS
WANTED
SHF
DIDN'T COLLECT THAT MUCH... BUT IT'S TIME TO GO BACK.
?

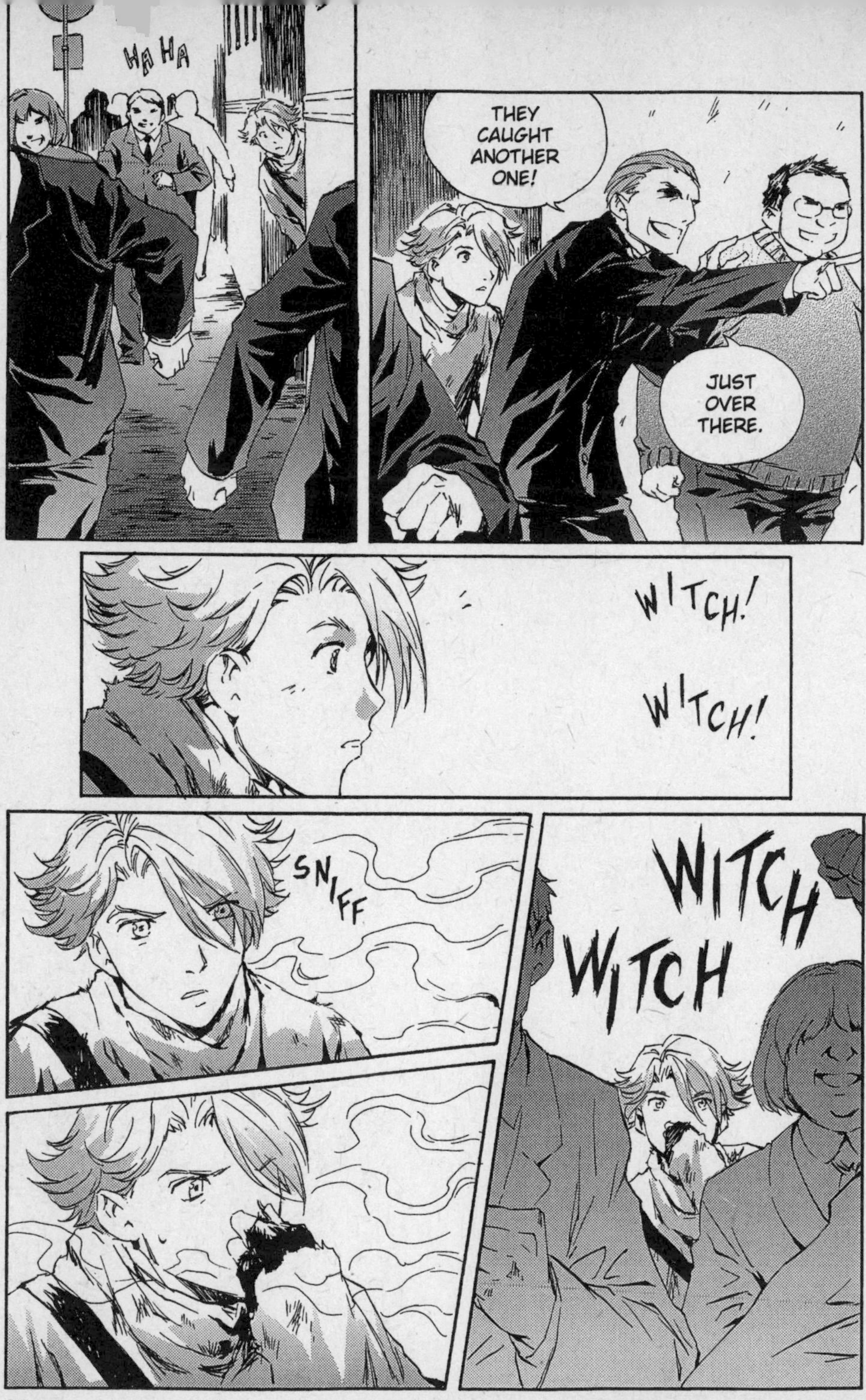
HA HA
THEY CAUGHT ANOTHER ONE!
JUST OVER THERE.
WITCH!
WITCH!
SNIFF
WITCH
WITCH

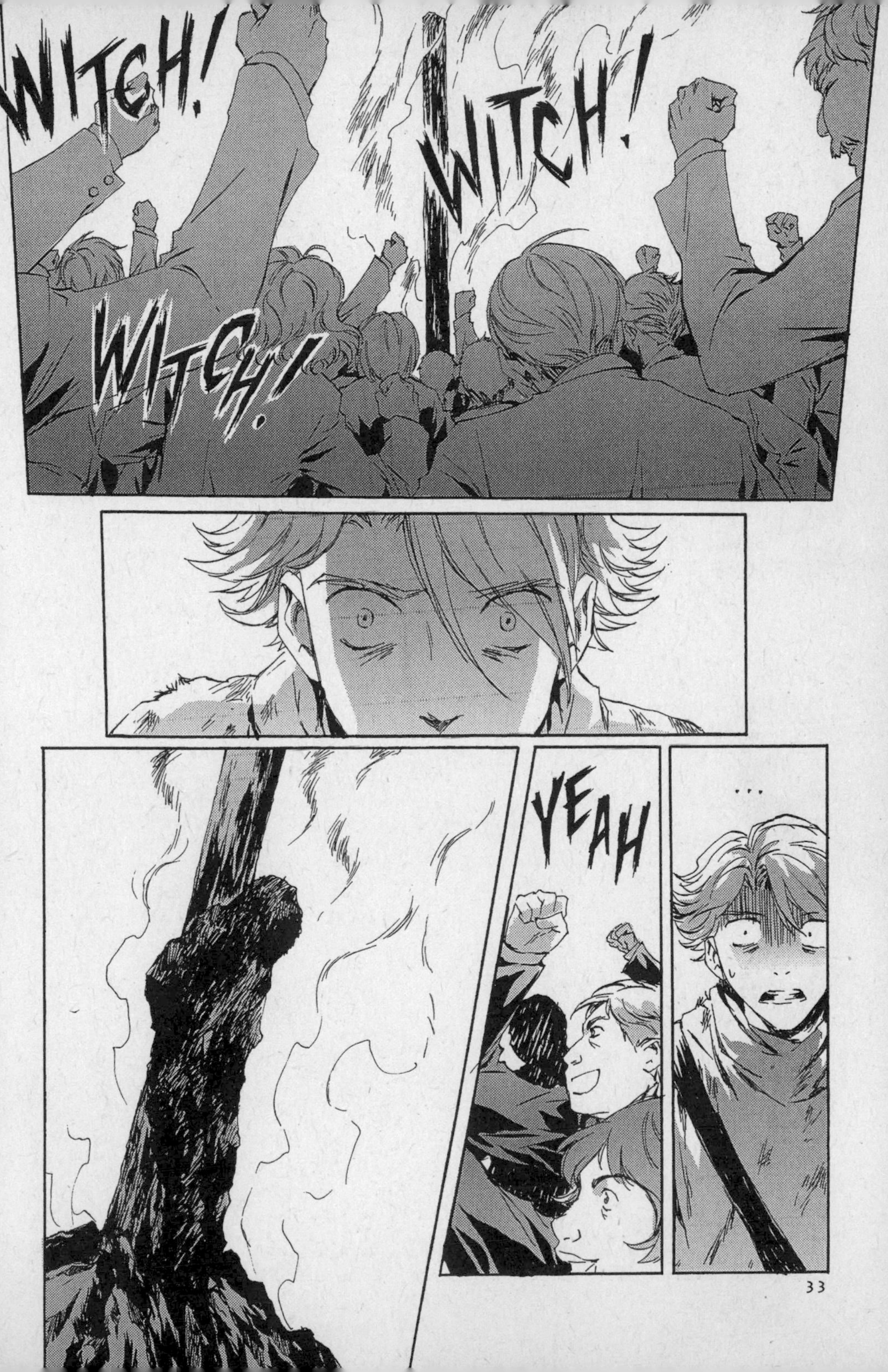
WITCH!
WITCH!
WITCH!
YEAH
...

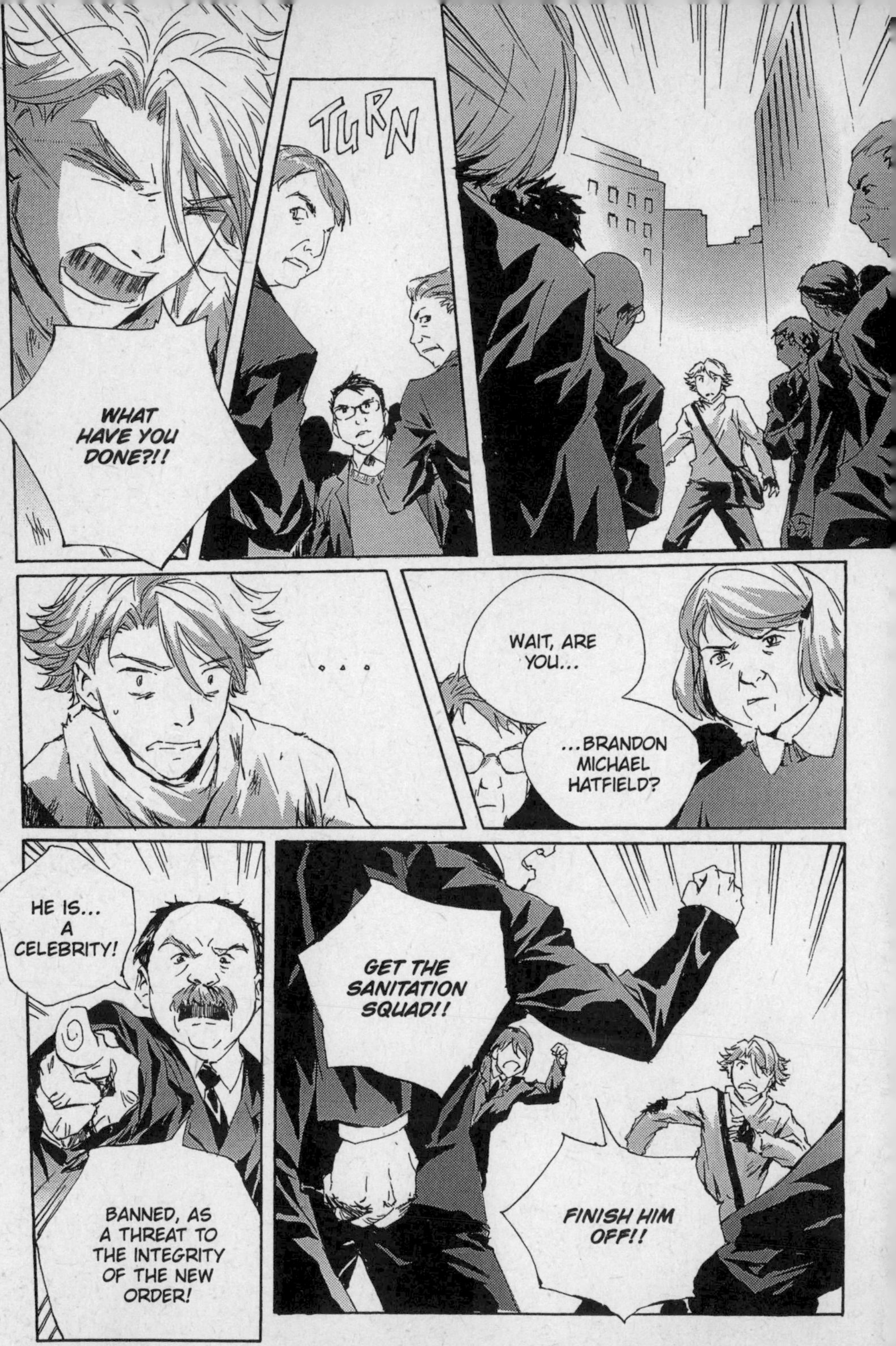
WHAT HAVE YOU DONE?!!
TURN
...
WAIT, ARE YOU...
...BRANDON MICHAEL HATFIELD?
HE IS... A CELEBRITY!
BANNED, AS A THREAT TO THE INTEGRITY OF THE NEW ORDER!
GET THE SANITATION SQUAD!!
FINISH HIM OFF!!

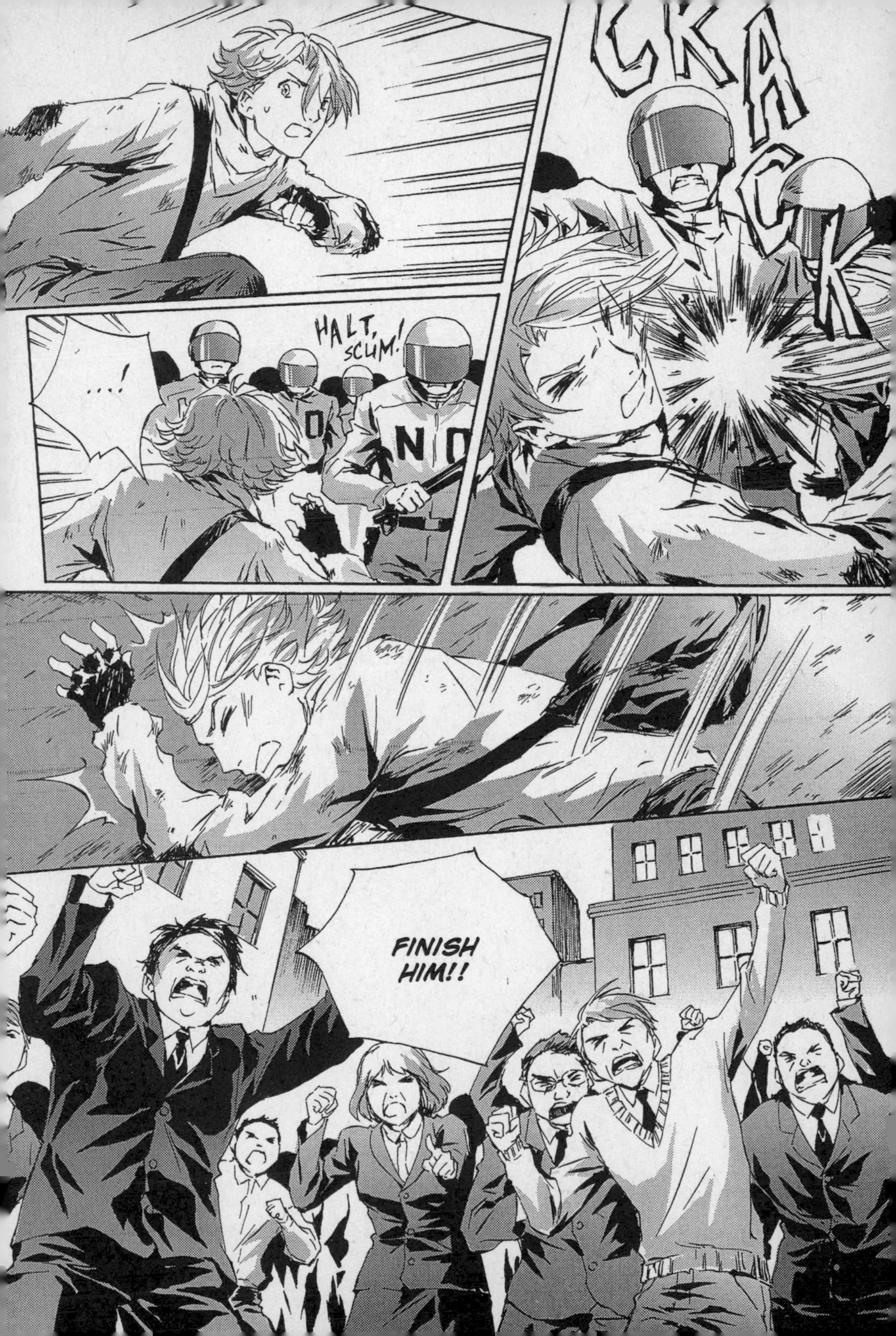

...!
HALT, SCUM!
CKACK
FINISH HIM!!

WITCH & WIZARD

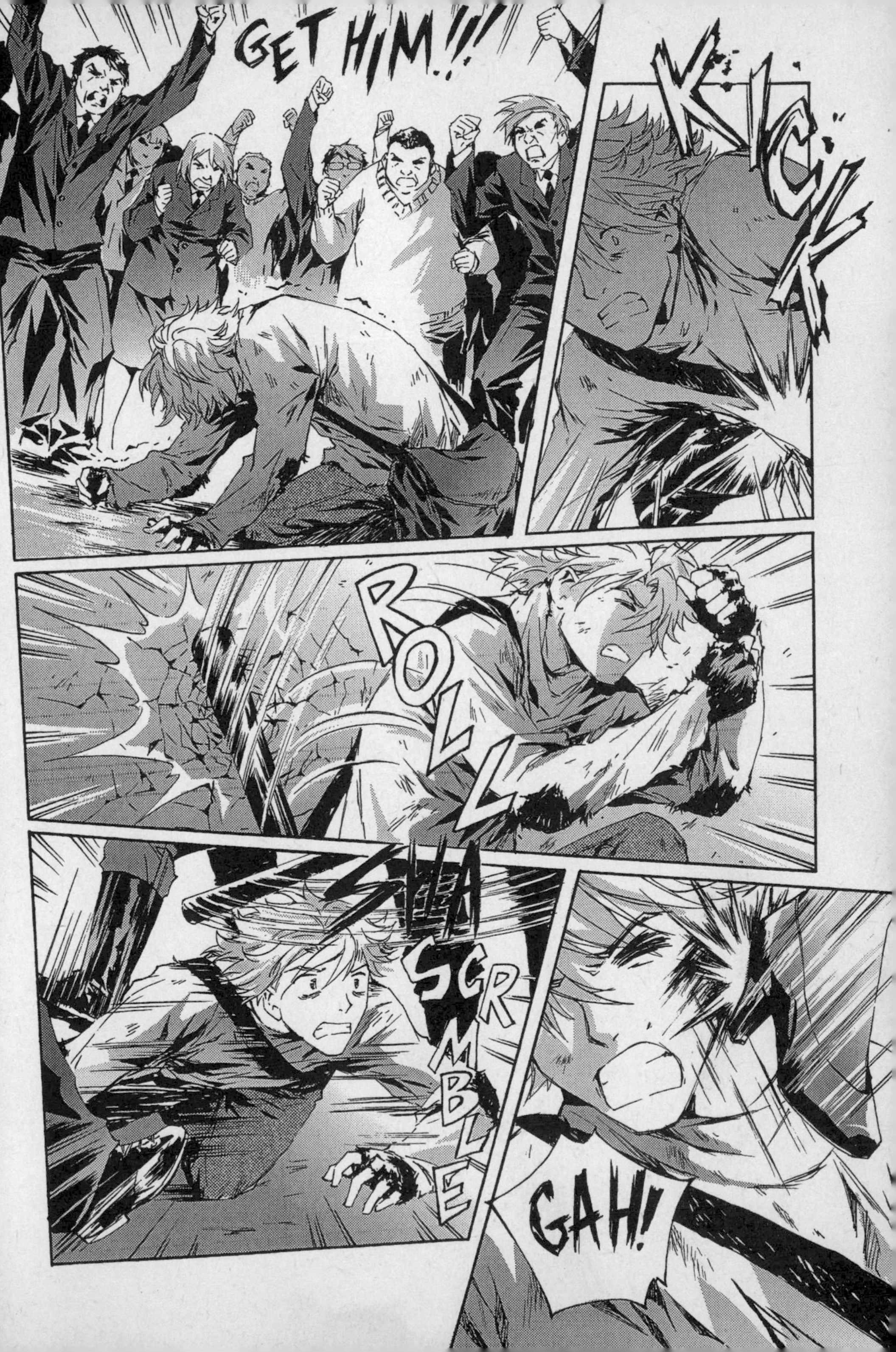
KICK
GET HIM!!!
ROLL
SHA
SCRAMBLE
GAH!

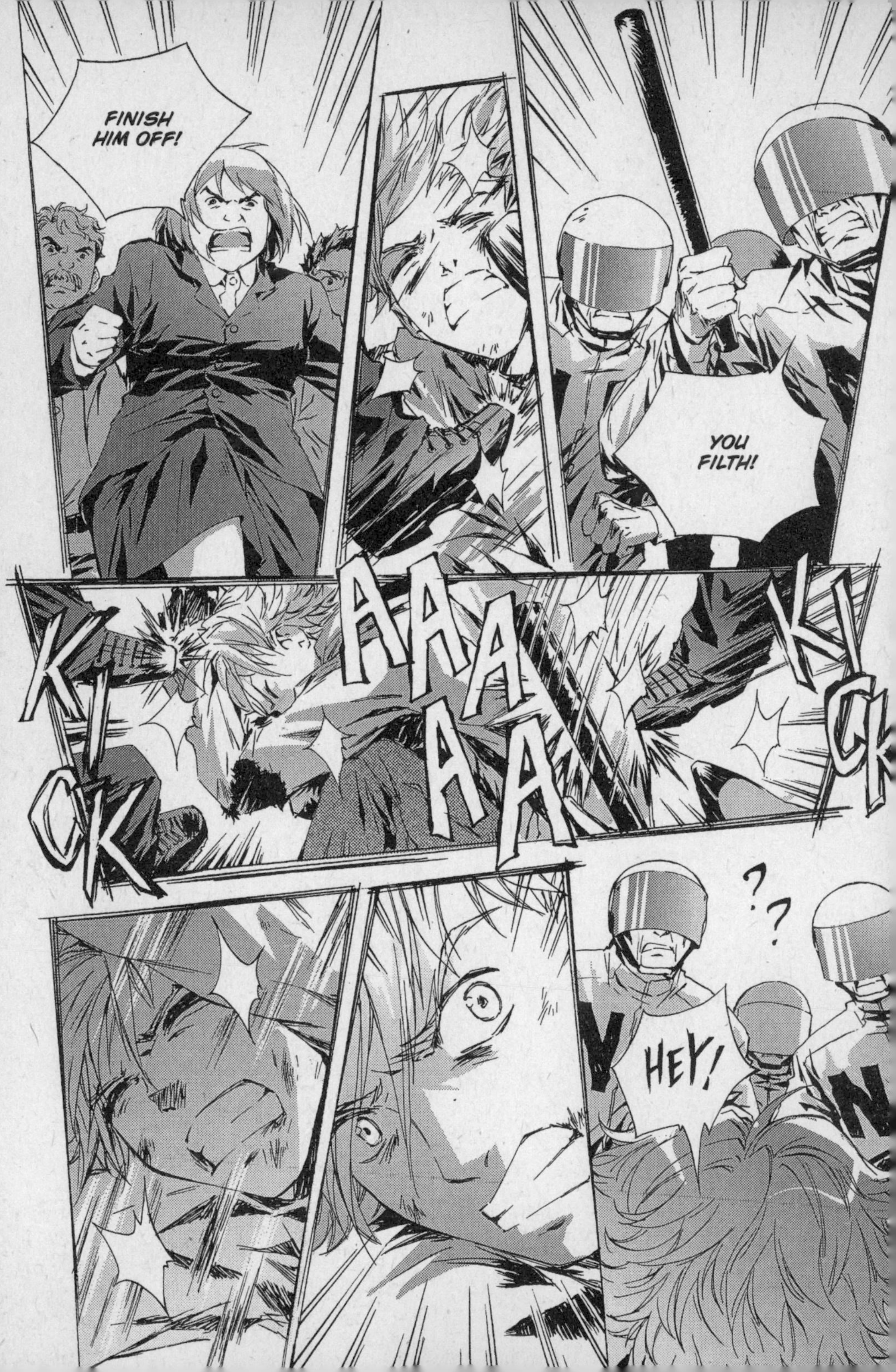
YOU FILTH!
FINISH HIM OFF!
KICK
AAAAA
KICK
??
HEY!

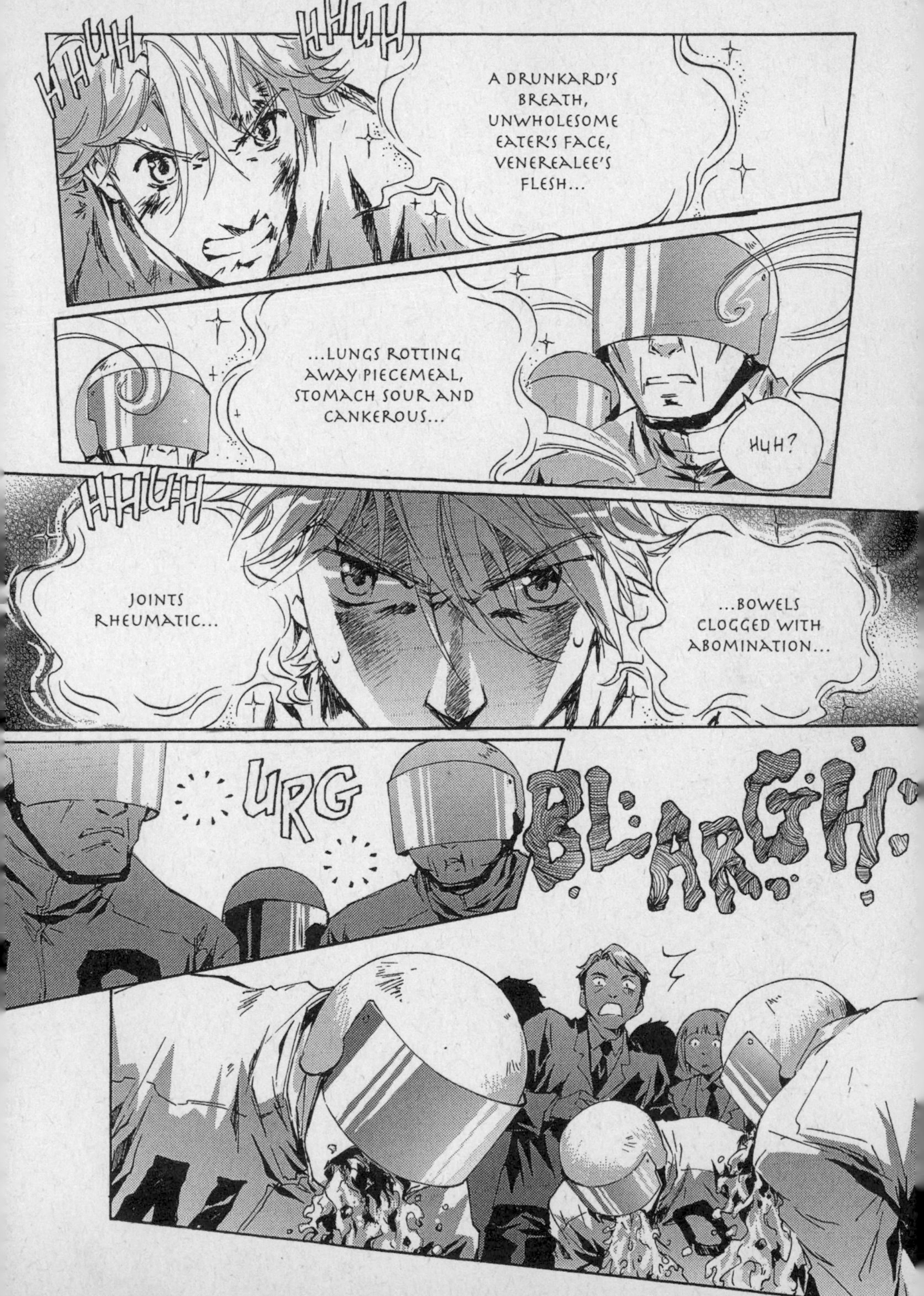
HHUH
HHUH
A DRUNKARD'S BREATH, UNWHOLESOME EATER'S FACE, VENEREALEE'S FLESH...
...LUNGS ROTTING AWAY PIECEMEAL, STOMACH SOUR AND CANKEROUS...
HUH?
HHUH
JOINTS RHEUMATIC...
...BOWELS CLOGGED WITH ABOMINATION...
URG
BLARGH!

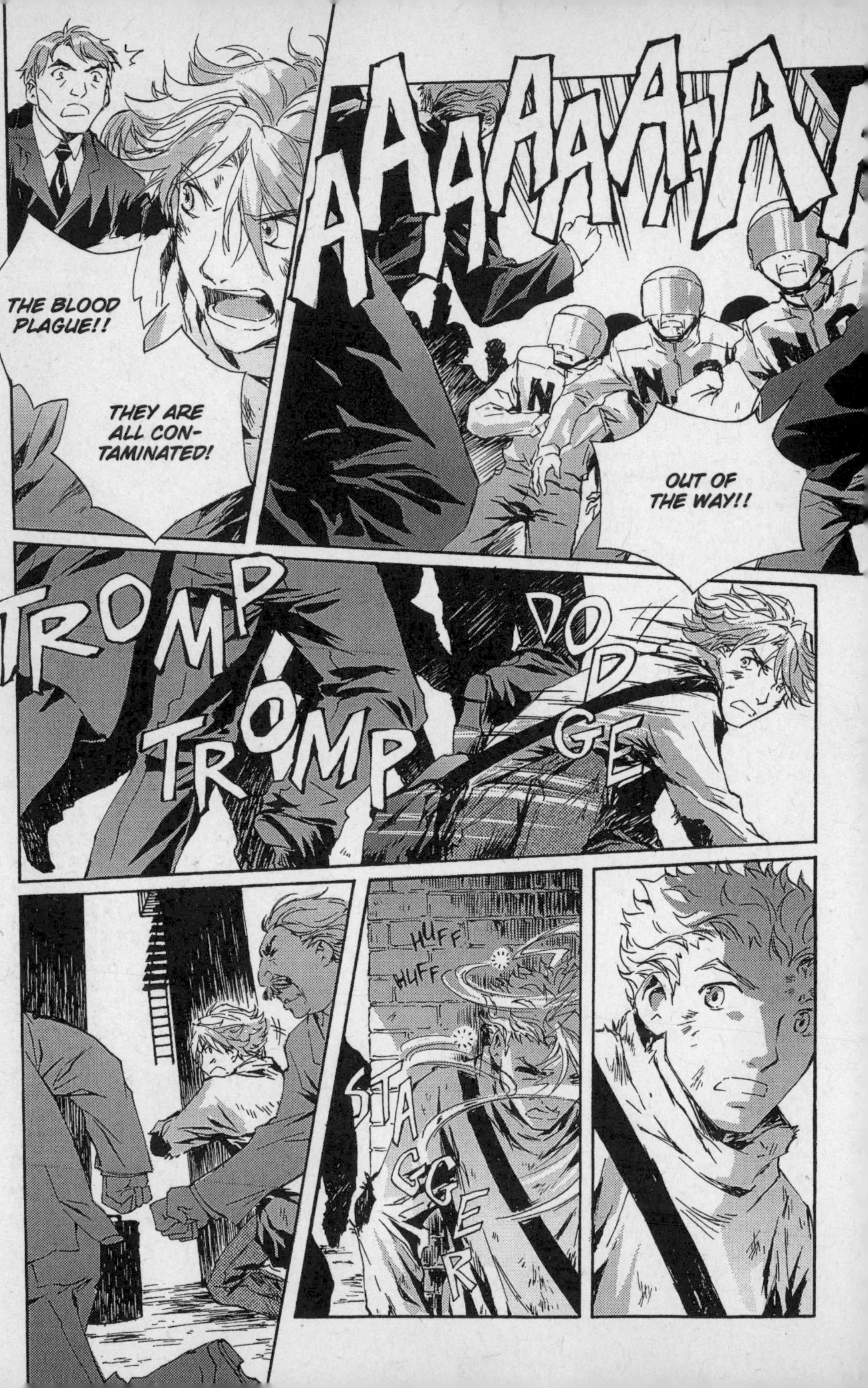
THE BLOOD PLAGUE!!
THEY ARE ALL CON-TAMINATED!
AAAAAAAA
OUT OF THE WAY!!
TROMP
TROMP
DODGE
HUFF
HUFF
STAGGER

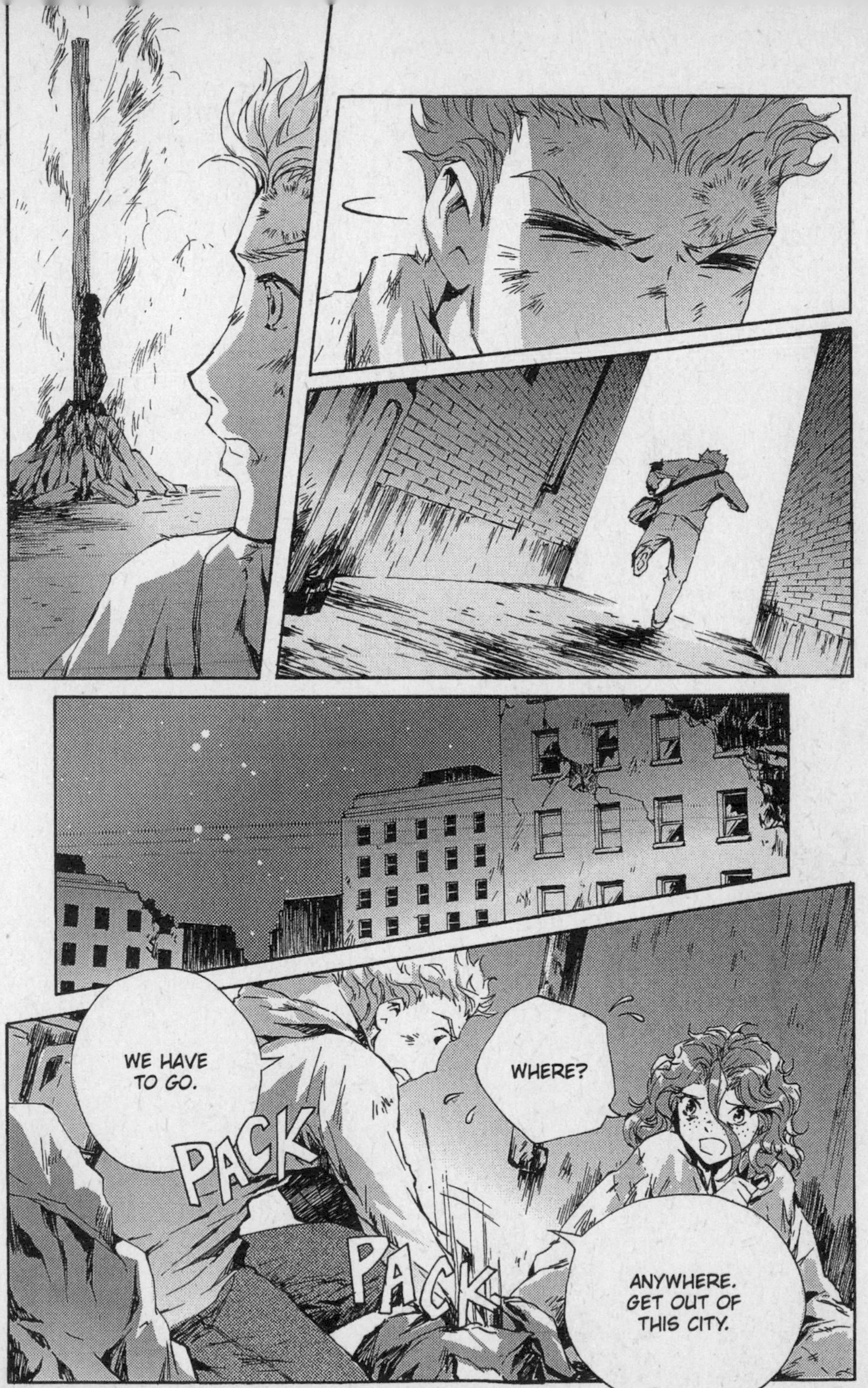
WE HAVE TO GO.
WHERE?
PACK
PACK
ANYWHERE. GET OUT OF THIS CITY.

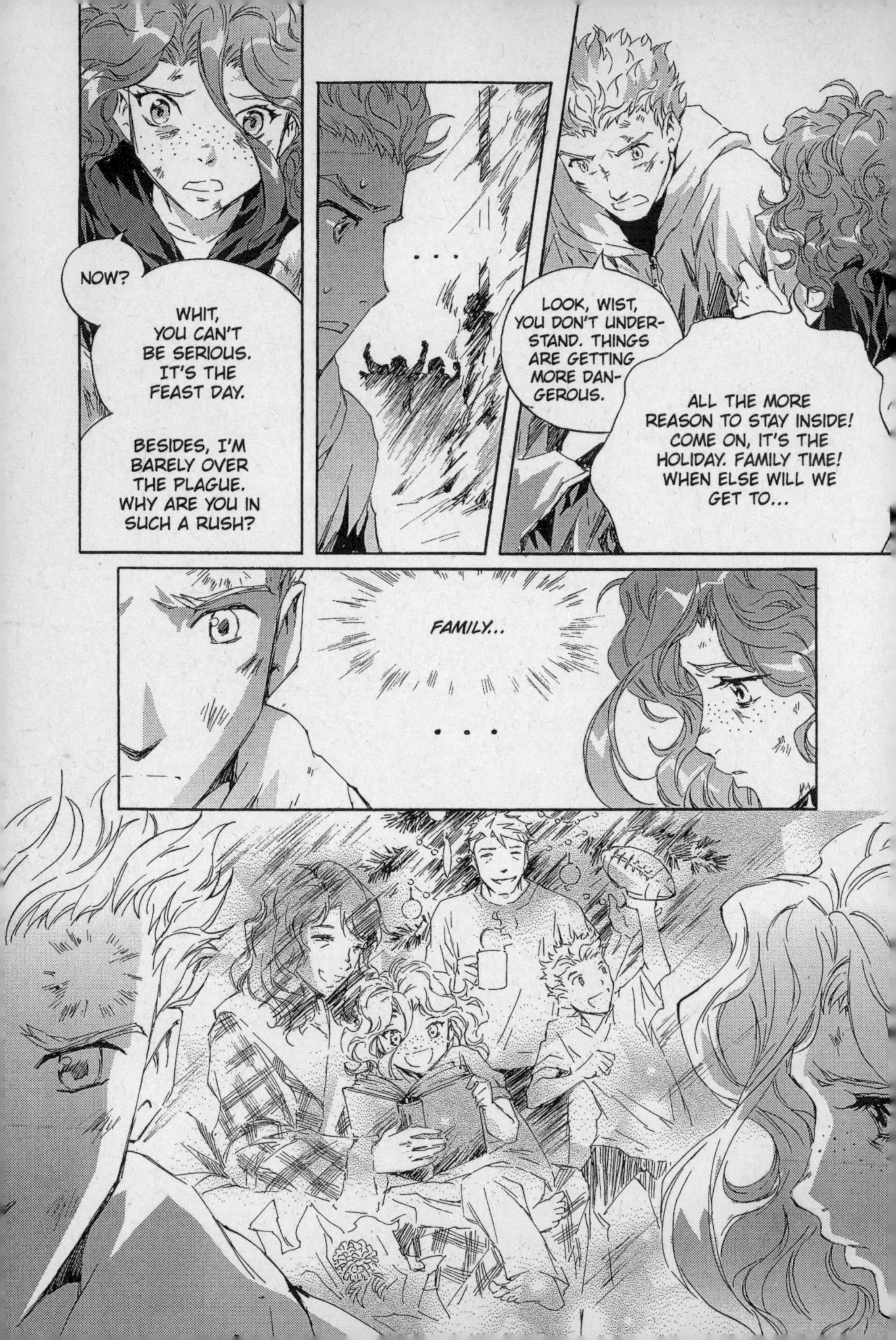
NOW?
WHIT, YOU CAN'T BE SERIOUS. IT'S THE FEAST DAY.
BESIDES, I'M BARELY OVER THE PLAGUE. WHY ARE YOU IN SUCH A RUSH?
...
LOOK, WIST, YOU DON'T UNDER-STAND. THINGS ARE GETTING MORE DAN-GEROUS.
ALL THE MORE REASON TO STAY INSIDE! COME ON, IT'S THE HOLIDAY. FAMILY TIME! WHEN ELSE WILL WE GET TO...
FAMILY...
...

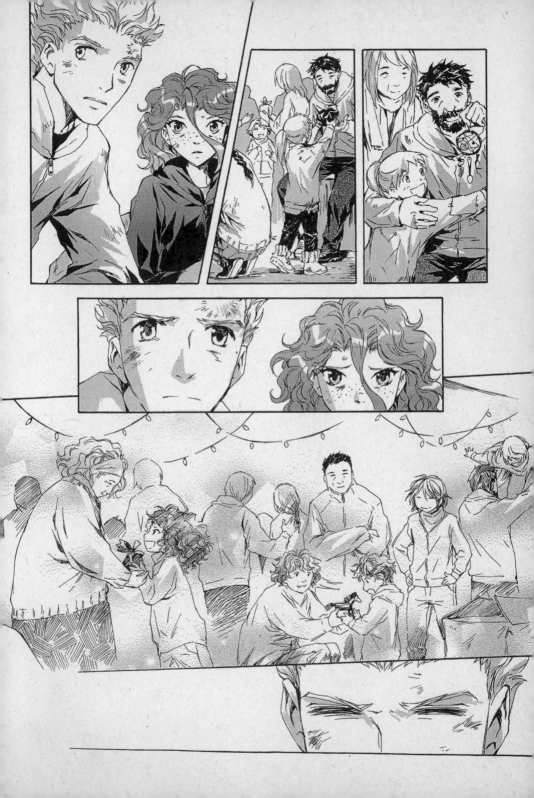

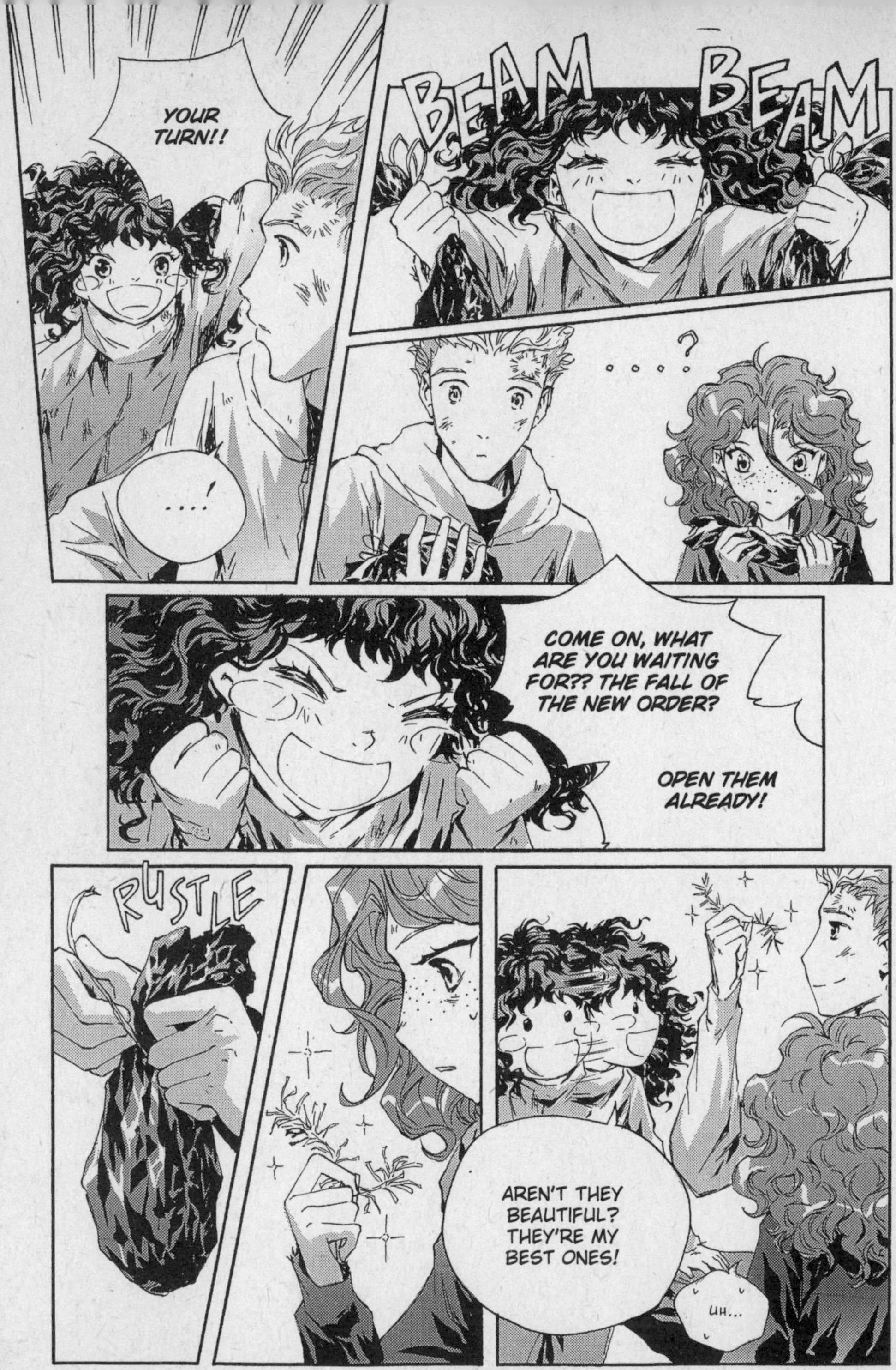
YOUR TURN!!
...!
BEAM BEAM
...?
COME ON, WHAT ARE YOU WAITING FOR?? THE FALL OF THE NEW ORDER?
OPEN THEM ALREADY!
RUSTLE
AREN'T THEY BEAUTIFUL? THEY'RE MY BEST ONES!
UH...

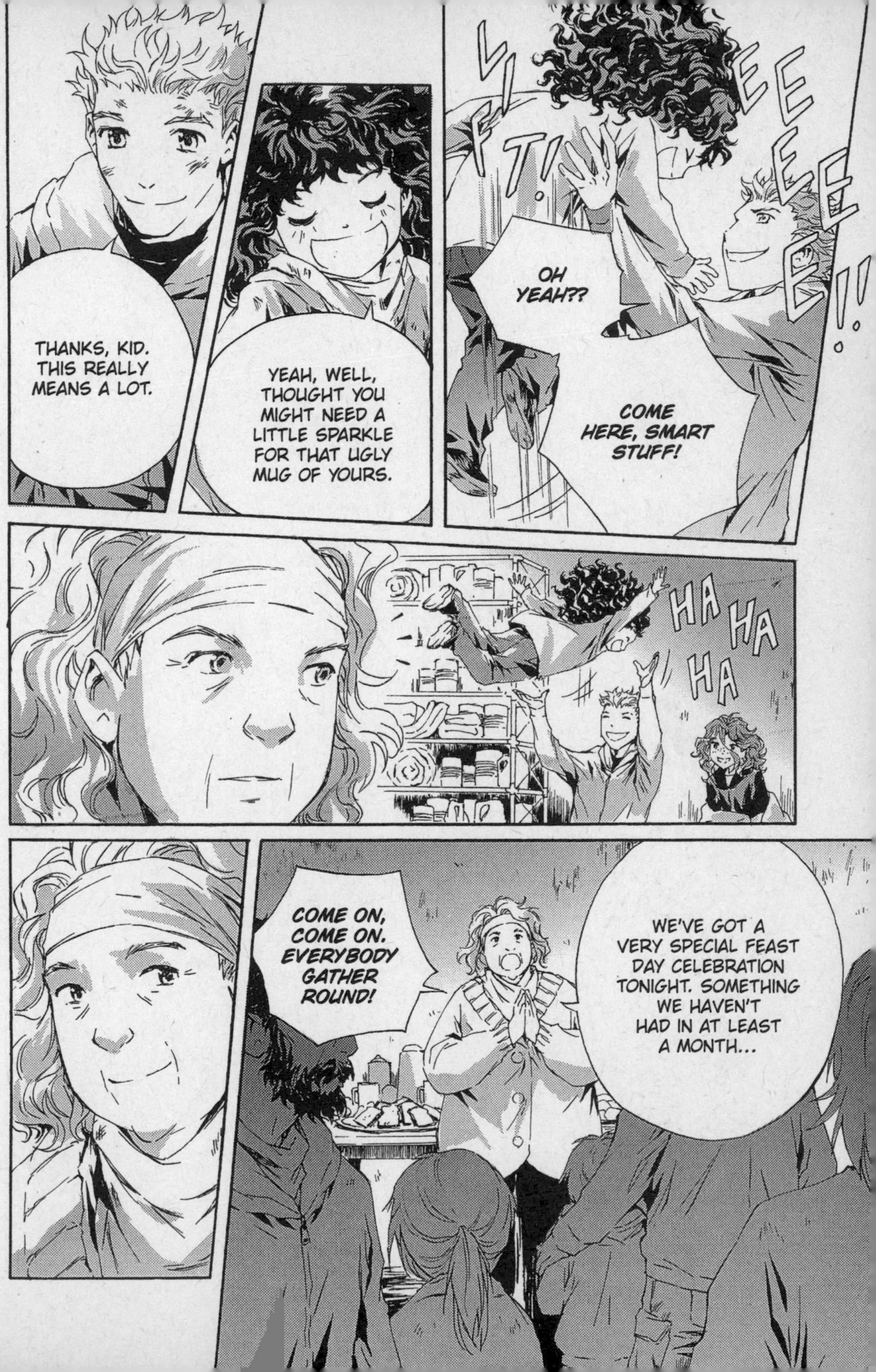
THANKS, KID. THIS REALLY MEANS A LOT.
YEAH, WELL, THOUGHT YOU MIGHT NEED A LITTLE SPARKLE FOR THAT UGLY MUG OF YOURS.
LIFT!!
OH YEAH??
EEEEE!!
COME HERE, SMART STUFF!
HA HA HA HA
COME ON, COME ON. EVERYBODY GATHER ROUND!
WE'VE GOT A VERY SPECIAL FEAST DAY CELEBRATION TONIGHT. SOMETHING WE HAVEN'T HAD IN AT LEAST A MONTH...

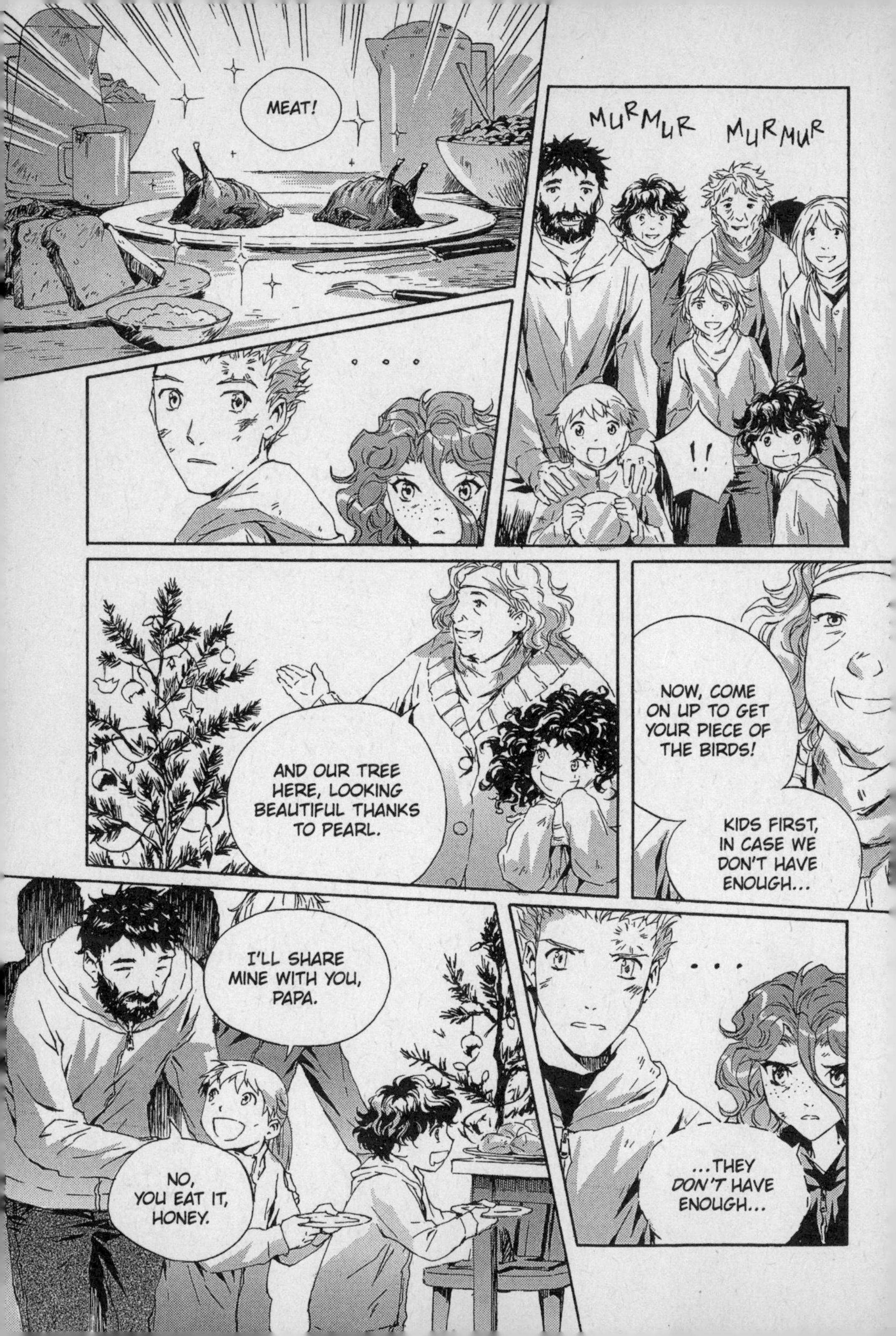
MEAT!
MURMUR MURMUR
. . .
!!
AND OUR TREE HERE, LOOKING BEAUTIFUL THANKS TO PEARL.
NOW, COME ON UP TO GET YOUR PIECE OF THE BIRDS!
KIDS FIRST, IN CASE WE DON'T HAVE ENOUGH...
I'LL SHARE MINE WITH YOU, PAPA.
NO, YOU EAT IT, HONEY.
. . .
...THEY *DON'T* HAVE ENOUGH...

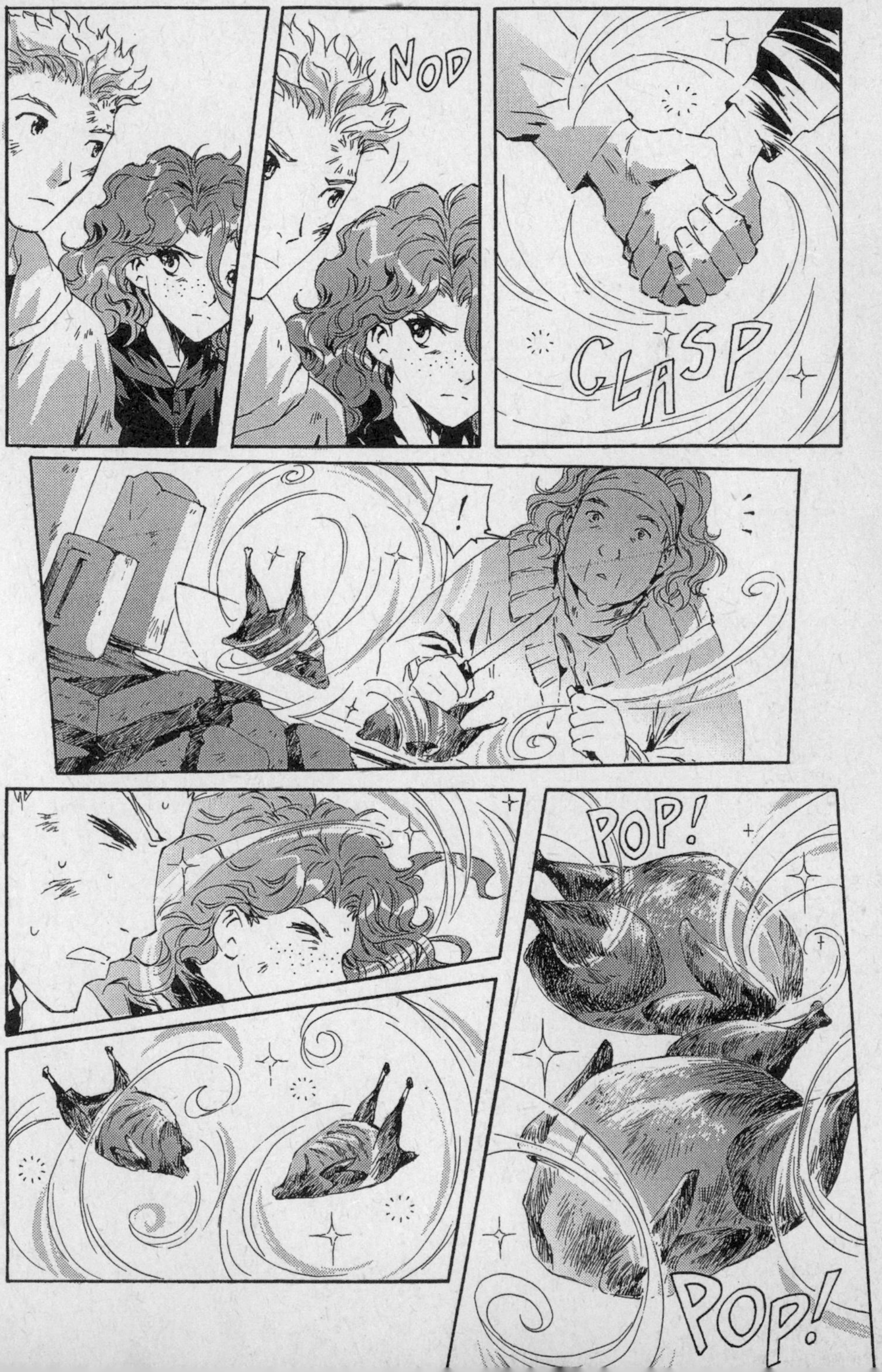
NOD
CLASP
!
POP!
POP!

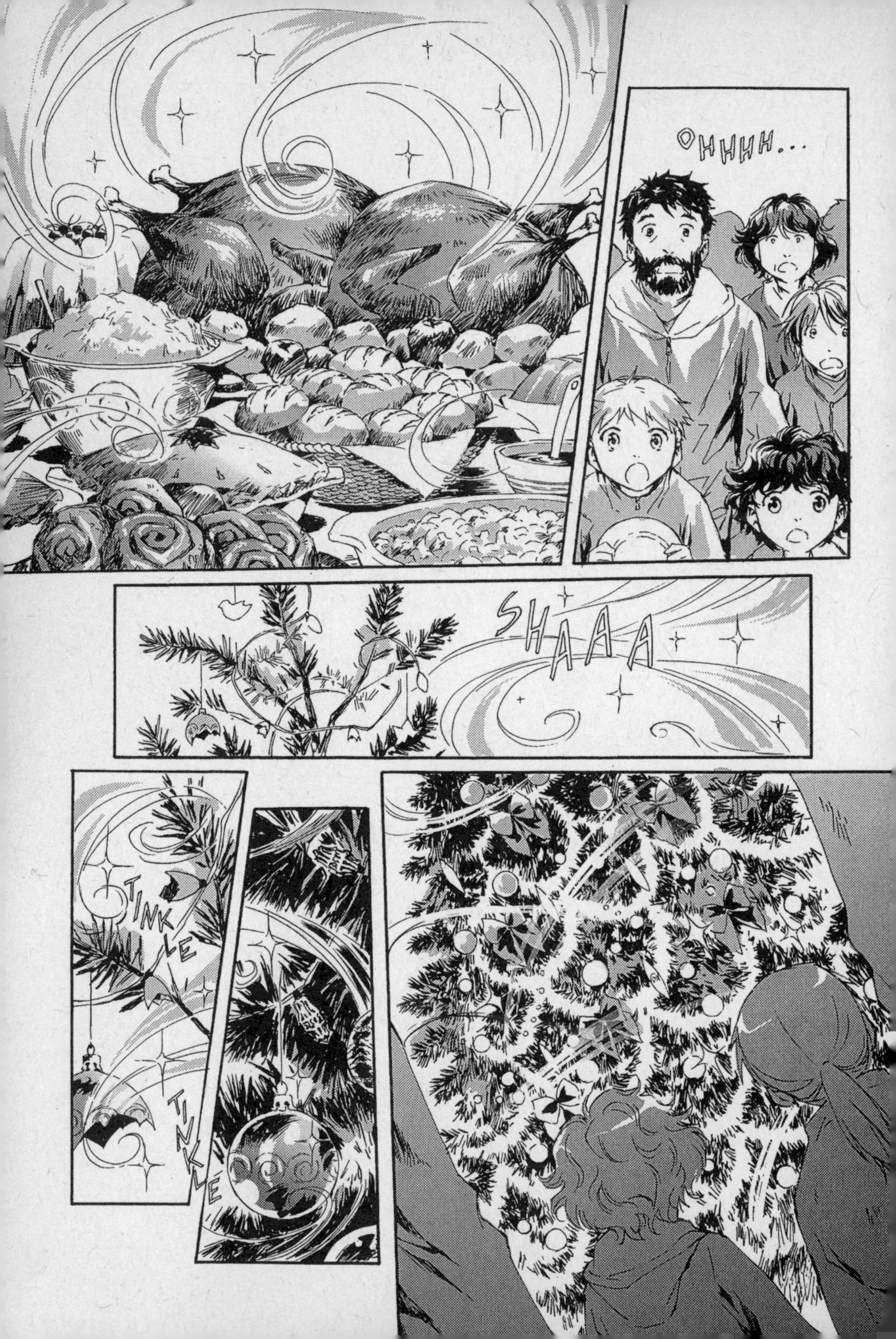
OHHHH...
SHAAA
TINKLE
TINKLE

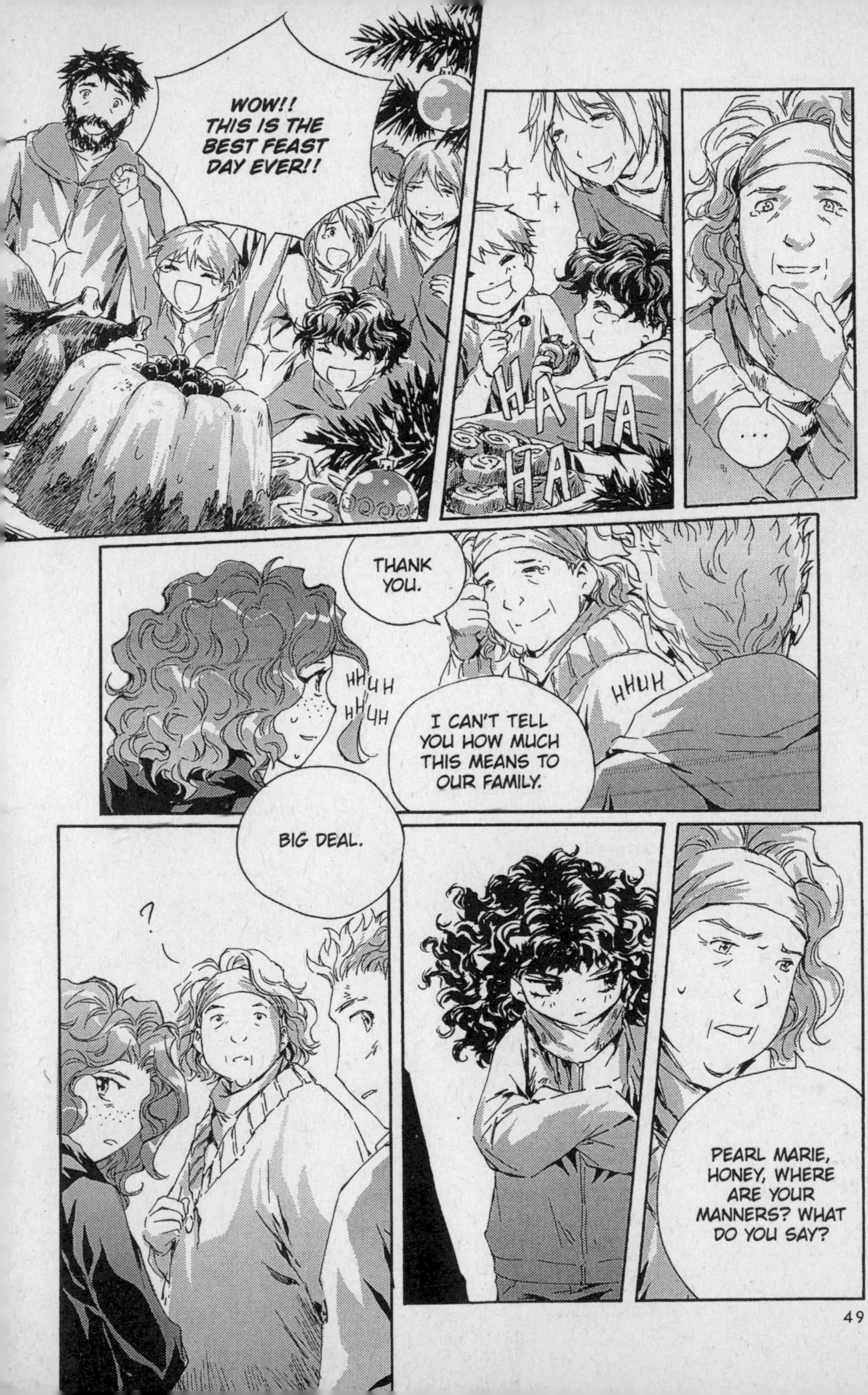
WOW!! THIS IS THE BEST FEAST DAY EVER!!
HA HA HA HA
...
THANK YOU.
HHUH HHUH
HHUH
I CAN'T TELL YOU HOW MUCH THIS MEANS TO OUR FAMILY.
BIG DEAL.
?
PEARL MARIE, HONEY, WHERE ARE YOUR MANNERS? WHAT DO YOU SAY?

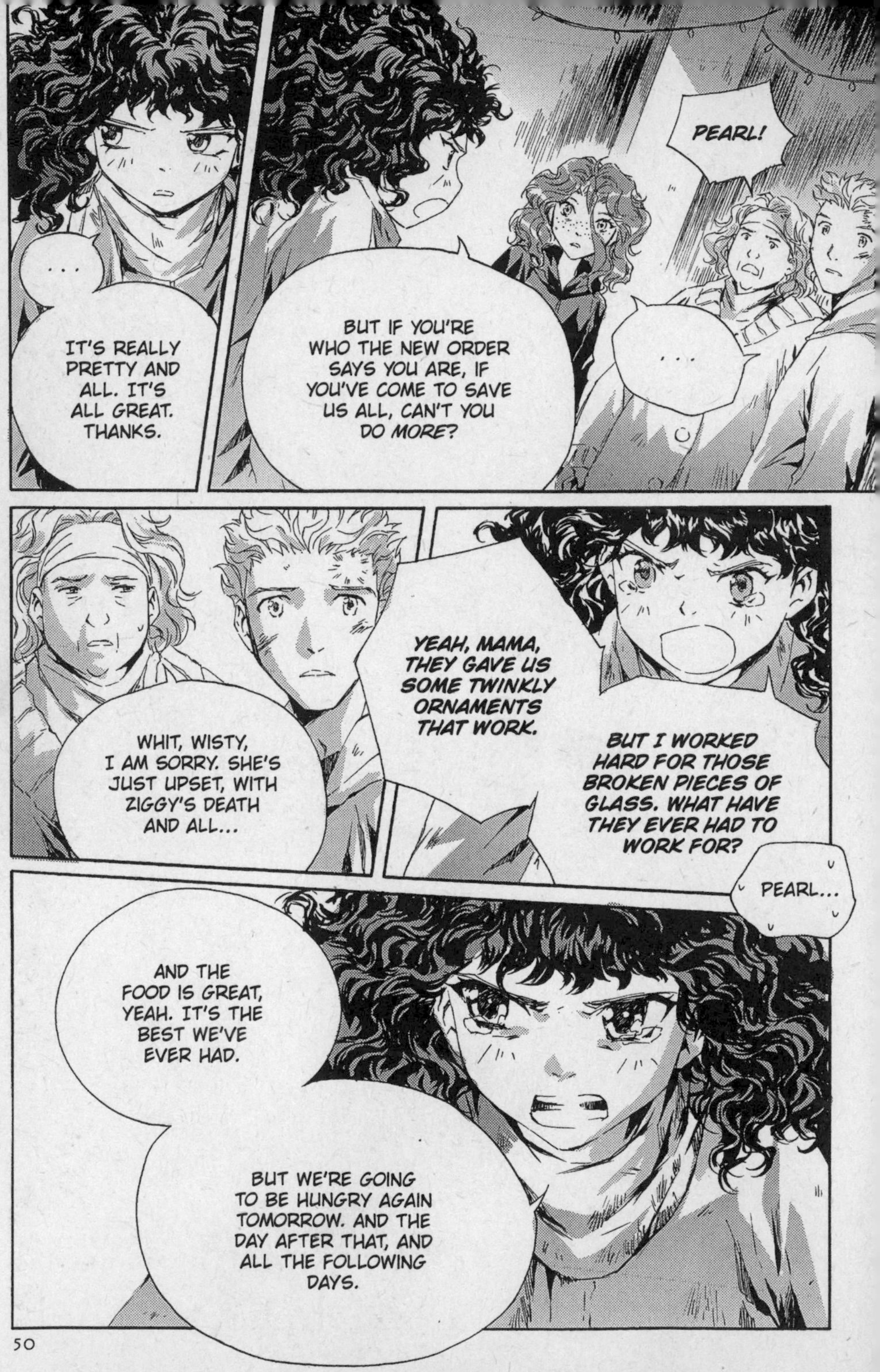
...
IT'S REALLY PRETTY AND ALL. IT'S ALL GREAT. THANKS.
BUT IF YOU'RE WHO THE NEW ORDER SAYS YOU ARE, IF YOU'VE COME TO SAVE US ALL, CAN'T YOU DO *MORE*?
PEARL!
...
WHIT, WISTY, I AM SORRY. SHE'S JUST UPSET, WITH ZIGGY'S DEATH AND ALL...
YEAH, MAMA, THEY GAVE US SOME TWINKLY ORNAMENTS THAT WORK.
BUT I WORKED HARD FOR THOSE BROKEN PIECES OF GLASS. WHAT HAVE THEY EVER HAD TO WORK FOR?
PEARL...
AND THE FOOD IS GREAT, YEAH. IT'S THE BEST WE'VE EVER HAD.
BUT WE'RE GOING TO BE HUNGRY AGAIN TOMORROW. AND THE DAY AFTER THAT, AND ALL THE FOLLOWING DAYS.

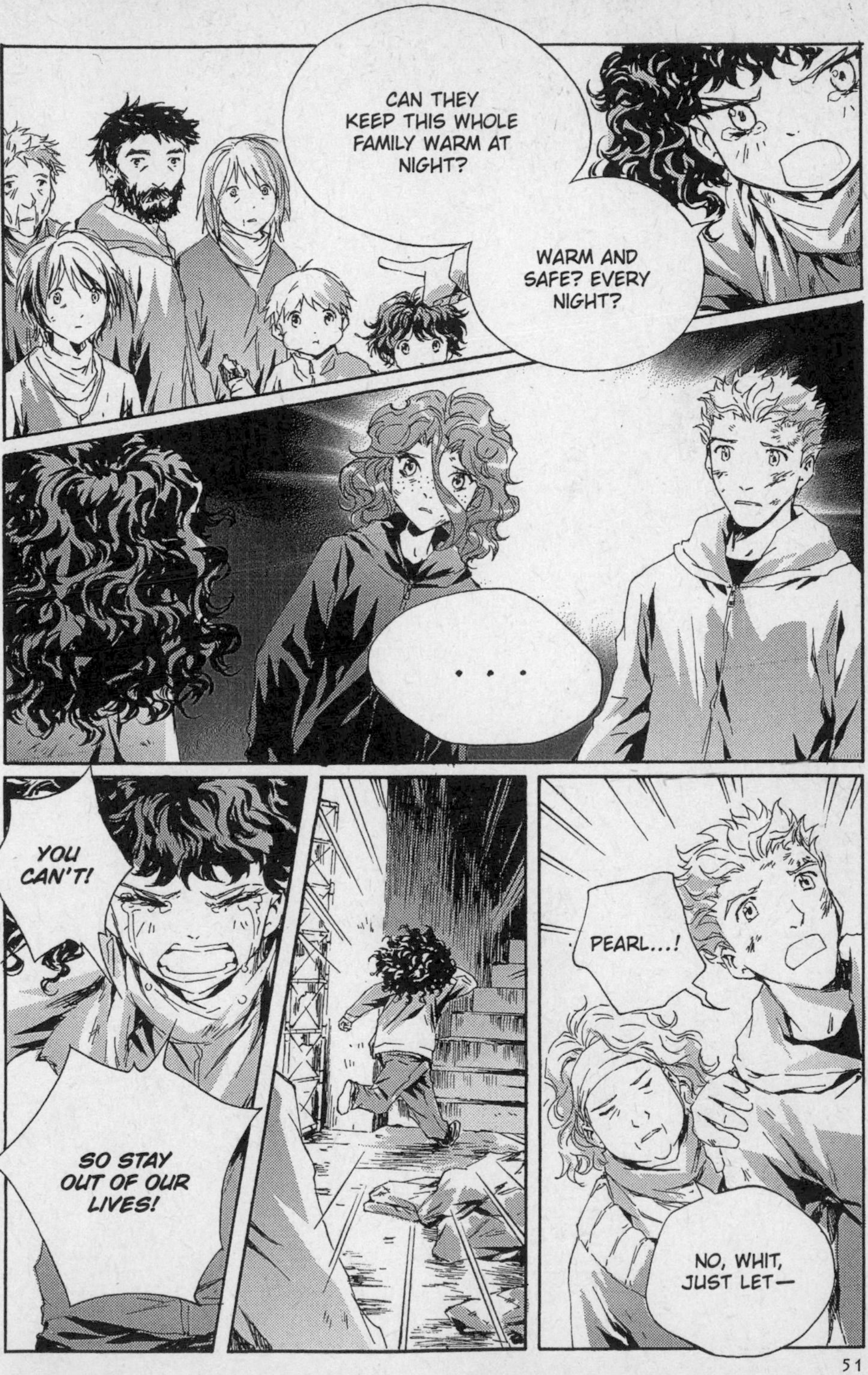
CAN THEY KEEP THIS WHOLE FAMILY WARM AT NIGHT?
WARM AND SAFE? EVERY NIGHT?
. . .
YOU CAN'T!
SO STAY OUT OF OUR LIVES!
PEARL...!
NO, WHIT, JUST LET—

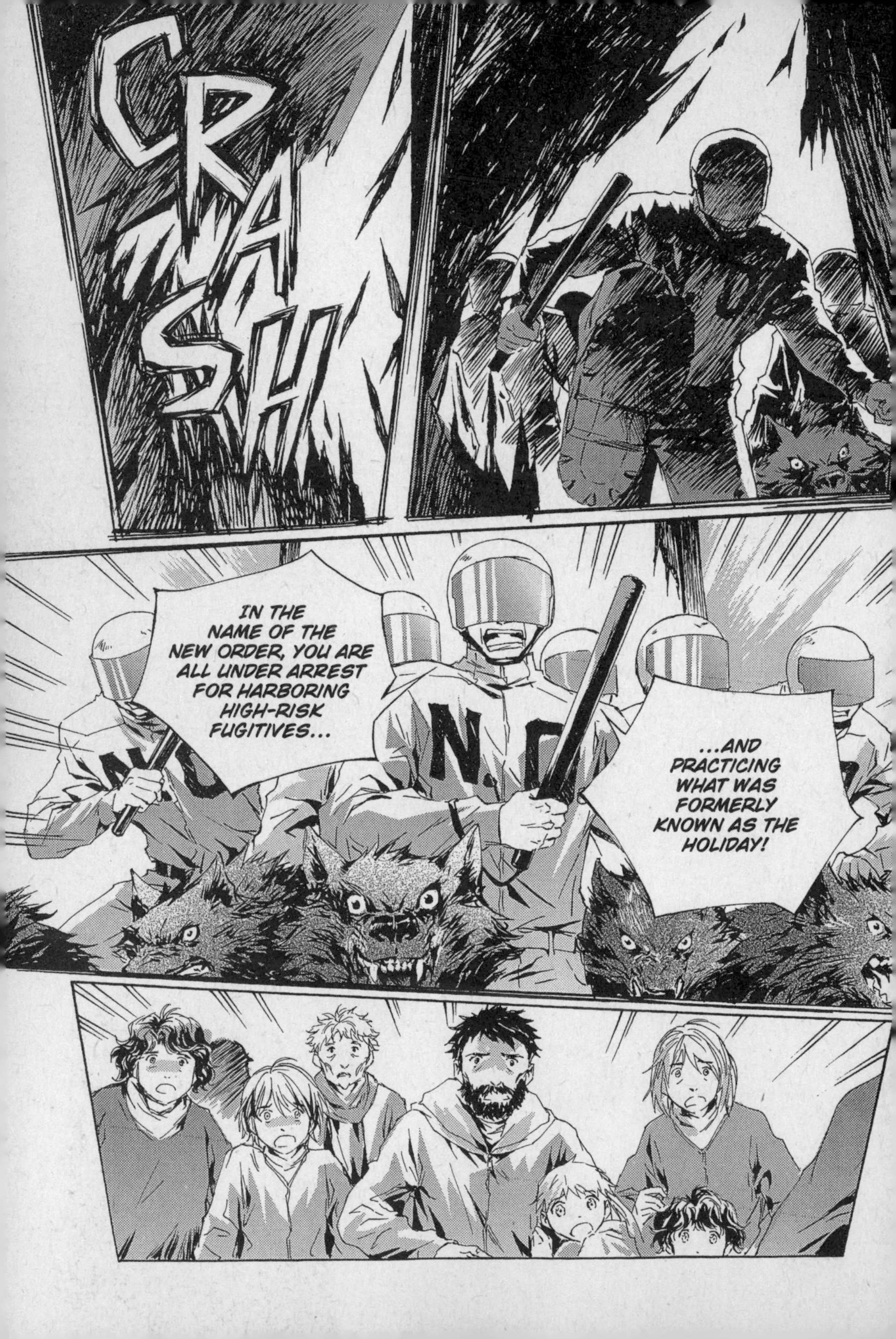
CRASH
IN THE NAME OF THE NEW ORDER, YOU ARE ALL UNDER ARREST FOR HARBORING HIGH-RISK FUGITIVES...
...AND PRACTICING WHAT WAS FORMERLY KNOWN AS THE HOLIDAY!

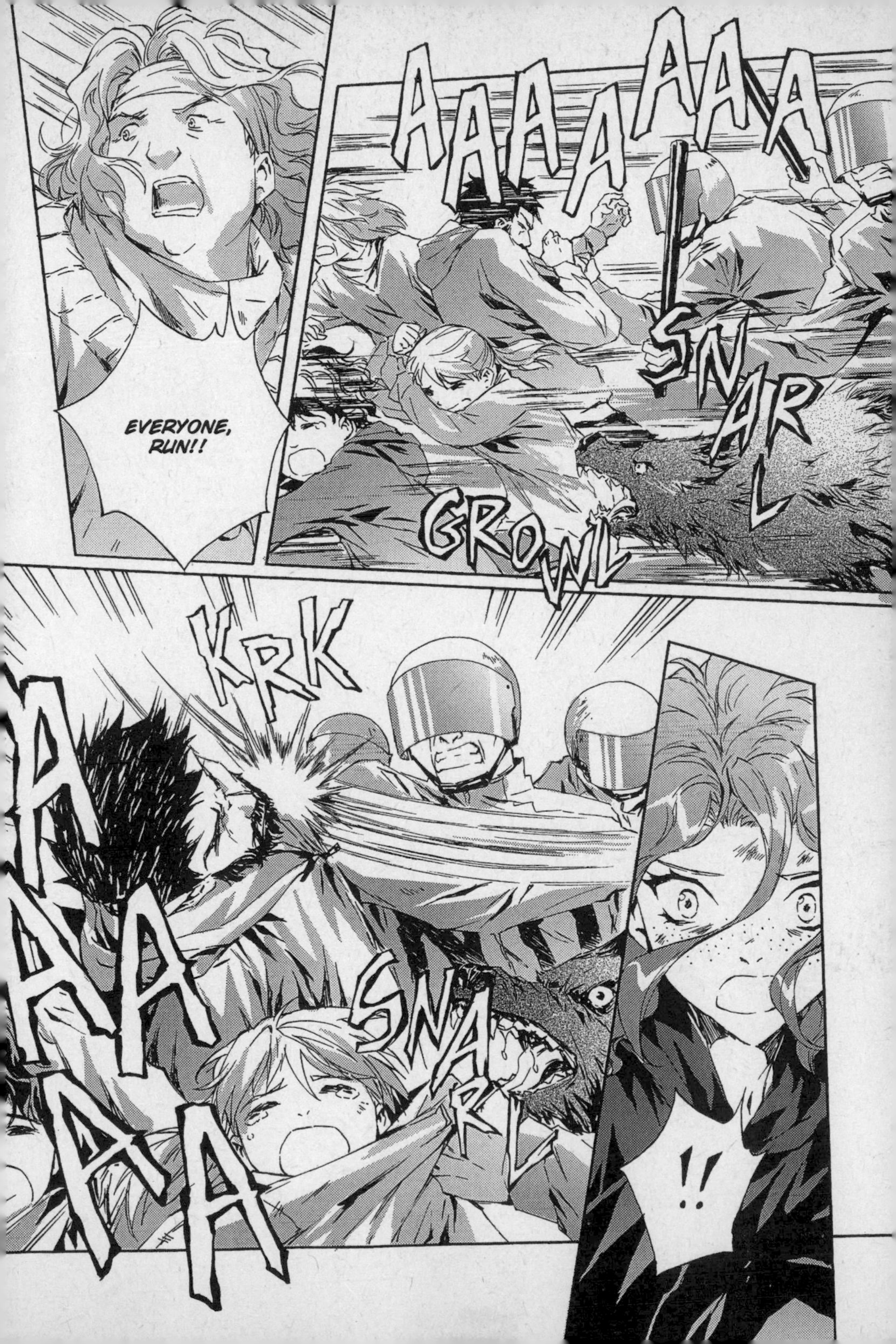
AAAAAAAA
EVERYONE, RUN!!
SNARL
GROWL
KRK
AAAAA
SNARL
!!

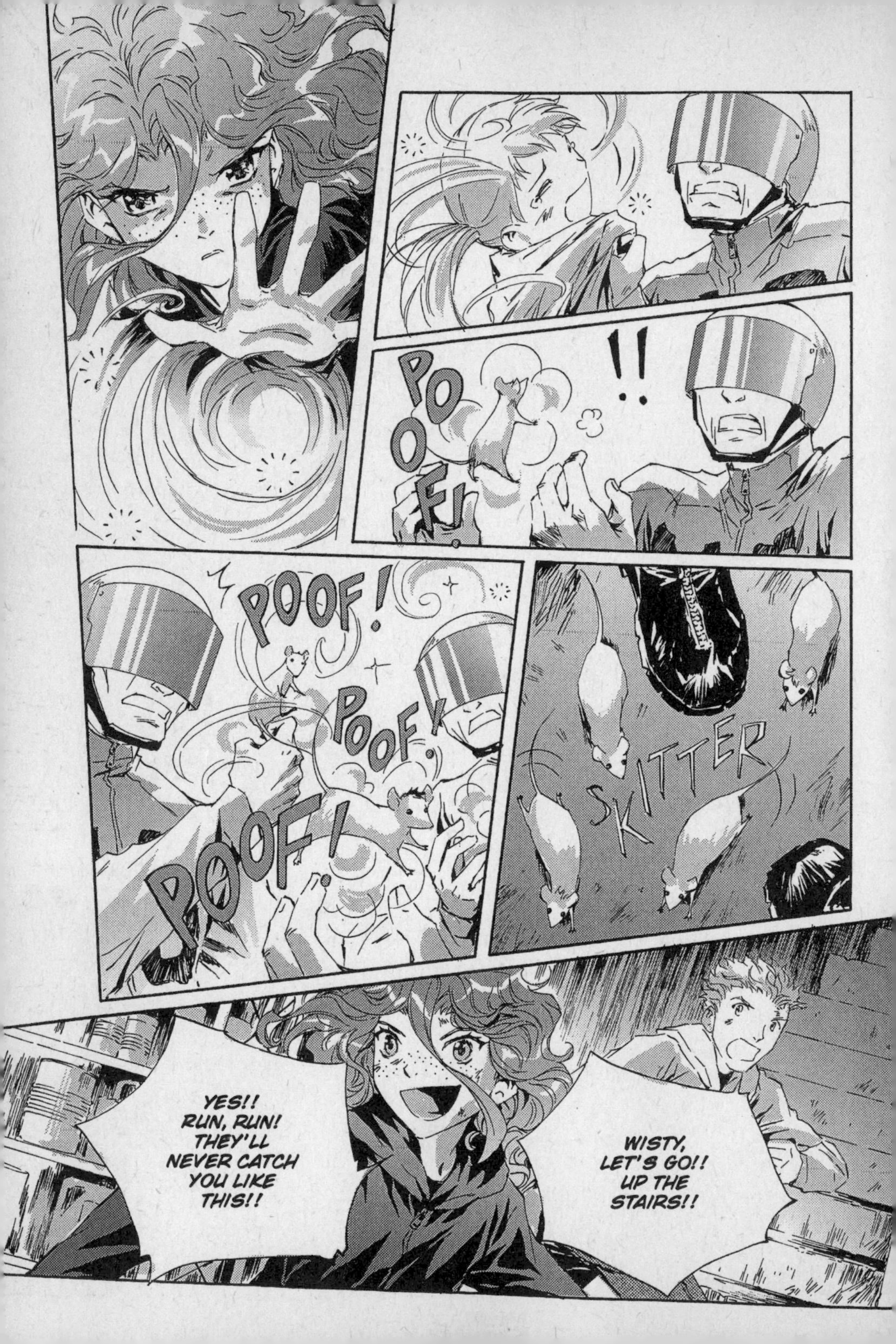
POOF!
!!
POOF!
POOF!
POOF!
SKITTER
YES!! RUN, RUN! THEY'LL NEVER CATCH YOU LIKE THIS!!
WISTY, LET'S GO!! UP THE STAIRS!!

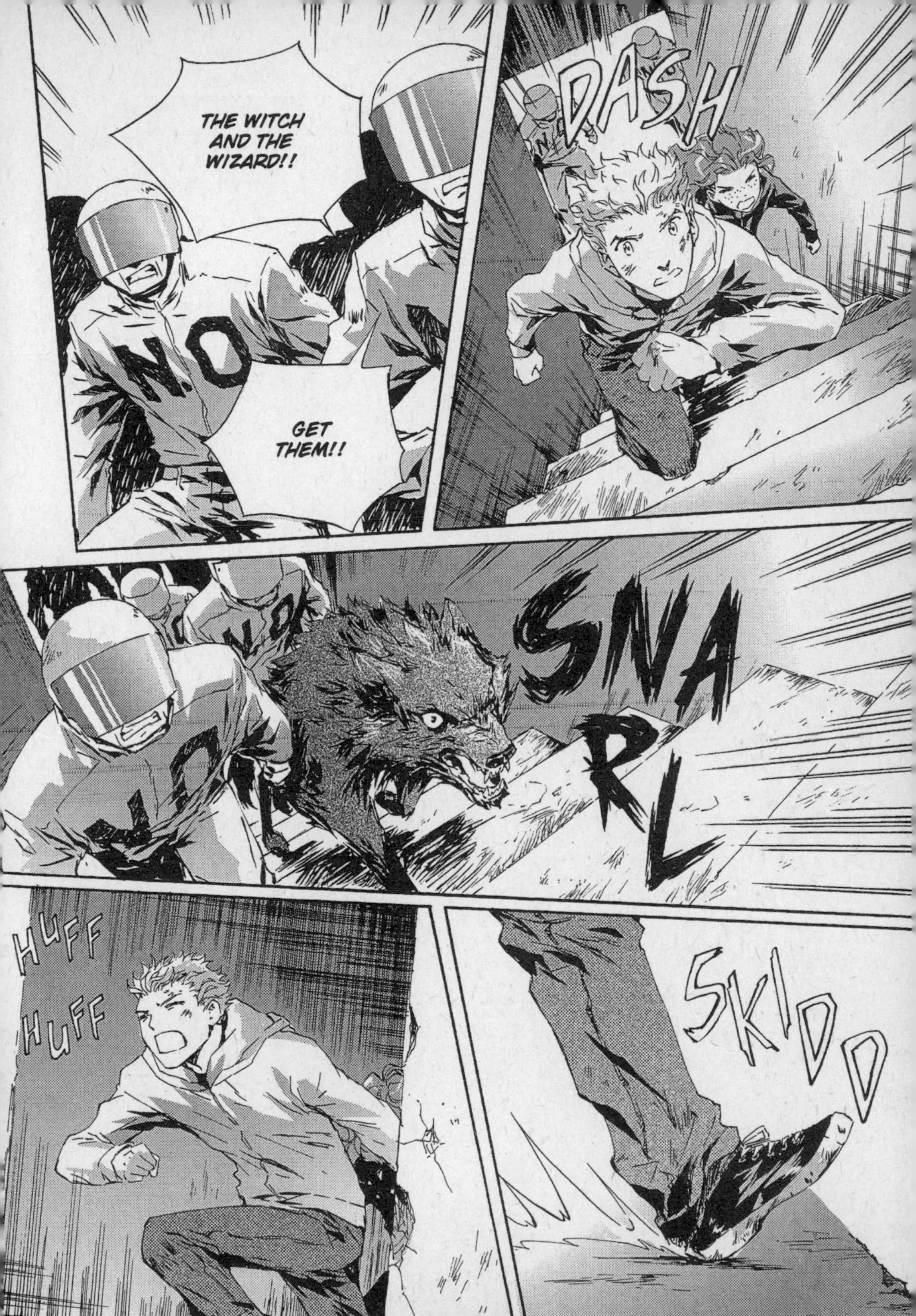
THE WITCH AND THE WIZARD!!
NO
GET THEM!!
DASH
SNARL
HUFF HUFF
SKIDD

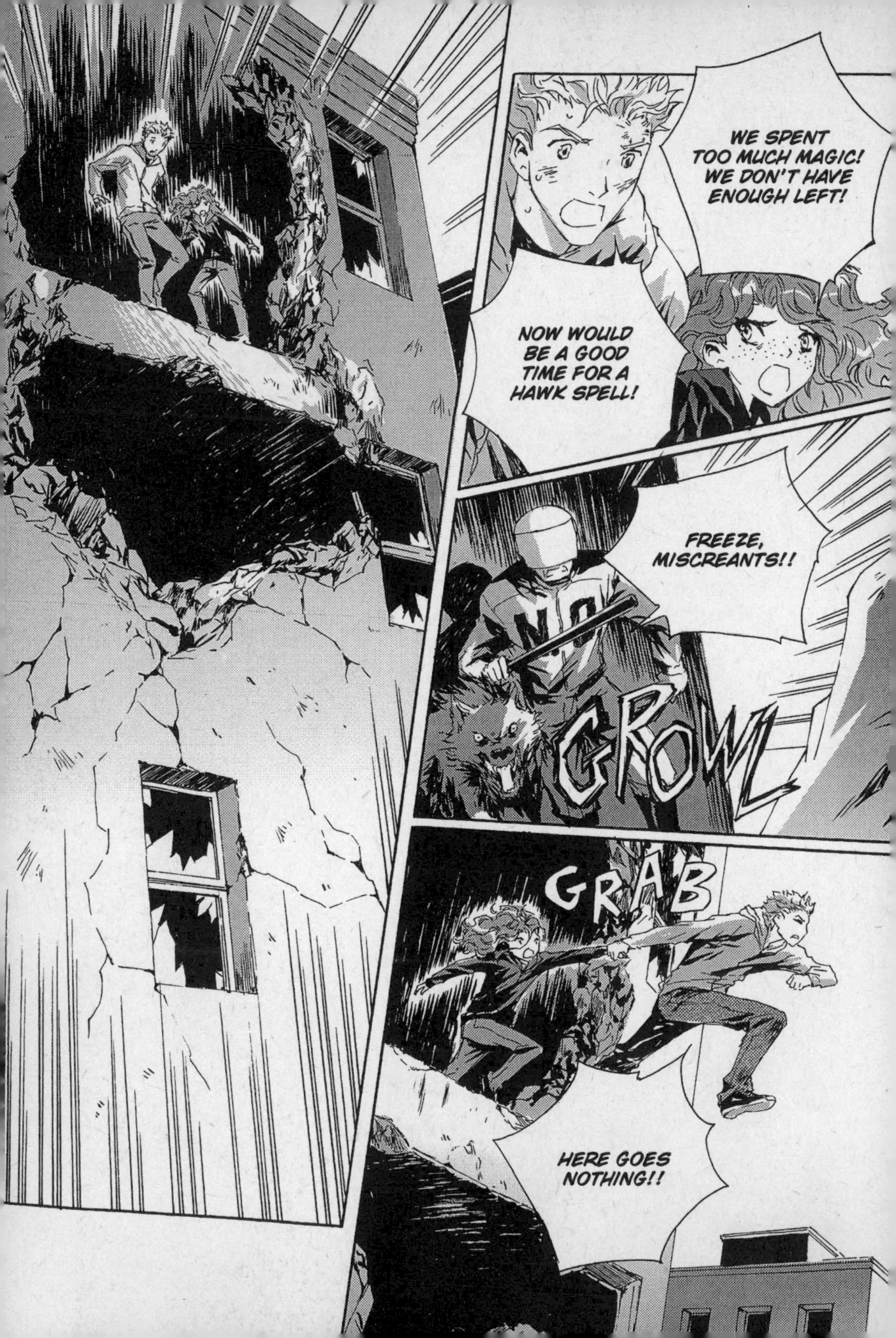
WE SPENT TOO MUCH MAGIC! WE DON'T HAVE ENOUGH LEFT!
NOW WOULD BE A GOOD TIME FOR A HAWK SPELL!
FREEZE, MISCREANTS!!
GROWL
GRAB
HERE GOES NOTHING!!

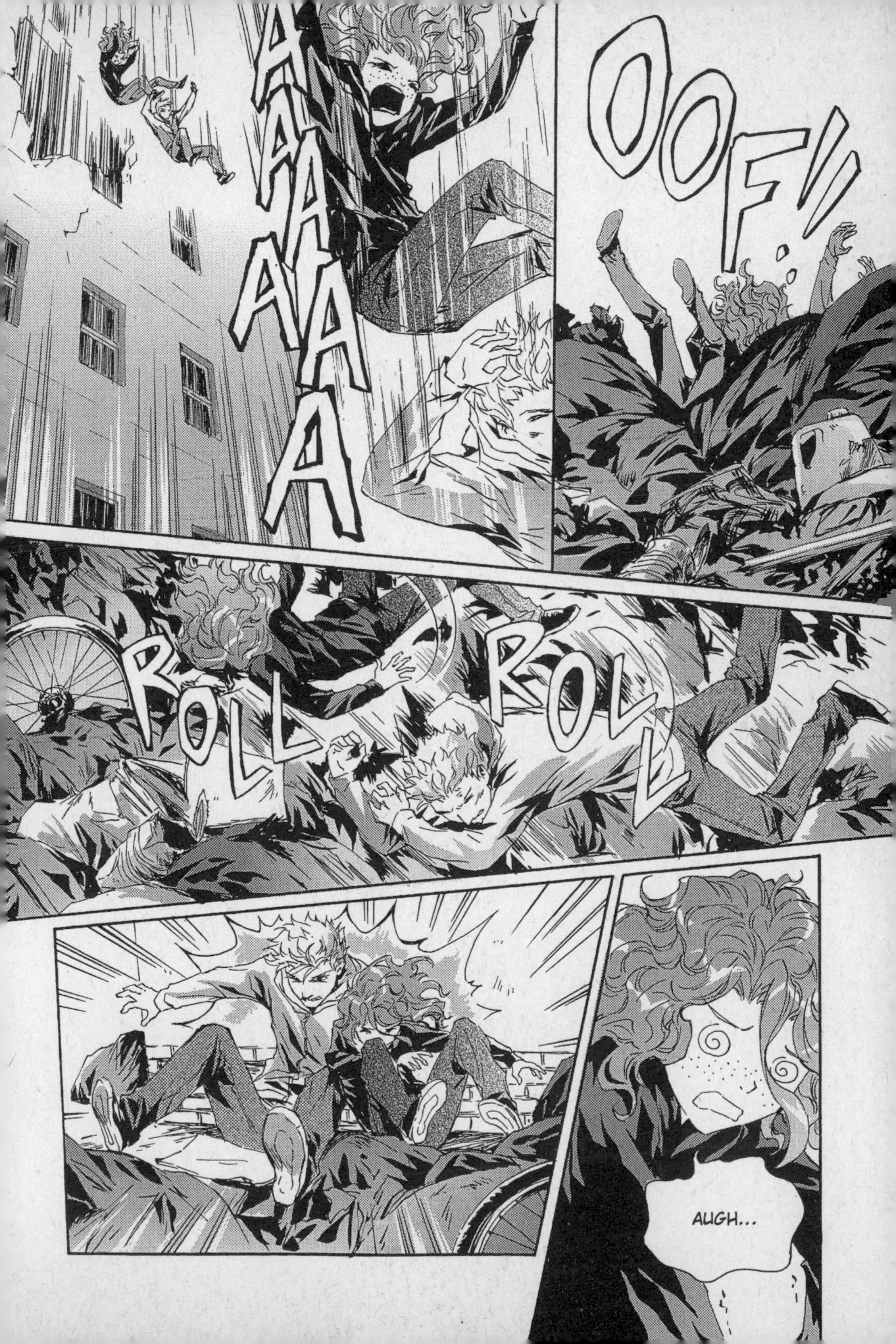
AAAAAAAA
OOF!!
ROLL
ROLL
AUGH...

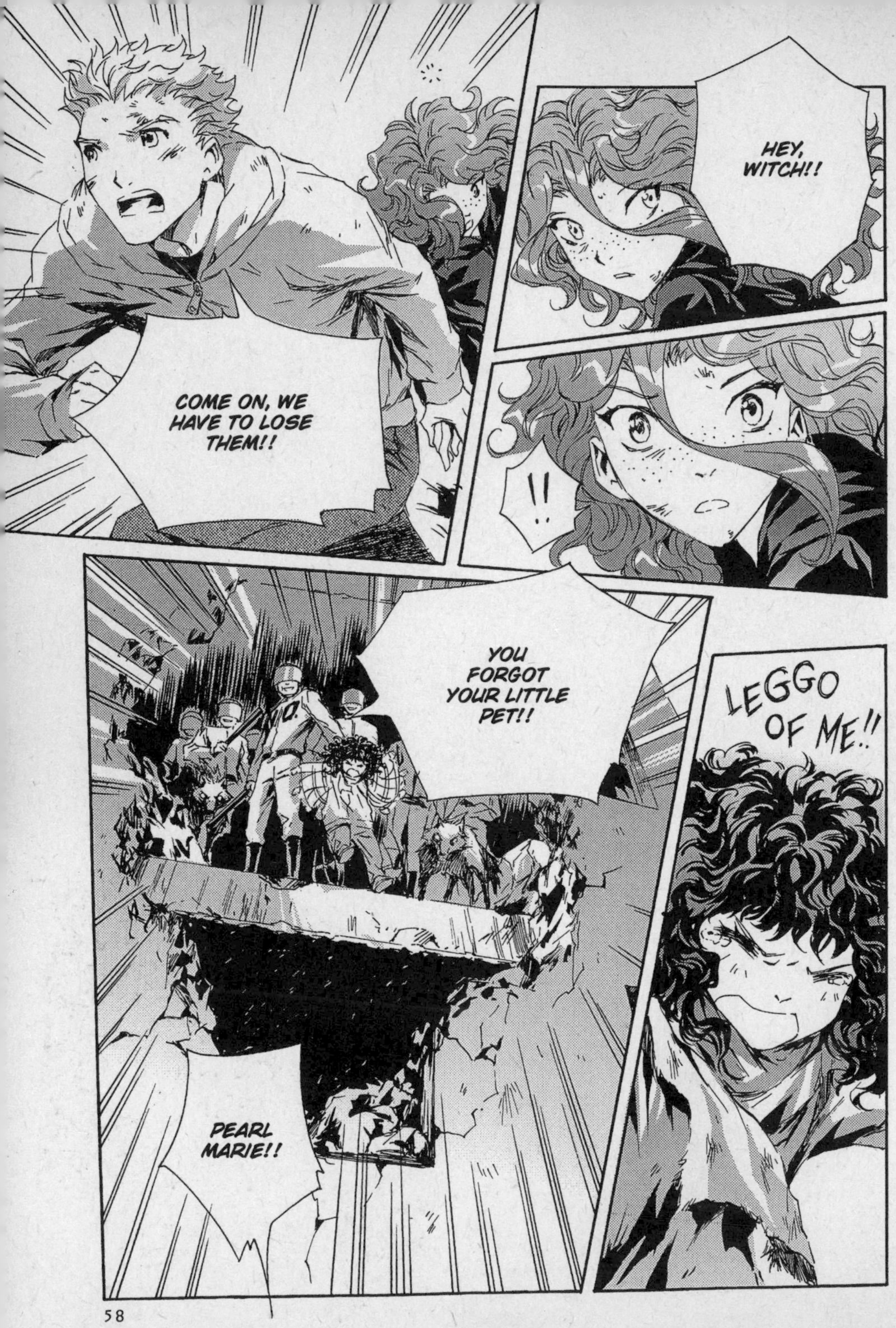

HEY, WITCH!!
!!
COME ON, WE HAVE TO LOSE THEM!!
YOU FORGOT YOUR LITTLE PET!!
LEGGO OF ME!!
PEARL MARIE!!

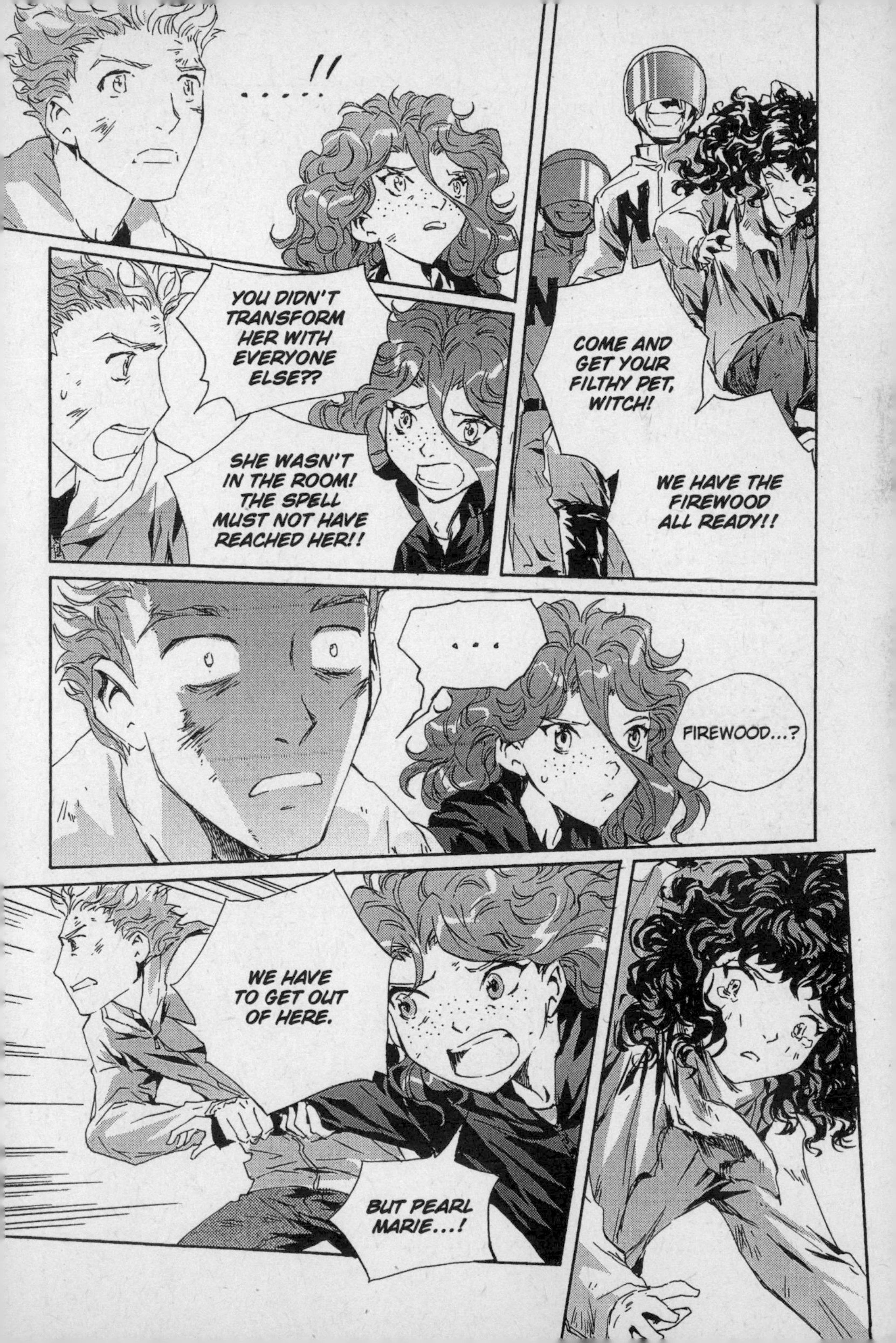
.....!!
YOU DIDN'T TRANSFORM HER WITH EVERYONE ELSE??
SHE WASN'T IN THE ROOM! THE SPELL MUST NOT HAVE REACHED HER!!
COME AND GET YOUR FILTHY PET, WITCH!
WE HAVE THE FIREWOOD ALL READY!!
...
FIREWOOD...?
WE HAVE TO GET OUT OF HERE.
BUT PEARL MARIE...!

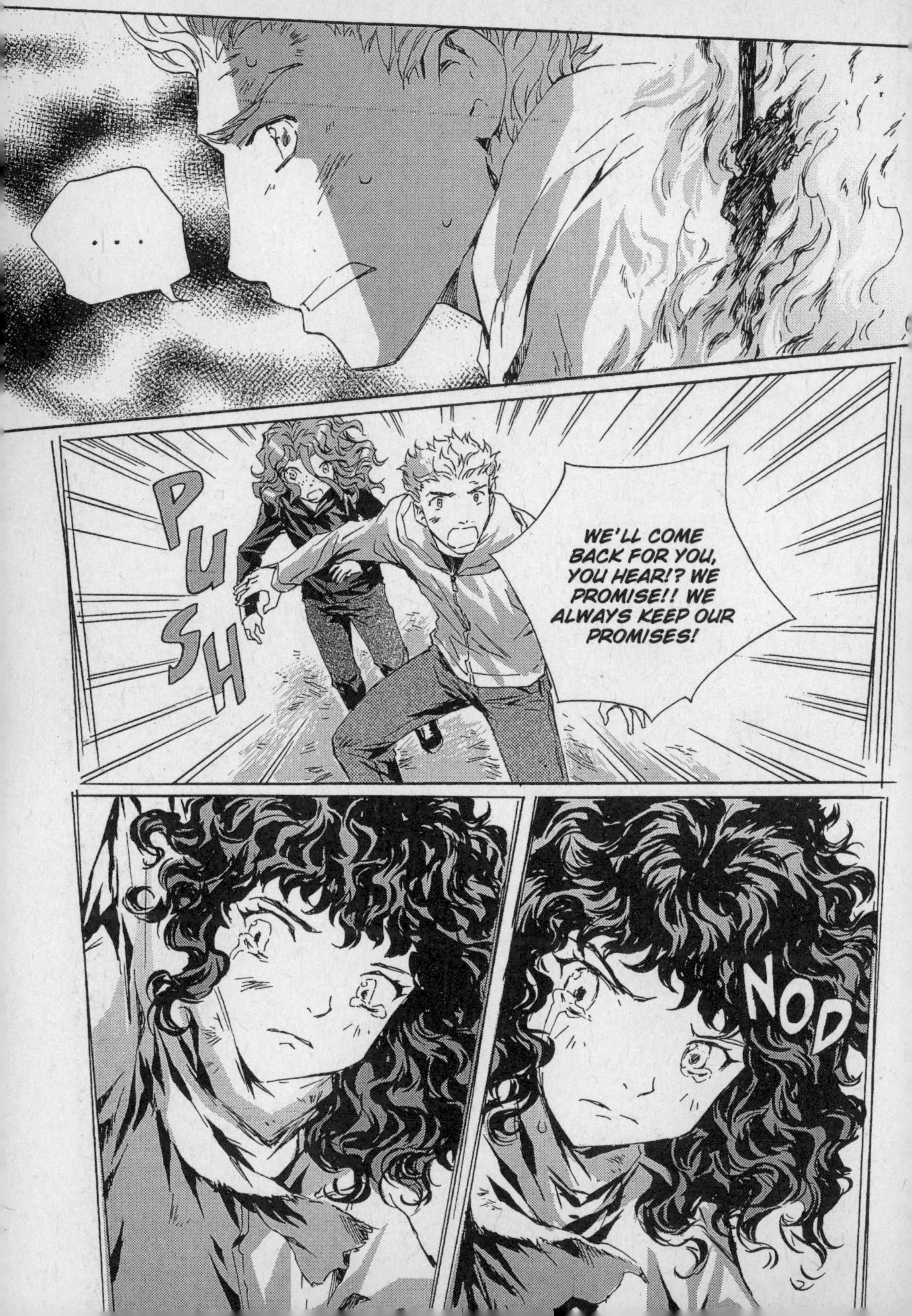
...
PUSH
WE'LL COME BACK FOR YOU, YOU HEAR!? WE PROMISE!! WE ALWAYS KEEP OUR PROMISES!
NOD

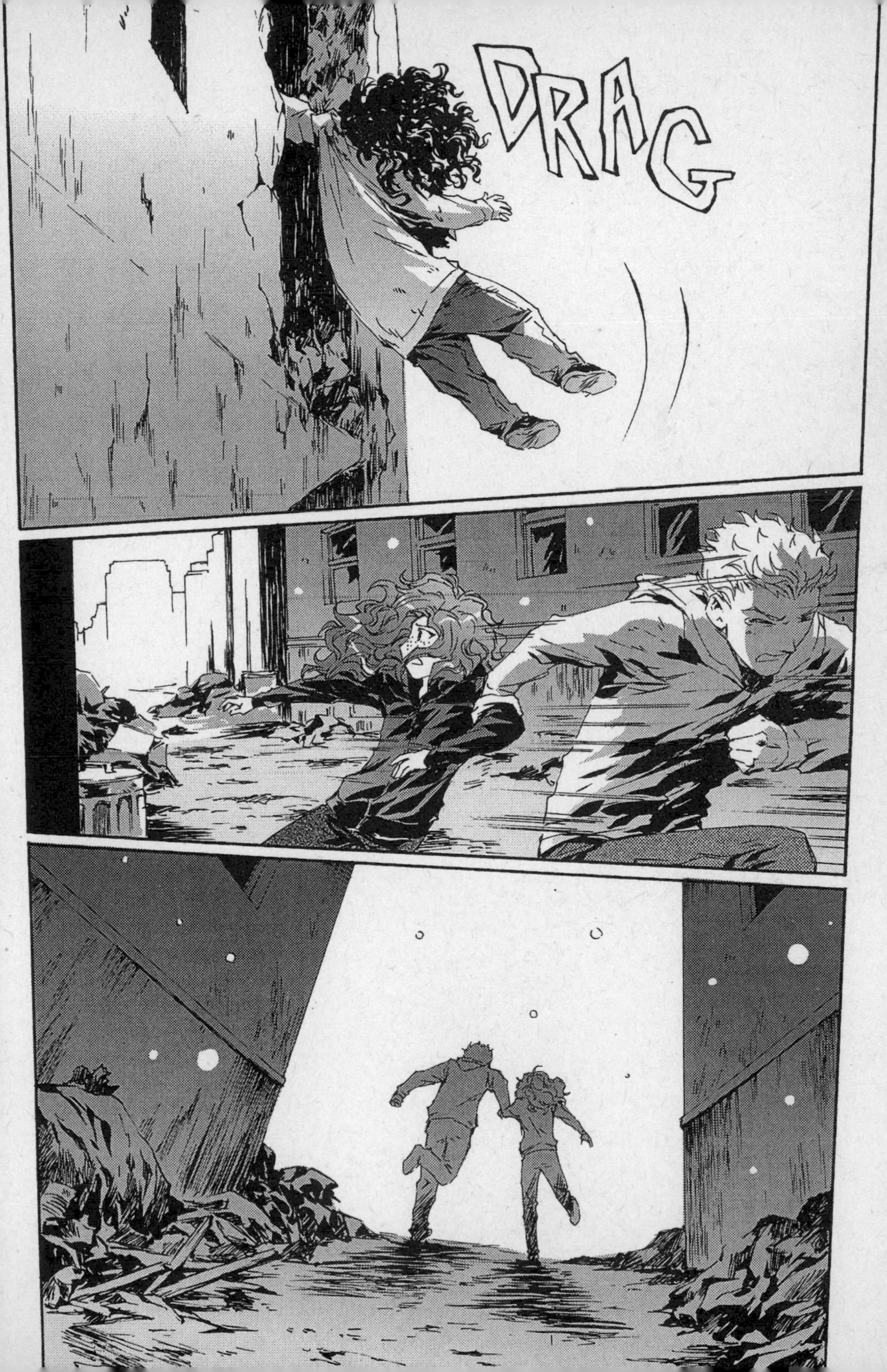
DRAG

WITCH & WIZARD

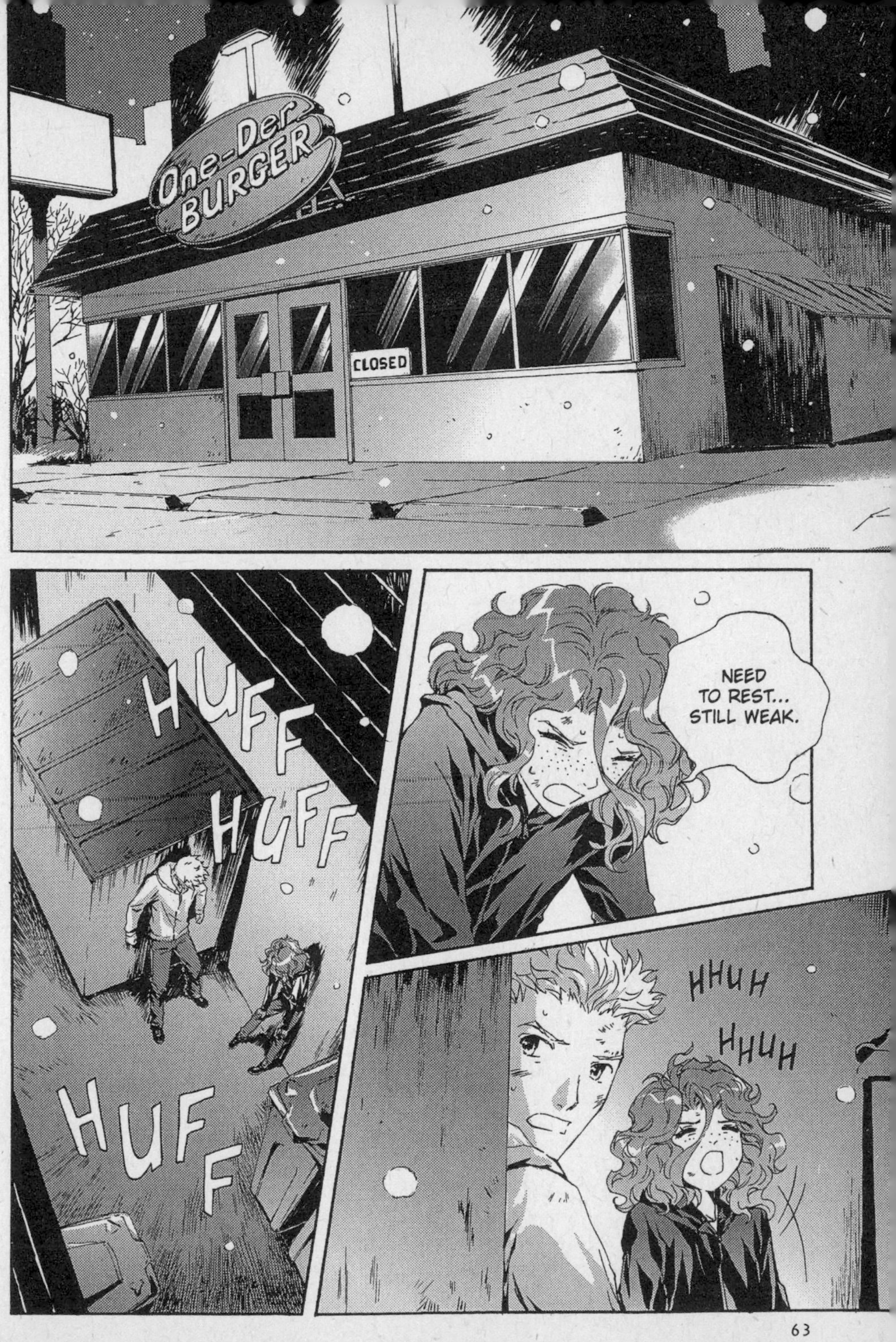
One-Der BURGER
CLOSED
HUFF HUFF
HUFF
NEED TO REST... STILL WEAK.
HHUH HHUH

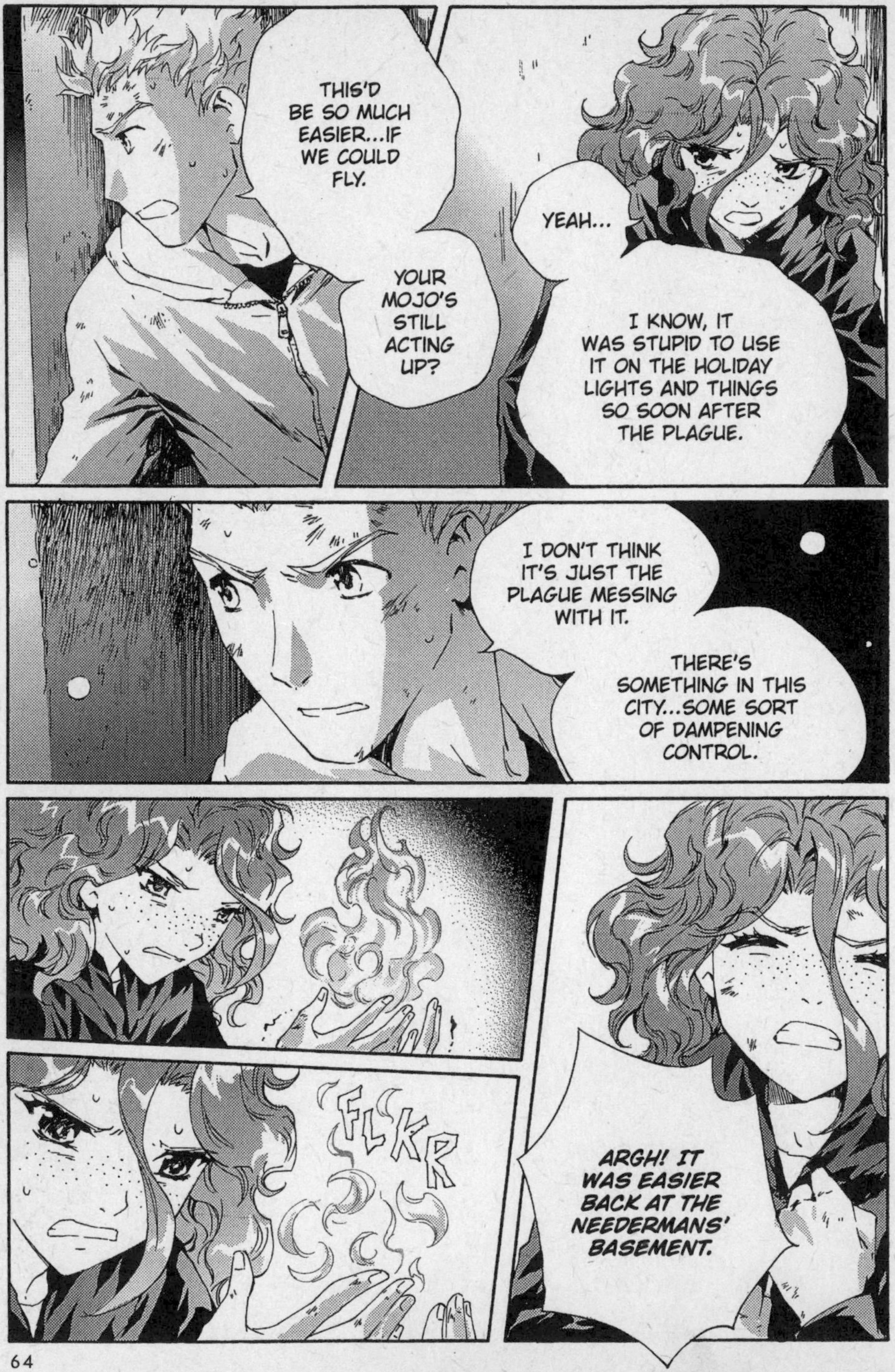
THIS'D BE SO MUCH EASIER...IF WE COULD FLY.
YEAH...
YOUR MOJO'S STILL ACTING UP?
I KNOW, IT WAS STUPID TO USE IT ON THE HOLIDAY LIGHTS AND THINGS SO SOON AFTER THE PLAGUE.
I DON'T THINK IT'S JUST THE PLAGUE MESSING WITH IT.
THERE'S SOMETHING IN THIS CITY...SOME SORT OF DAMPENING CONTROL.
FLKR
ARGH! IT WAS EASIER BACK AT THE NEEDERMANS' BASEMENT.

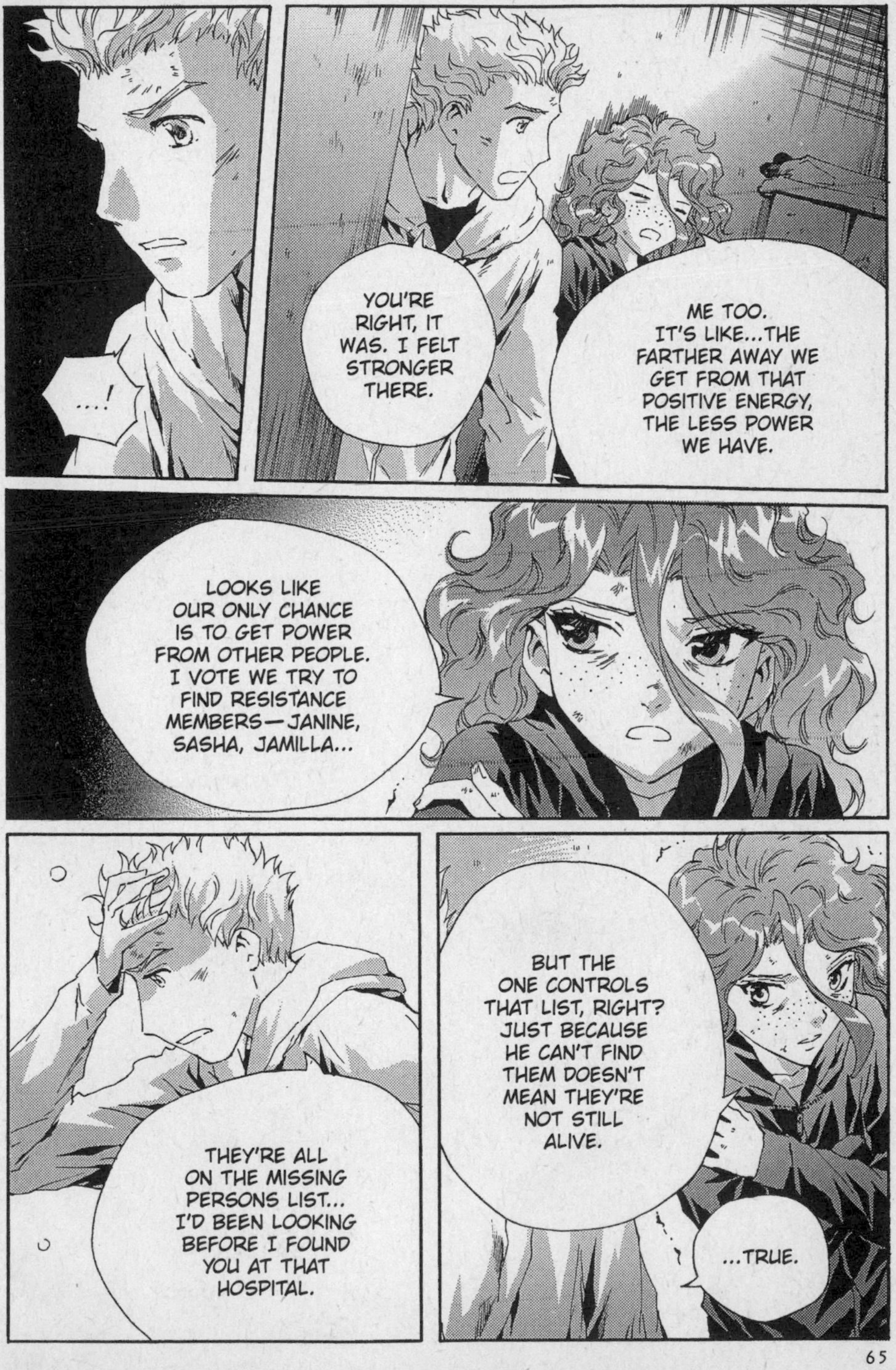
...!
YOU'RE RIGHT, IT WAS. I FELT STRONGER THERE.
ME TOO. IT'S LIKE...THE FARTHER AWAY WE GET FROM THAT POSITIVE ENERGY, THE LESS POWER WE HAVE.
LOOKS LIKE OUR ONLY CHANCE IS TO GET POWER FROM OTHER PEOPLE. I VOTE WE TRY TO FIND RESISTANCE MEMBERS—JANINE, SASHA, JAMILLA...
THEY'RE ALL ON THE MISSING PERSONS LIST... I'D BEEN LOOKING BEFORE I FOUND YOU AT THAT HOSPITAL.
BUT THE ONE CONTROLS THAT LIST, RIGHT? JUST BECAUSE HE CAN'T FIND THEM DOESN'T MEAN THEY'RE NOT STILL ALIVE.
...TRUE.

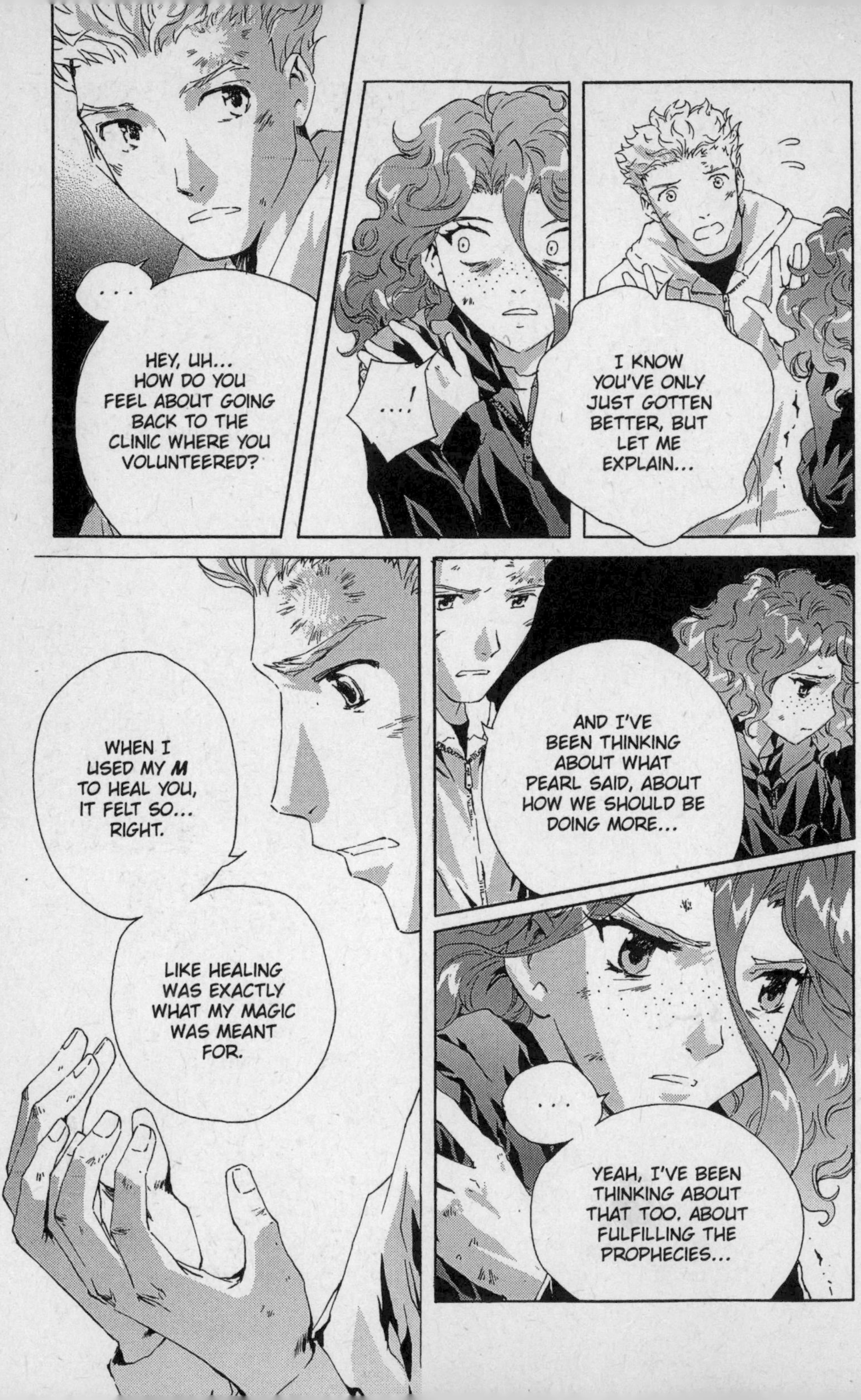
...
HEY, UH... HOW DO YOU FEEL ABOUT GOING BACK TO THE CLINIC WHERE YOU VOLUNTEERED?
...!
I KNOW YOU'VE ONLY JUST GOTTEN BETTER, BUT LET ME EXPLAIN...
WHEN I USED MY M TO HEAL YOU, IT FELT SO... RIGHT.
LIKE HEALING WAS EXACTLY WHAT MY MAGIC WAS MEANT FOR.
AND I'VE BEEN THINKING ABOUT WHAT PEARL SAID, ABOUT HOW WE SHOULD BE DOING MORE...
...
YEAH, I'VE BEEN THINKING ABOUT THAT TOO. ABOUT FULFILLING THE PROPHECIES...

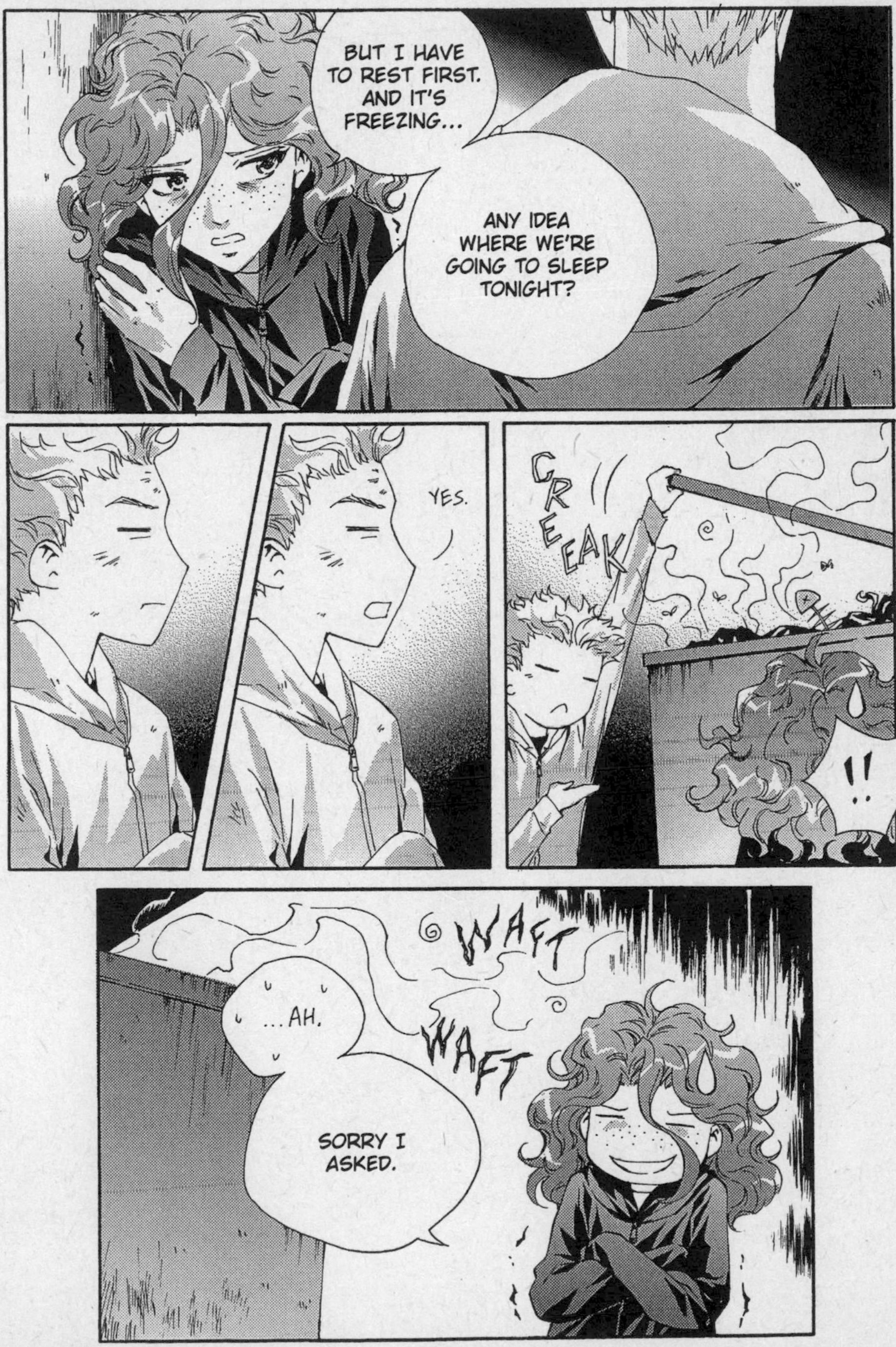
BUT I HAVE TO REST FIRST. AND IT'S FREEZING...
ANY IDEA WHERE WE'RE GOING TO SLEEP TONIGHT?
YES.
CREEAK
!!
WAFT
WAFT
...AH.
SORRY I ASKED.

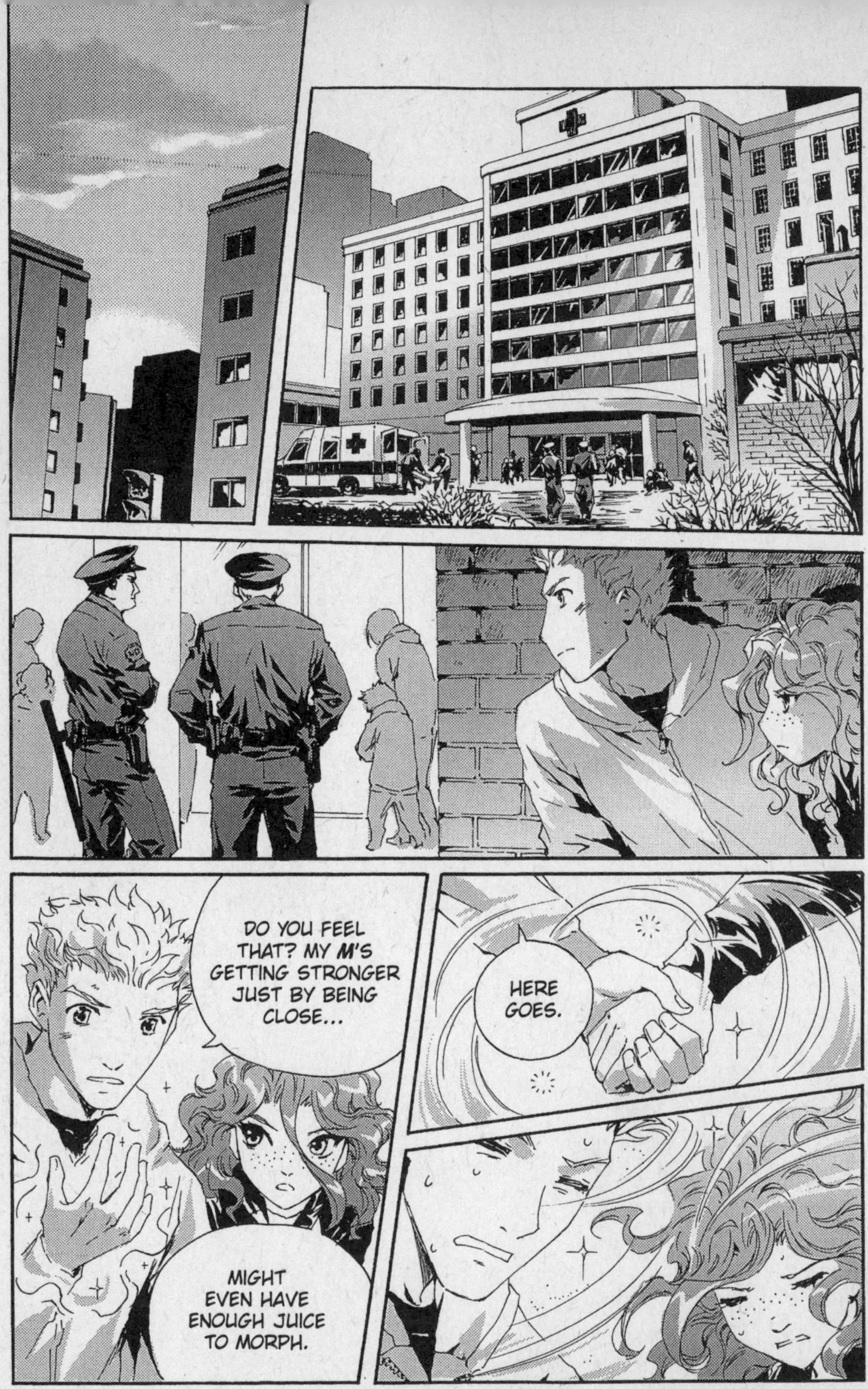
DO YOU FEEL THAT? MY M'S GETTING STRONGER JUST BY BEING CLOSE...
MIGHT EVEN HAVE ENOUGH JUICE TO MORPH.
HERE GOES.

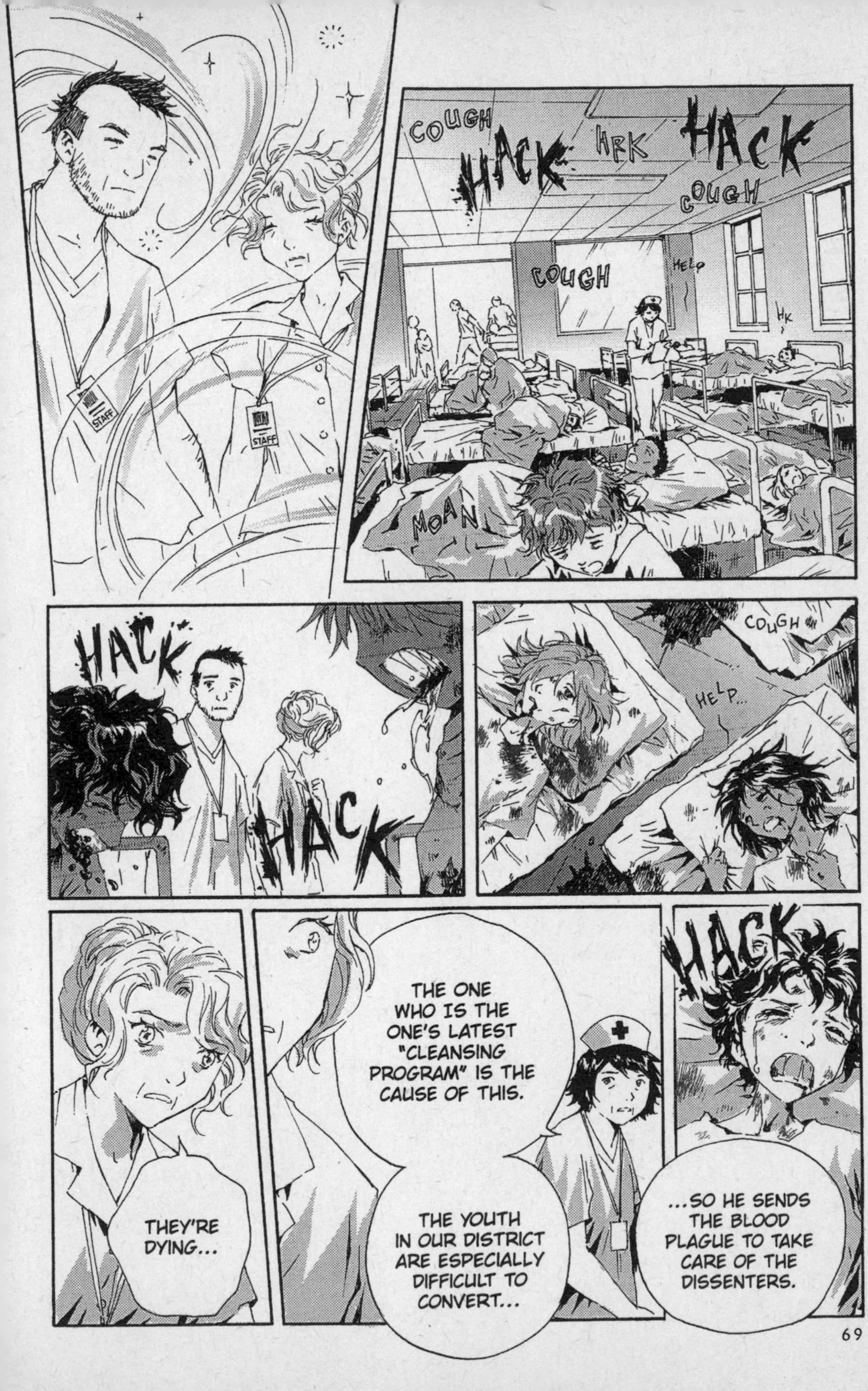
COUGH
HACK
HRK
HACK
COUGH
COUGH
HELP
HK
MOAN
HACK
HACK
COUGH
HELP...
HACK
THEY'RE DYING...
THE ONE WHO IS THE ONE'S LATEST "CLEANSING PROGRAM" IS THE CAUSE OF THIS.
THE YOUTH IN OUR DISTRICT ARE ESPECIALLY DIFFICULT TO CONVERT...
...SO HE SENDS THE BLOOD PLAGUE TO TAKE CARE OF THE DISSENTERS.

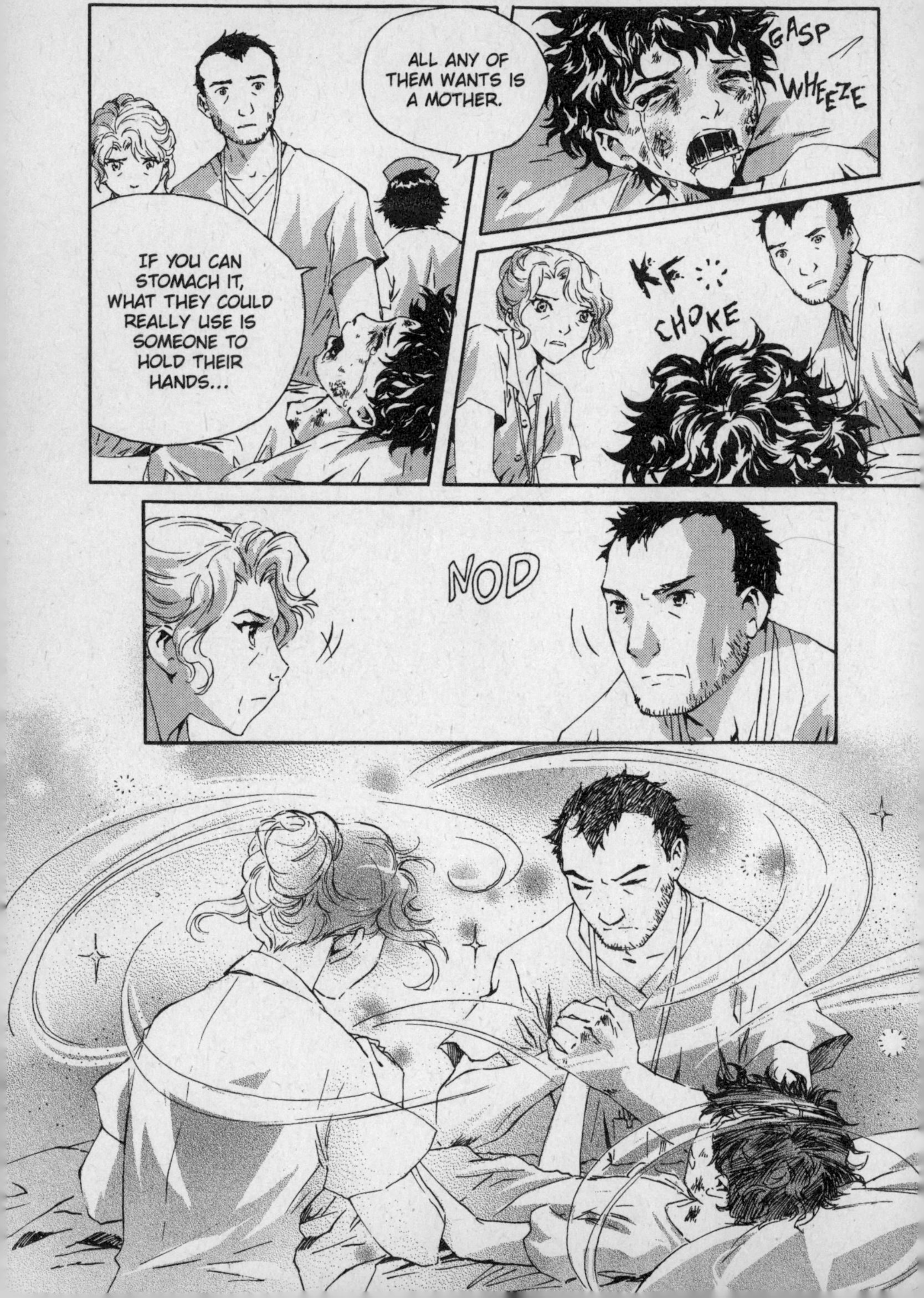

ALL ANY OF THEM WANTS IS A MOTHER.
IF YOU CAN STOMACH IT, WHAT THEY COULD REALLY USE IS SOMEONE TO HOLD THEIR HANDS...
GASP
WHEEZE
KF
CHOKE
NOD

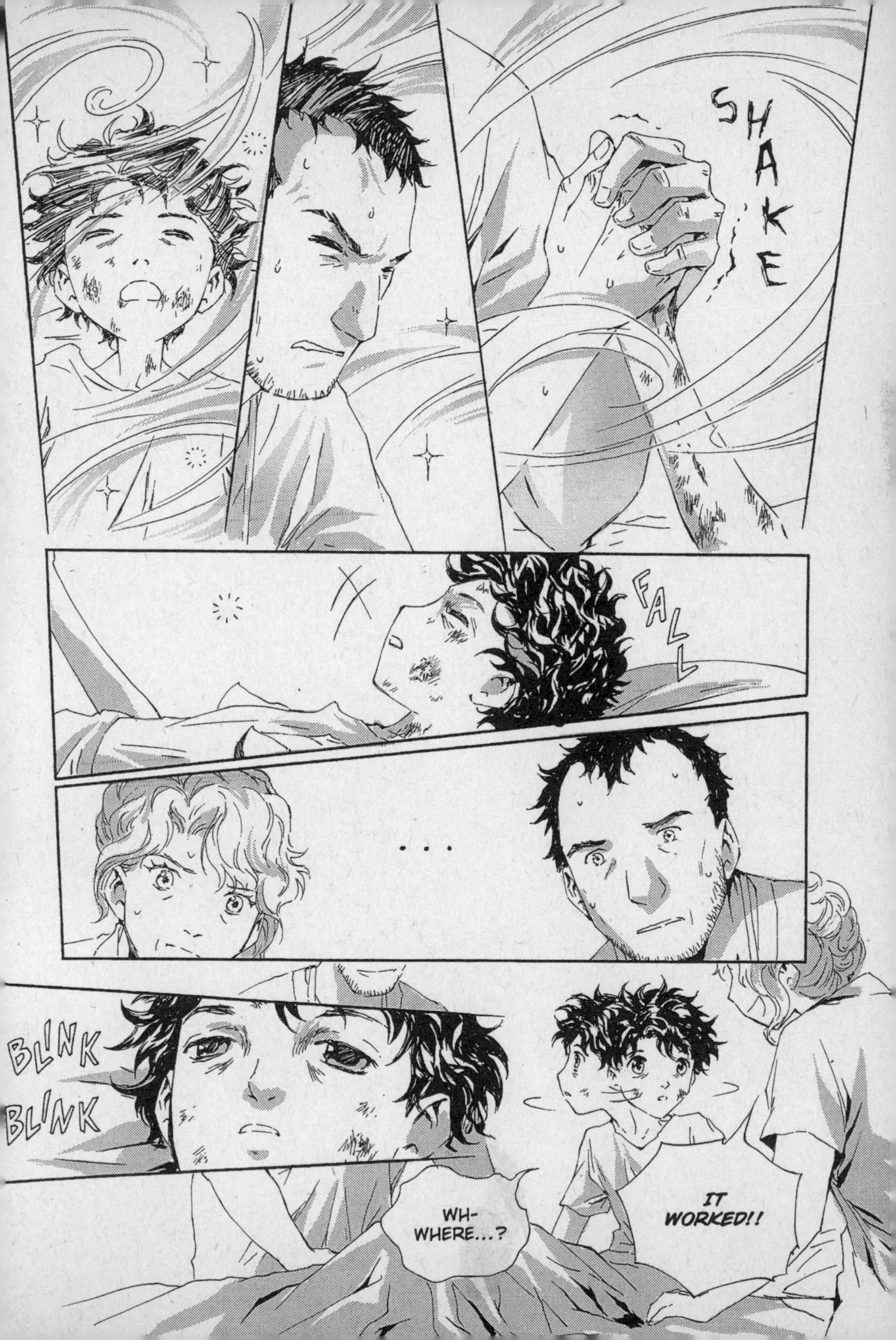
SHAKE
FALL
...
BLINK
BLINK
IT WORKED!!
WH- WHERE...?

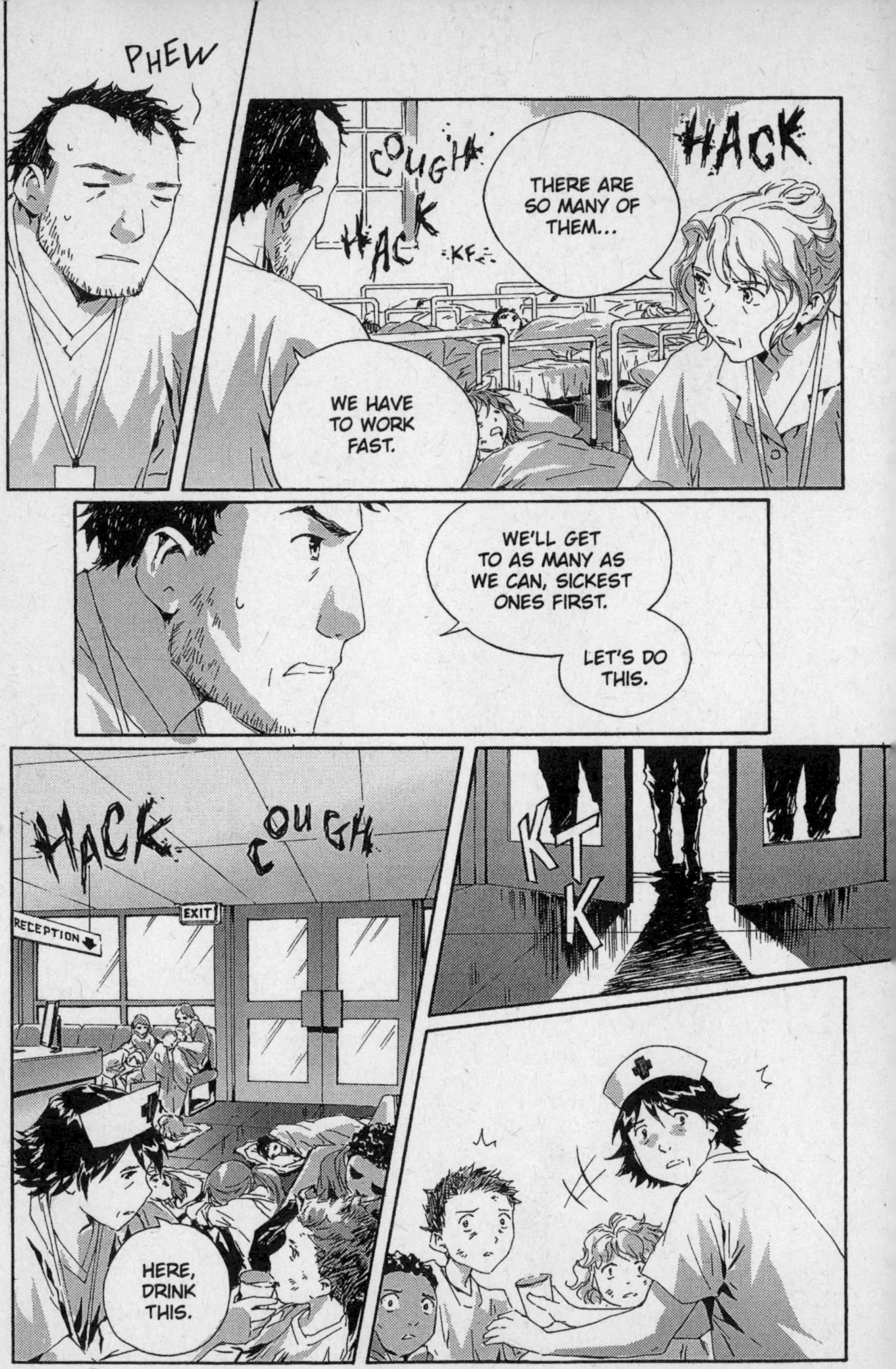
PHEW
COUGH
HACK
KF
THERE ARE SO MANY OF THEM...
HACK
WE HAVE TO WORK FAST.
WE'LL GET TO AS MANY AS WE CAN, SICKEST ONES FIRST.
LET'S DO THIS.
HACK
COUGH
RECEPTION
EXIT
KTK
HERE, DRINK THIS.

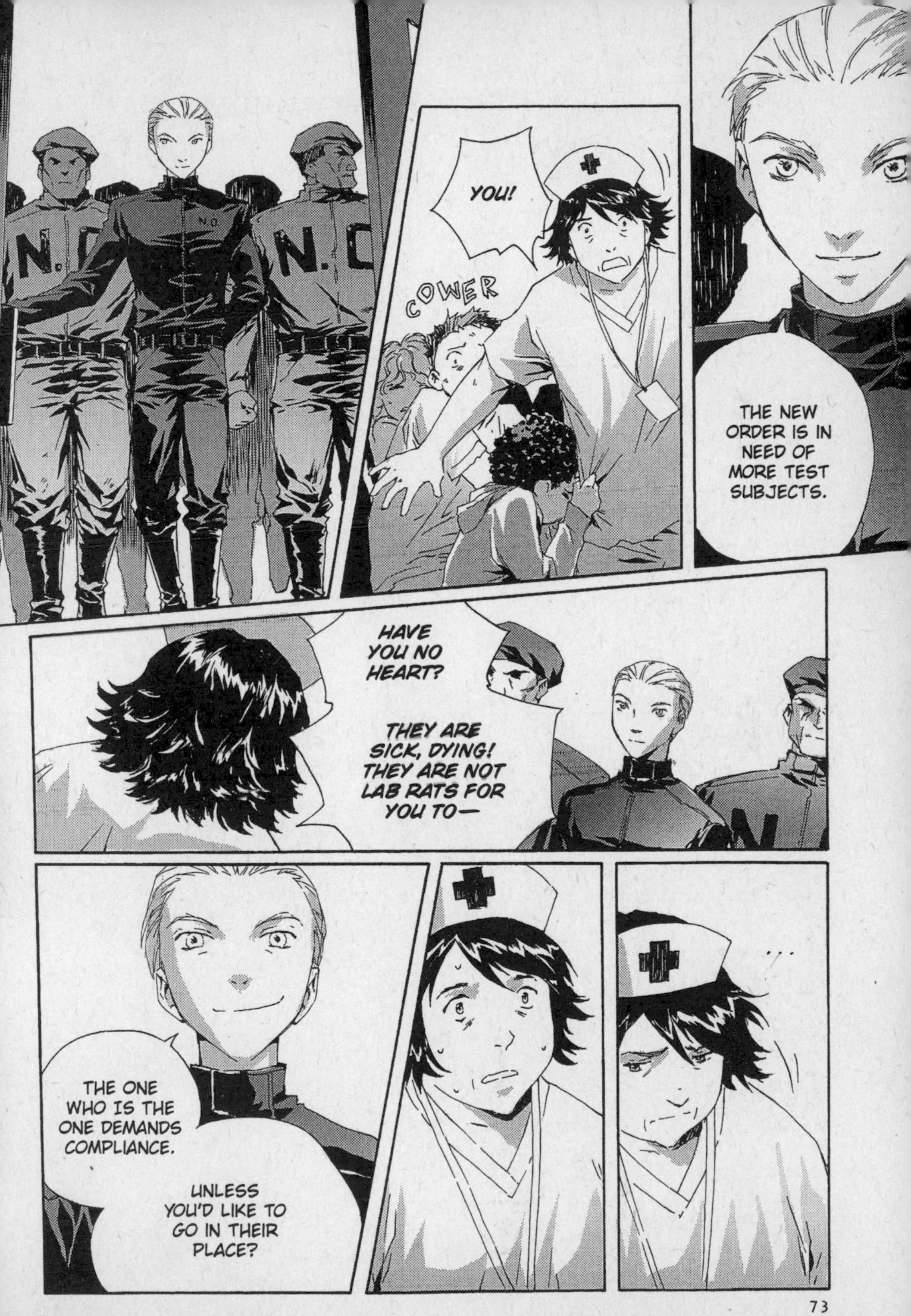
YOU!
COWER
THE NEW ORDER IS IN NEED OF MORE TEST SUBJECTS.
HAVE YOU NO HEART?
THEY ARE SICK, DYING! THEY ARE NOT LAB RATS FOR YOU TO—
THE ONE WHO IS THE ONE DEMANDS COMPLIANCE.
UNLESS YOU'D LIKE TO GO IN THEIR PLACE?
...

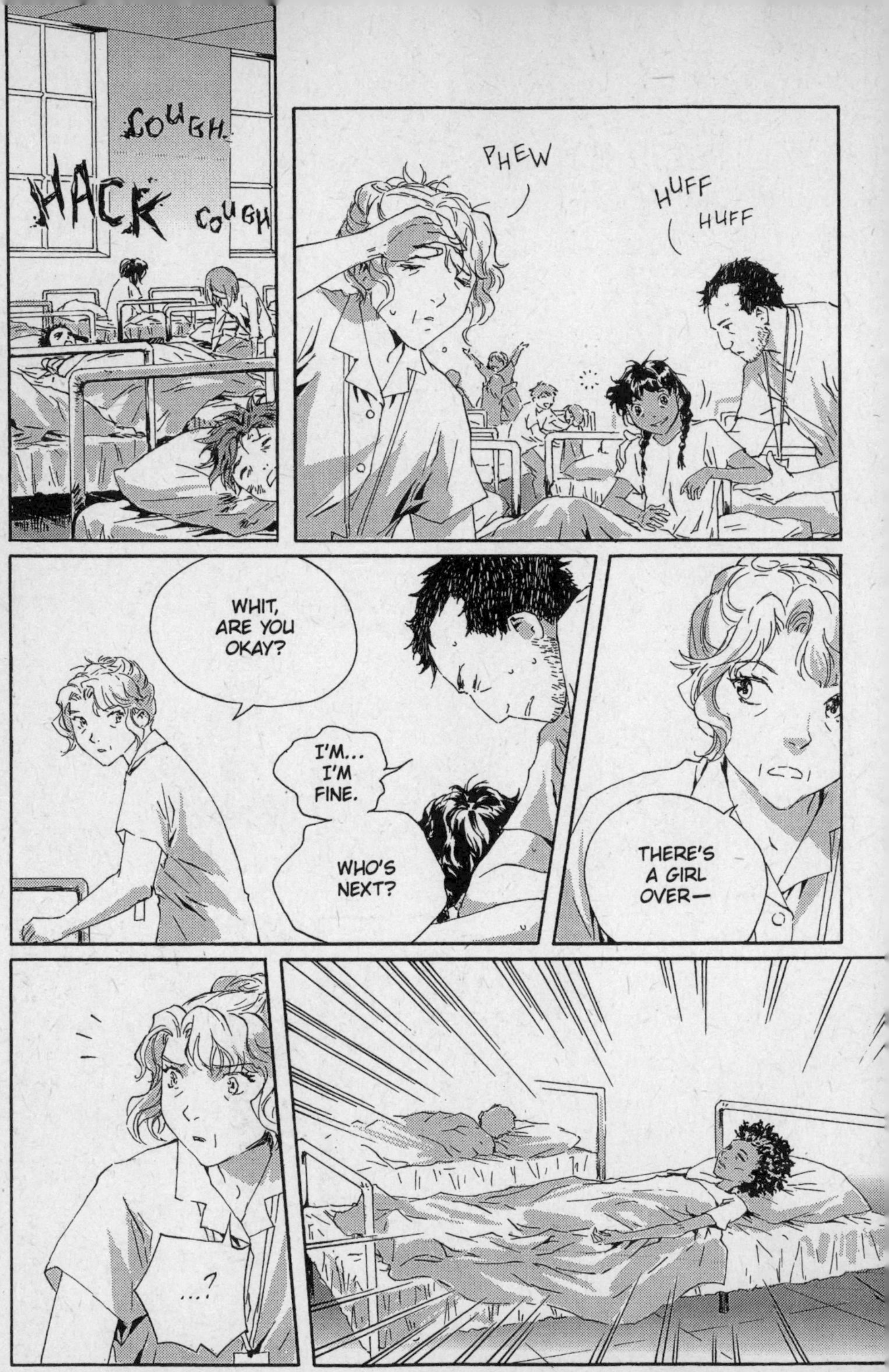
COUGH
HACK
COUGH
PHEW
HUFF
HUFF
WHIT, ARE YOU OKAY?
I'M... I'M FINE.
WHO'S NEXT?
THERE'S A GIRL OVER—
...?

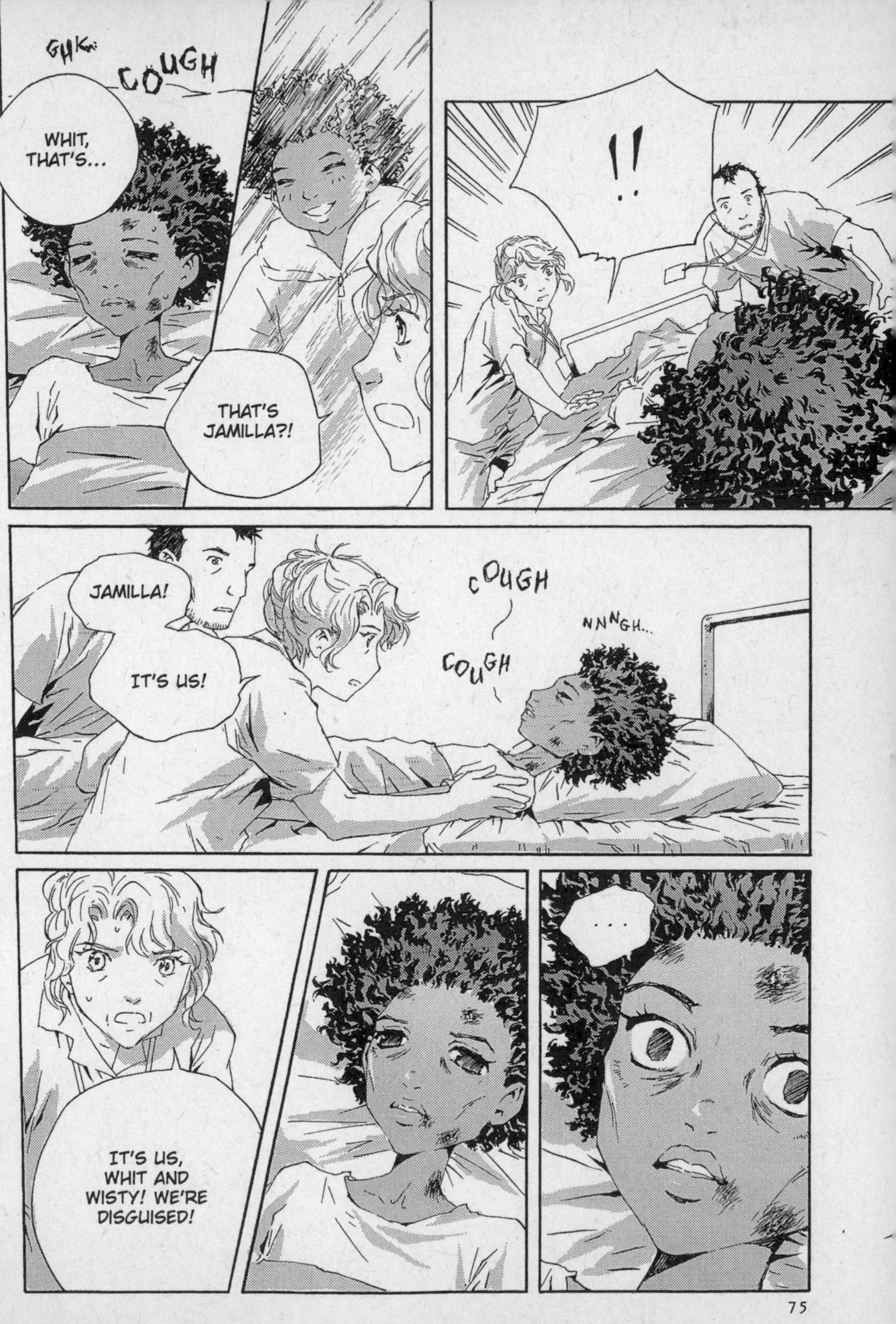
GHK-
COUGH
WHIT, THAT'S...
THAT'S JAMILLA?!
!!
JAMILLA!
IT'S US!
COUGH
COUGH
NNNGH...
IT'S US, WHIT AND WISTY! WE'RE DISGUISED!
...

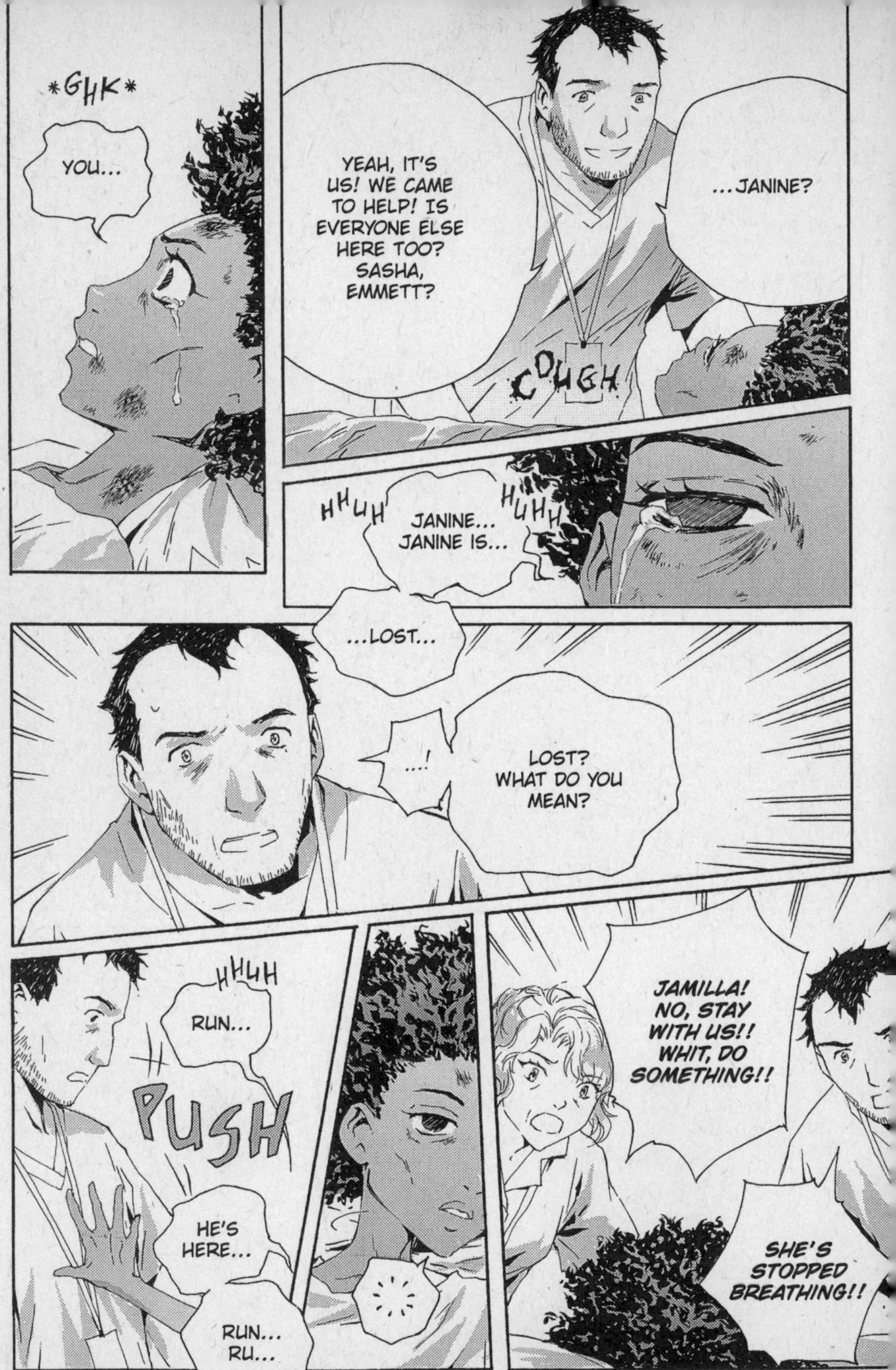
GHK
YOU...
YEAH, IT'S US! WE CAME TO HELP! IS EVERYONE ELSE HERE TOO? SASHA, EMMETT?
...JANINE?
COUGH
HHUH
JANINE... JANINE IS...
HUHH
...LOST...
...!
LOST? WHAT DO YOU MEAN?
HHUH
RUN...
PUSH
HE'S HERE...
RUN... RU...
JAMILLA! NO, STAY WITH US!! WHIT, DO SOMETHING!!
SHE'S STOPPED BREATHING!!

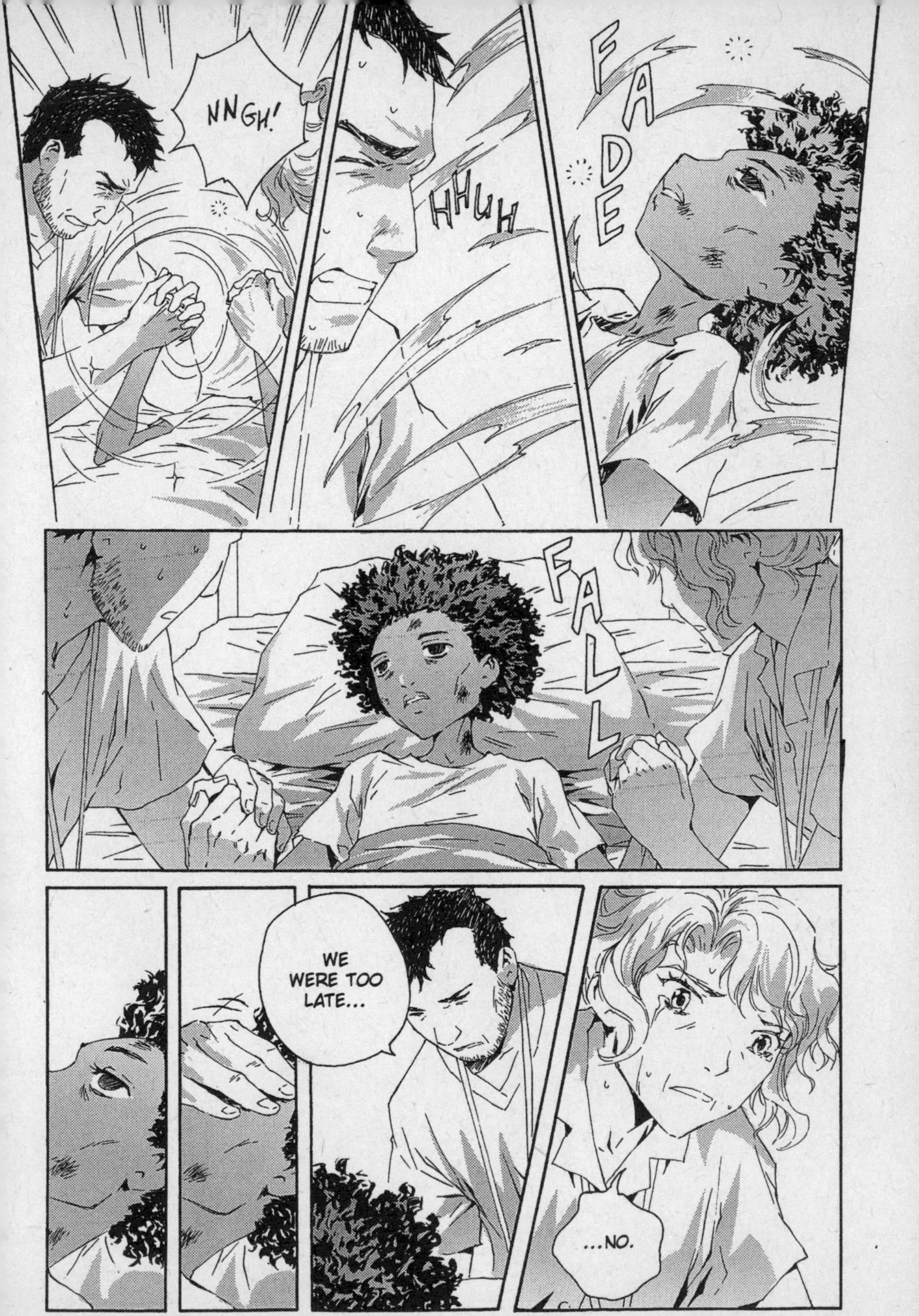
NNGH!
HHUH
FADE
FALL
WE WERE TOO LATE...
...NO.

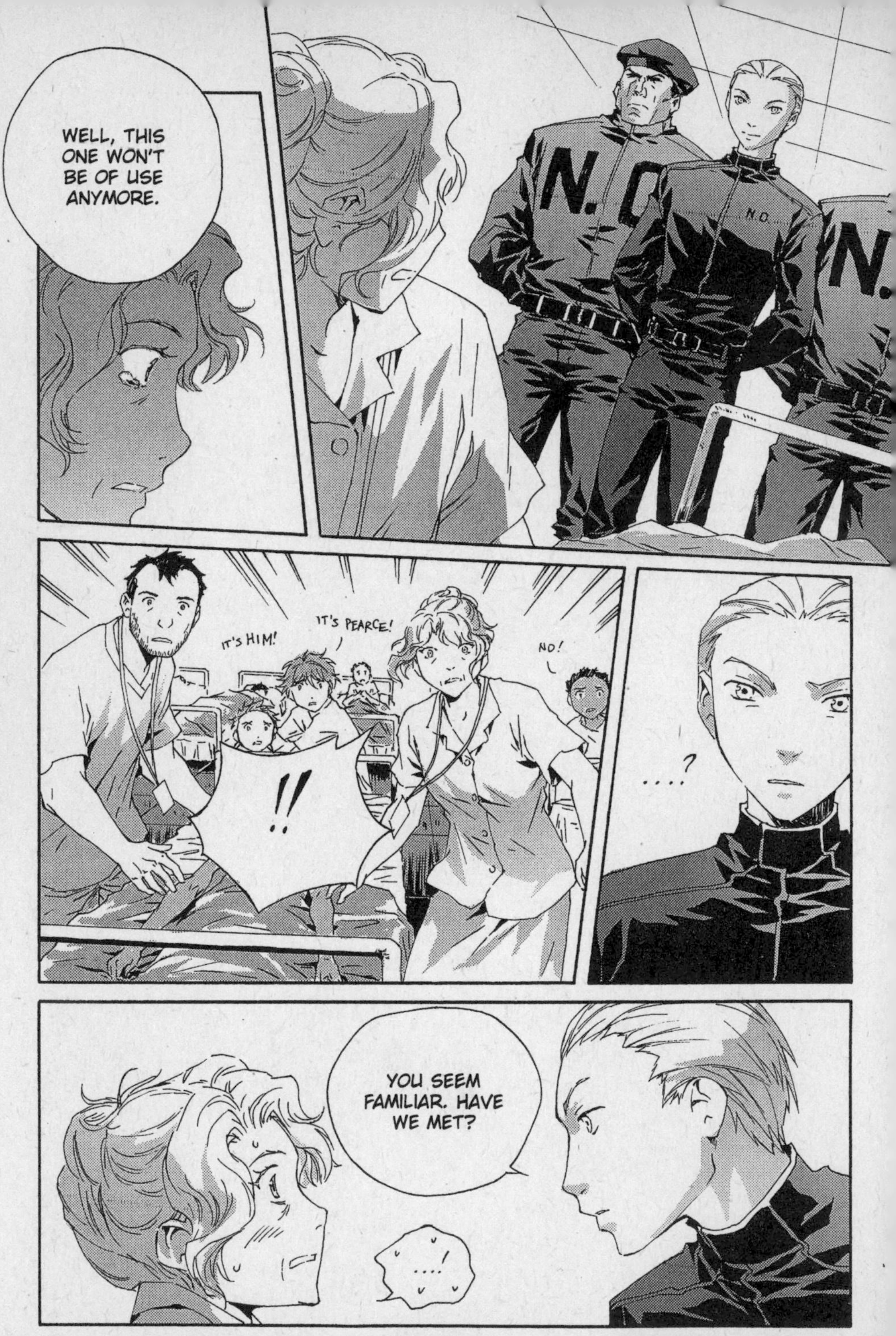

WELL, THIS ONE WON'T BE OF USE ANYMORE.
IT'S HIM!
IT'S PEARCE!
NO!
!!
....?
YOU SEEM FAMILIAR. HAVE WE MET?
....!

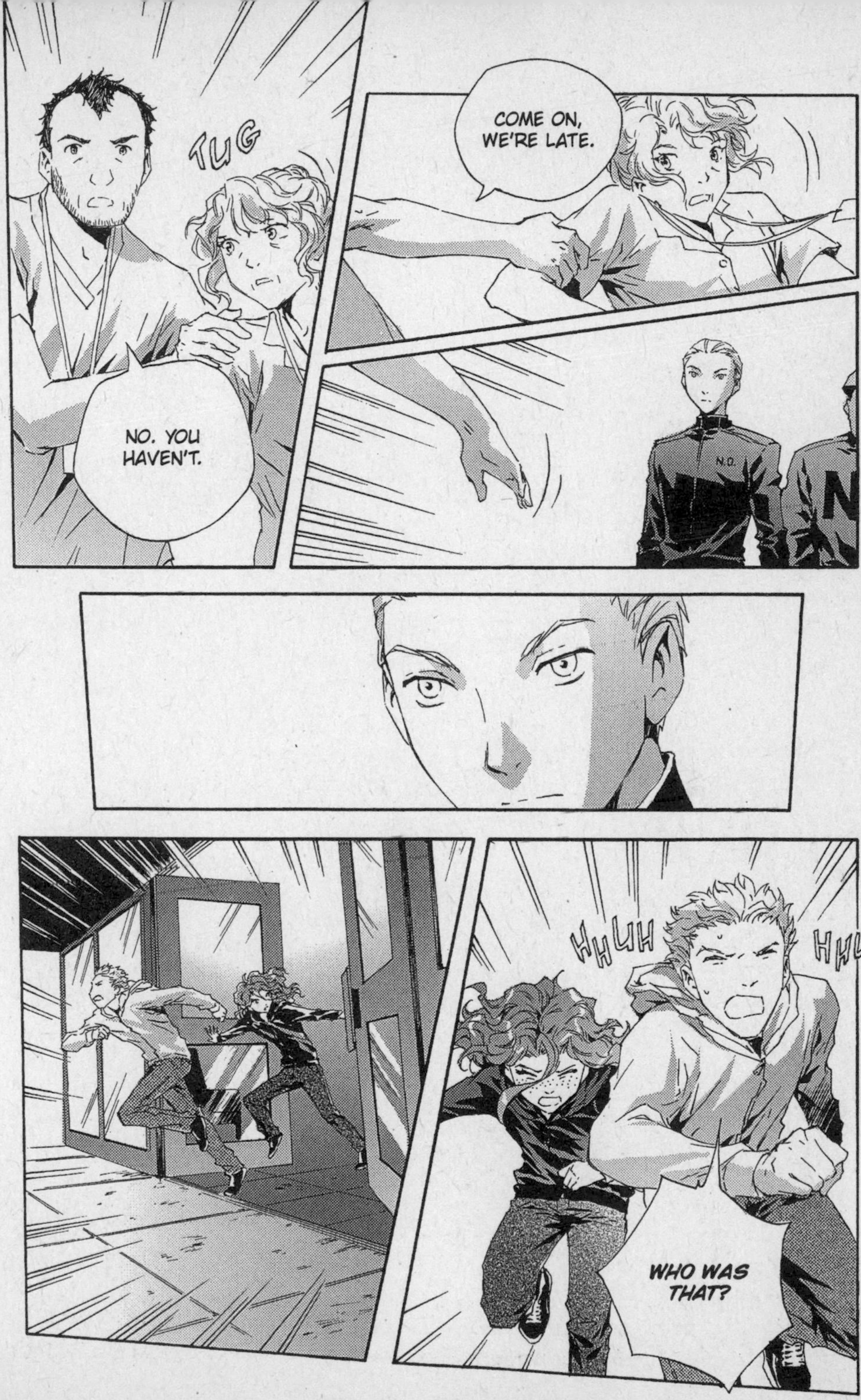
TUG
NO. YOU HAVEN'T.
COME ON, WE'RE LATE.
N.O.
HHUH
HHUH
WHO WAS THAT?

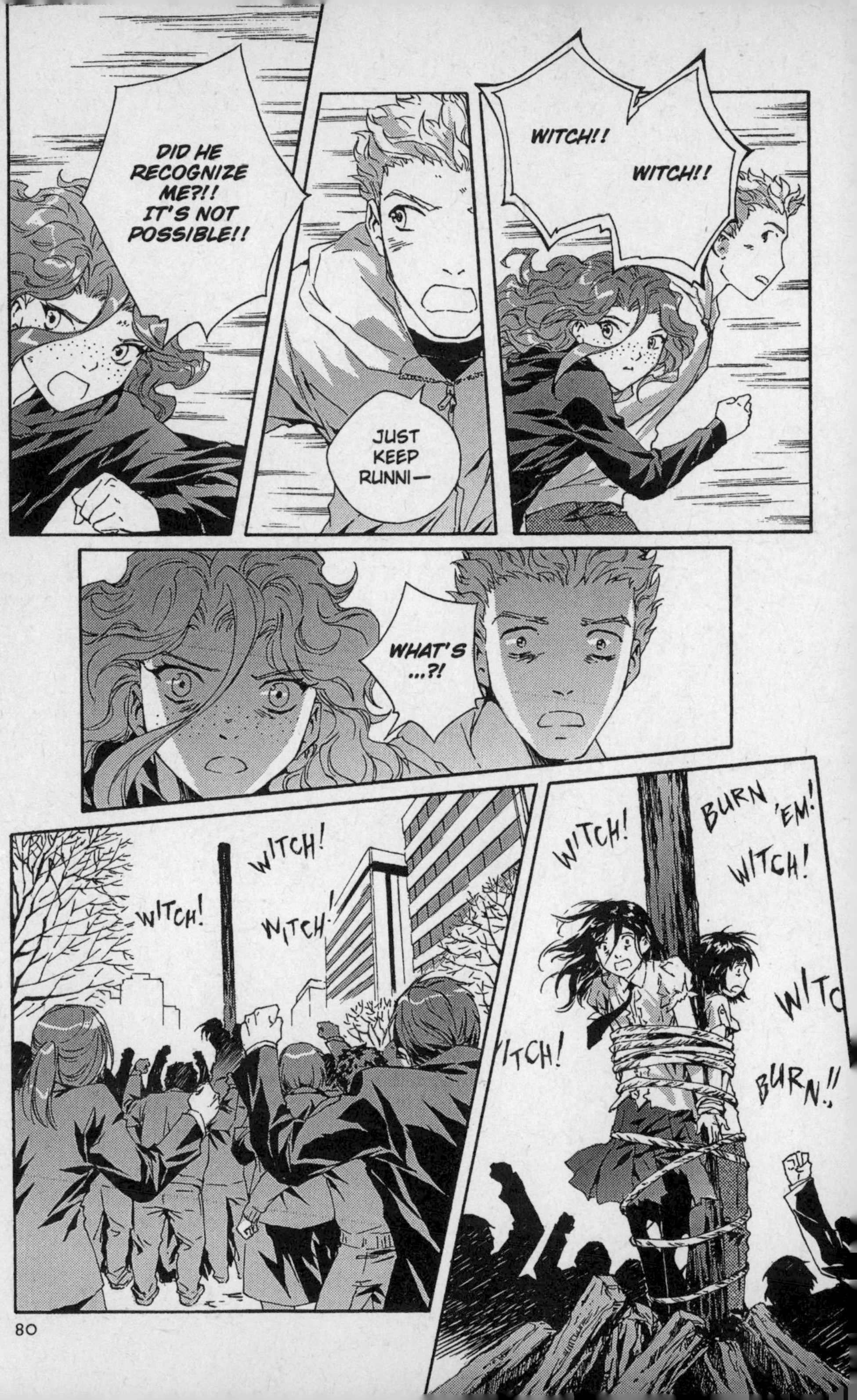
DID HE RECOGNIZE ME?!! IT'S NOT POSSIBLE!!
JUST KEEP RUNNI—
WITCH!!
WITCH!!
WHAT'S ...?!
WITCH!
WITCH!
WITCH!
WITCH!
BURN 'EM!
WITCH!
WITC
ITCH!
BURN!!

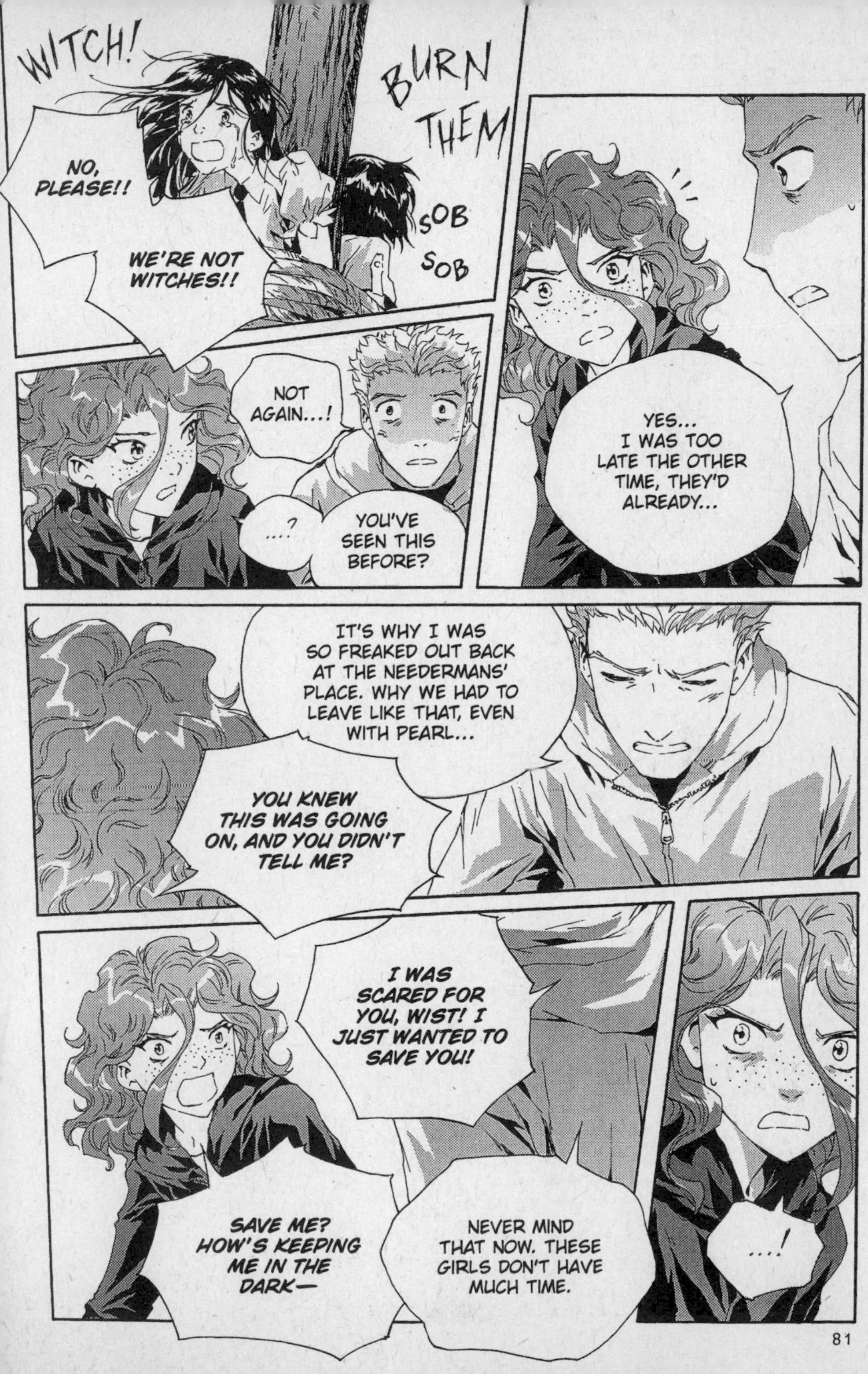

WITCH!
BURN THEM
NO, PLEASE!!
WE'RE NOT WITCHES!!
SOB SOB
NOT AGAIN...!
...?
YOU'VE SEEN THIS BEFORE?
YES... I WAS TOO LATE THE OTHER TIME, THEY'D ALREADY...
IT'S WHY I WAS SO FREAKED OUT BACK AT THE NEEDERMANS' PLACE. WHY WE HAD TO LEAVE LIKE THAT, EVEN WITH PEARL...
YOU KNEW THIS WAS GOING ON, AND YOU DIDN'T TELL ME?
I WAS SCARED FOR YOU, WIST! I JUST WANTED TO SAVE YOU!
SAVE ME? HOW'S KEEPING ME IN THE DARK—
NEVER MIND THAT NOW. THESE GIRLS DON'T HAVE MUCH TIME.
...!

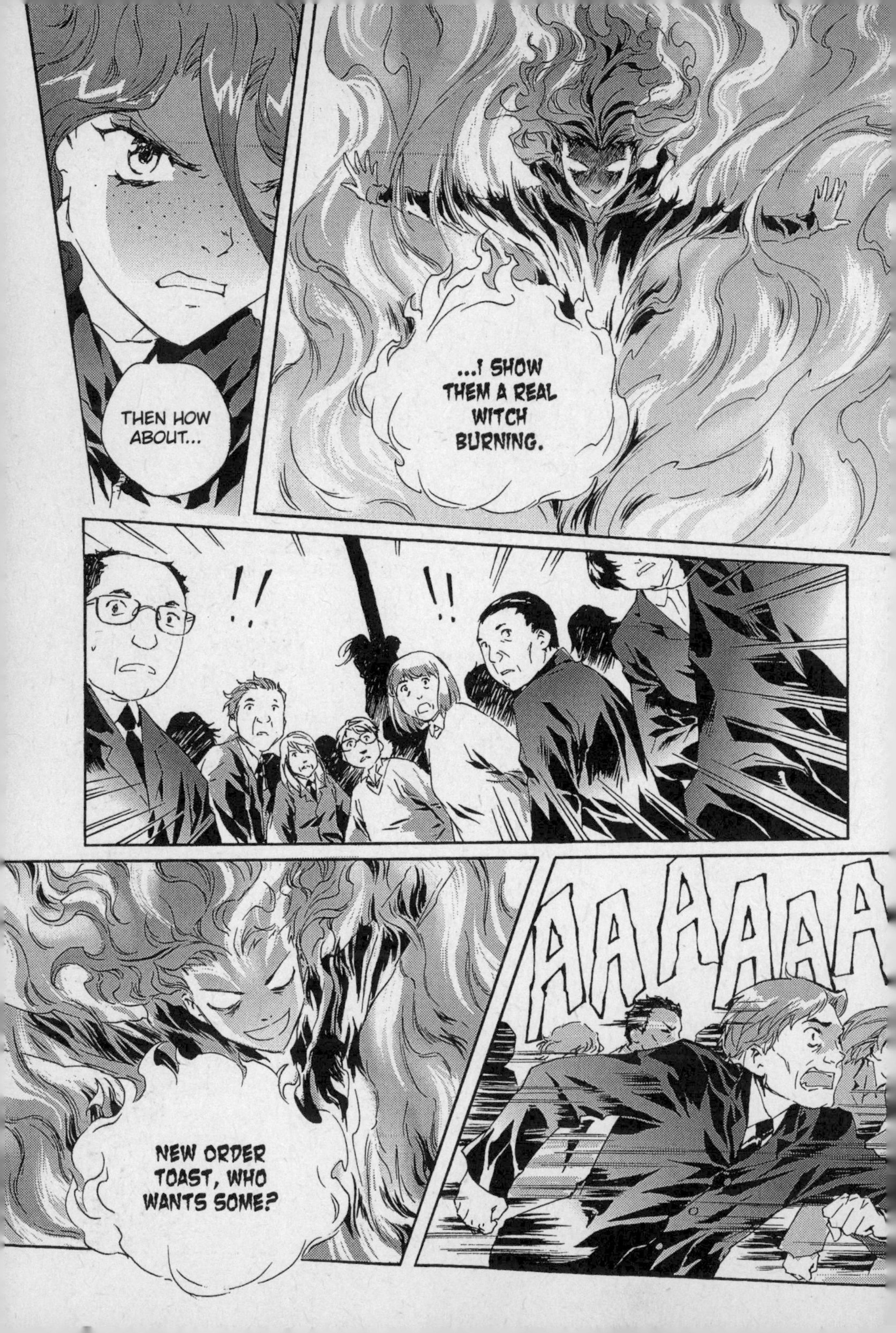
THEN HOW ABOUT...
...I SHOW THEM A REAL WITCH BURNING.
!!
!!
NEW ORDER TOAST, WHO WANTS SOME?
AAAAAA

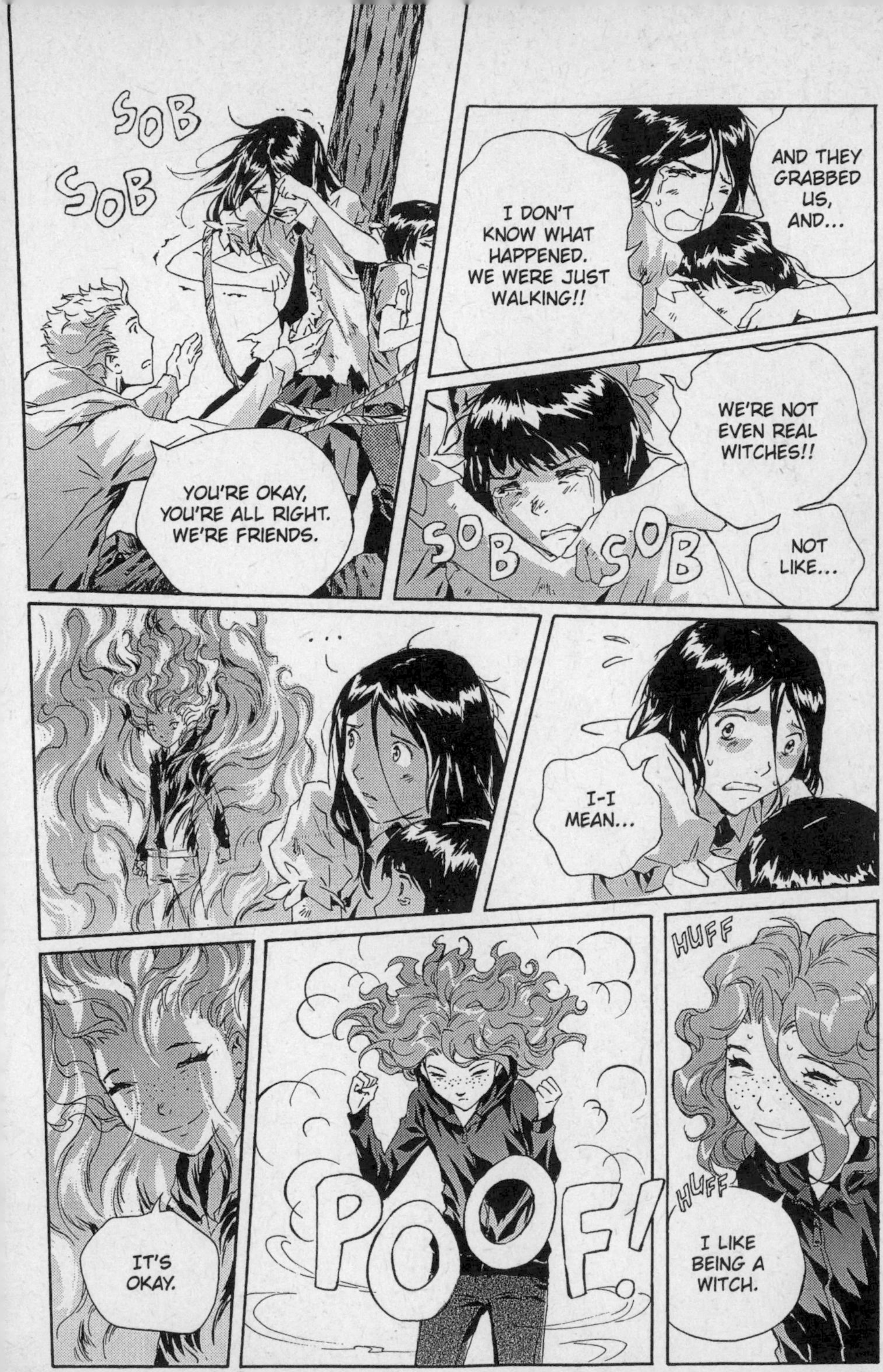
SOB
SOB
YOU'RE OKAY, YOU'RE ALL RIGHT. WE'RE FRIENDS.
I DON'T KNOW WHAT HAPPENED. WE WERE JUST WALKING!!
AND THEY GRABBED US, AND...
WE'RE NOT EVEN REAL WITCHES!!
SOB SOB
NOT LIKE...
. . .
I-I MEAN...
IT'S OKAY.
POOF!
HUFF
HUFF
I LIKE BEING A WITCH.

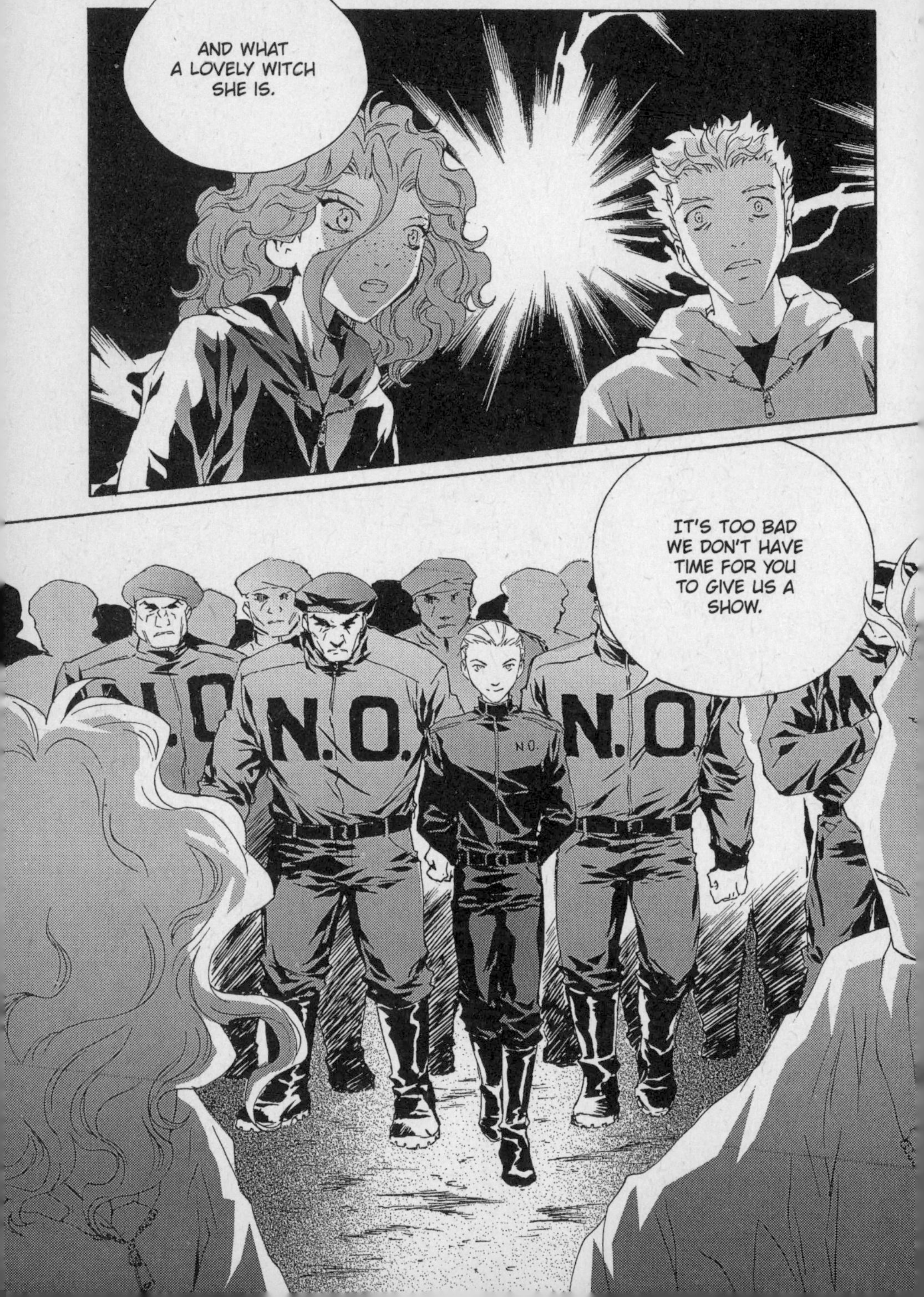
AND WHAT A LOVELY WITCH SHE IS.
IT'S TOO BAD WE DON'T HAVE TIME FOR YOU TO GIVE US A SHOW.
N.O.
N.O.
N.O.

WITCH & WIZARD

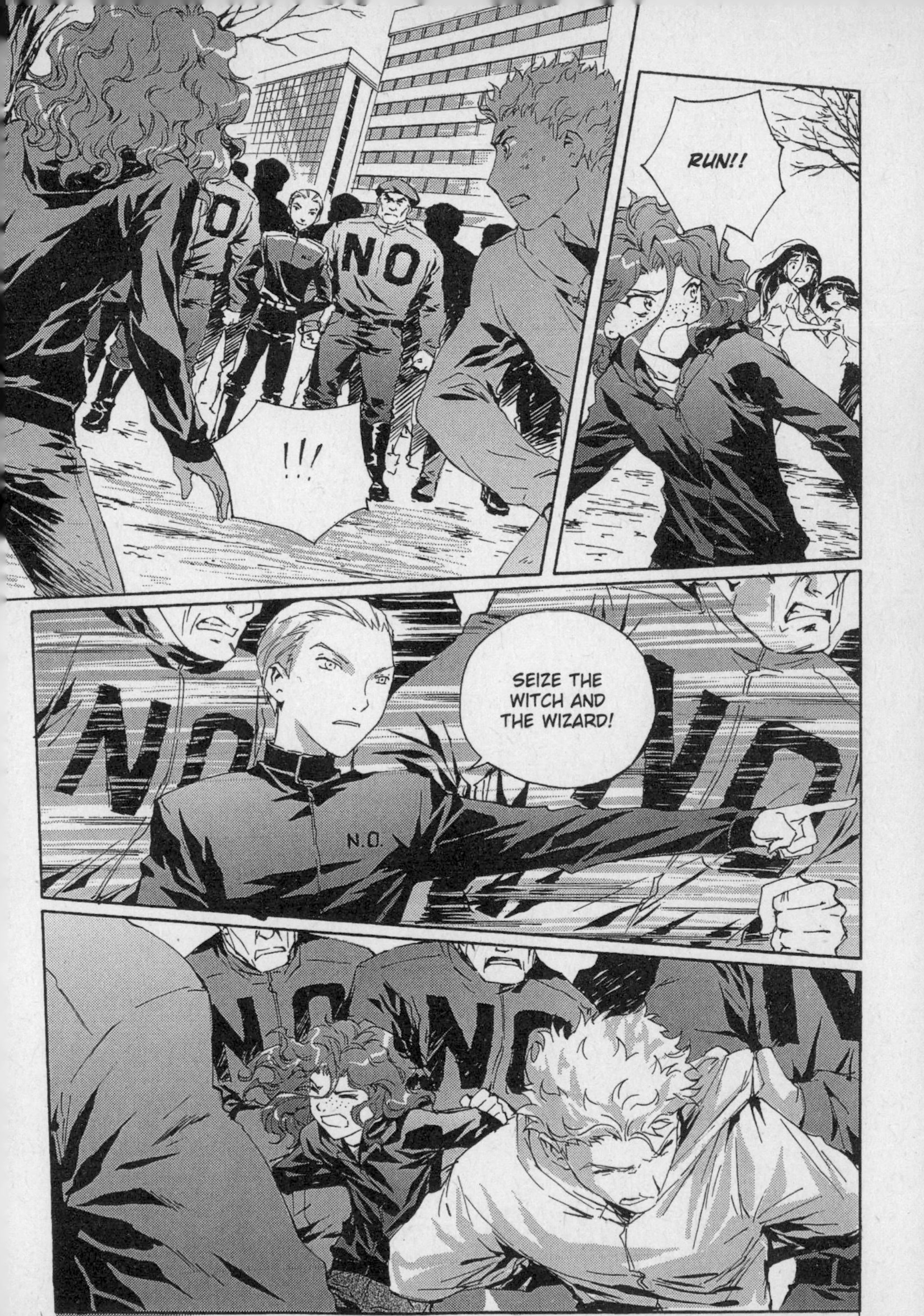

!!!
RUN!!
SEIZE THE WITCH AND THE WIZARD!

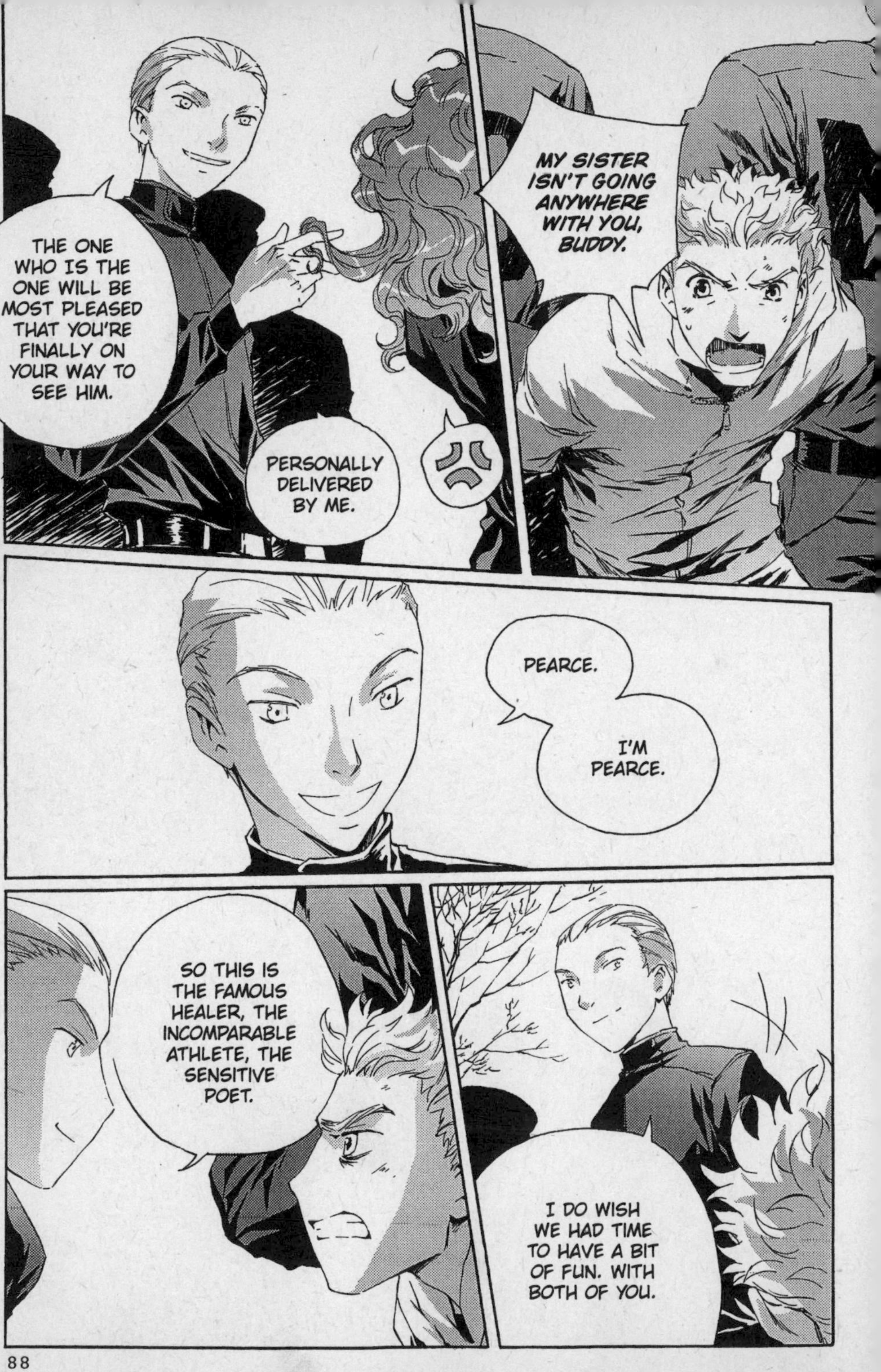

THE ONE WHO IS THE ONE WILL BE MOST PLEASED THAT YOU'RE FINALLY ON YOUR WAY TO SEE HIM.
PERSONALLY DELIVERED BY ME.
MY SISTER ISN'T GOING ANYWHERE WITH YOU, BUDDY.
PEARCE.
I'M PEARCE.
SO THIS IS THE FAMOUS HEALER, THE INCOMPARABLE ATHLETE, THE SENSITIVE POET.
I DO WISH WE HAD TIME TO HAVE A BIT OF FUN. WITH BOTH OF YOU.

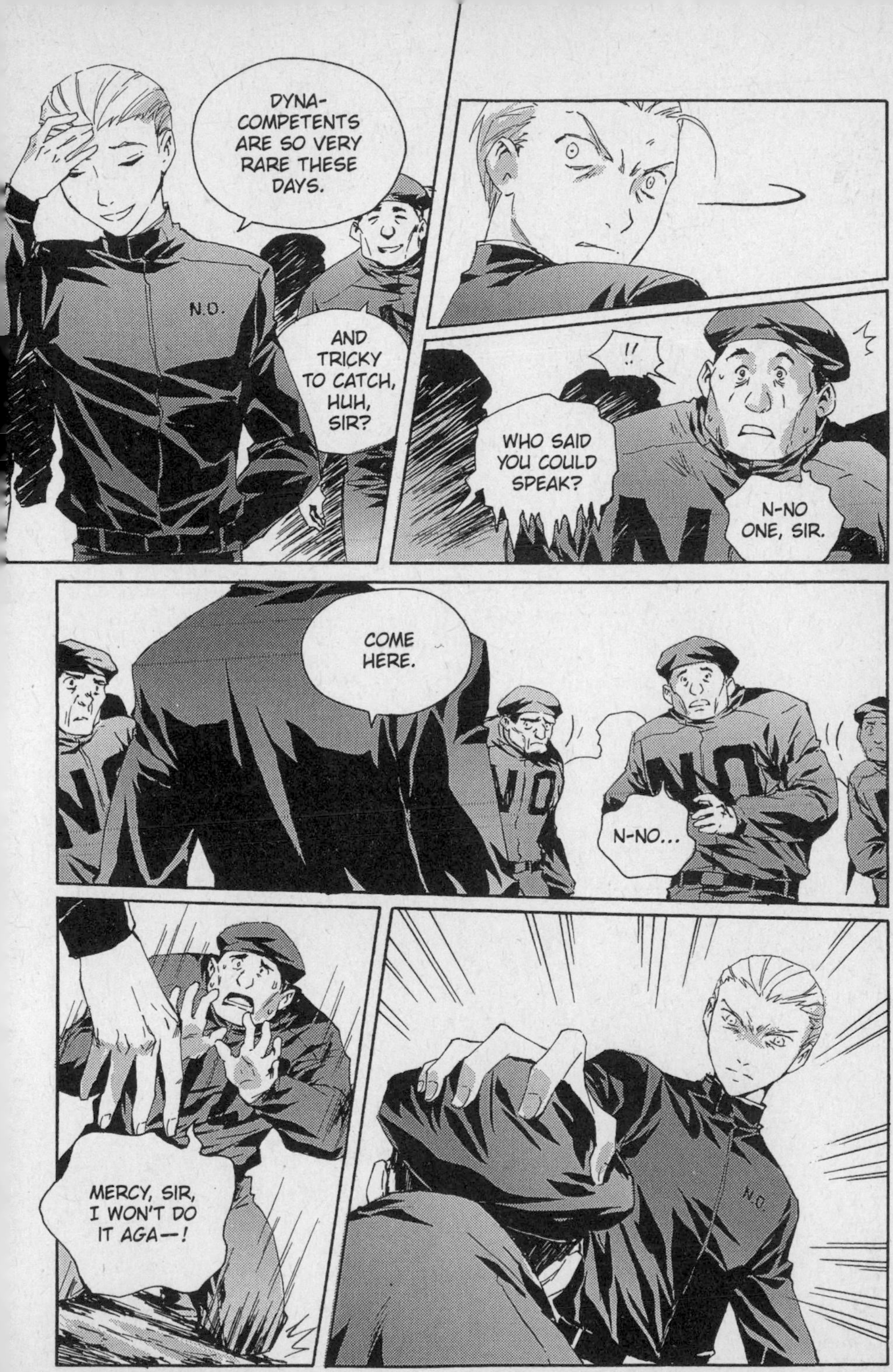
DYNA-COMPETENTS ARE SO VERY RARE THESE DAYS.
AND TRICKY TO CATCH, HUH, SIR?
!!
WHO SAID YOU COULD SPEAK?
N-NO ONE, SIR.
COME HERE.
N-NO...
MERCY, SIR, I WON'T DO IT AGA--!

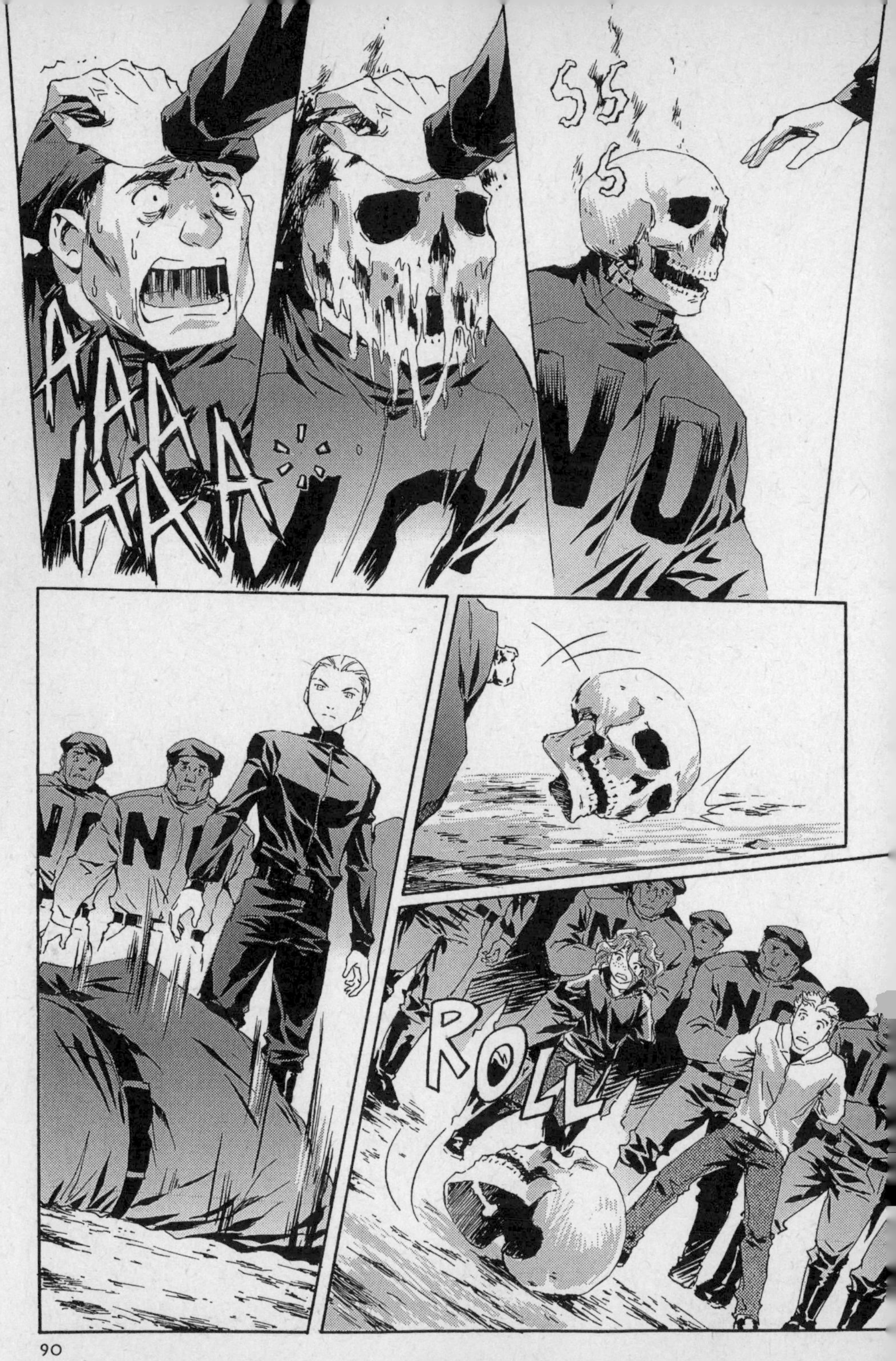
AAAAHAA
SSS
S
ROLL

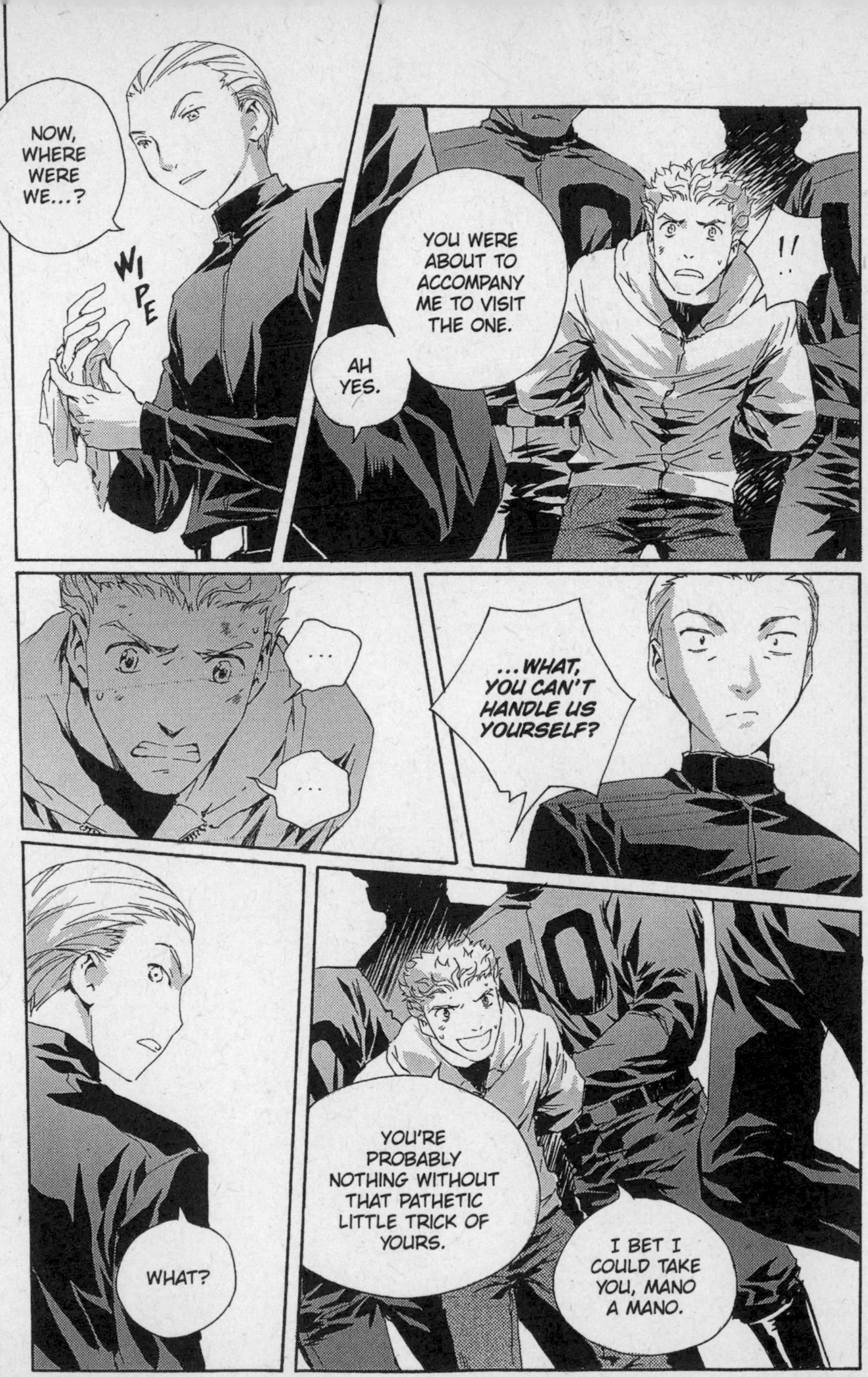
NOW, WHERE WERE WE...?
WIPE
YOU WERE ABOUT TO ACCOMPANY ME TO VISIT THE ONE.
AH YES.
!!
...
...
...WHAT, YOU CAN'T HANDLE US YOURSELF?
WHAT?
YOU'RE PROBABLY NOTHING WITHOUT THAT PATHETIC LITTLE TRICK OF YOURS.
I BET I COULD TAKE YOU, MANO A MANO.

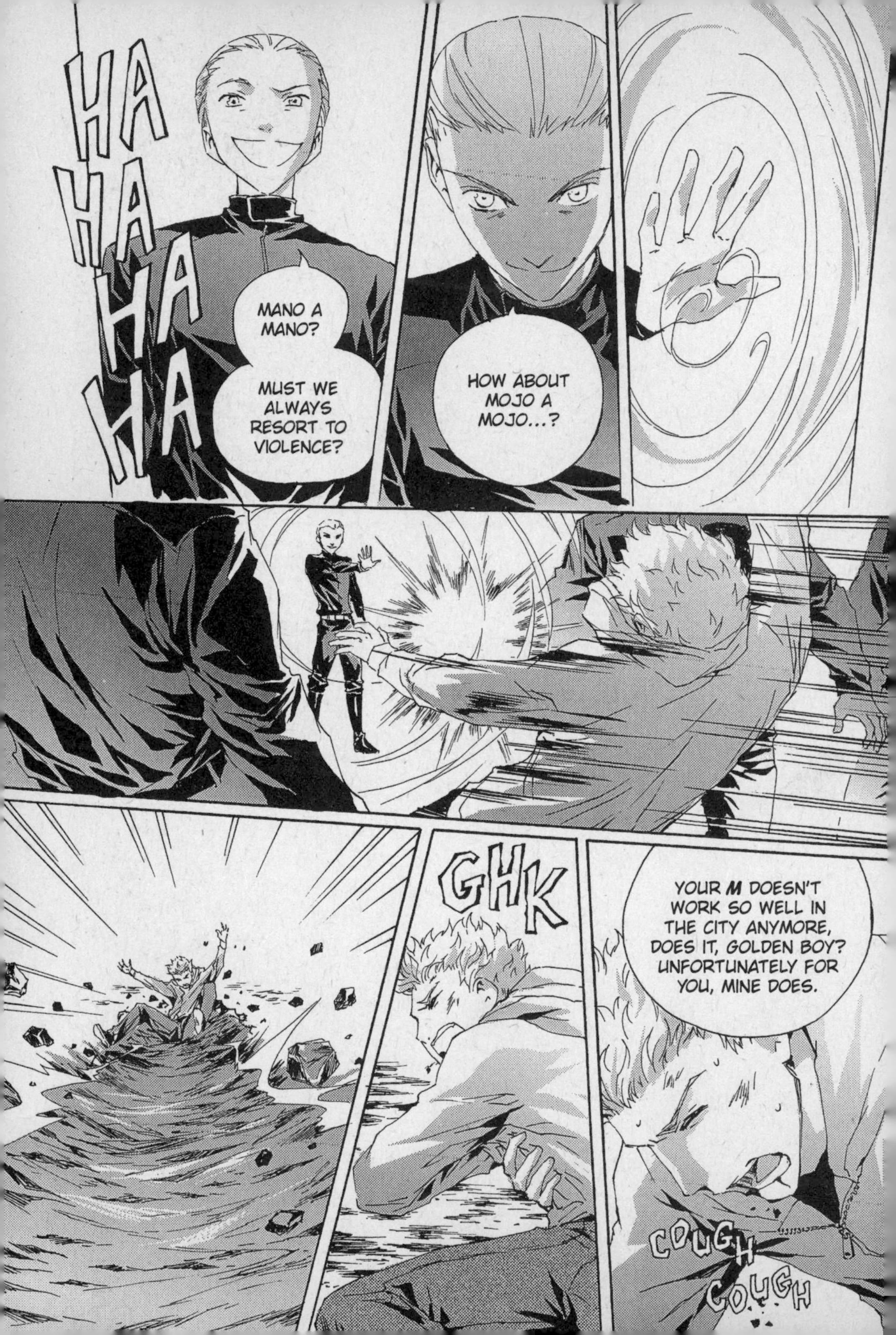

HA HA HA HA HA
MANO A MANO?
MUST WE ALWAYS RESORT TO VIOLENCE?
HOW ABOUT MOJO A MOJO...?
GHK
YOUR *M* DOESN'T WORK SO WELL IN THE CITY ANYMORE, DOES IT, GOLDEN BOY? UNFORTUNATELY FOR YOU, MINE DOES.
COUGH COUGH

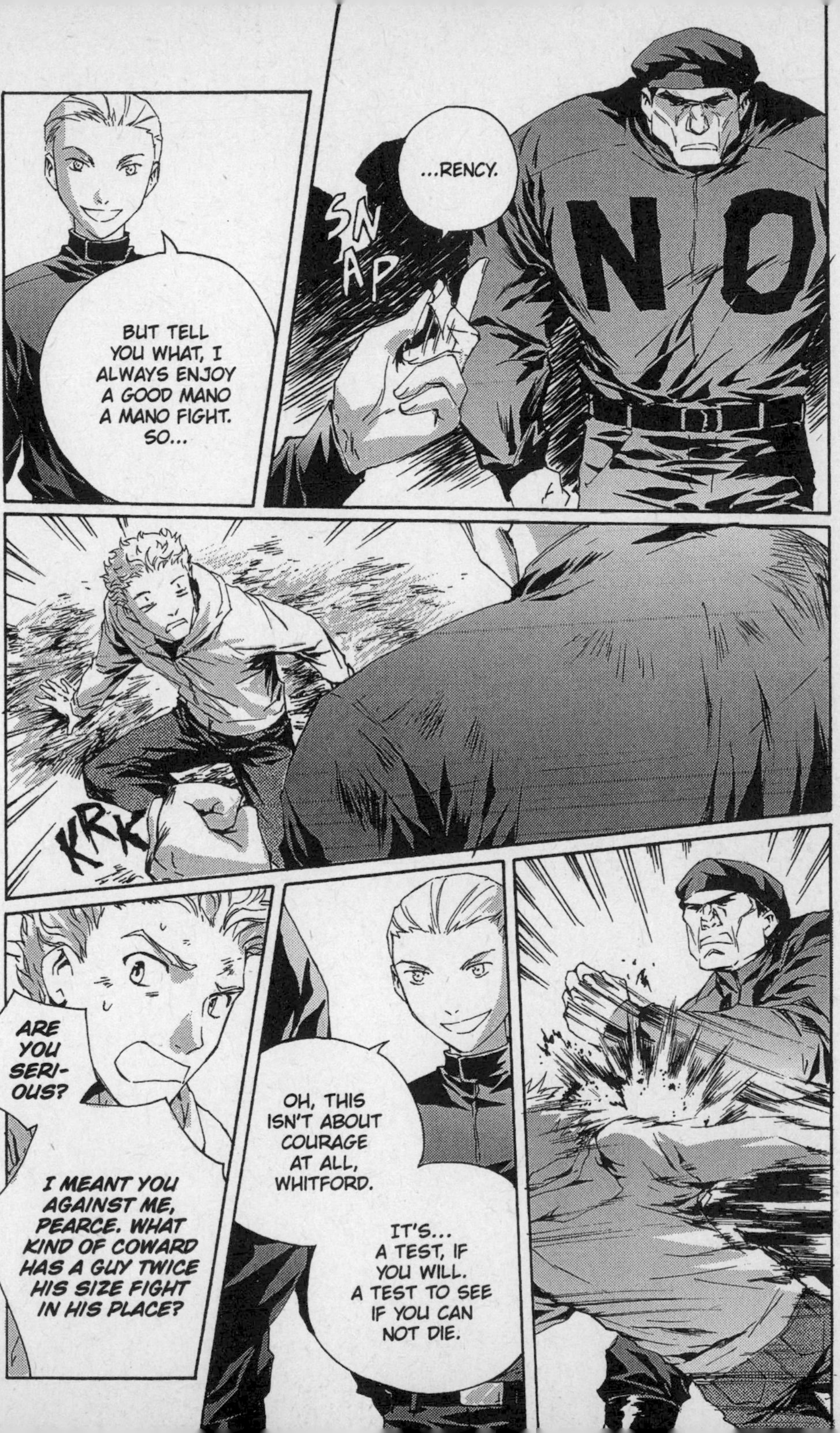
BUT TELL YOU WHAT, I ALWAYS ENJOY A GOOD MANO A MANO FIGHT. SO...
...RENCY.
SNAP
KRK
ARE YOU SERI-OUS?
I MEANT YOU AGAINST ME, PEARCE. WHAT KIND OF COWARD HAS A GUY TWICE HIS SIZE FIGHT IN HIS PLACE?
OH, THIS ISN'T ABOUT COURAGE AT ALL, WHITFORD.
IT'S... A TEST, IF YOU WILL. A TEST TO SEE IF YOU CAN NOT DIE.

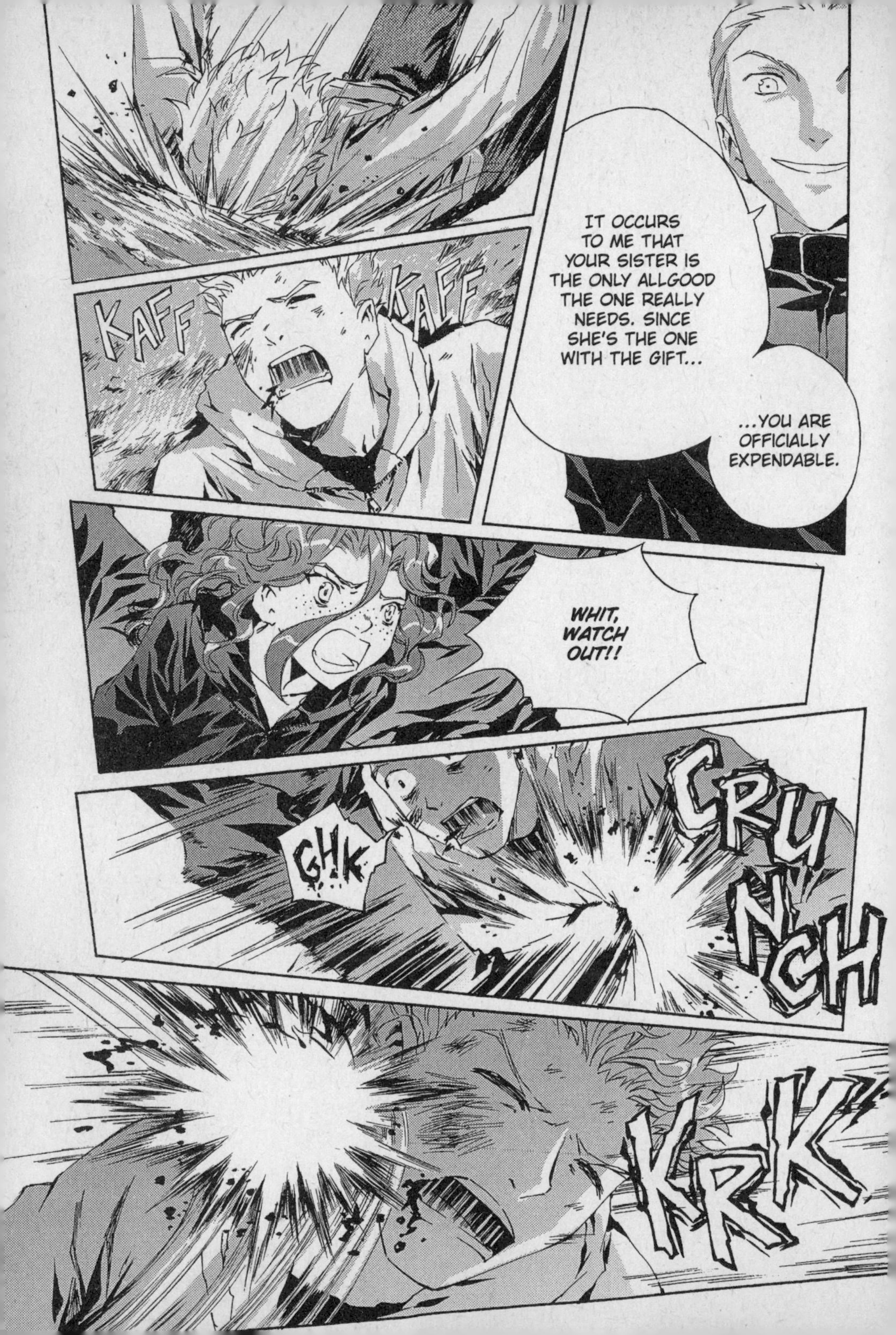
KAFF KAFF
IT OCCURS TO ME THAT YOUR SISTER IS THE ONLY ALLGOOD THE ONE REALLY NEEDS. SINCE SHE'S THE ONE WITH THE GIFT...
...YOU ARE OFFICIALLY EXPENDABLE.
WHIT, WATCH OUT!!
GHK
CRUNCH
KRK

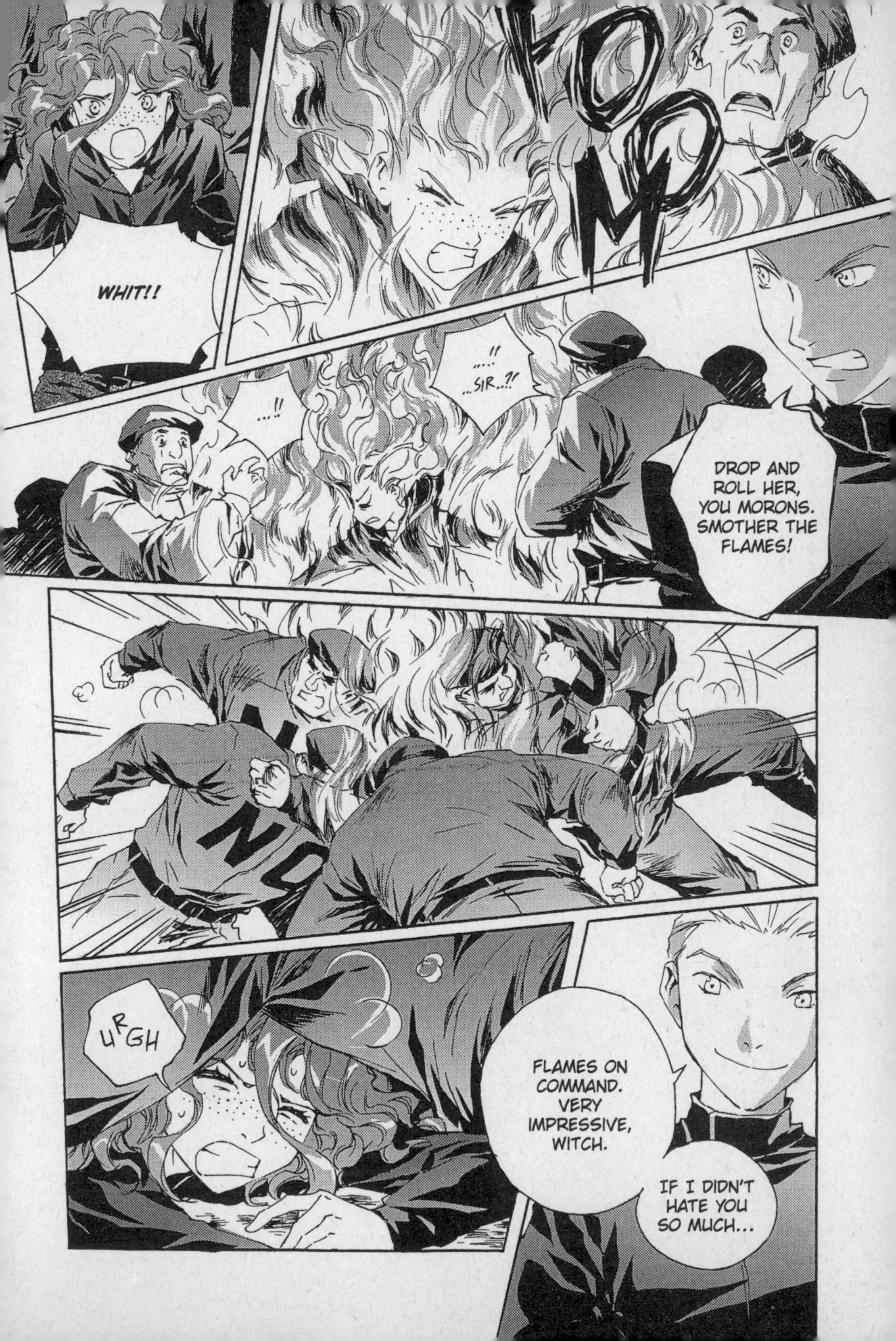
WHIT!!
FOOMP
...!!
...!!
...SIR...?!
DROP AND ROLL HER, YOU MORONS. SMOTHER THE FLAMES!
URGH
FLAMES ON COMMAND. VERY IMPRESSIVE, WITCH.
IF I DIDN'T HATE YOU SO MUCH...

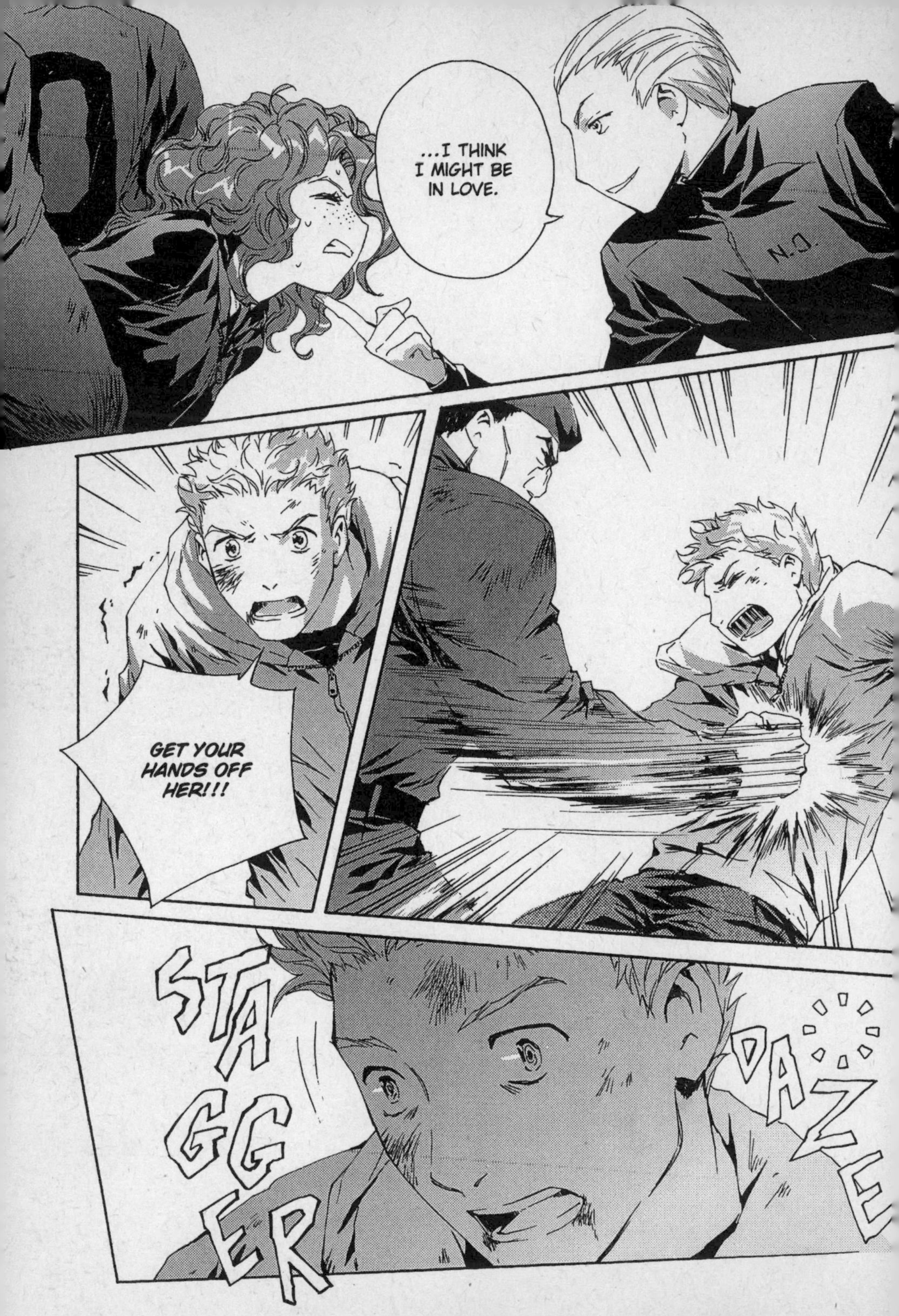
...I THINK I MIGHT BE IN LOVE.
N.O.
GET YOUR HANDS OFF HER!!!
STAGGER
DAZE

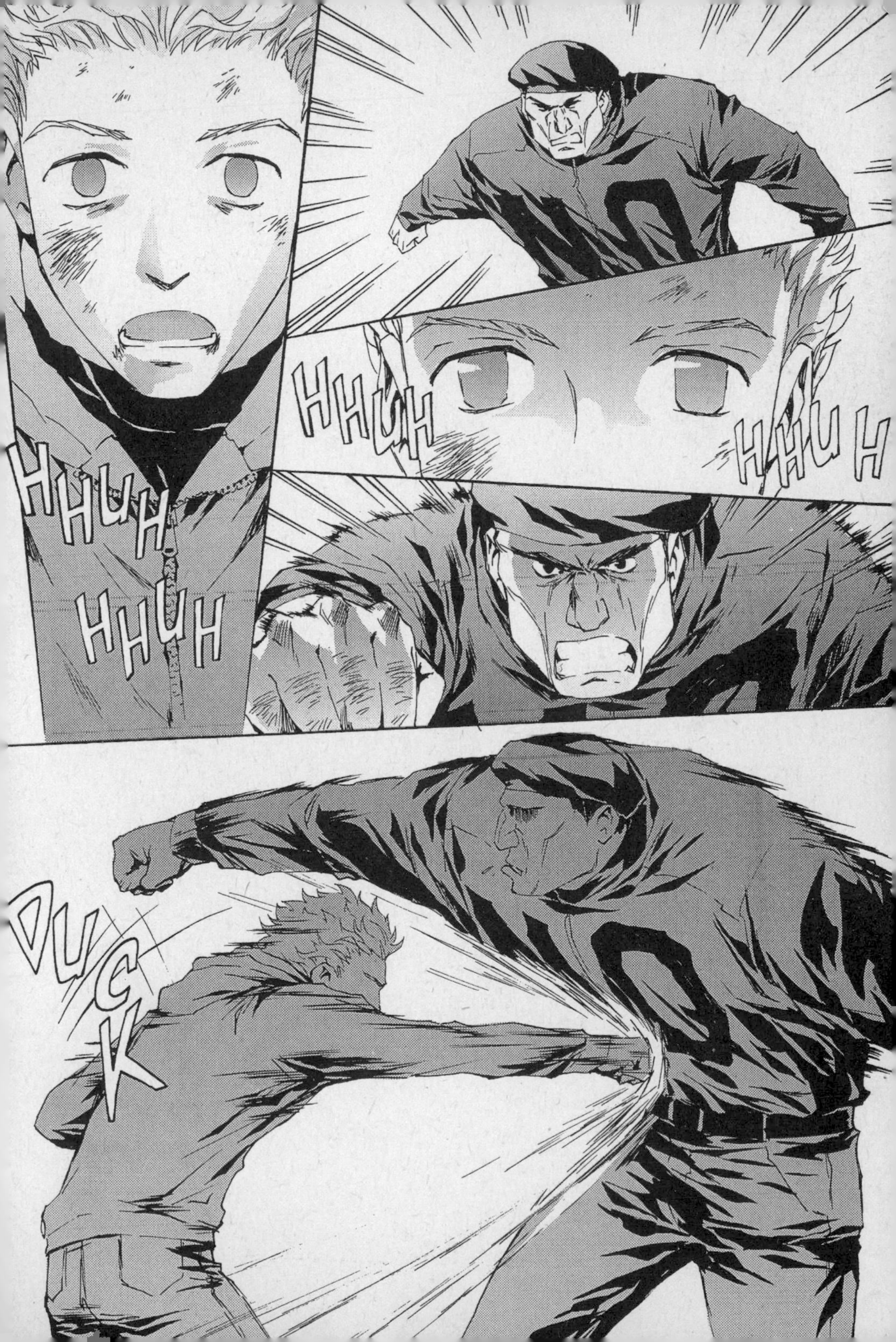
HHUH
HHUH
HHUH
HHUH
DUCK

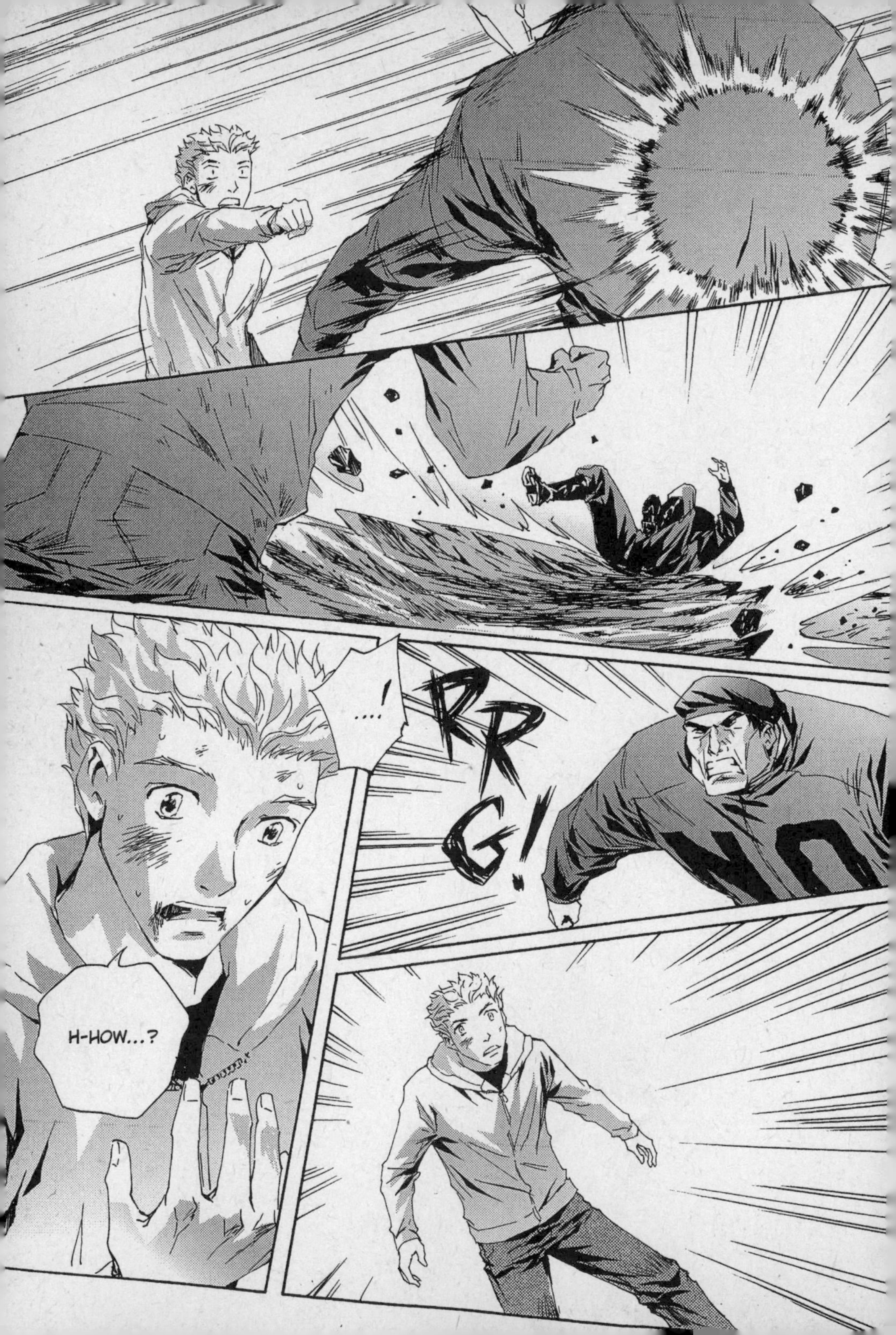
RRG!
....!
H-HOW...?

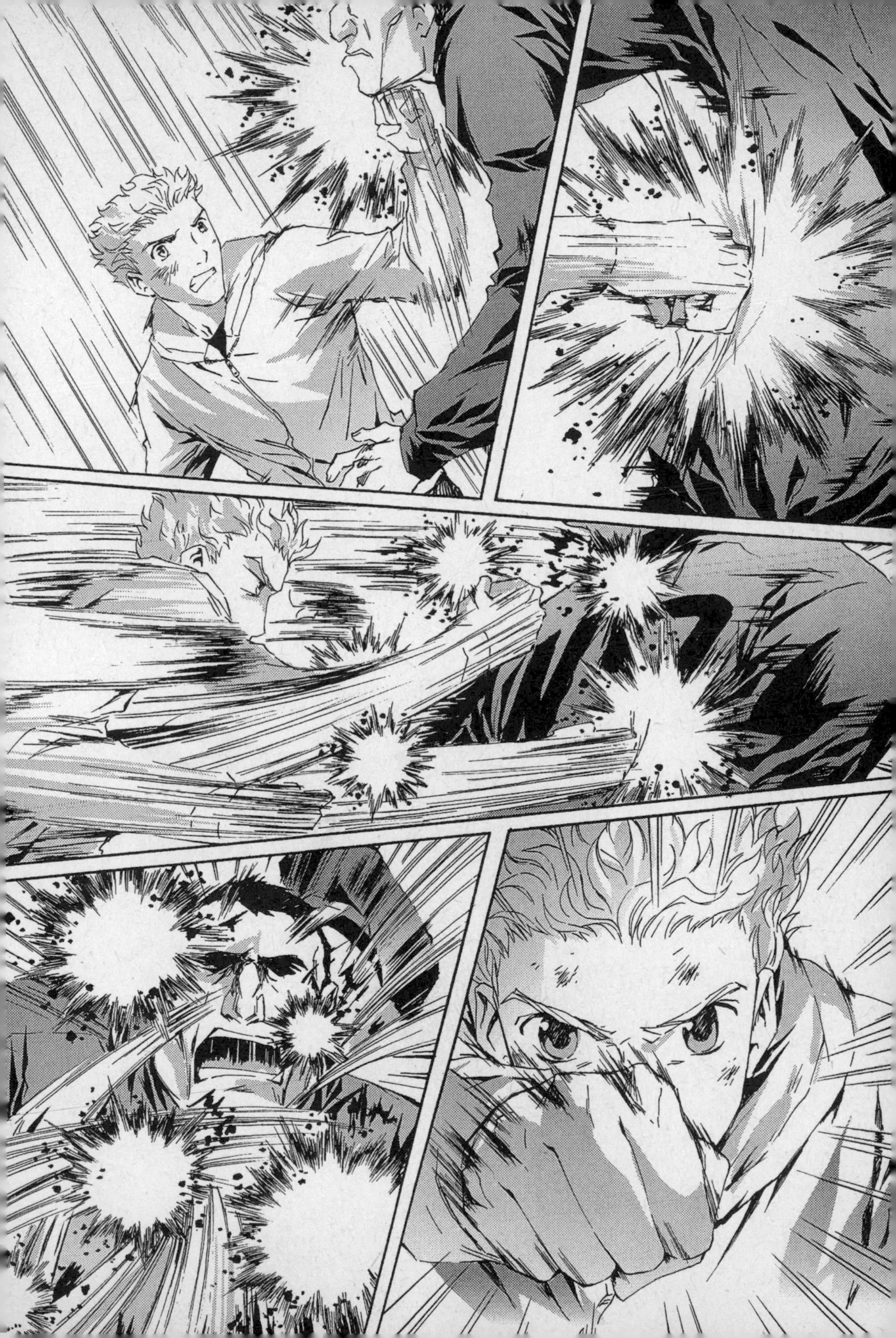

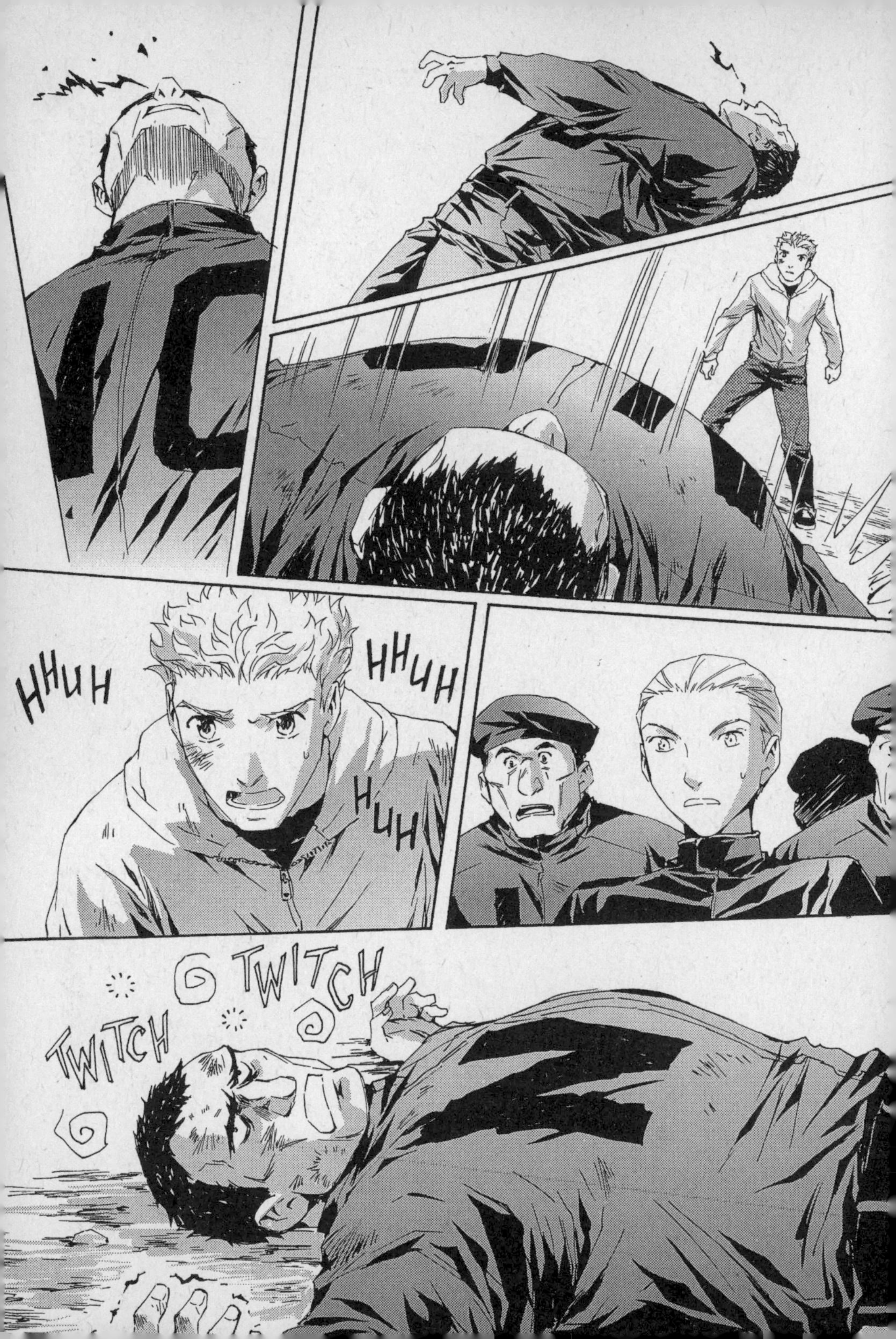
HHUH
HHUH
HUH
TWITCH
TWITCH

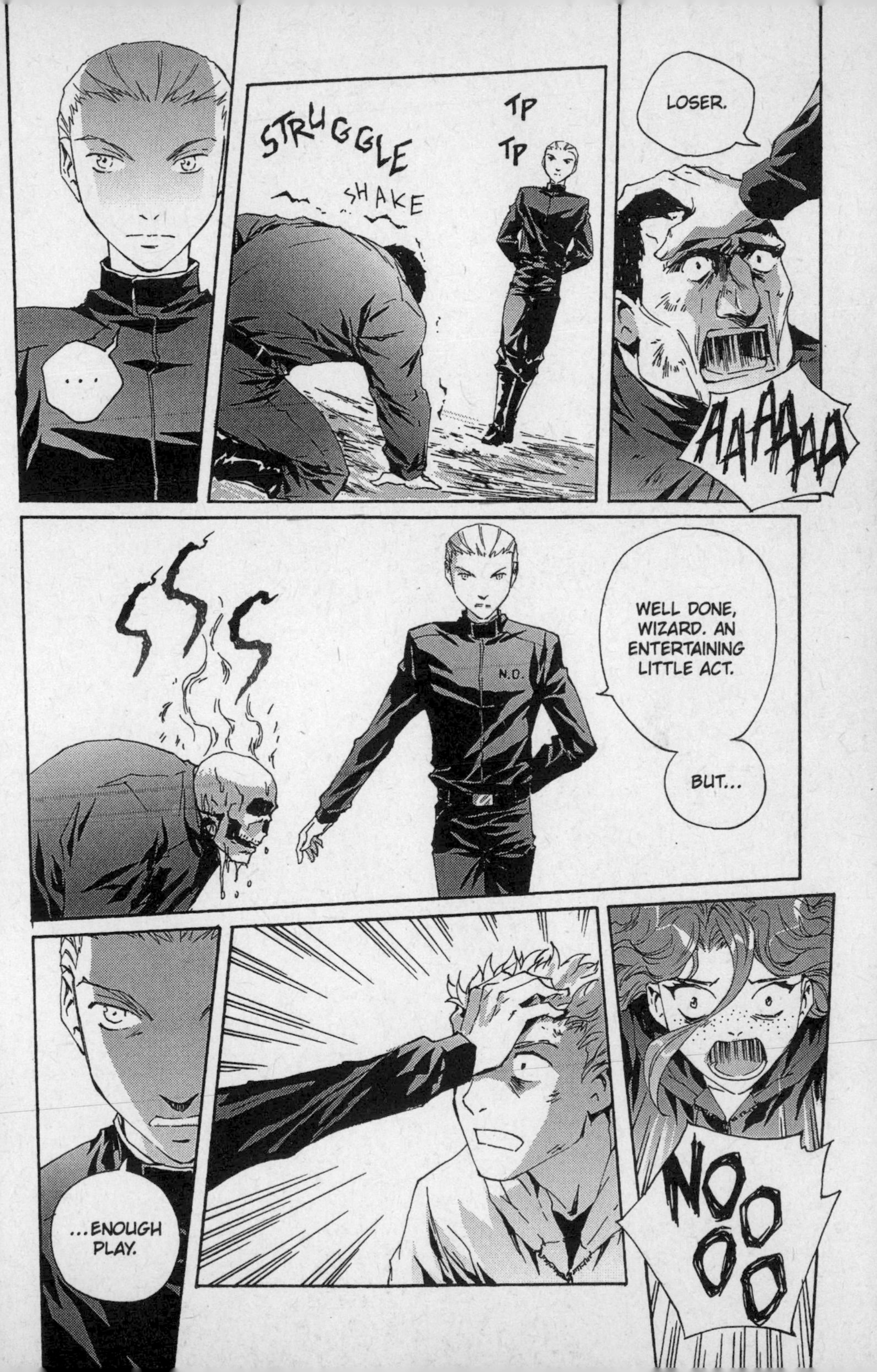
LOSER.
AAAAAA
TP
TP
STRUGGLE
SHAKE
...
WELL DONE, WIZARD. AN ENTERTAINING LITTLE ACT.
BUT...
SSS
NOOOOOO
...ENOUGH PLAY.

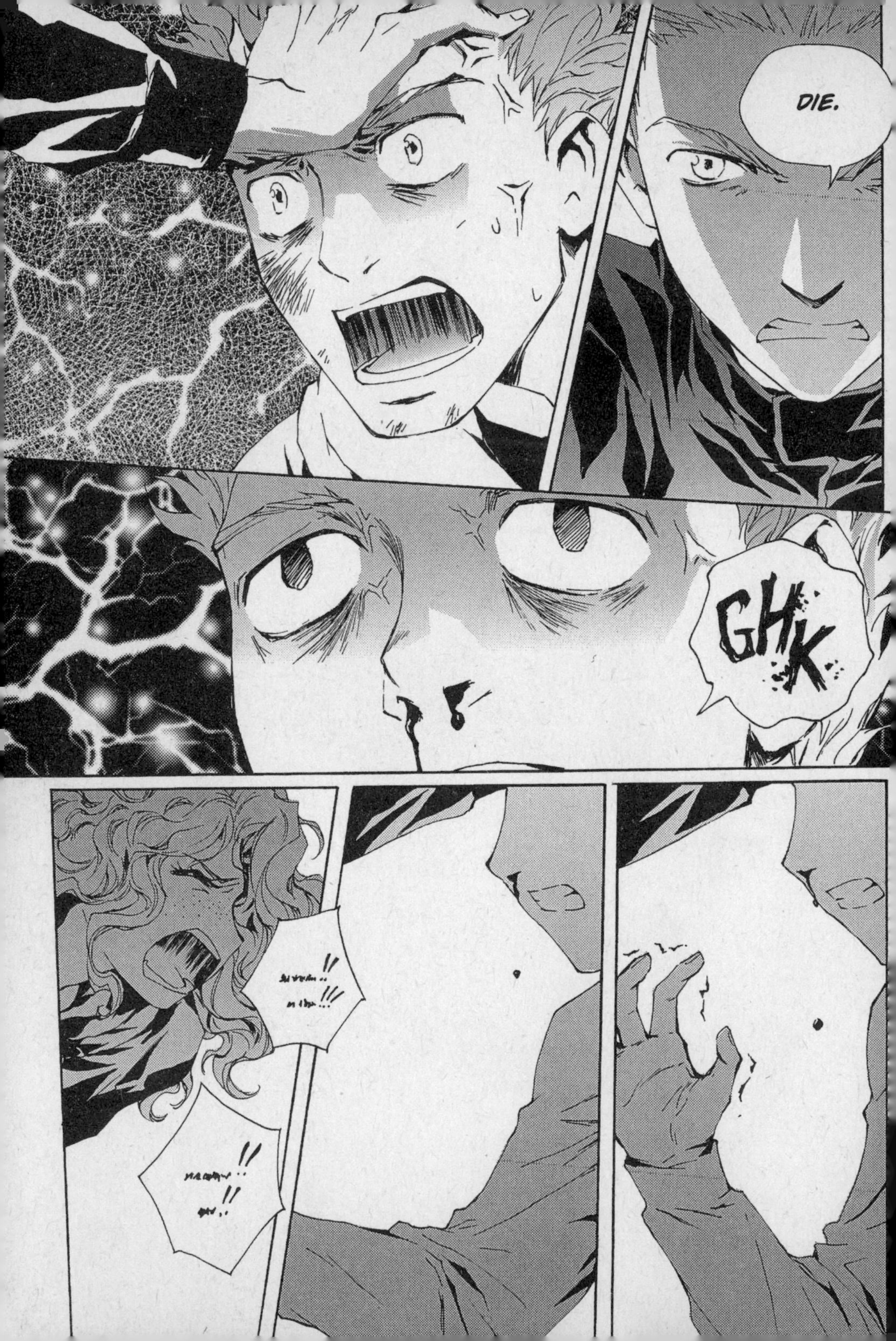
DIE.
GHK

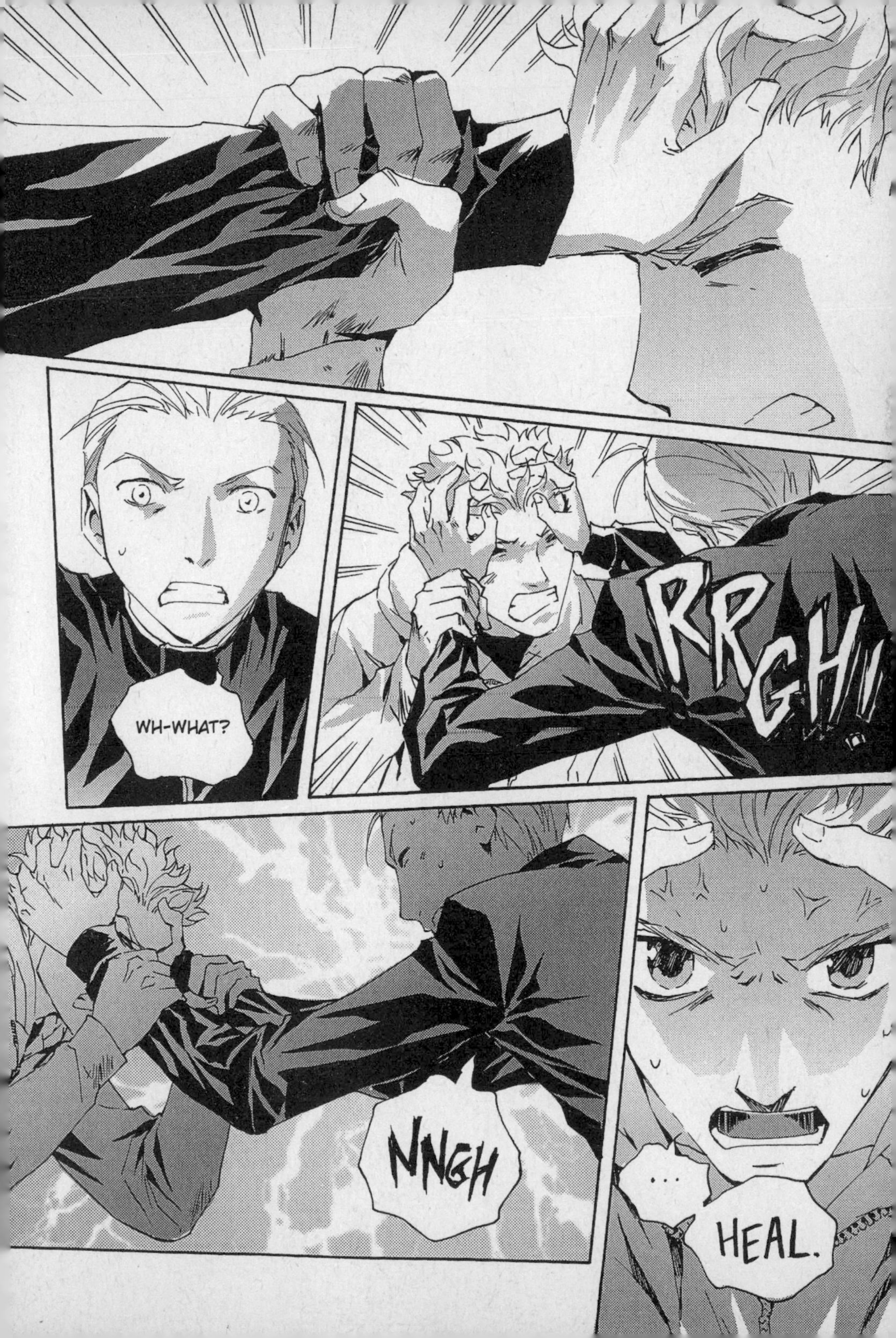
RRGH!!
WH-WHAT?
...
HEAL.
NNGH

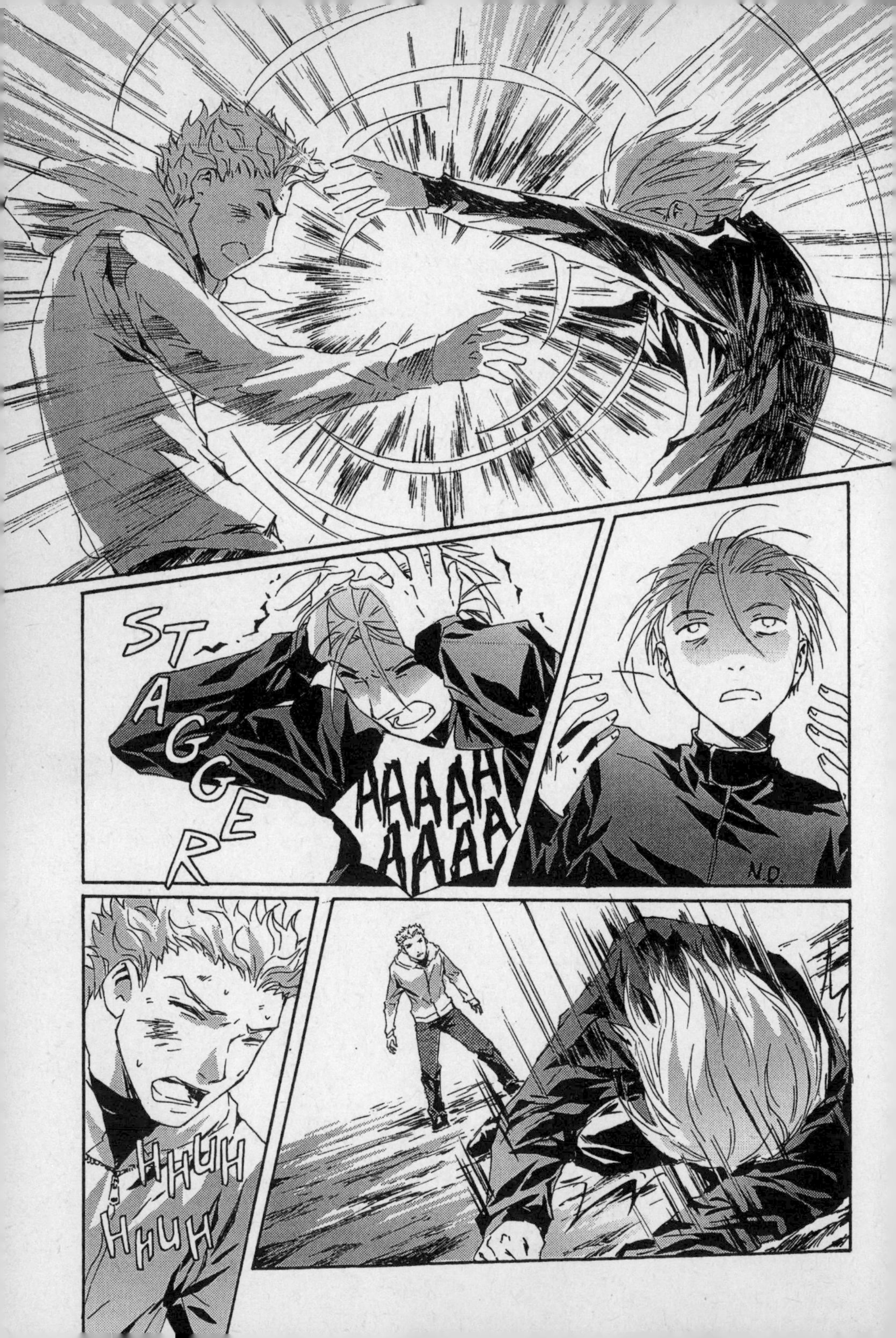
STAGGER
HAAAAHAAAA
N.D.
HHUH HHUH

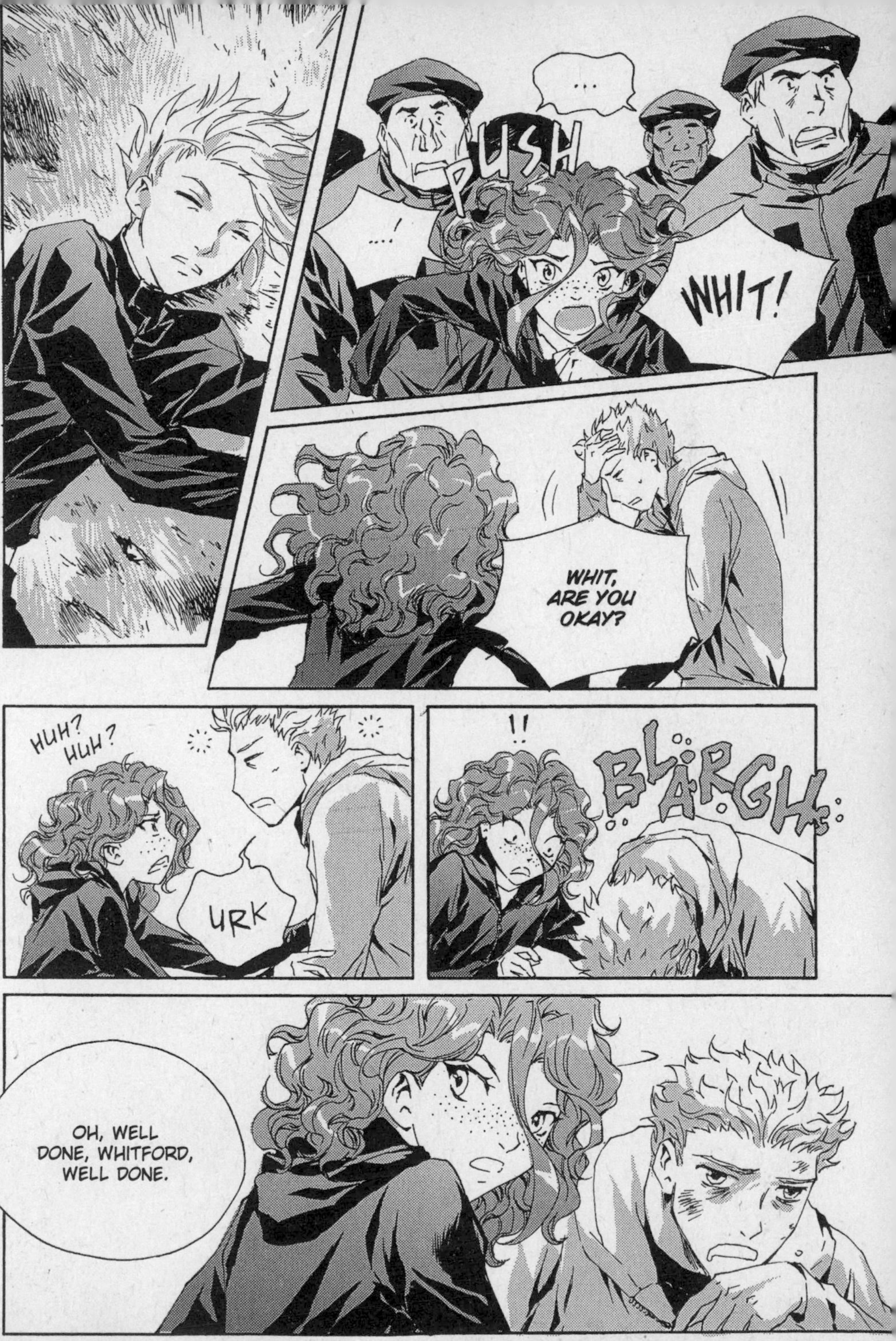
...
PUSH
...!
WHIT!
WHIT, ARE YOU OKAY?
HUH? HUH?
URK
!!
BLÄRGH
OH, WELL DONE, WHITFORD, WELL DONE.

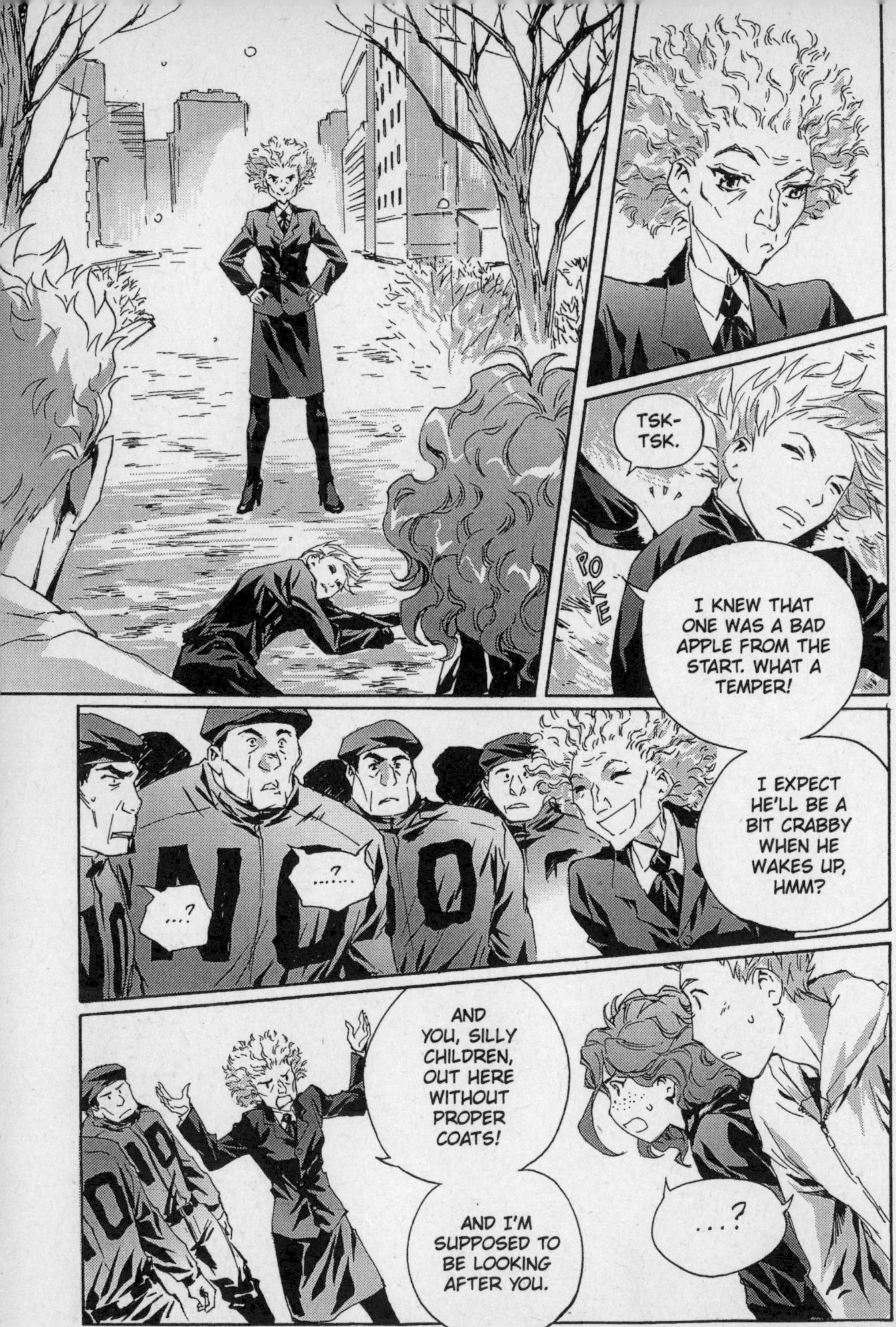
TSK-TSK.
POKE
I KNEW THAT ONE WAS A BAD APPLE FROM THE START. WHAT A TEMPER!
I EXPECT HE'LL BE A BIT CRABBY WHEN HE WAKES UP, HMM?
......?
....?
AND YOU, SILLY CHILDREN, OUT HERE WITHOUT PROPER COATS!
AND I'M SUPPOSED TO BE LOOKING AFTER YOU.
...?

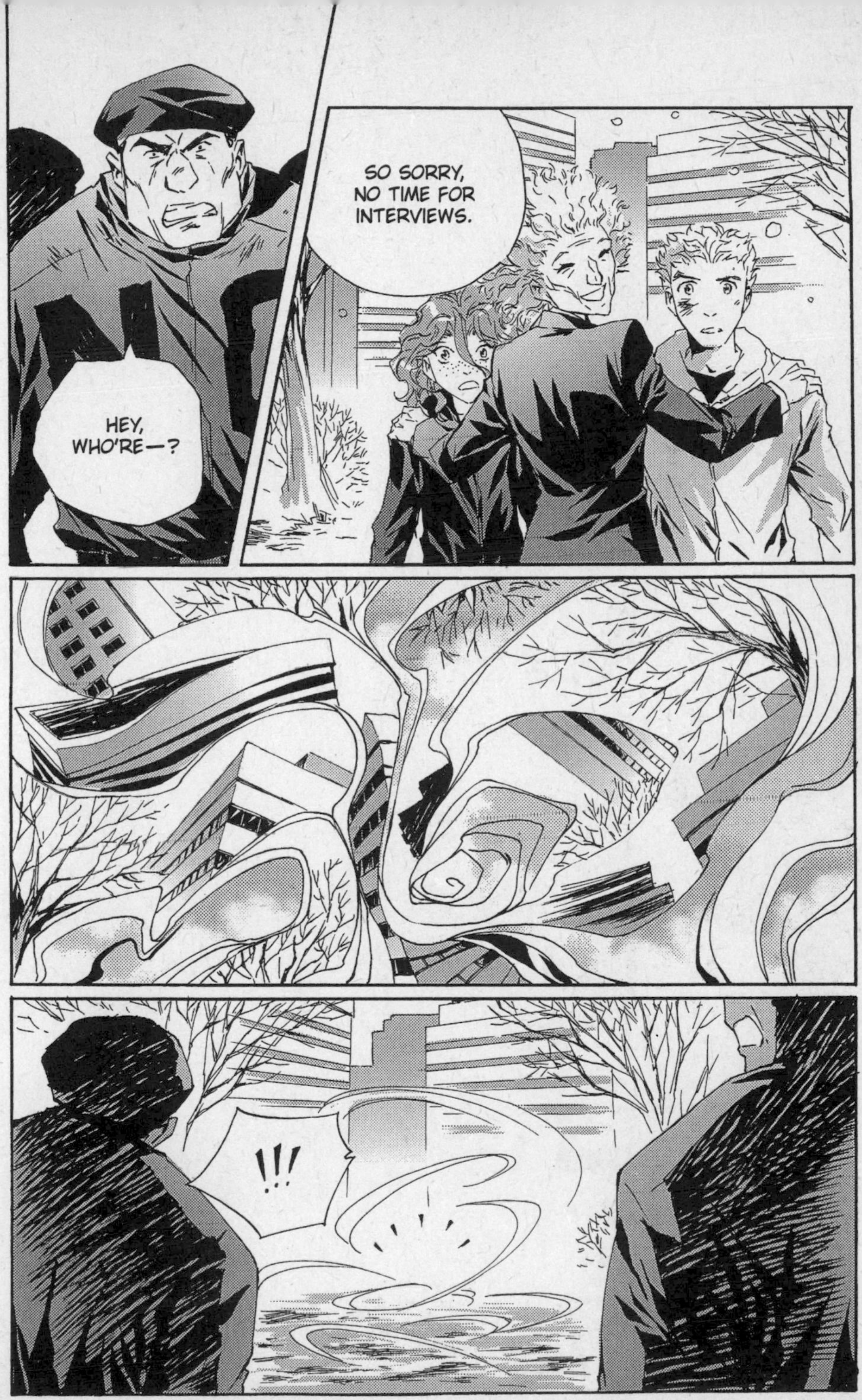
HEY, WHO'RE—?
SO SORRY, NO TIME FOR INTERVIEWS.
!!!

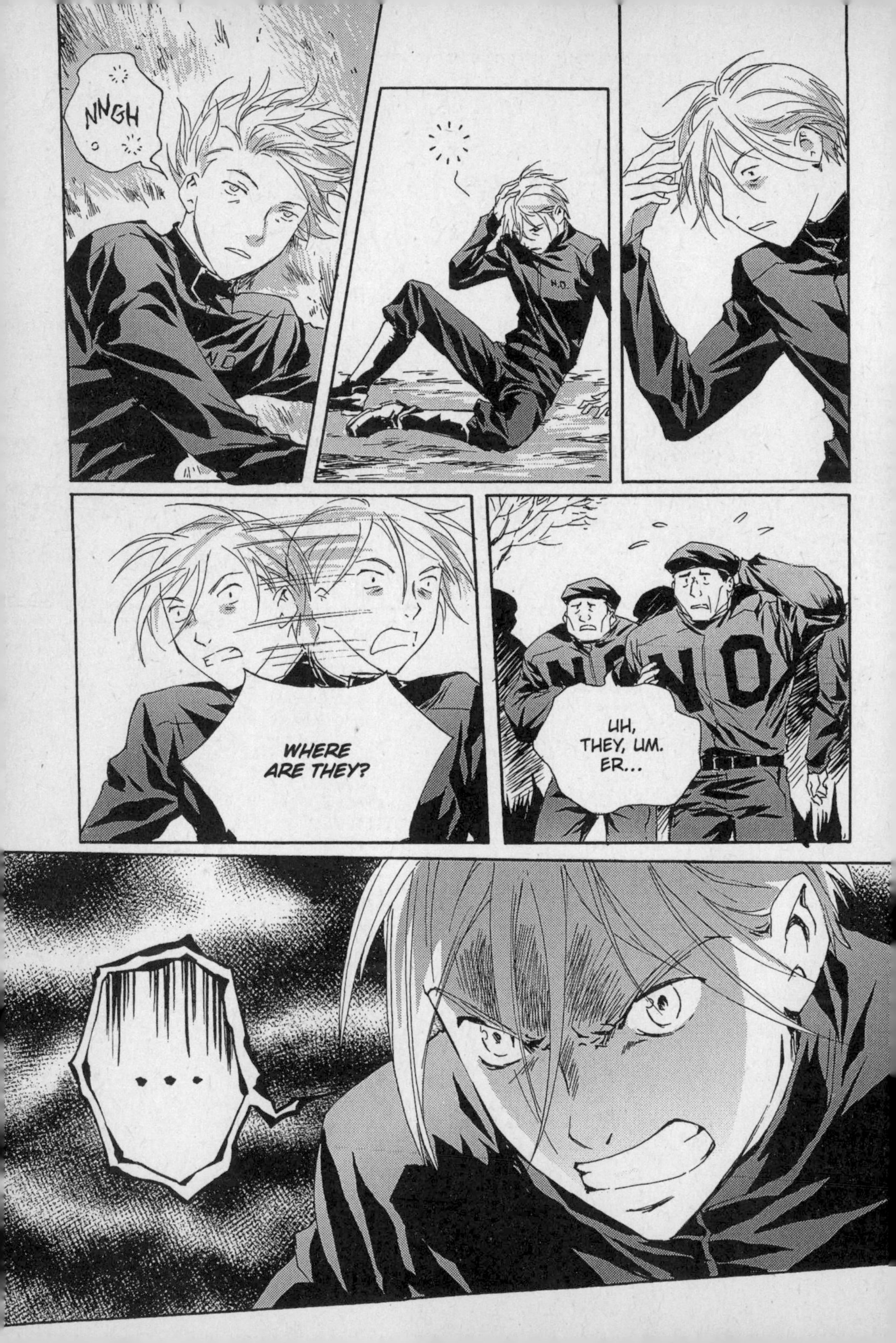
NNGH
WHERE ARE THEY?
UH, THEY, UM. ER...
...

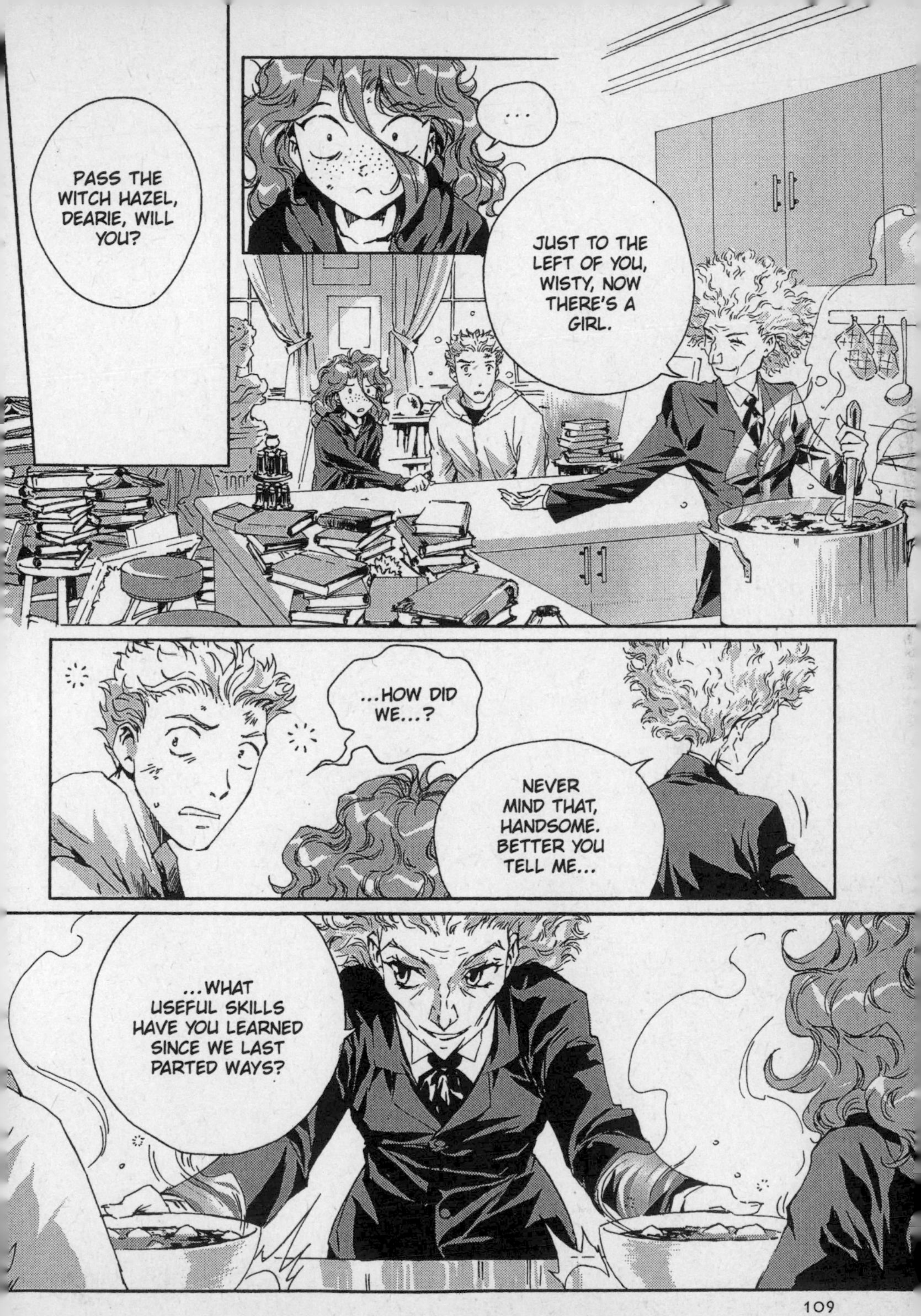
PASS THE WITCH HAZEL, DEARIE, WILL YOU?
...
JUST TO THE LEFT OF YOU, WISTY, NOW THERE'S A GIRL.
...HOW DID WE...?
NEVER MIND THAT, HANDSOME. BETTER YOU TELL ME...
...WHAT USEFUL SKILLS HAVE YOU LEARNED SINCE WE LAST PARTED WAYS?

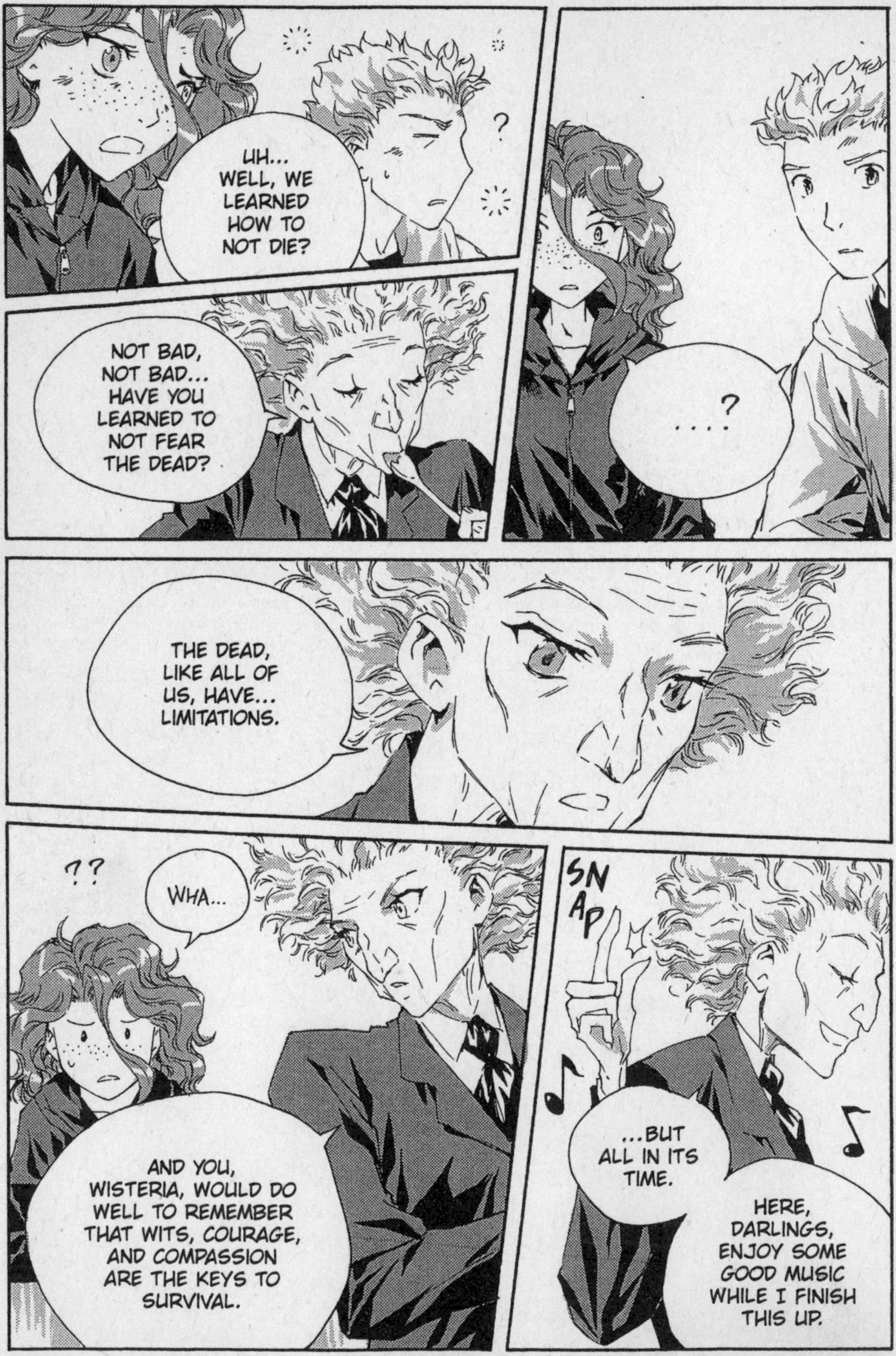
UH... WELL, WE LEARNED HOW TO NOT DIE?
?
NOT BAD, NOT BAD... HAVE YOU LEARNED TO NOT FEAR THE DEAD?
...?
THE DEAD, LIKE ALL OF US, HAVE... LIMITATIONS.
??
WHA...
AND YOU, WISTERIA, WOULD DO WELL TO REMEMBER THAT WITS, COURAGE, AND COMPASSION ARE THE KEYS TO SURVIVAL.
SNAP
...BUT ALL IN ITS TIME.
HERE, DARLINGS, ENJOY SOME GOOD MUSIC WHILE I FINISH THIS UP.

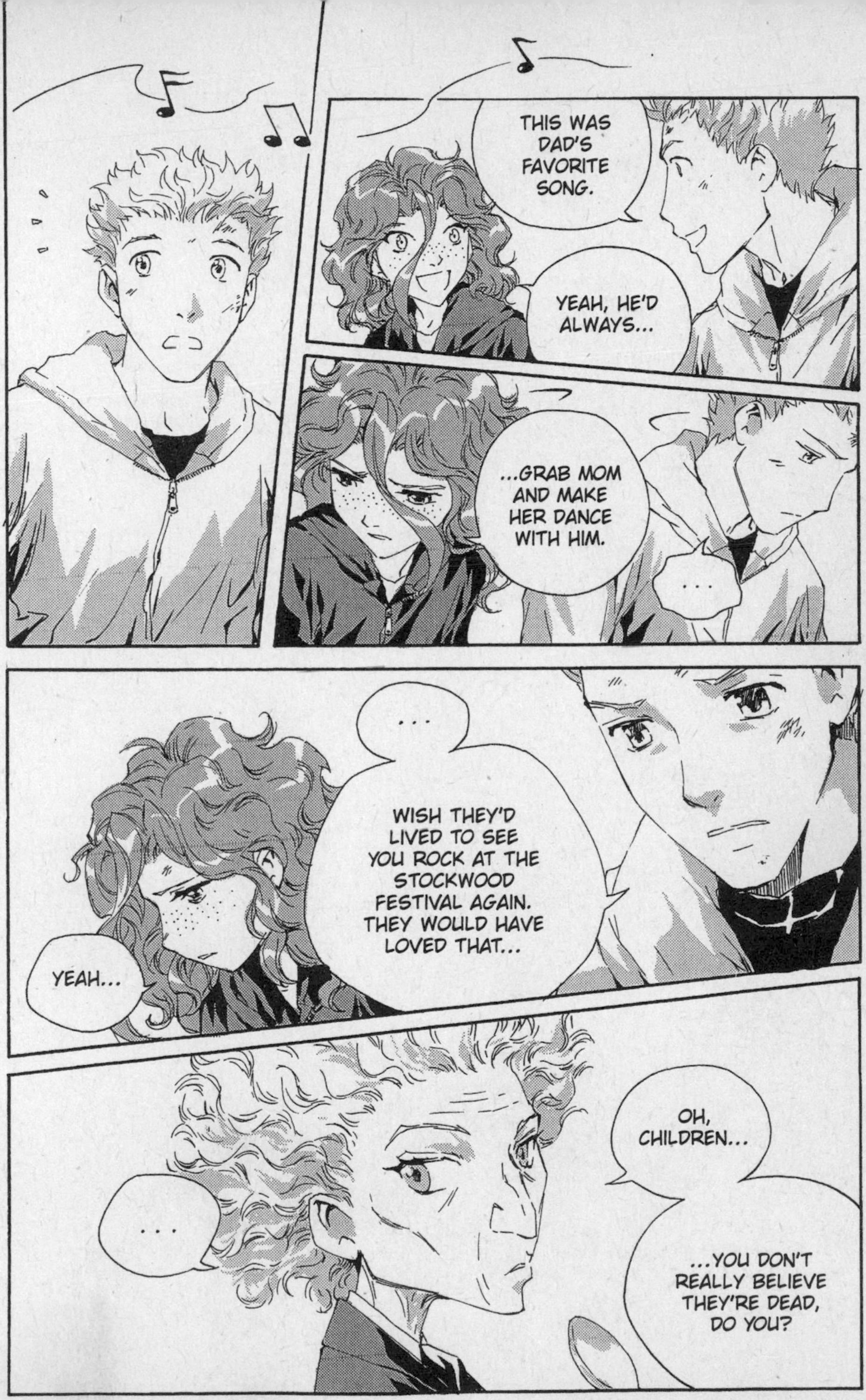
THIS WAS DAD'S FAVORITE SONG.
YEAH, HE'D ALWAYS...
...GRAB MOM AND MAKE HER DANCE WITH HIM.
...
...
WISH THEY'D LIVED TO SEE YOU ROCK AT THE STOCKWOOD FESTIVAL AGAIN. THEY WOULD HAVE LOVED THAT...
YEAH...
OH, CHILDREN...
...
...YOU DON'T REALLY BELIEVE THEY'RE DEAD, DO YOU?

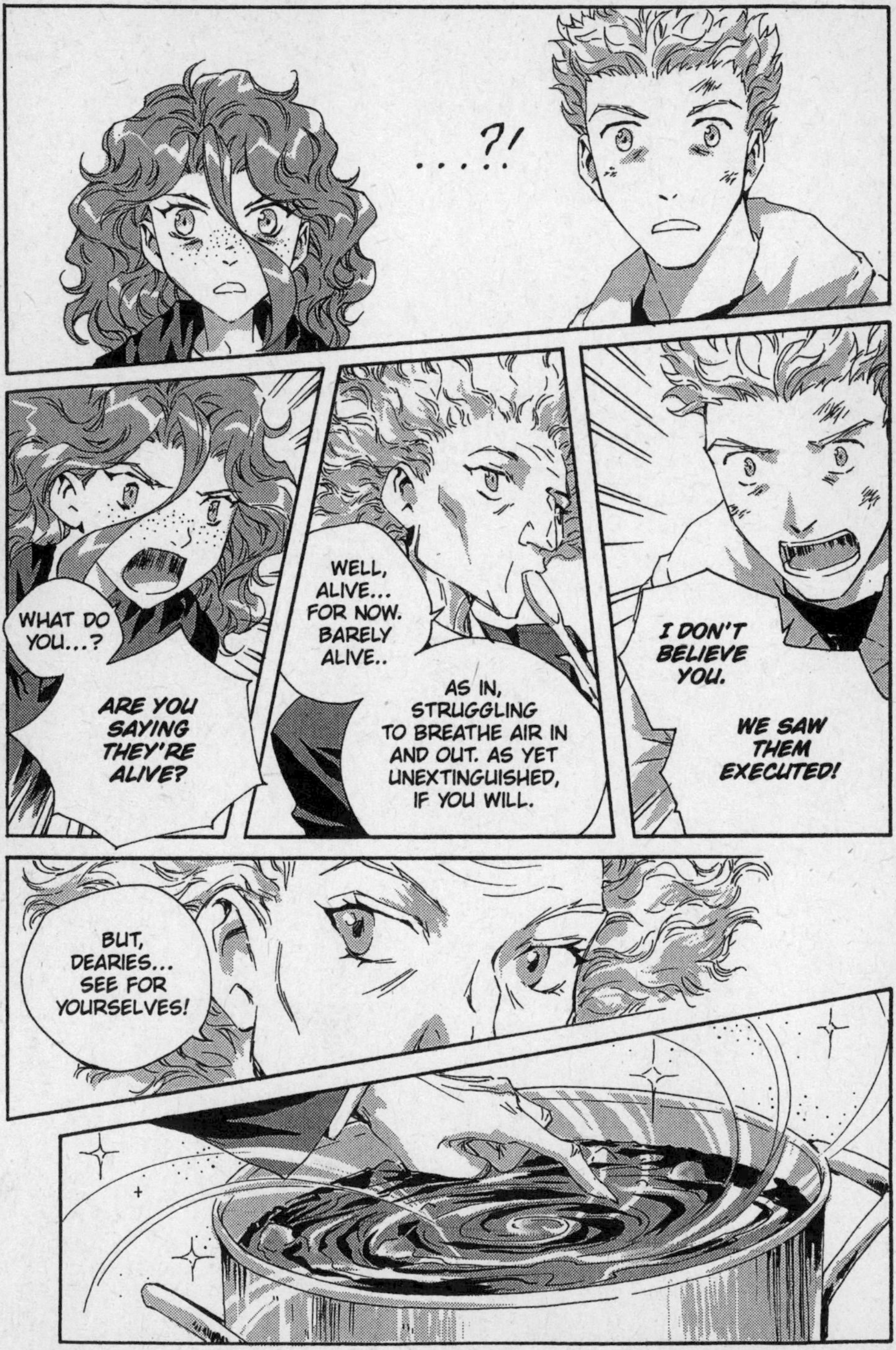

...?!
WHAT DO YOU...?
ARE YOU SAYING THEY'RE ALIVE?
WELL, ALIVE... FOR NOW. BARELY ALIVE..
AS IN, STRUGGLING TO BREATHE AIR IN AND OUT. AS YET UNEXTINGUISHED, IF YOU WILL.
I DON'T BELIEVE YOU.
WE SAW THEM EXECUTED!
BUT, DEARIES... SEE FOR YOURSELVES!

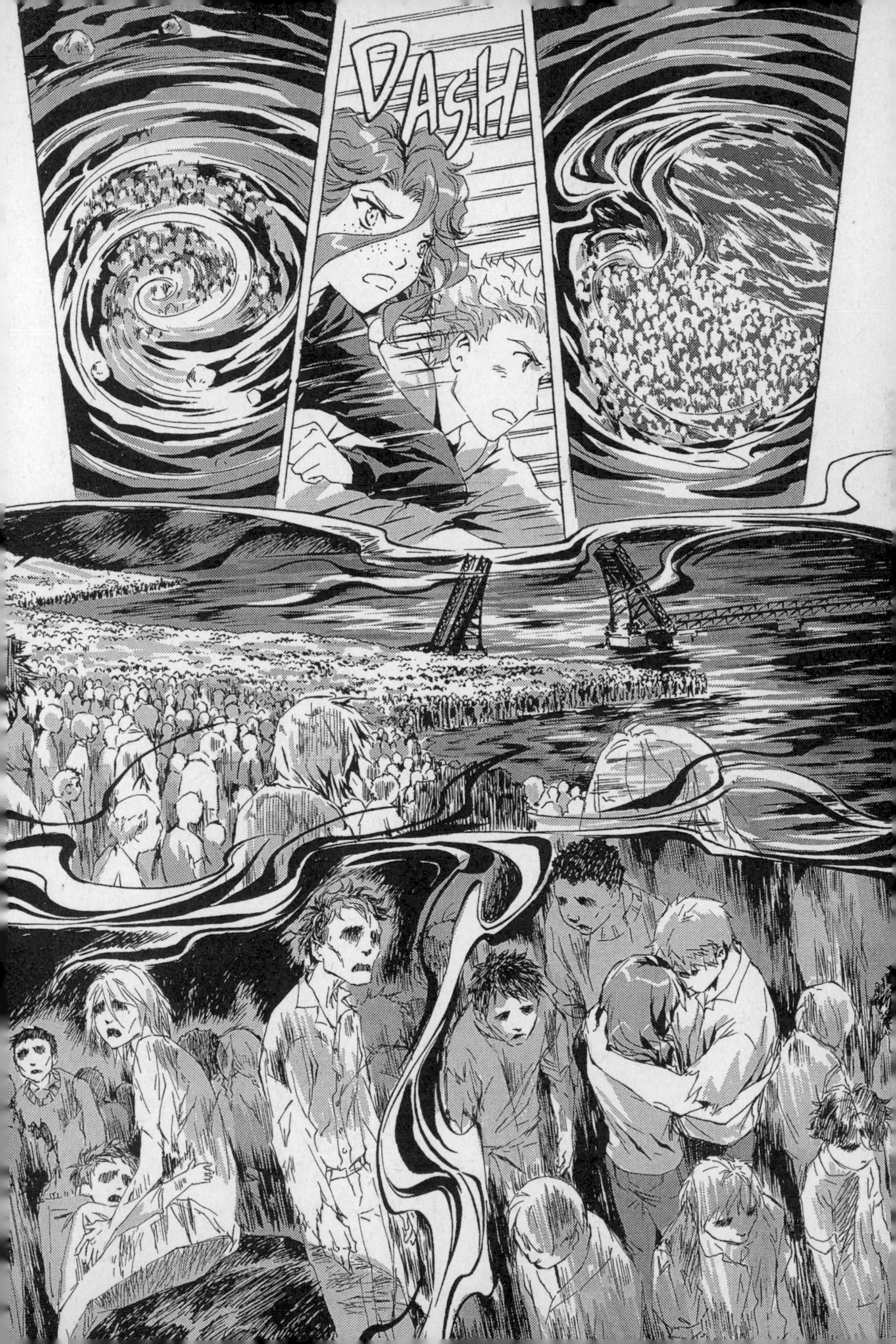
DASH

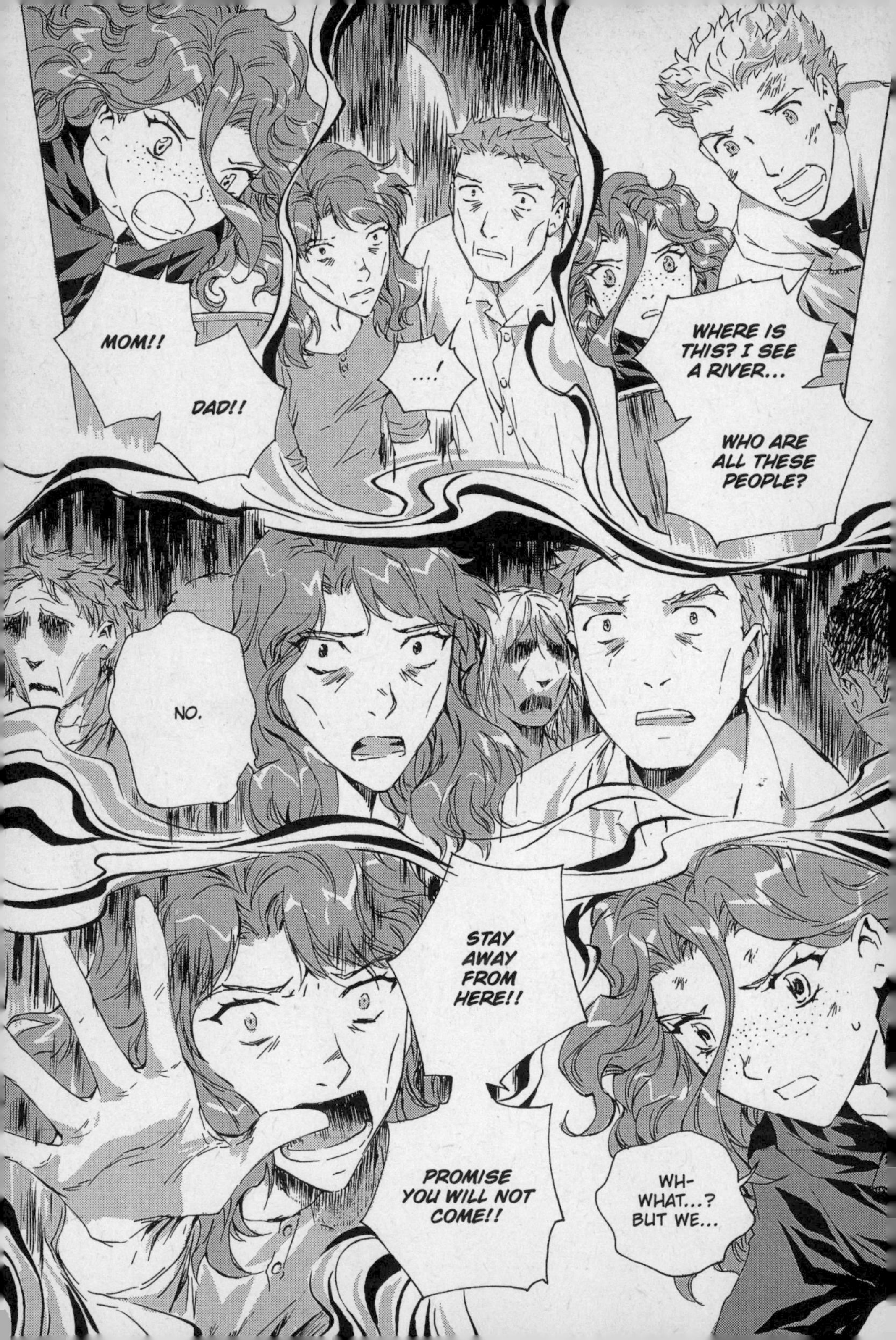
MOM!!
DAD!!
....!
WHERE IS THIS? I SEE A RIVER...
WHO ARE ALL THESE PEOPLE?
NO.
STAY AWAY FROM HERE!!
PROMISE YOU WILL NOT COME!!
WH- WHAT...? BUT WE...

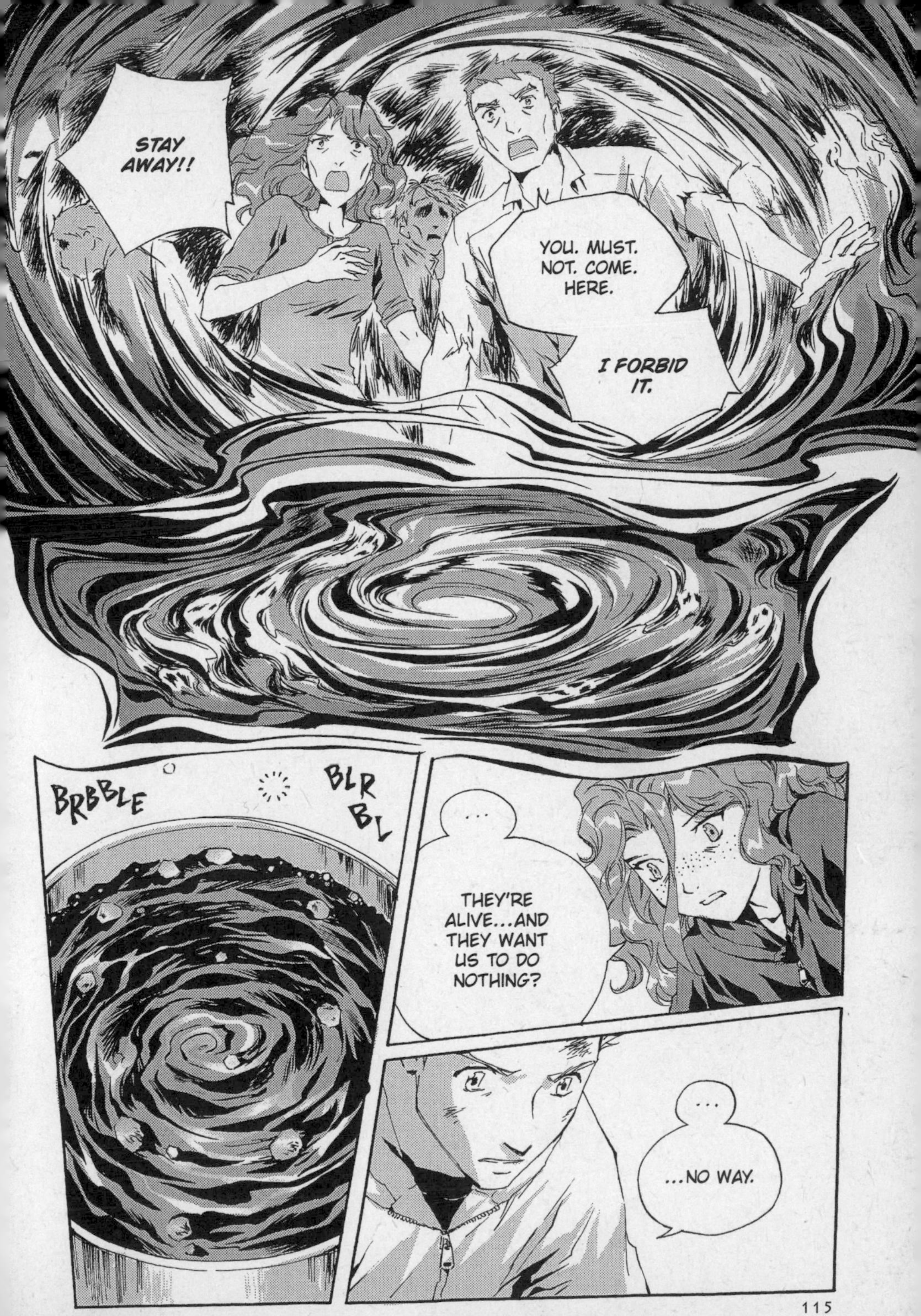
STAY AWAY!!
YOU. MUST. NOT. COME. HERE.
I FORBID IT.
BRBBLE
BLR BL
...
THEY'RE ALIVE...AND THEY WANT US TO DO NOTHING?
...
...NO WAY.

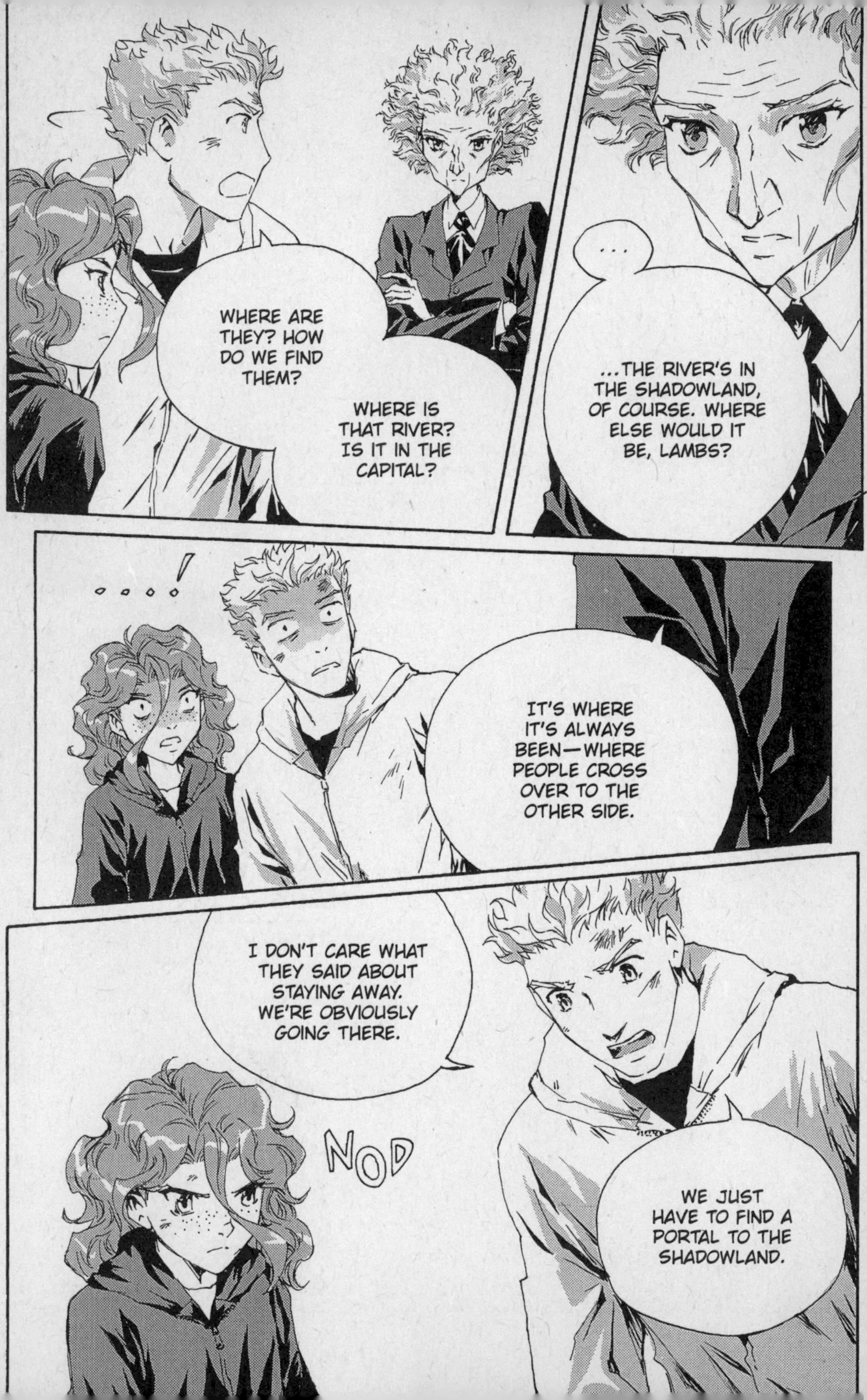
WHERE ARE THEY? HOW DO WE FIND THEM?
WHERE IS THAT RIVER? IS IT IN THE CAPITAL?
...
...THE RIVER'S IN THE SHADOWLAND, OF COURSE. WHERE ELSE WOULD IT BE, LAMBS?
....!
IT'S WHERE IT'S ALWAYS BEEN—WHERE PEOPLE CROSS OVER TO THE OTHER SIDE.
I DON'T CARE WHAT THEY SAID ABOUT STAYING AWAY. WE'RE OBVIOUSLY GOING THERE.
NOD
WE JUST HAVE TO FIND A PORTAL TO THE SHADOWLAND.

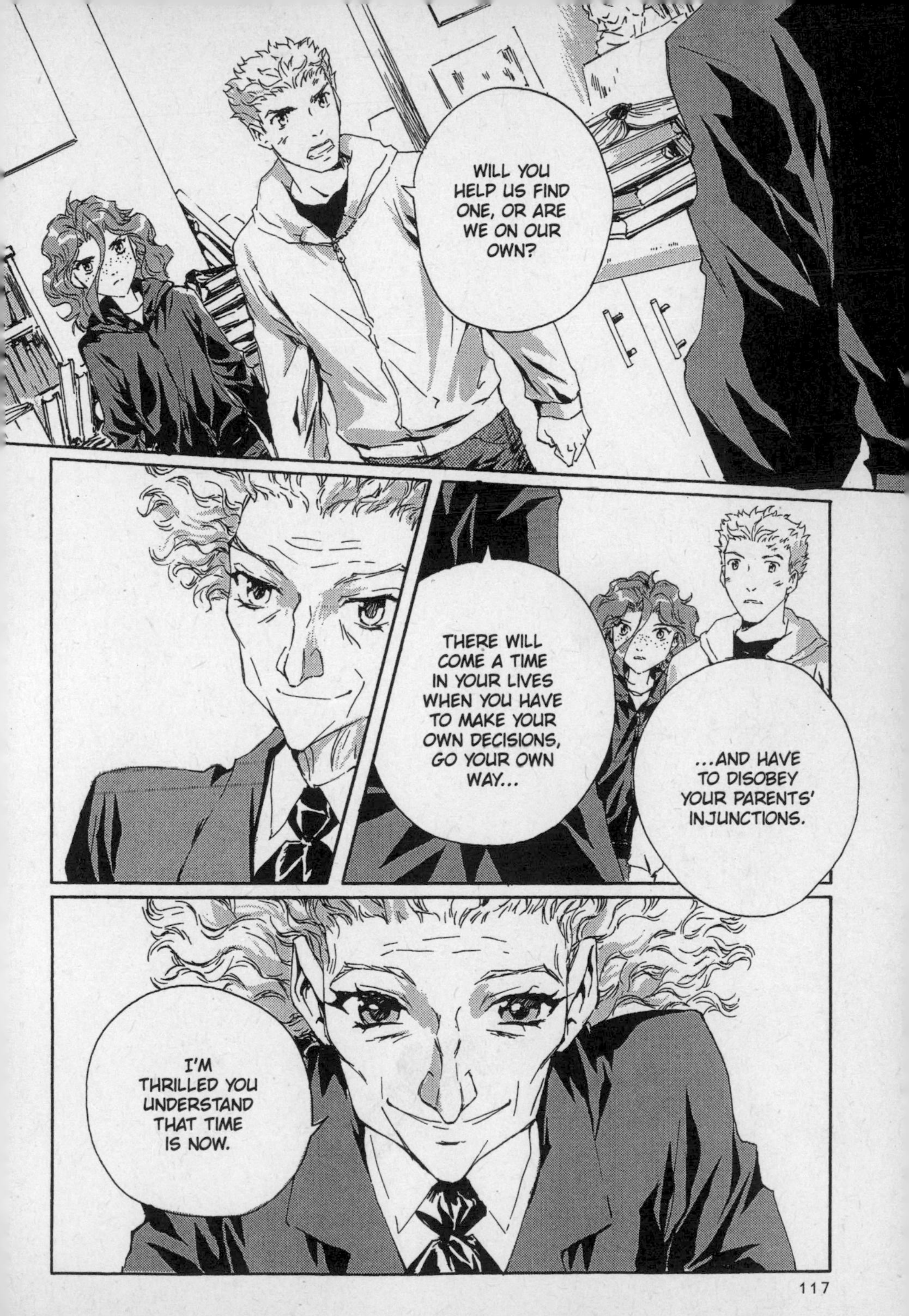
WILL YOU HELP US FIND ONE, OR ARE WE ON OUR OWN?
THERE WILL COME A TIME IN YOUR LIVES WHEN YOU HAVE TO MAKE YOUR OWN DECISIONS, GO YOUR OWN WAY...
...AND HAVE TO DISOBEY YOUR PARENTS' INJUNCTIONS.
I'M THRILLED YOU UNDERSTAND THAT TIME IS NOW.

WITCH & WIZARD

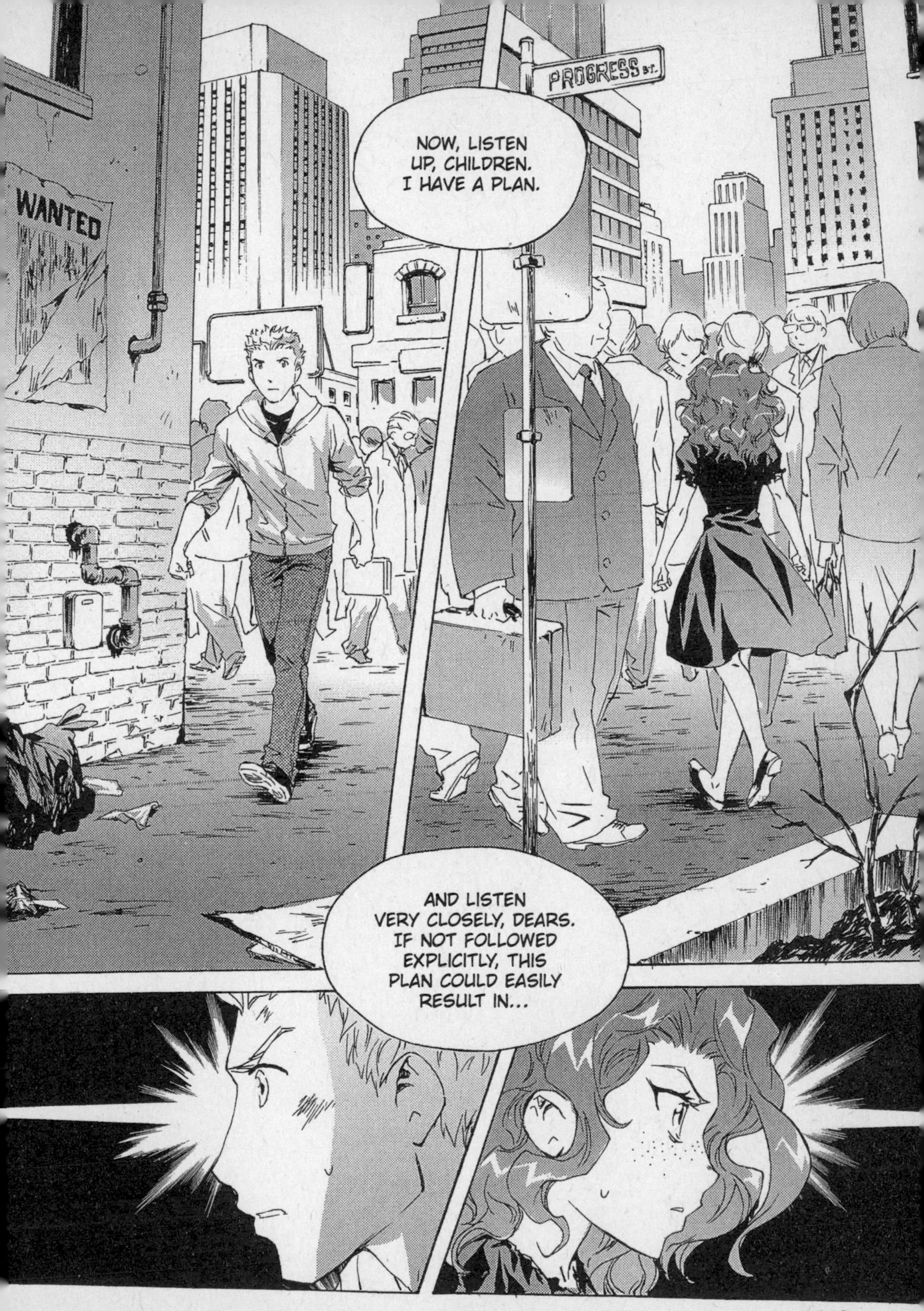
PROGRESS ST.
WANTED
NOW, LISTEN UP, CHILDREN. I HAVE A PLAN.
AND LISTEN VERY CLOSELY, DEARS. IF NOT FOLLOWED EXPLICITLY, THIS PLAN COULD EASILY RESULT IN...

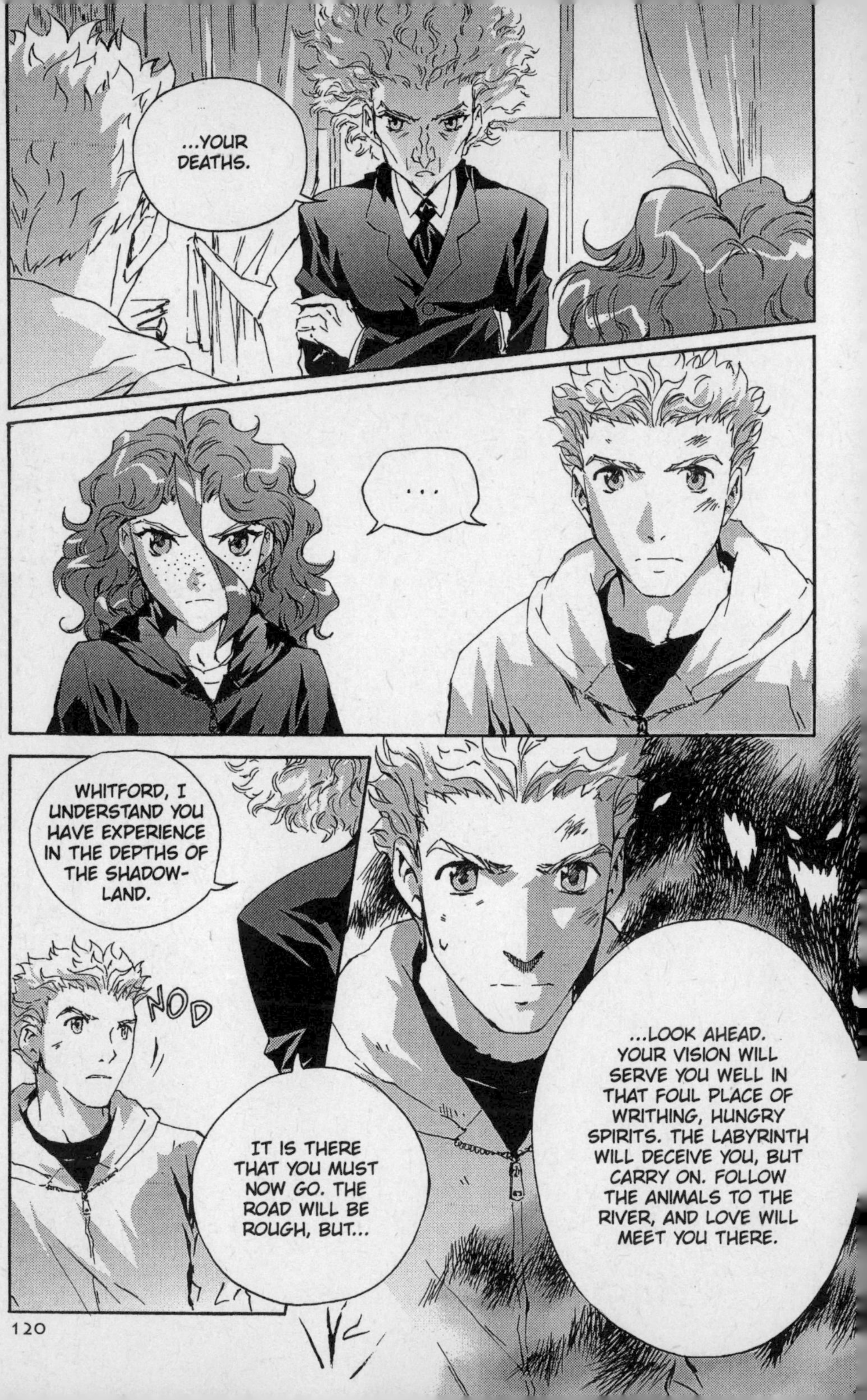
...YOUR DEATHS.
. . .
WHITFORD, I UNDERSTAND YOU HAVE EXPERIENCE IN THE DEPTHS OF THE SHADOW-LAND.
NOD
IT IS THERE THAT YOU MUST NOW GO. THE ROAD WILL BE ROUGH, BUT...
...LOOK AHEAD. YOUR VISION WILL SERVE YOU WELL IN THAT FOUL PLACE OF WRITHING, HUNGRY SPIRITS. THE LABYRINTH WILL DECEIVE YOU, BUT CARRY ON. FOLLOW THE ANIMALS TO THE RIVER, AND LOVE WILL MEET YOU THERE.

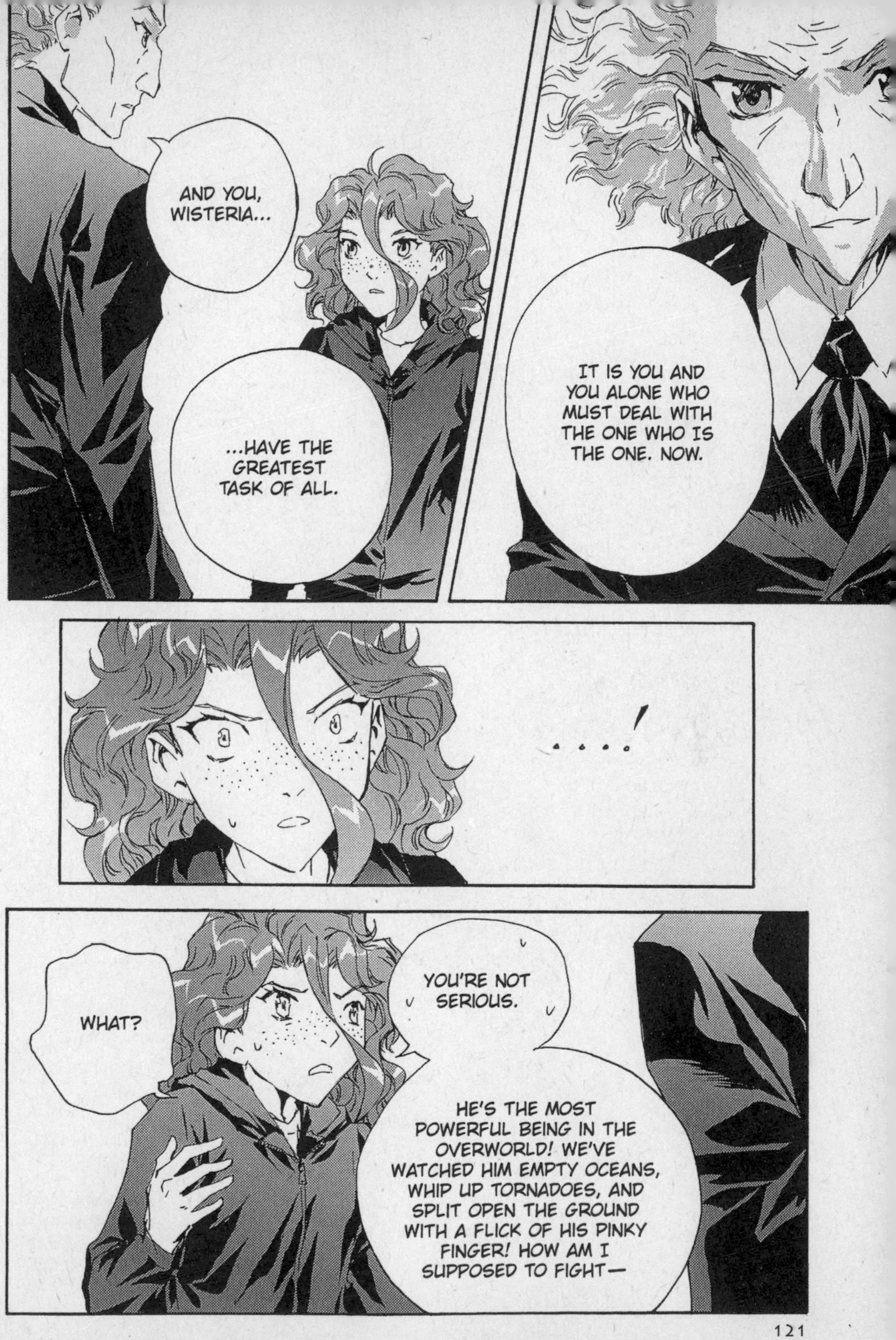
AND YOU, WISTERIA...
...HAVE THE GREATEST TASK OF ALL.
IT IS YOU AND YOU ALONE WHO MUST DEAL WITH THE ONE WHO IS THE ONE. NOW.
....!
WHAT?
YOU'RE NOT SERIOUS.
HE'S THE MOST POWERFUL BEING IN THE OVERWORLD! WE'VE WATCHED HIM EMPTY OCEANS, WHIP UP TORNADOES, AND SPLIT OPEN THE GROUND WITH A FLICK OF HIS PINKY FINGER! HOW AM I SUPPOSED TO FIGHT—

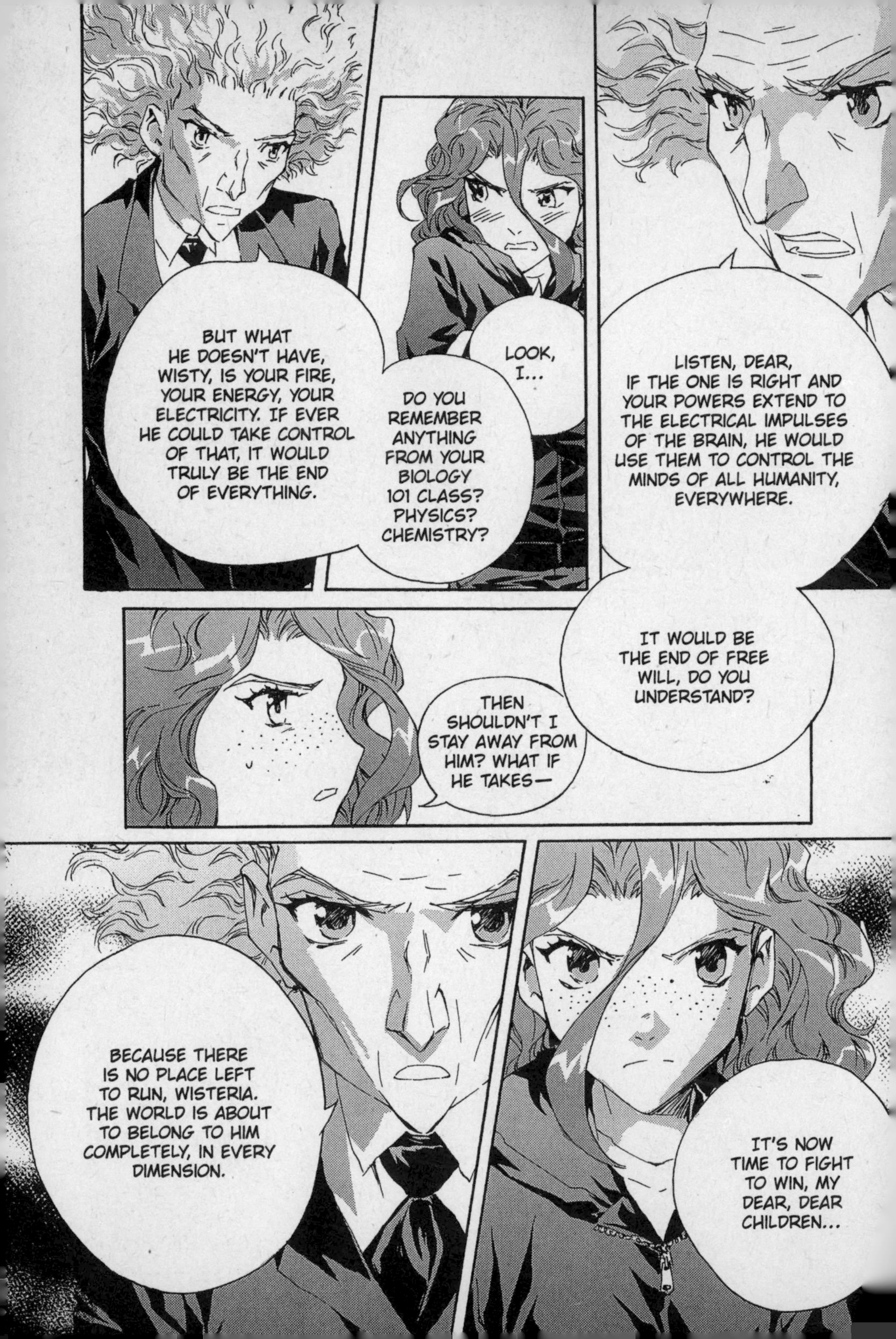
BUT WHAT HE DOESN'T HAVE, WISTY, IS YOUR FIRE, YOUR ENERGY, YOUR ELECTRICITY. IF EVER HE COULD TAKE CONTROL OF THAT, IT WOULD TRULY BE THE END OF EVERYTHING.
LOOK, I...
DO YOU REMEMBER ANYTHING FROM YOUR BIOLOGY 101 CLASS? PHYSICS? CHEMISTRY?
LISTEN, DEAR, IF THE ONE IS RIGHT AND YOUR POWERS EXTEND TO THE ELECTRICAL IMPULSES OF THE BRAIN, HE WOULD USE THEM TO CONTROL THE MINDS OF ALL HUMANITY, EVERYWHERE.
IT WOULD BE THE END OF FREE WILL, DO YOU UNDERSTAND?
THEN SHOULDN'T I STAY AWAY FROM HIM? WHAT IF HE TAKES—
BECAUSE THERE IS NO PLACE LEFT TO RUN, WISTERIA. THE WORLD IS ABOUT TO BELONG TO HIM COMPLETELY, IN EVERY DIMENSION.
IT'S NOW TIME TO FIGHT TO WIN, MY DEAR, DEAR CHILDREN...

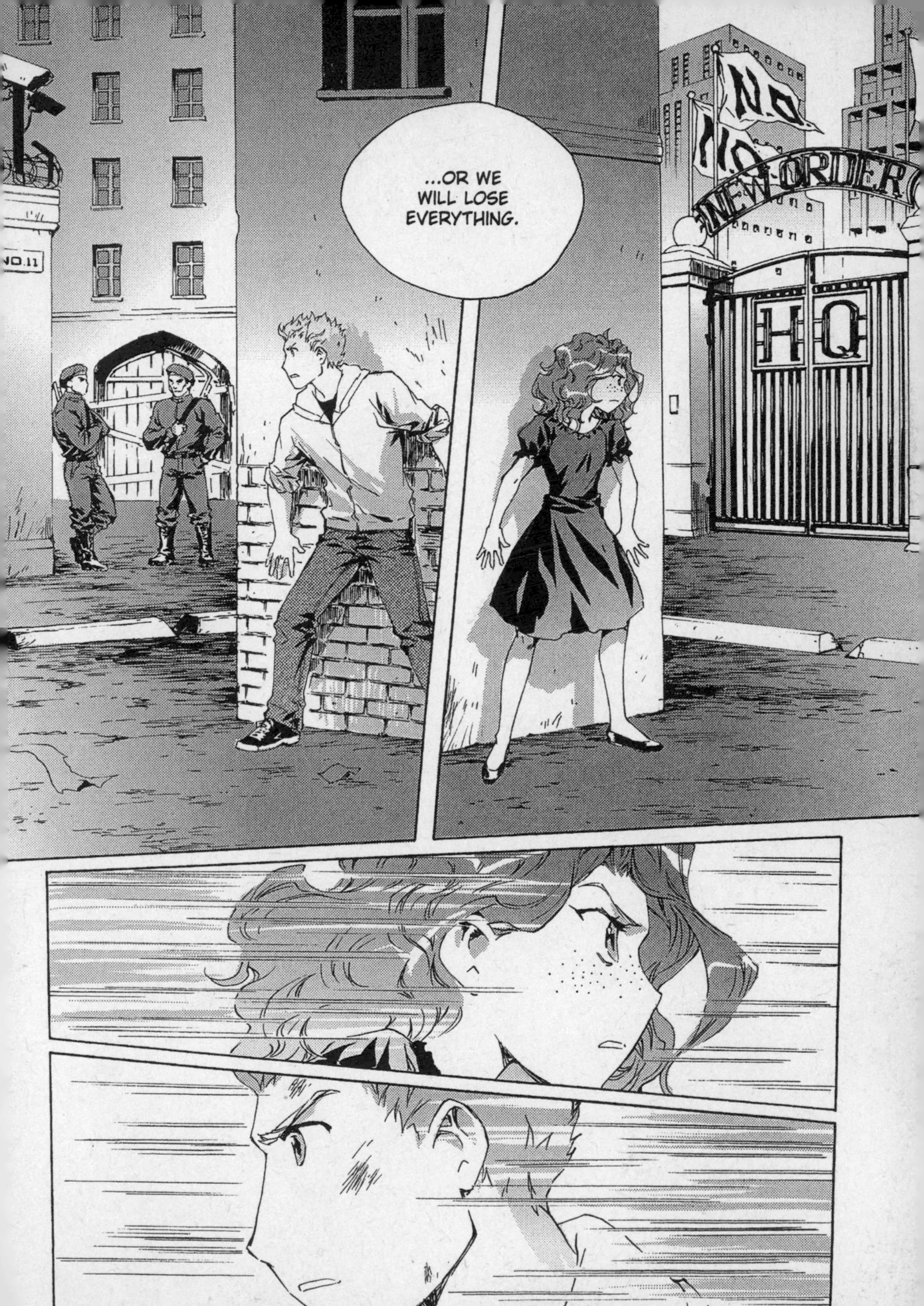
NO.11
...OR WE WILL LOSE EVERYTHING.
NEW ORDER
HQ

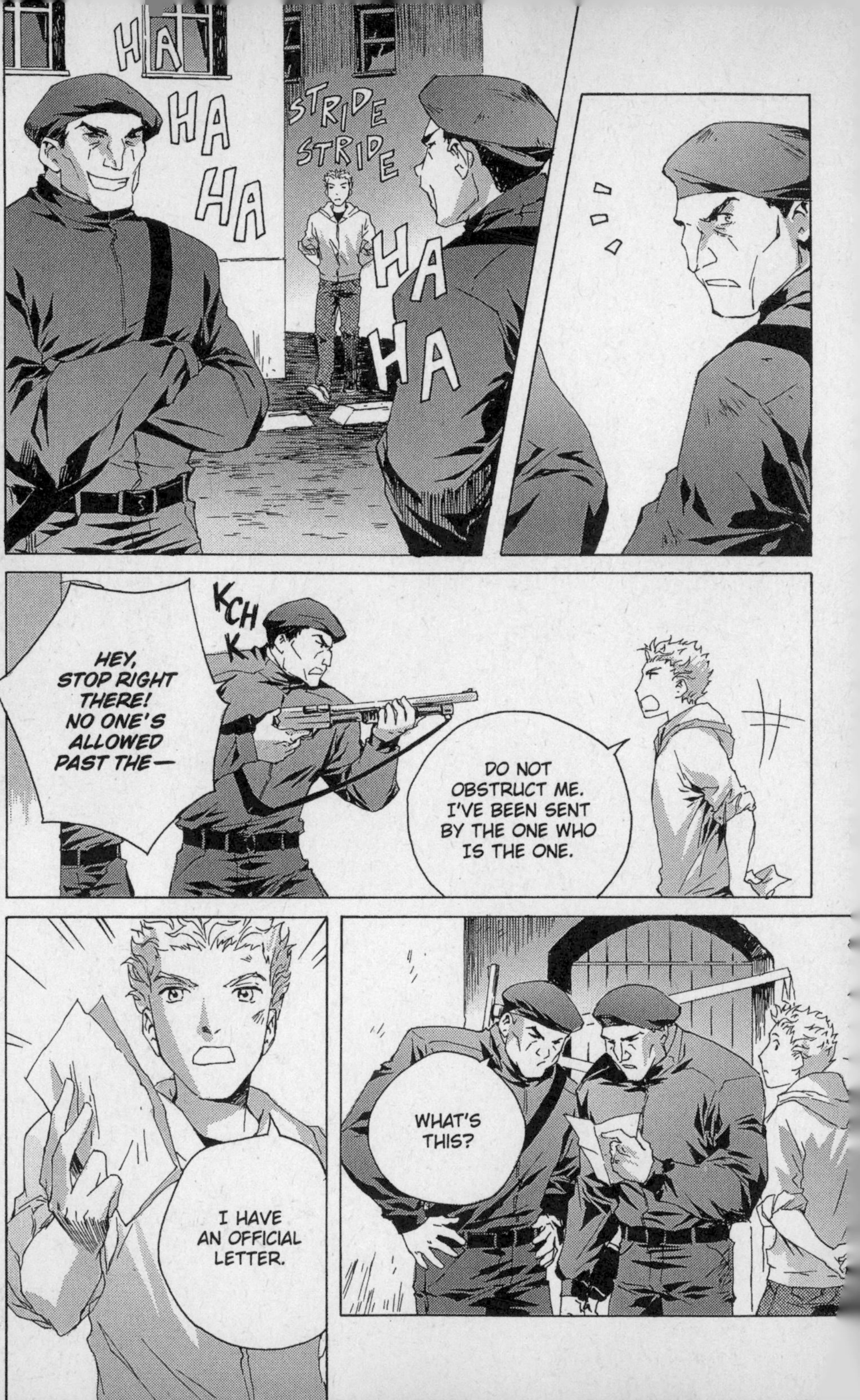
HA HA HA HA
STRIDE STRIDE
HA HA HA
KCHK
HEY, STOP RIGHT THERE! NO ONE'S ALLOWED PAST THE—
DO NOT OBSTRUCT ME. I'VE BEEN SENT BY THE ONE WHO IS THE ONE.
I HAVE AN OFFICIAL LETTER.
WHAT'S THIS?

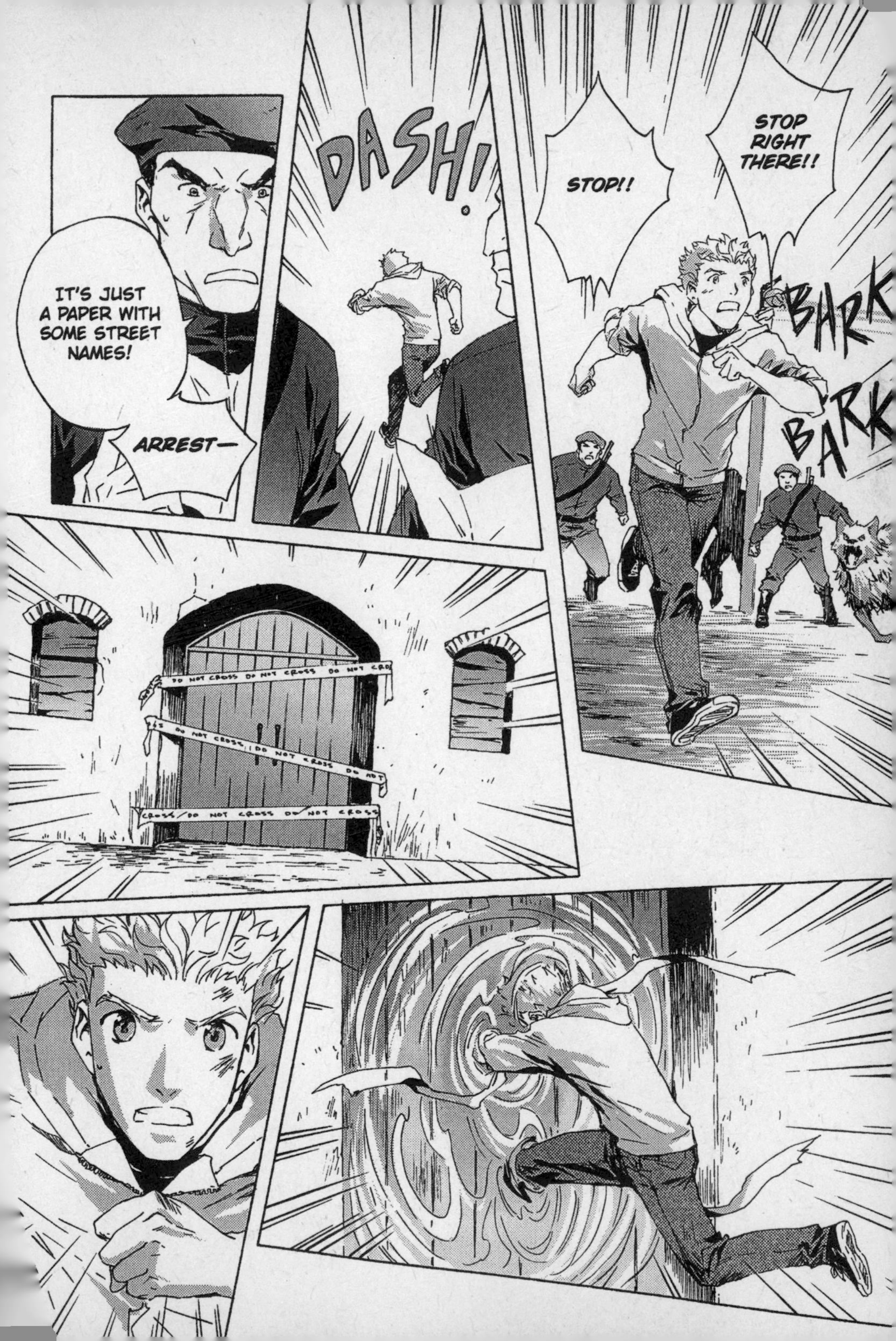
IT'S JUST A PAPER WITH SOME STREET NAMES!
ARREST—
DASH!
STOP!!
STOP RIGHT THERE!!
BARK
BARK
DO NOT CROSS DO NOT CROSS
DO NOT CROSS DO NOT CROSS DO NOT
CROSS DO NOT CROSS DO NOT CROSS

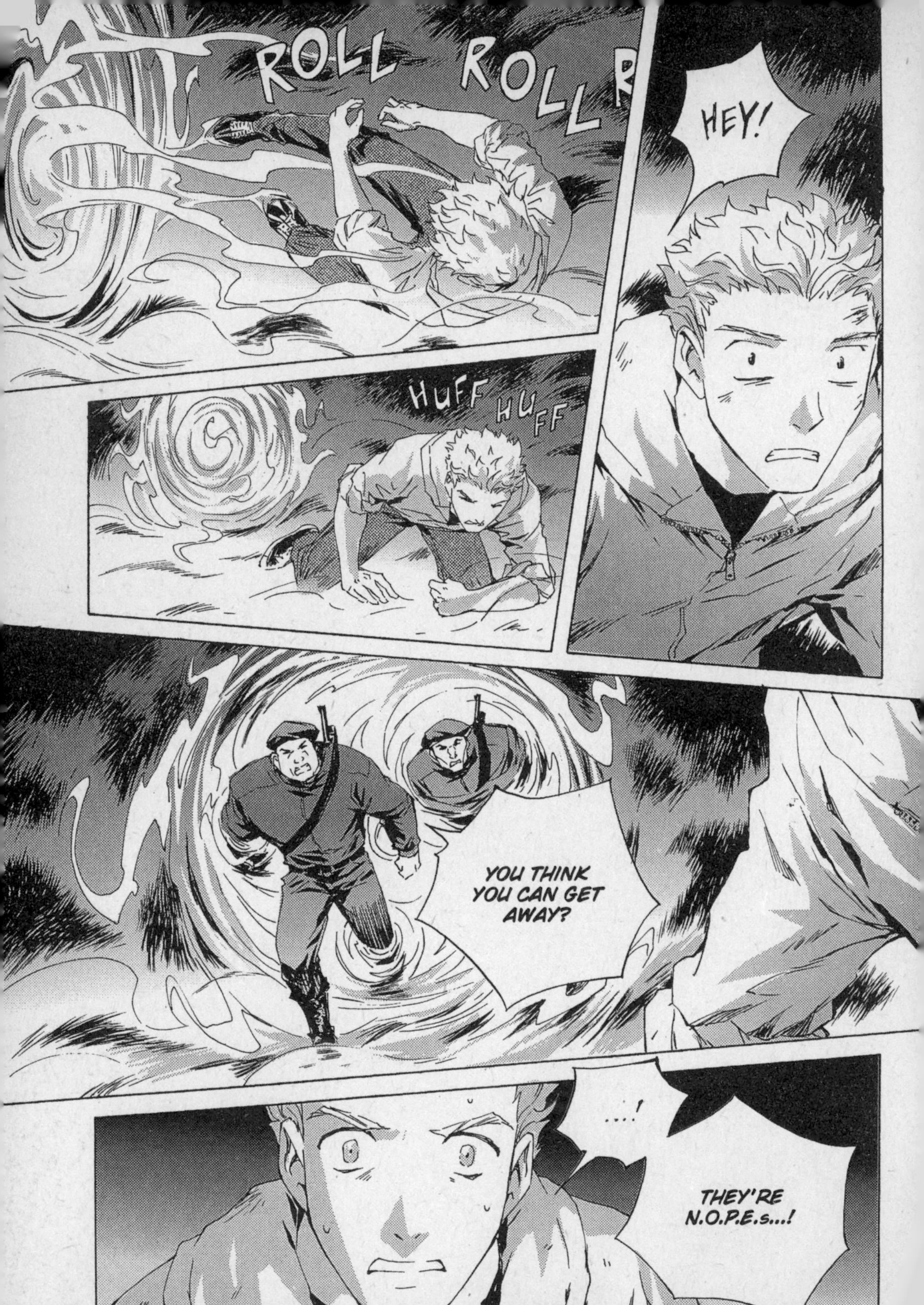
HEY!
ROLL ROLL R
HUFF HUFF
YOU THINK YOU CAN GET AWAY?
...!
THEY'RE N.O.P.E.s...!

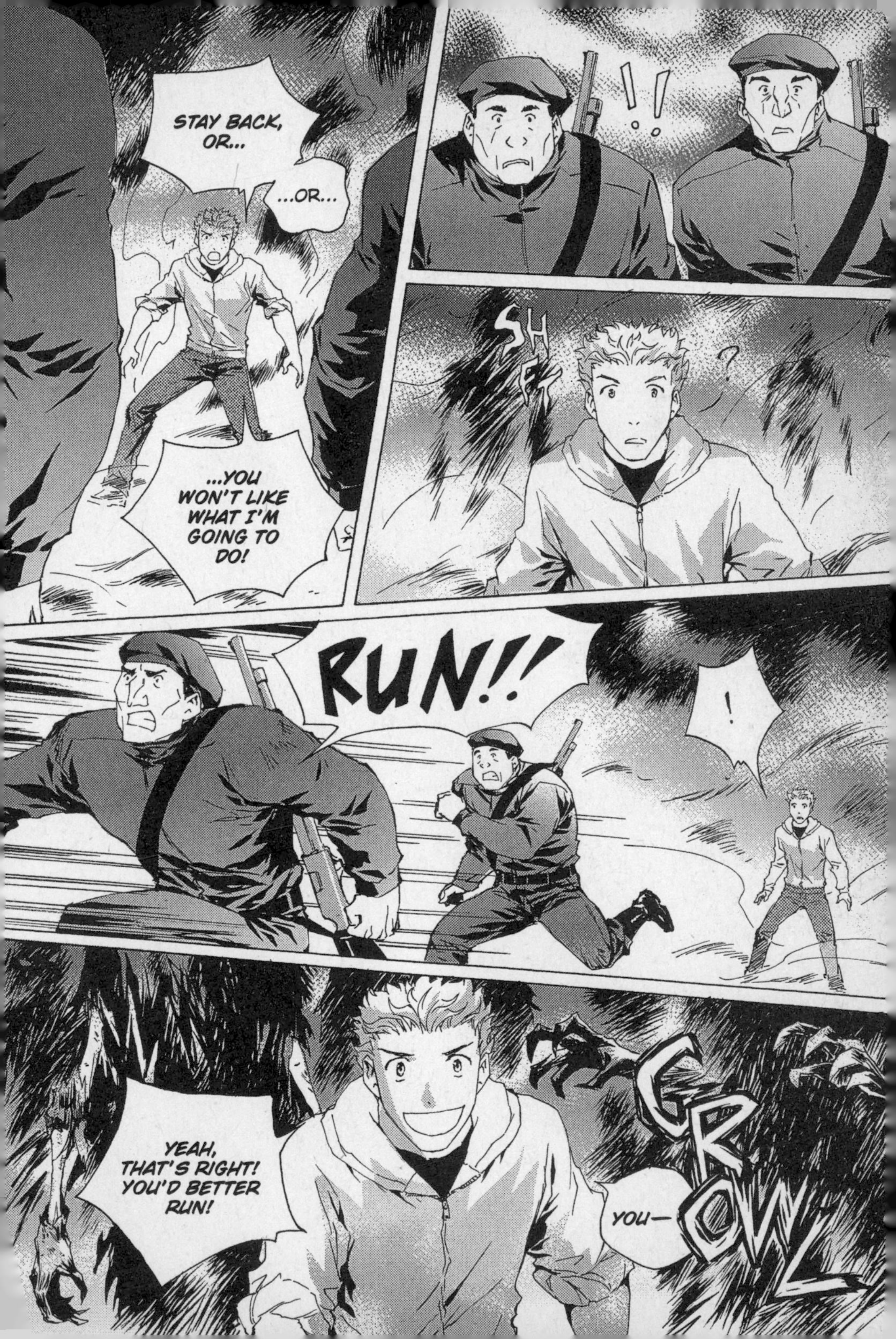
STAY BACK, OR...
...OR...
...YOU WON'T LIKE WHAT I'M GOING TO DO!
!!
SHIFT
?
RUN!!
!
YEAH, THAT'S RIGHT! YOU'D BETTER RUN!
YOU—
GROWL

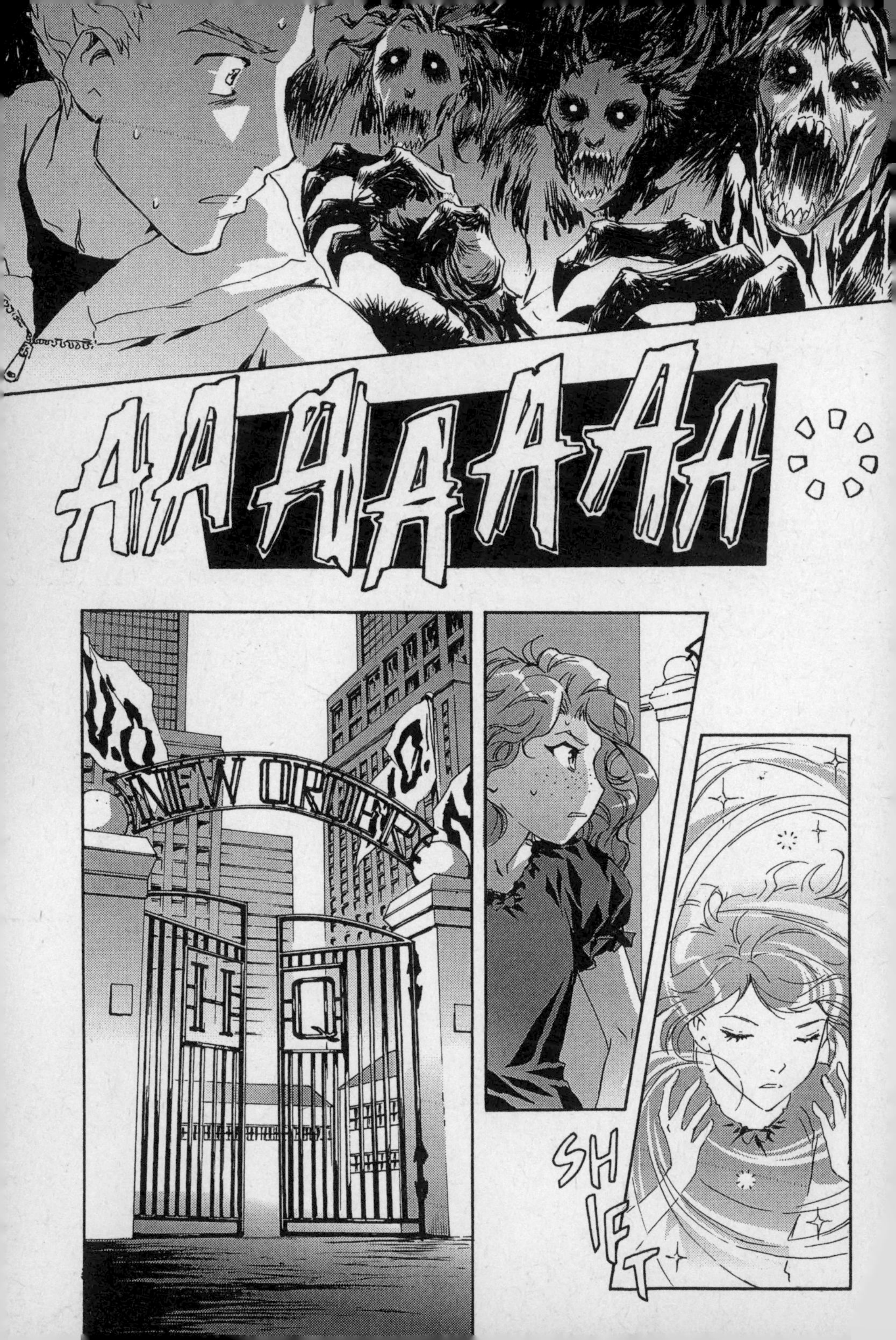
AAAAAAAA
NEW ORDER
N.O.
HQ
SHIFT

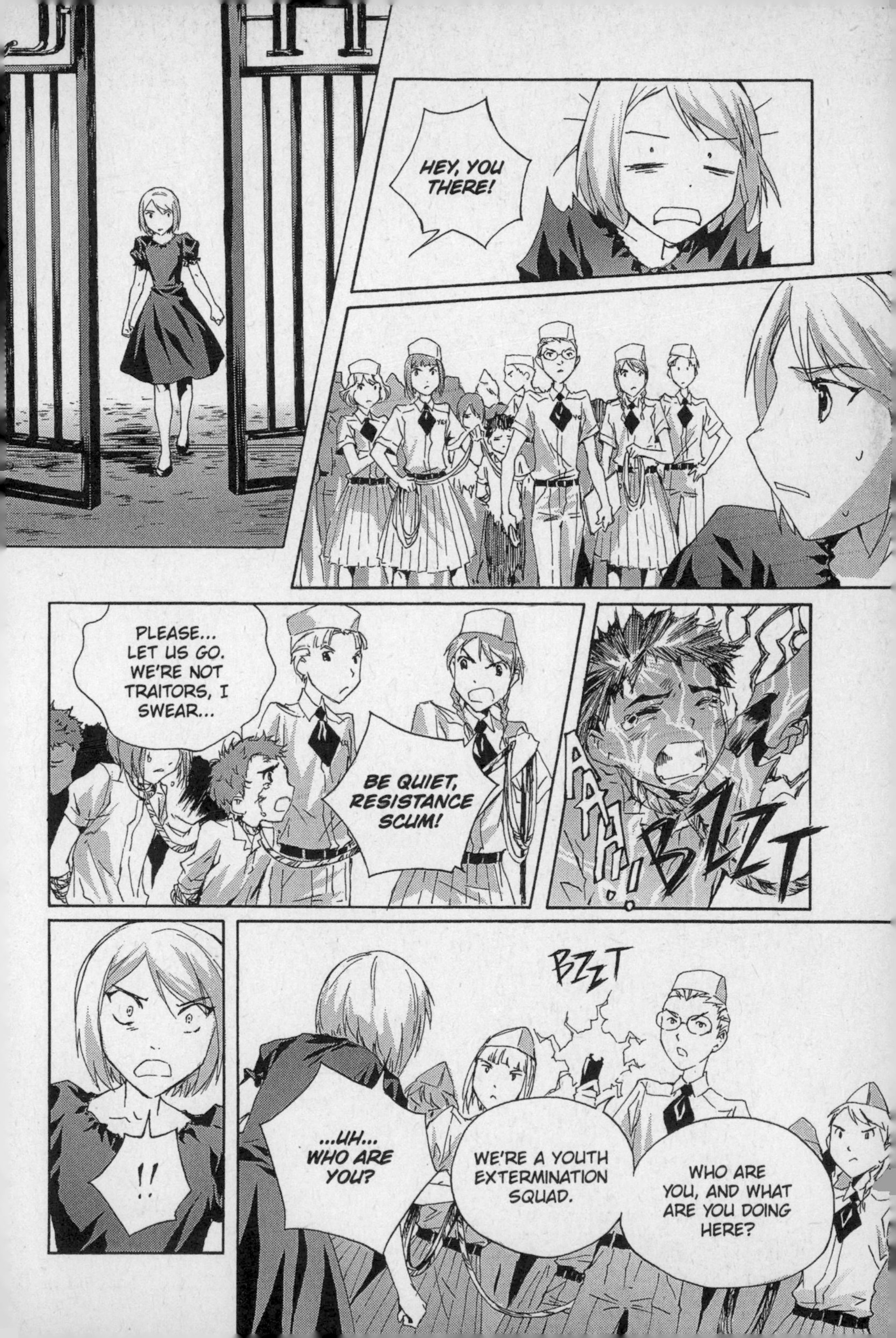
HEY, YOU THERE!
PLEASE... LET US GO. WE'RE NOT TRAITORS, I SWEAR...
BE QUIET, RESISTANCE SCUM!
AAH...!
BZZZT
BZZT
!!
...UH... WHO ARE YOU?
WE'RE A YOUTH EXTERMINATION SQUAD.
WHO ARE YOU, AND WHAT ARE YOU DOING HERE?

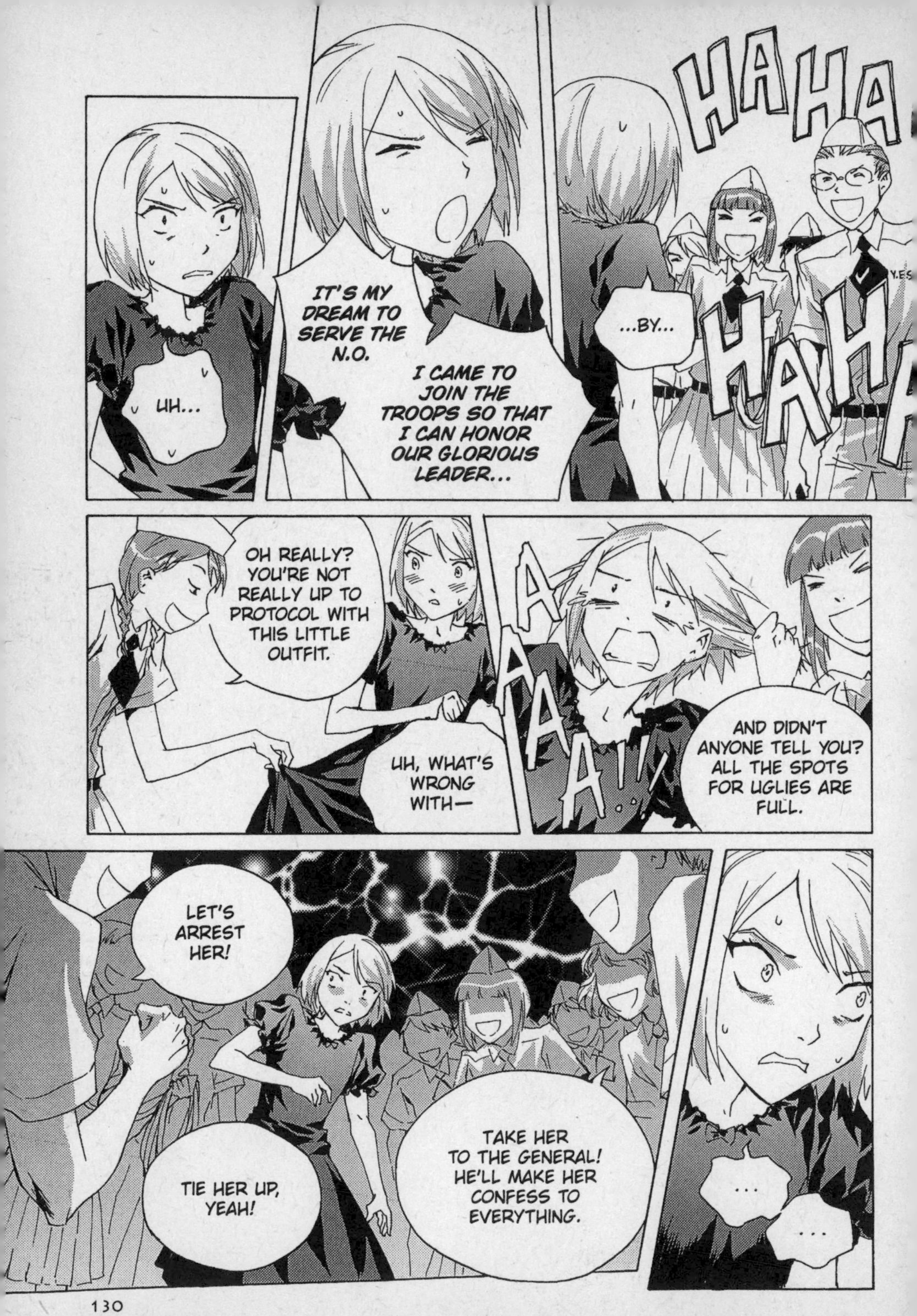
UH...
IT'S MY DREAM TO SERVE THE N.O.
I CAME TO JOIN THE TROOPS SO THAT I CAN HONOR OUR GLORIOUS LEADER...
...BY...
HAHAHA
HAHAHA
OH REALLY? YOU'RE NOT REALLY UP TO PROTOCOL WITH THIS LITTLE OUTFIT.
UH, WHAT'S WRONG WITH—
AAAAA!!
AND DIDN'T ANYONE TELL YOU? ALL THE SPOTS FOR UGLIES ARE FULL.
LET'S ARREST HER!
TIE HER UP, YEAH!
TAKE HER TO THE GENERAL! HE'LL MAKE HER CONFESS TO EVERYTHING.
...
...

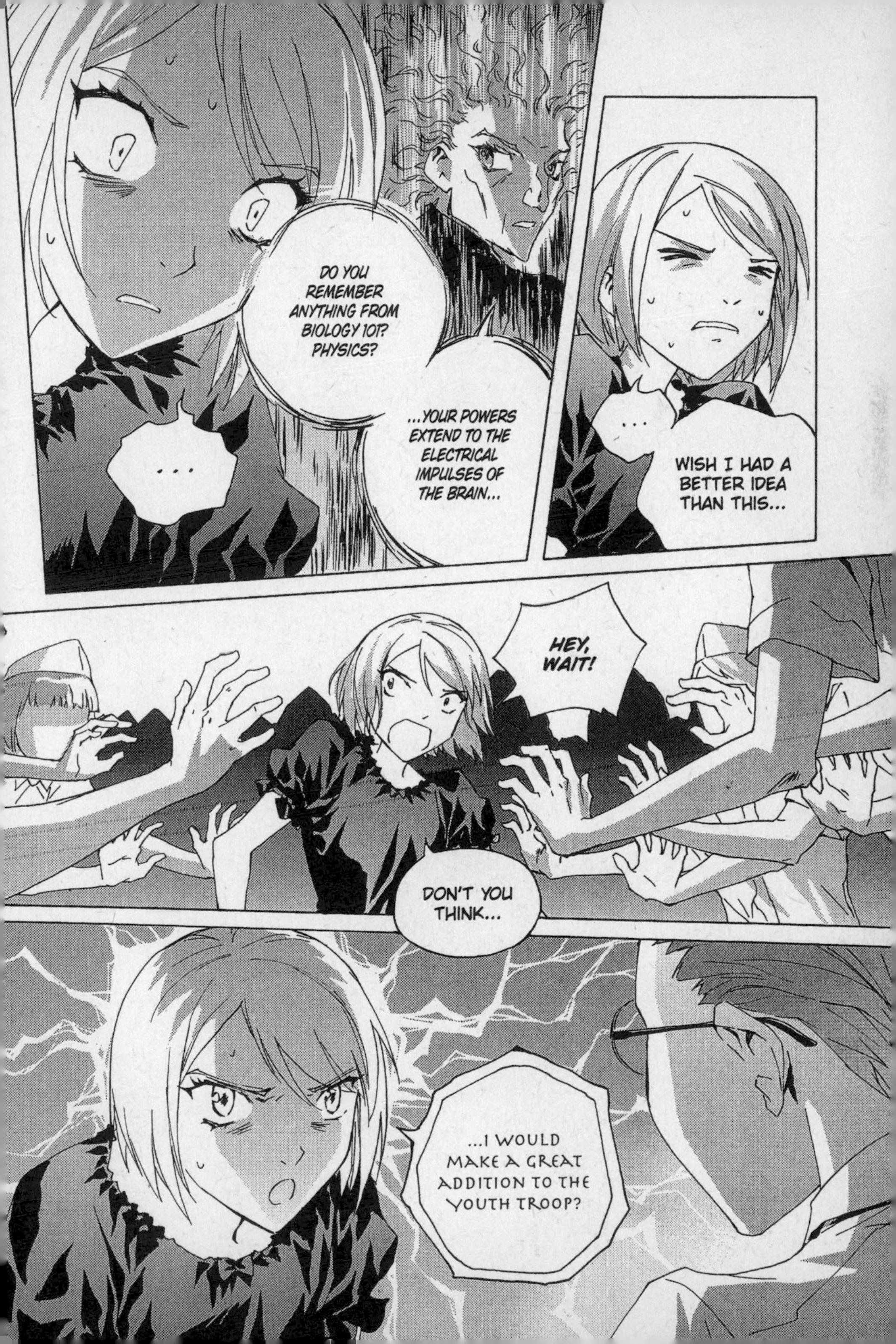
DO YOU REMEMBER ANYTHING FROM BIOLOGY 101? PHYSICS?
...YOUR POWERS EXTEND TO THE ELECTRICAL IMPULSES OF THE BRAIN...
...
...
WISH I HAD A BETTER IDEA THAN THIS...
HEY, WAIT!
DON'T YOU THINK...
...I WOULD MAKE A GREAT ADDITION TO THE YOUTH TROOP?

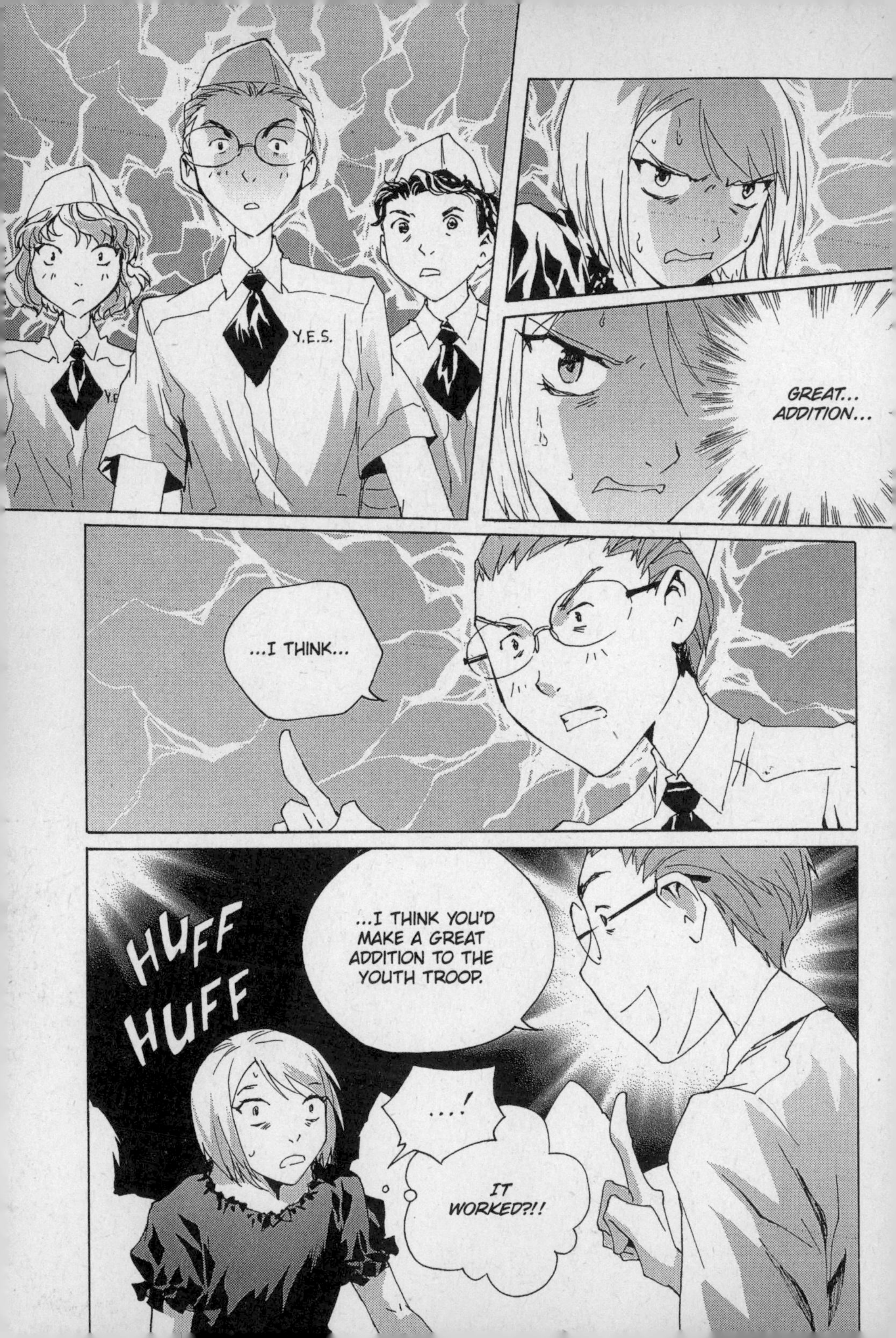
Y.E.S.
GREAT... ADDITION...
...I THINK...
HUFF HUFF
...I THINK YOU'D MAKE A GREAT ADDITION TO THE YOUTH TROOP.
...!
IT WORKED?!!

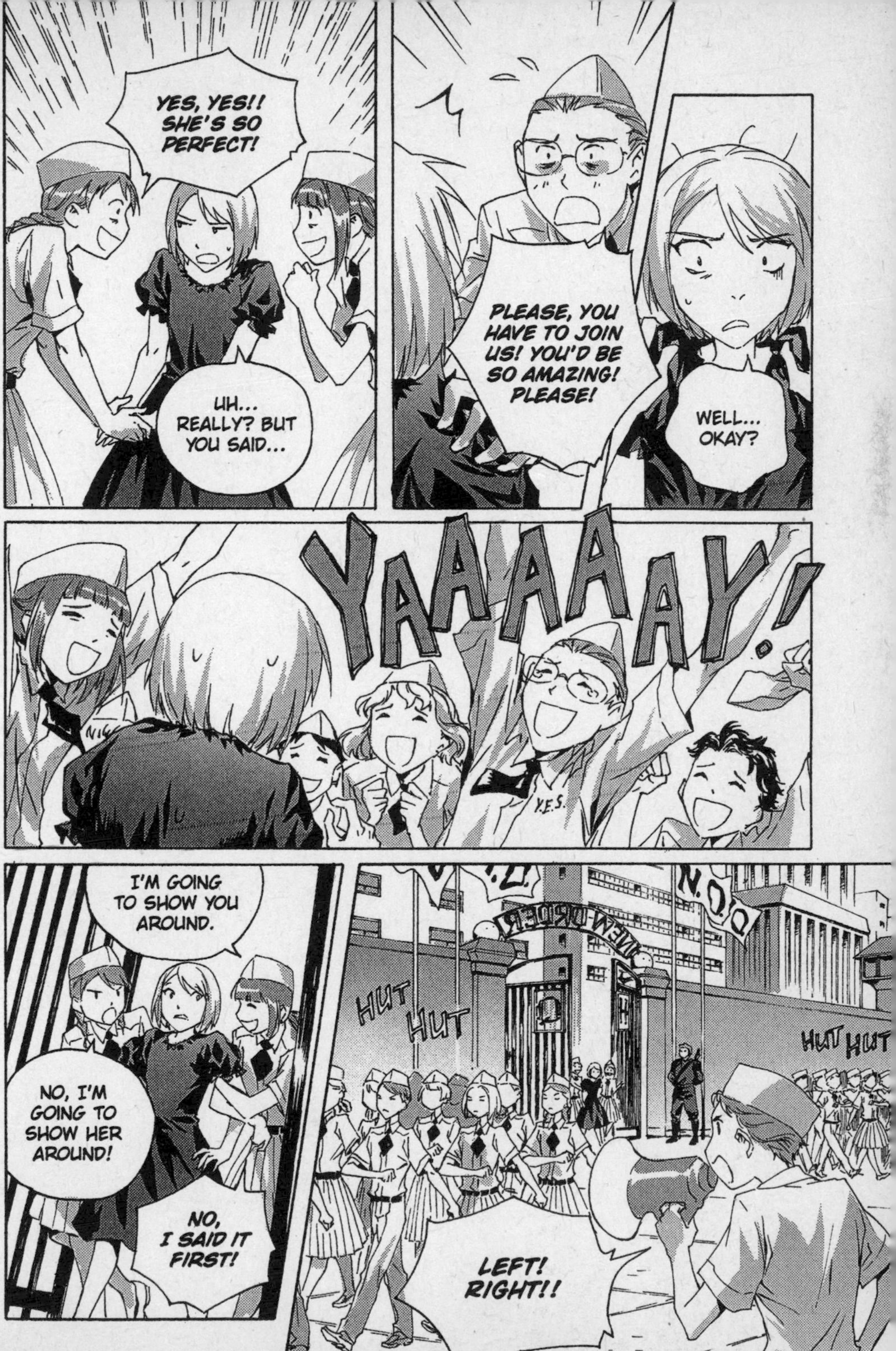
YES, YES!! SHE'S SO PERFECT!
UH... REALLY? BUT YOU SAID...
PLEASE, YOU HAVE TO JOIN US! YOU'D BE SO AMAZING! PLEASE!
WELL... OKAY?
YAAAAY!
Y.E.S.
I'M GOING TO SHOW YOU AROUND.
NO, I'M GOING TO SHOW HER AROUND!
NO, I SAID IT FIRST!
N.O.
NEW ORDER
HUT HUT
HUT HUT
LEFT! RIGHT!!

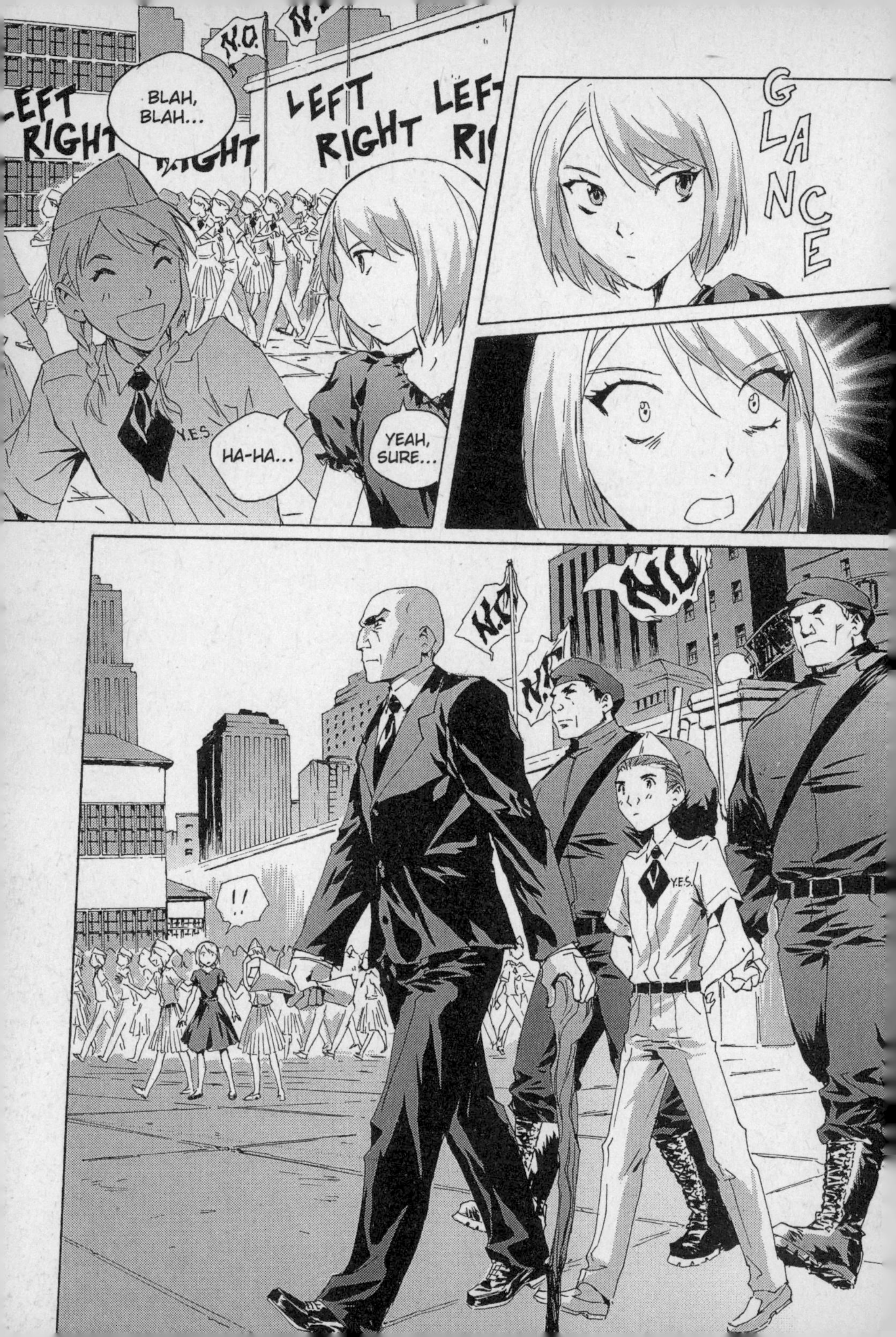
N.O.
LEFT RIGHT
BLAH, BLAH...
LEFT RIGHT
LEFT RIGHT
Y.E.S.
HA-HA...
YEAH, SURE...
GLANCE
N.O.
!!
Y.E.S.

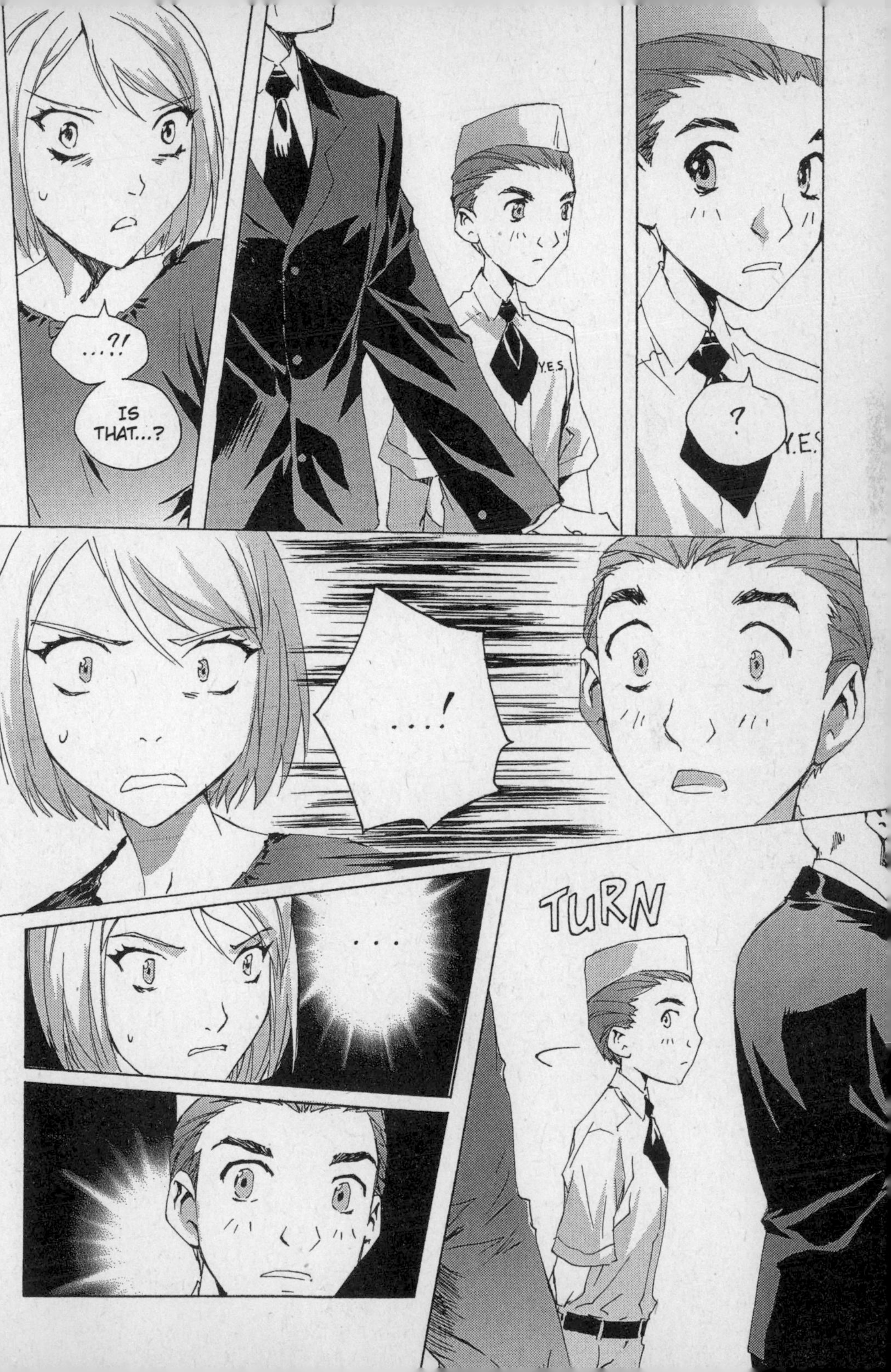
?
...?!
IS THAT...?
...!
TURN
...

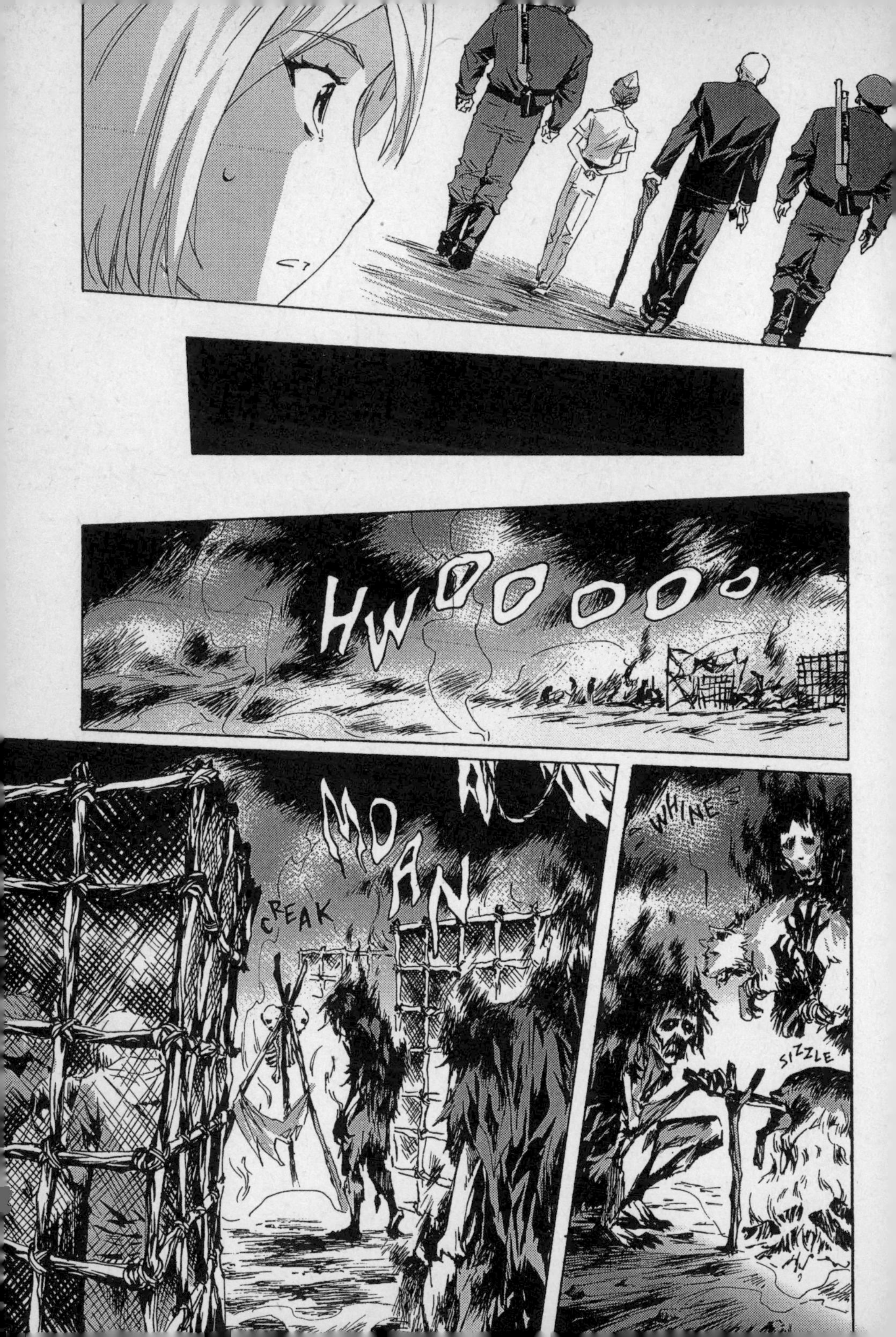
HWOOOOO
WHINE
SIZZLE
MOAN
CREAK

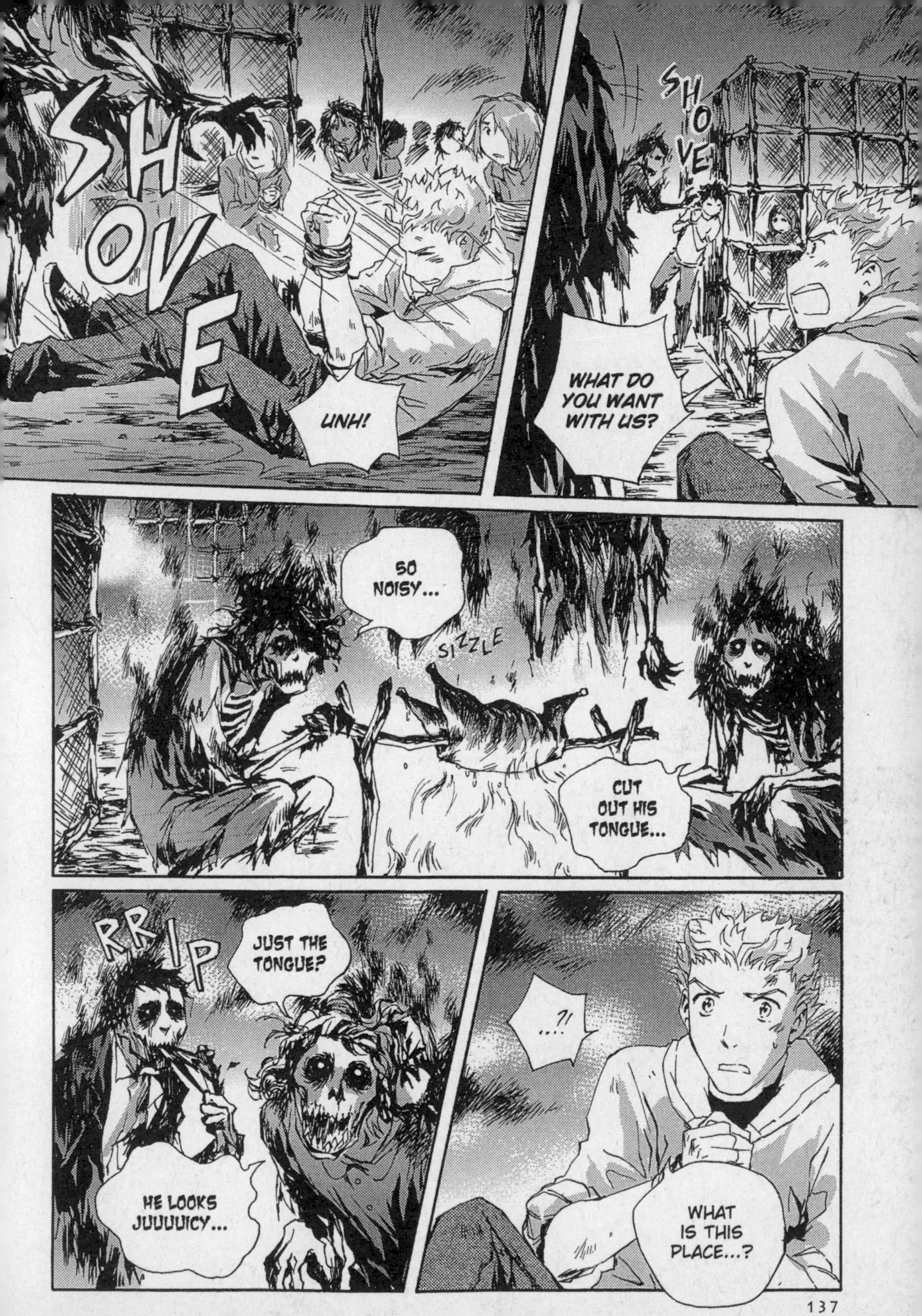
SHOVE
UNH!
SHOVE
WHAT DO YOU WANT WITH US?
SO NOISY...
SIZZLE
CUT OUT HIS TONGUE...
RRIP
JUST THE TONGUE?
HE LOOKS JUUUUICY...
...?!
WHAT IS THIS PLACE...?

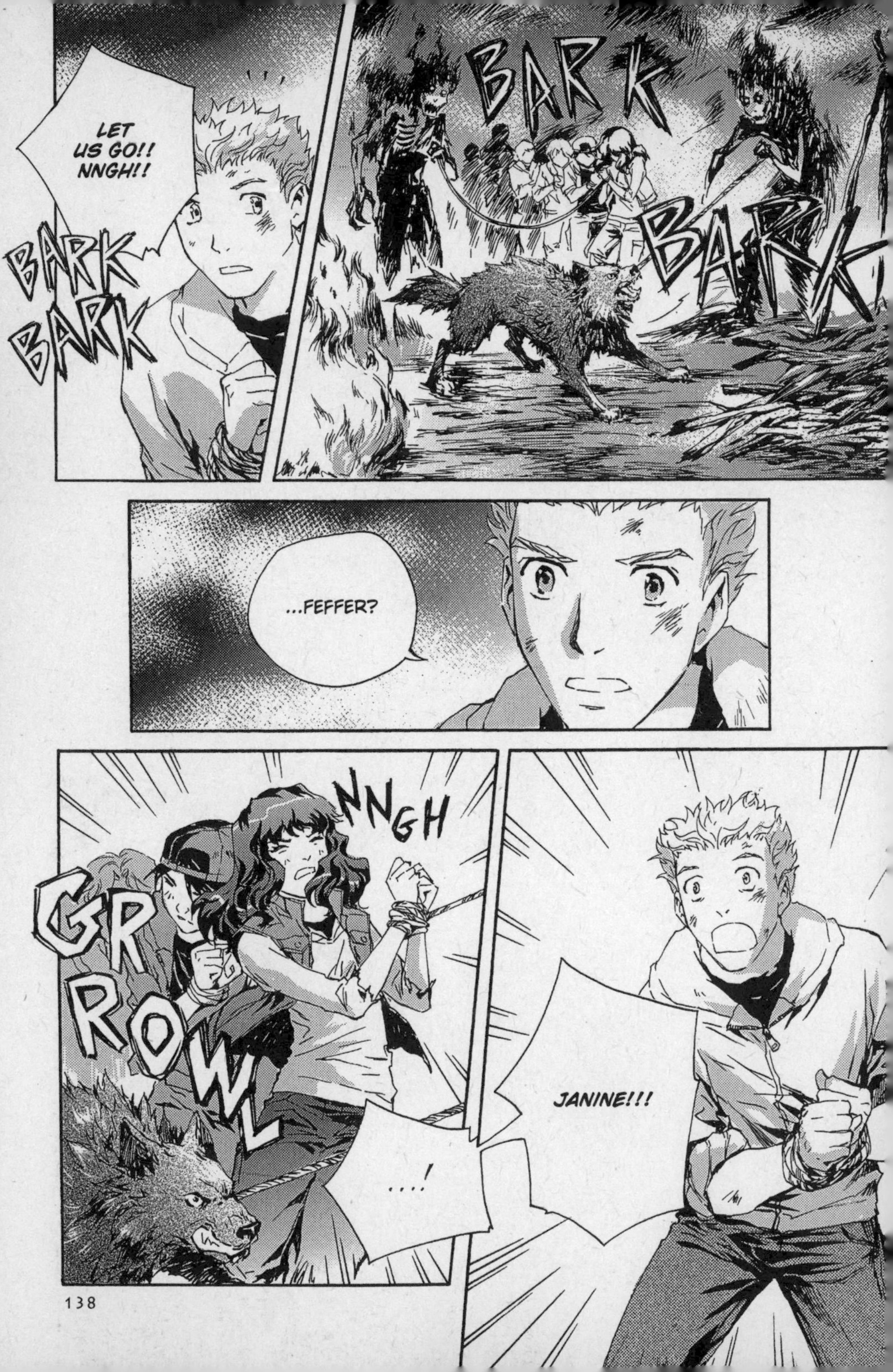
LET US GO!! NNGH!!
BARK BARK
BARK
BARK
...FEFFER?
NNGH
GROWL
...!
JANINE!!!

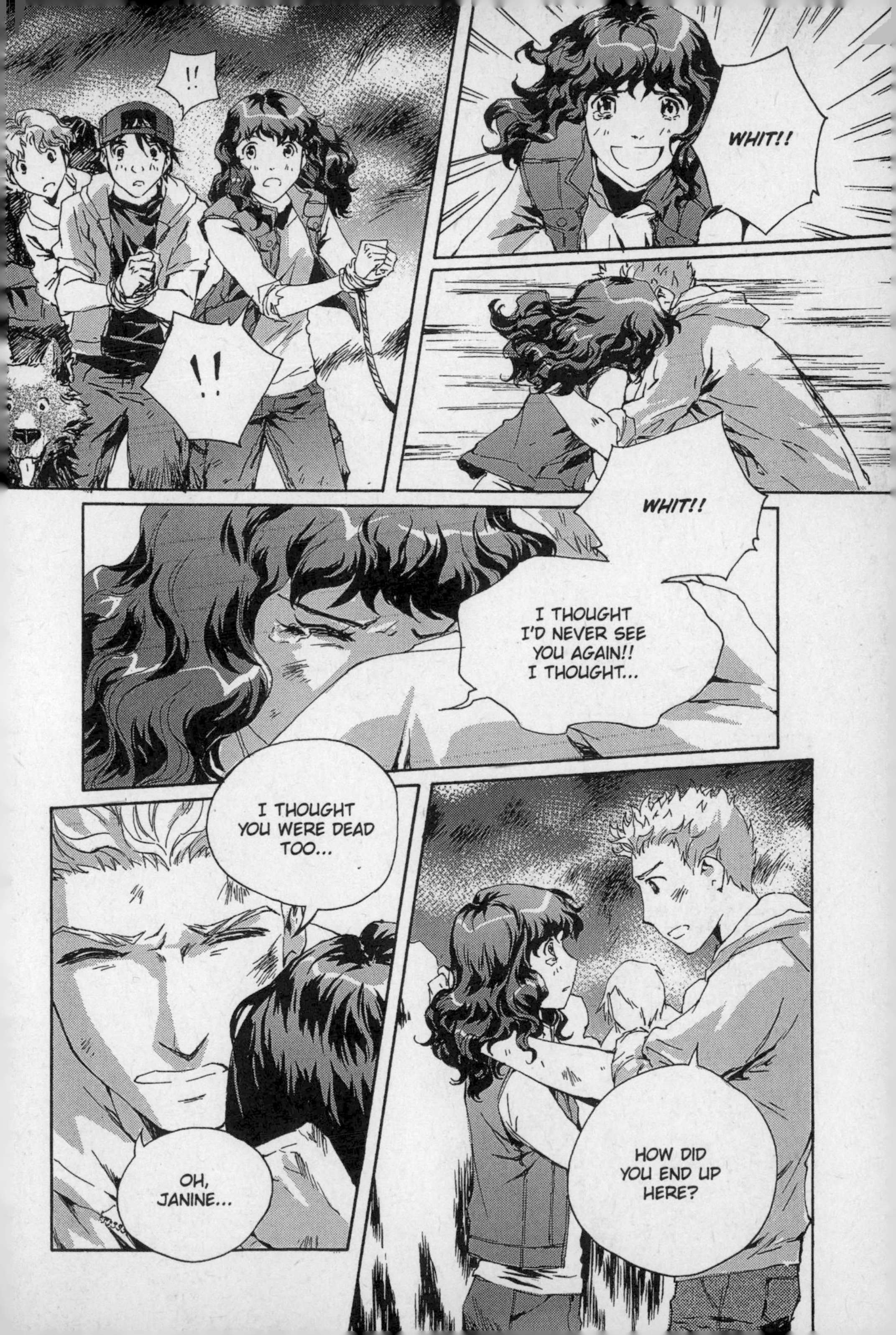
!!
!!
WHIT!!
WHIT!!
I THOUGHT I'D NEVER SEE YOU AGAIN!! I THOUGHT...
I THOUGHT YOU WERE DEAD TOO...
OH, JANINE...
HOW DID YOU END UP HERE?

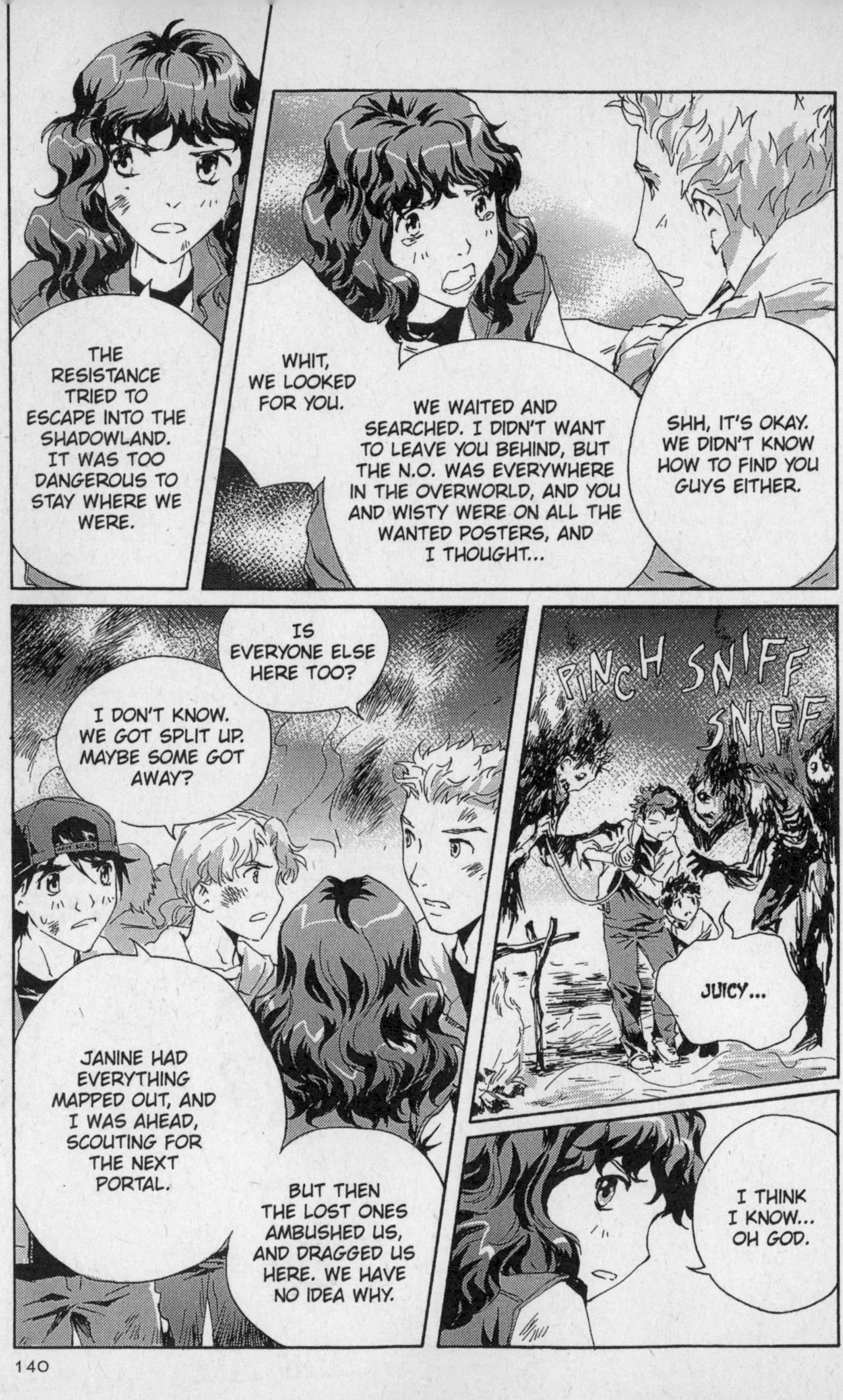
THE RESISTANCE TRIED TO ESCAPE INTO THE SHADOWLAND. IT WAS TOO DANGEROUS TO STAY WHERE WE WERE.
WHIT, WE LOOKED FOR YOU.
WE WAITED AND SEARCHED. I DIDN'T WANT TO LEAVE YOU BEHIND, BUT THE N.O. WAS EVERYWHERE IN THE OVERWORLD, AND YOU AND WISTY WERE ON ALL THE WANTED POSTERS, AND I THOUGHT...
SHH, IT'S OKAY. WE DIDN'T KNOW HOW TO FIND YOU GUYS EITHER.
IS EVERYONE ELSE HERE TOO?
I DON'T KNOW. WE GOT SPLIT UP. MAYBE SOME GOT AWAY?
JANINE HAD EVERYTHING MAPPED OUT, AND I WAS AHEAD, SCOUTING FOR THE NEXT PORTAL.
BUT THEN THE LOST ONES AMBUSHED US, AND DRAGGED US HERE. WE HAVE NO IDEA WHY.
PINCH SNIFF SNIFF
JUICY...
I THINK I KNOW... OH GOD.

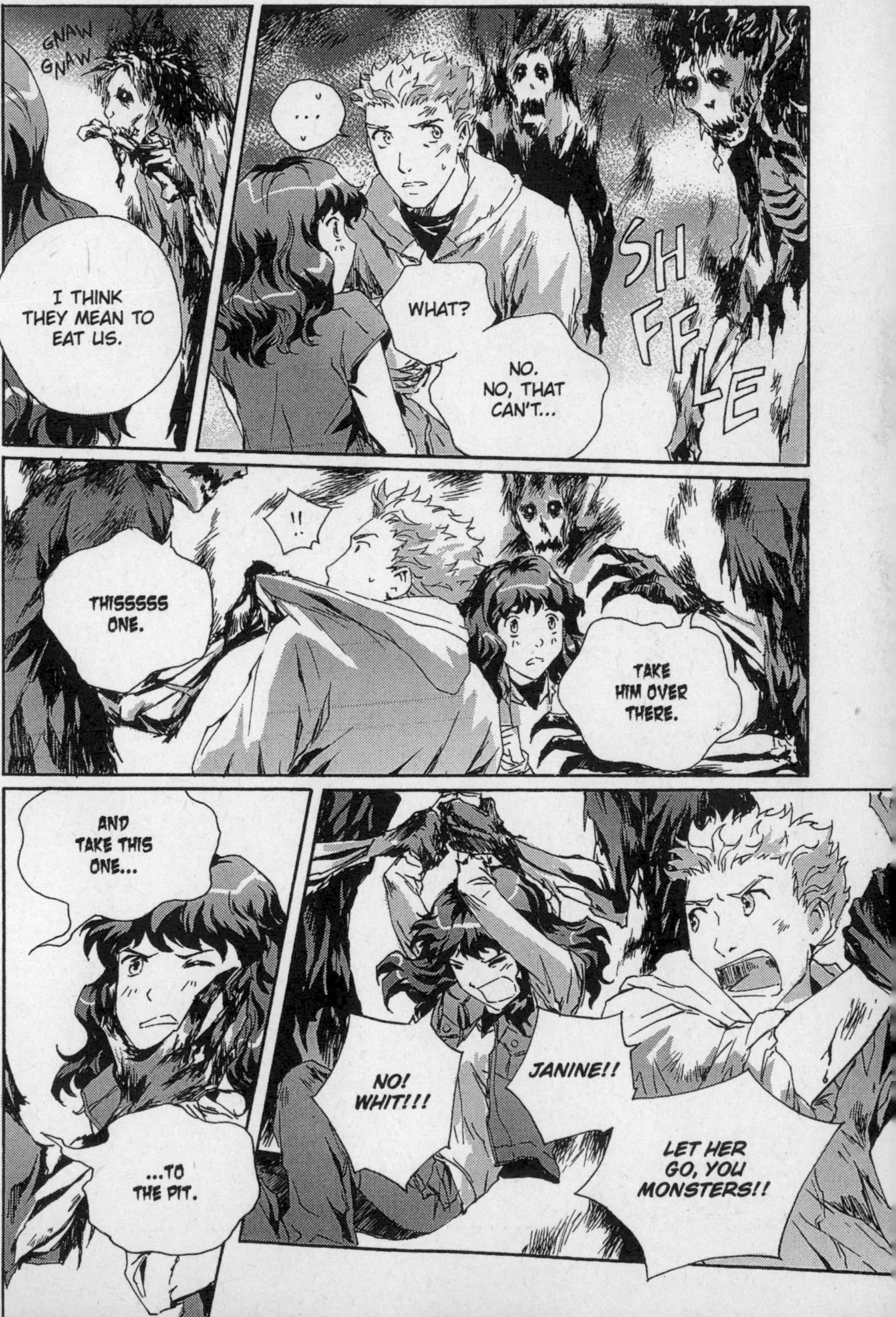
GNAW GNAW
I THINK THEY MEAN TO EAT US.
...
WHAT?
NO. NO, THAT CAN'T...
SHUFFLE
!!
THISSSSS ONE.
TAKE HIM OVER THERE.
AND TAKE THIS ONE...
...TO THE PIT.
NO! WHIT!!!
JANINE!!
LET HER GO, YOU MONSTERS!!

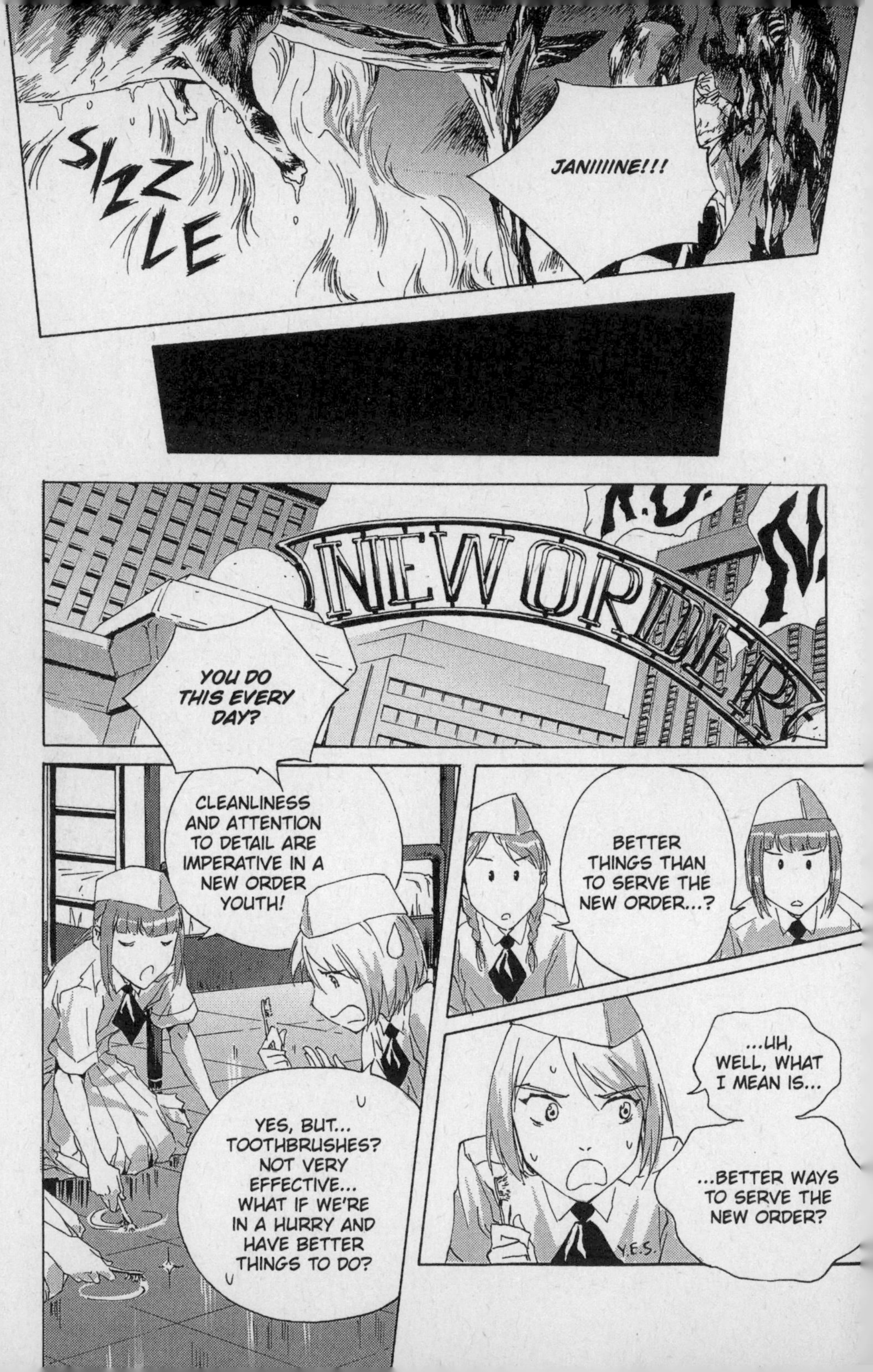

SIZZLE
JANIIIINE!!!
NEW ORDER
YOU DO THIS EVERY DAY?
CLEANLINESS AND ATTENTION TO DETAIL ARE IMPERATIVE IN A NEW ORDER YOUTH!
YES, BUT... TOOTHBRUSHES? NOT VERY EFFECTIVE... WHAT IF WE'RE IN A HURRY AND HAVE BETTER THINGS TO DO?
BETTER THINGS THAN TO SERVE THE NEW ORDER...?
...UH, WELL, WHAT I MEAN IS...
...BETTER WAYS TO SERVE THE NEW ORDER?
Y.E.S.

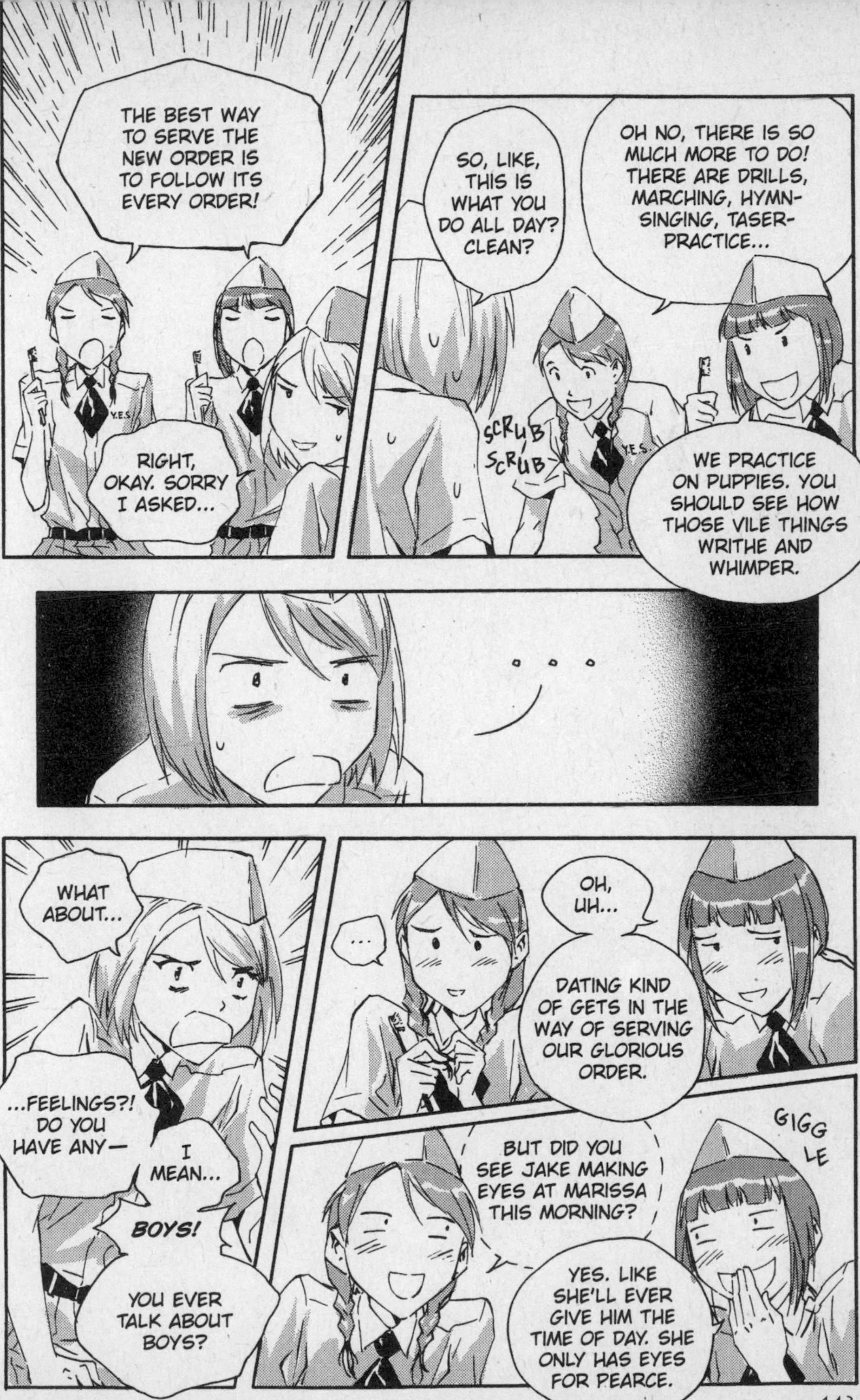
THE BEST WAY TO SERVE THE NEW ORDER IS TO FOLLOW ITS EVERY ORDER!
RIGHT, OKAY. SORRY I ASKED...
SO, LIKE, THIS IS WHAT YOU DO ALL DAY? CLEAN?
OH NO, THERE IS SO MUCH MORE TO DO! THERE ARE DRILLS, MARCHING, HYMN-SINGING, TASER-PRACTICE...
SCRUB SCRUB
WE PRACTICE ON PUPPIES. YOU SHOULD SEE HOW THOSE VILE THINGS WRITHE AND WHIMPER.
...
WHAT ABOUT...
...FEELINGS?! DO YOU HAVE ANY—
I MEAN...
BOYS!
YOU EVER TALK ABOUT BOYS?
...
OH, UH...
DATING KIND OF GETS IN THE WAY OF SERVING OUR GLORIOUS ORDER.
GIGGLE
BUT DID YOU SEE JAKE MAKING EYES AT MARISSA THIS MORNING?
YES. LIKE SHE'LL EVER GIVE HIM THE TIME OF DAY. SHE ONLY HAS EYES FOR PEARCE.

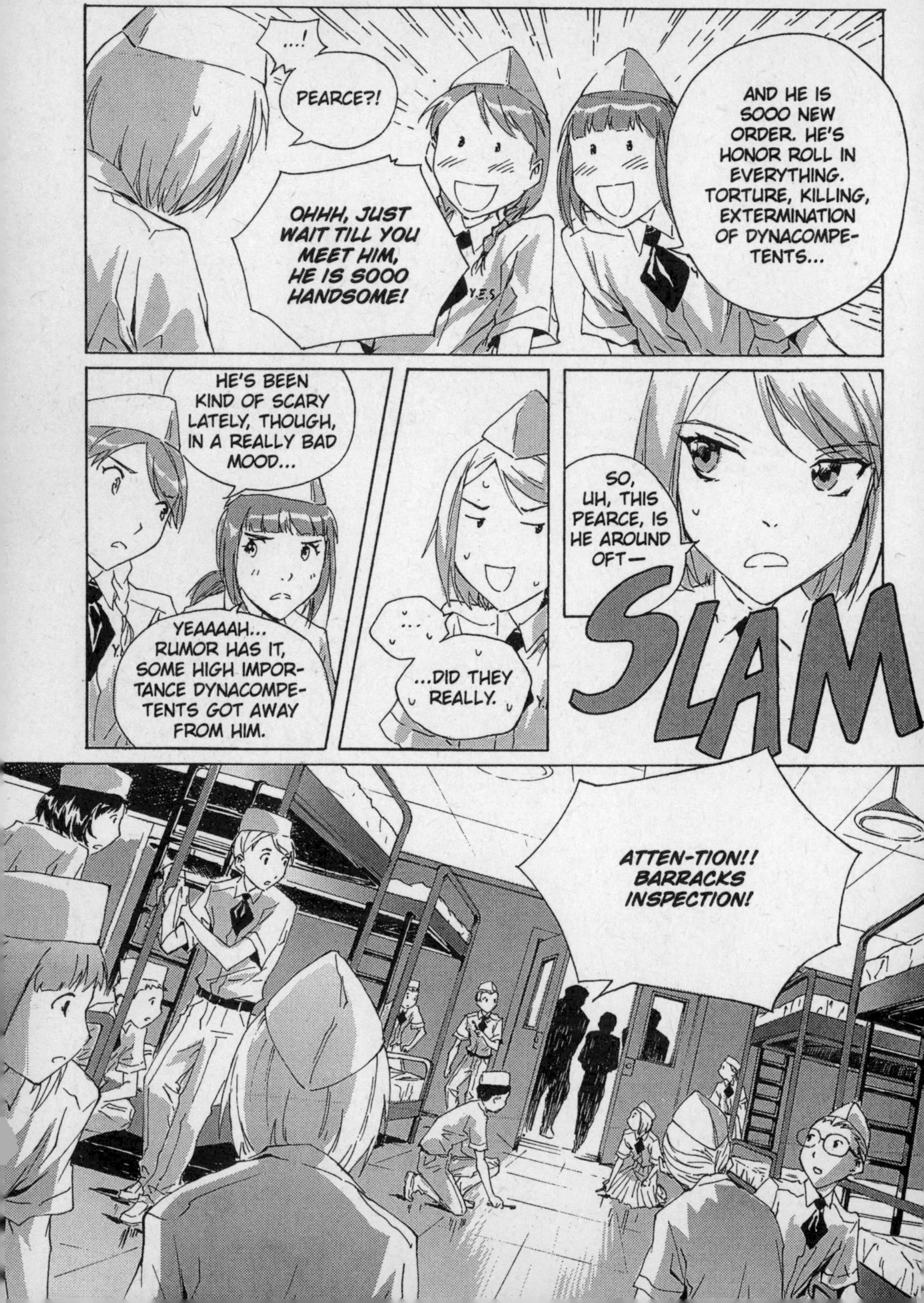
...!
PEARCE?!
OHHH, JUST WAIT TILL YOU MEET HIM, HE IS SOOO HANDSOME!
AND HE IS SOOO NEW ORDER. HE'S HONOR ROLL IN EVERYTHING. TORTURE, KILLING, EXTERMINATION OF DYNACOMPETENTS...
Y.E.S.
HE'S BEEN KIND OF SCARY LATELY, THOUGH, IN A REALLY BAD MOOD...
YEAAAAH... RUMOR HAS IT, SOME HIGH IMPORTANCE DYNACOMPETENTS GOT AWAY FROM HIM.
...
...DID THEY REALLY.
SO, UH, THIS PEARCE, IS HE AROUND OFT—
SLAM
ATTEN-TION!! BARRACKS INSPECTION!

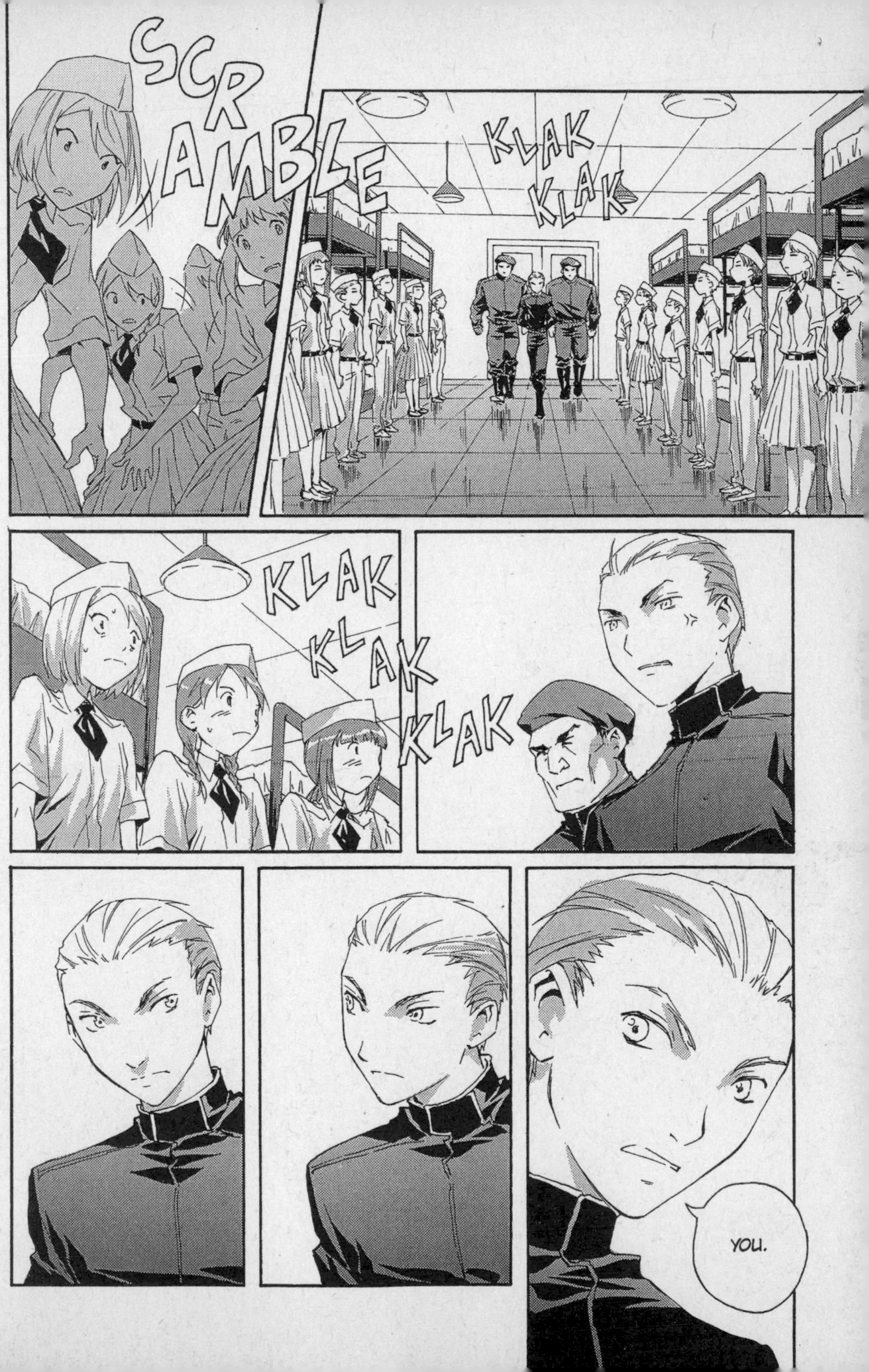
SCRAMBLE
KLAK KLAK
KLAK KLAK KLAK
YOU.

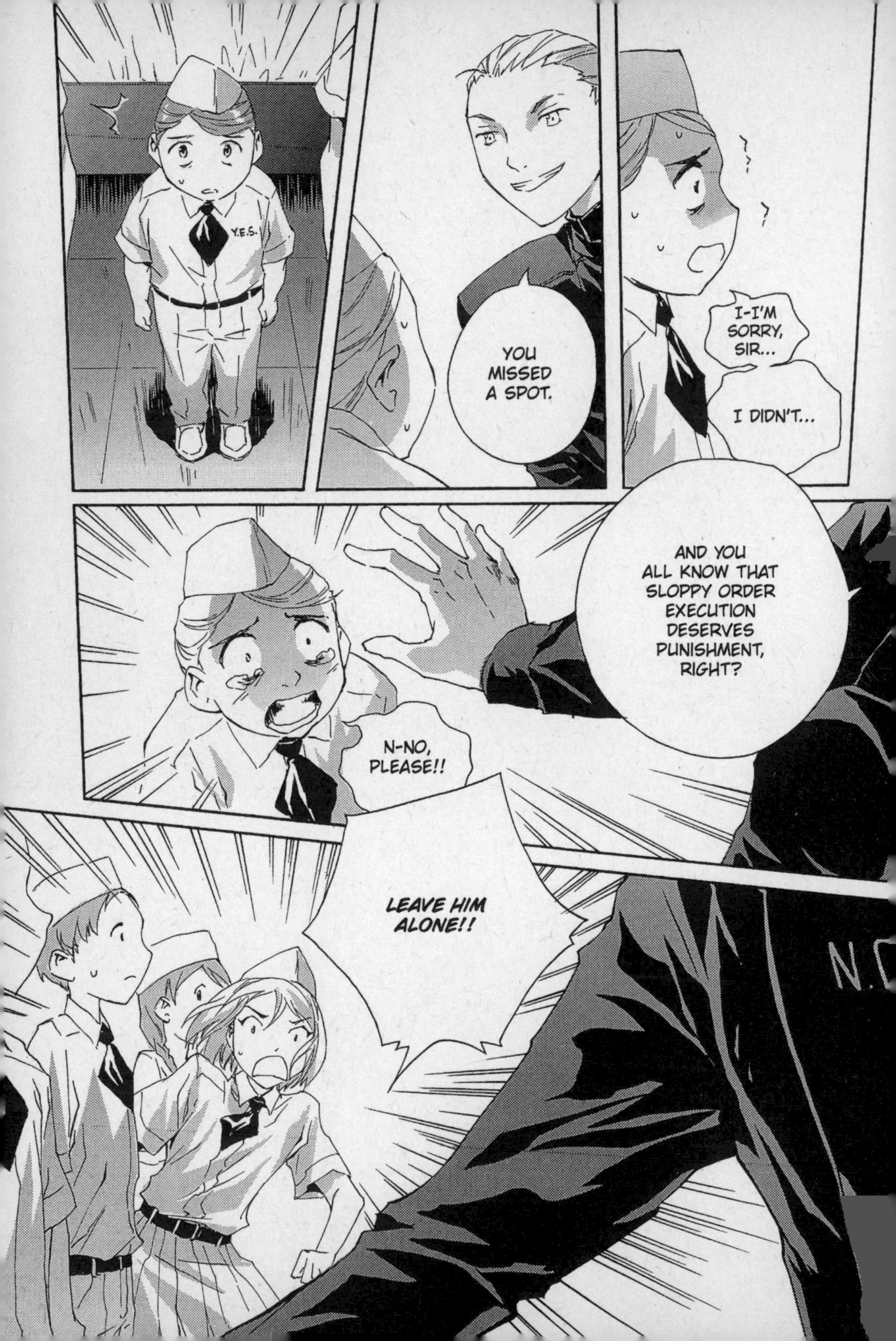
Y.E.S.
YOU MISSED A SPOT.
I-I'M SORRY, SIR...
I DIDN'T...
AND YOU ALL KNOW THAT SLOPPY ORDER EXECUTION DESERVES PUNISHMENT, RIGHT?
N-NO, PLEASE!!
LEAVE HIM ALONE!!

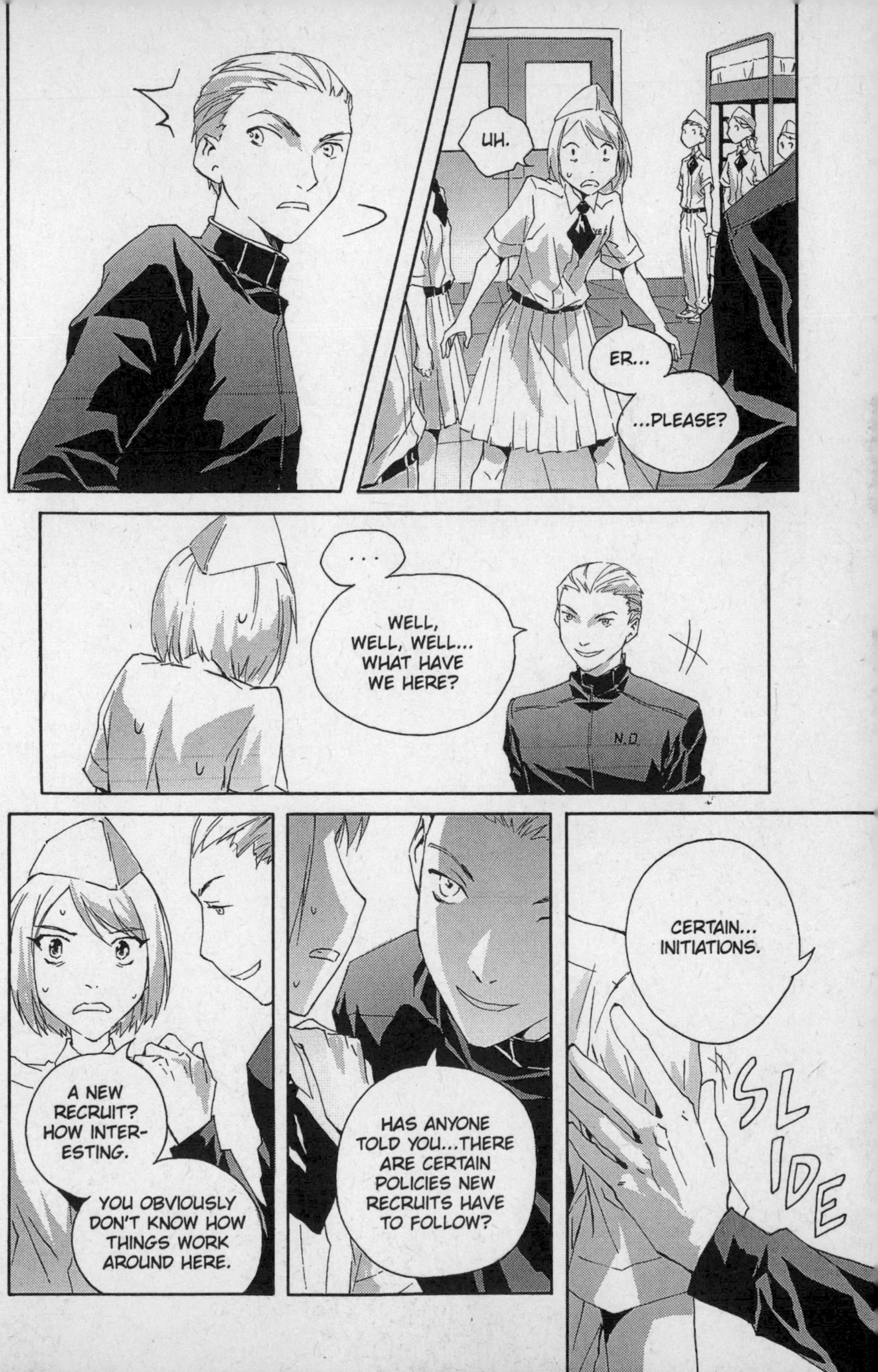
UH.
ER...
...PLEASE?
...
WELL, WELL, WELL... WHAT HAVE WE HERE?
A NEW RECRUIT? HOW INTER-ESTING.
YOU OBVIOUSLY DON'T KNOW HOW THINGS WORK AROUND HERE.
HAS ANYONE TOLD YOU...THERE ARE CERTAIN POLICIES NEW RECRUITS HAVE TO FOLLOW?
CERTAIN... INITIATIONS.
SLIDE

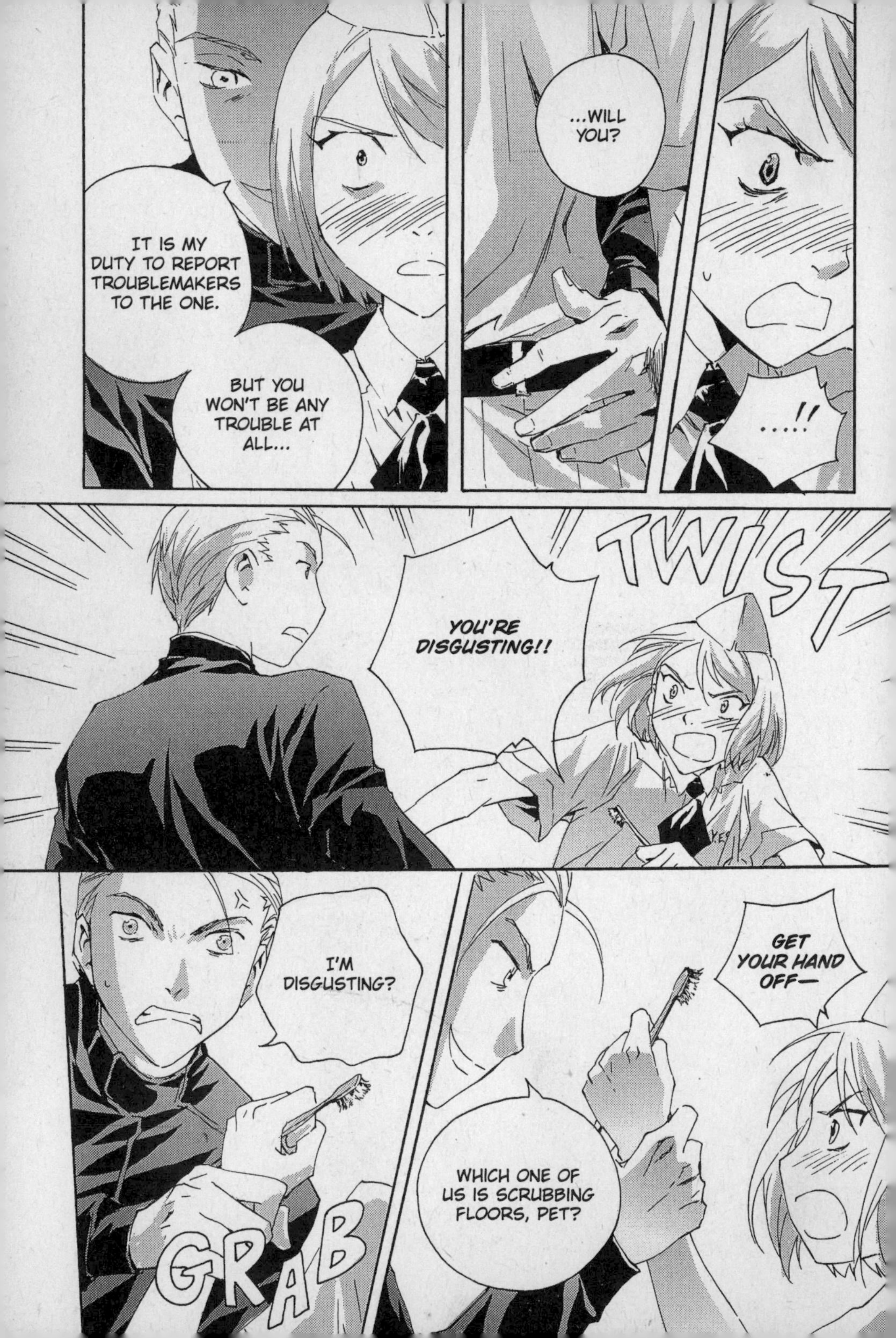
IT IS MY DUTY TO REPORT TROUBLEMAKERS TO THE ONE.
BUT YOU WON'T BE ANY TROUBLE AT ALL...
...WILL YOU?
....!!
YOU'RE DISGUSTING!!
TWIST
I'M DISGUSTING?
GET YOUR HAND OFF—
WHICH ONE OF US IS SCRUBBING FLOORS, PET?
GRAB

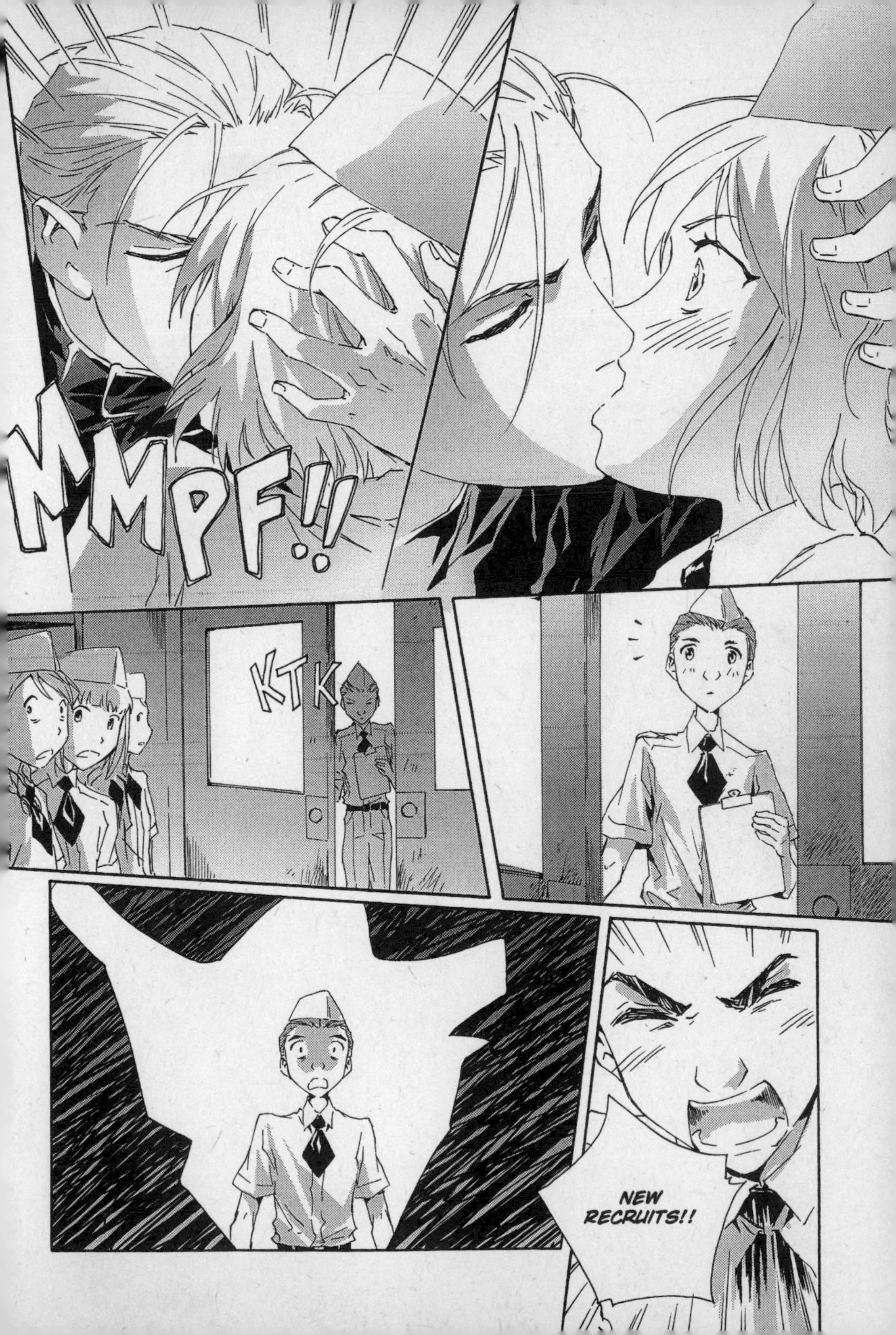
MMPF!!
KTK
NEW RECRUITS!!

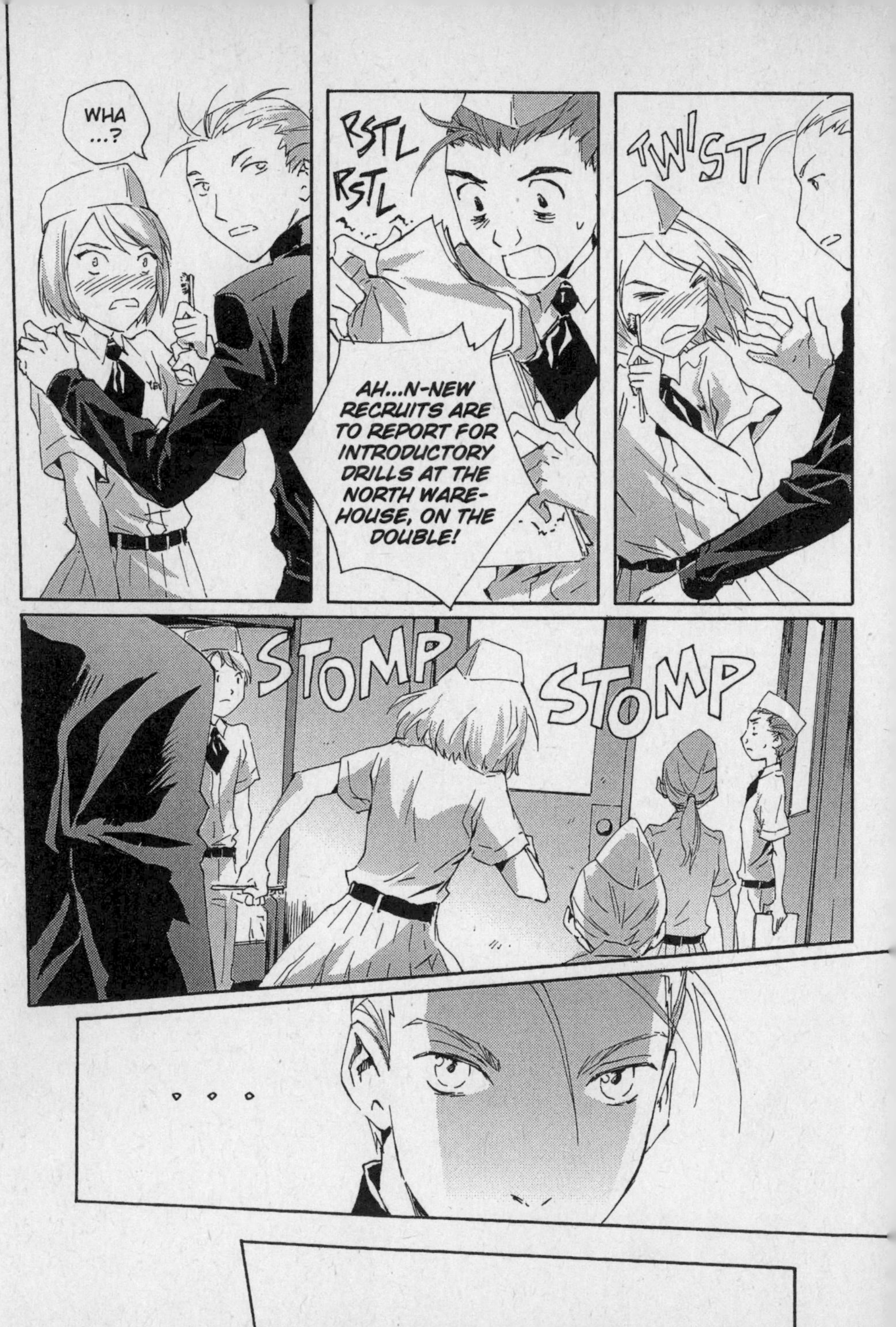
WHA ...?
RSTL RSTL
AH...N-NEW RECRUITS ARE TO REPORT FOR INTRODUCTORY DRILLS AT THE NORTH WARE-HOUSE, ON THE DOUBLE!
TWIST
STOMP
STOMP
...

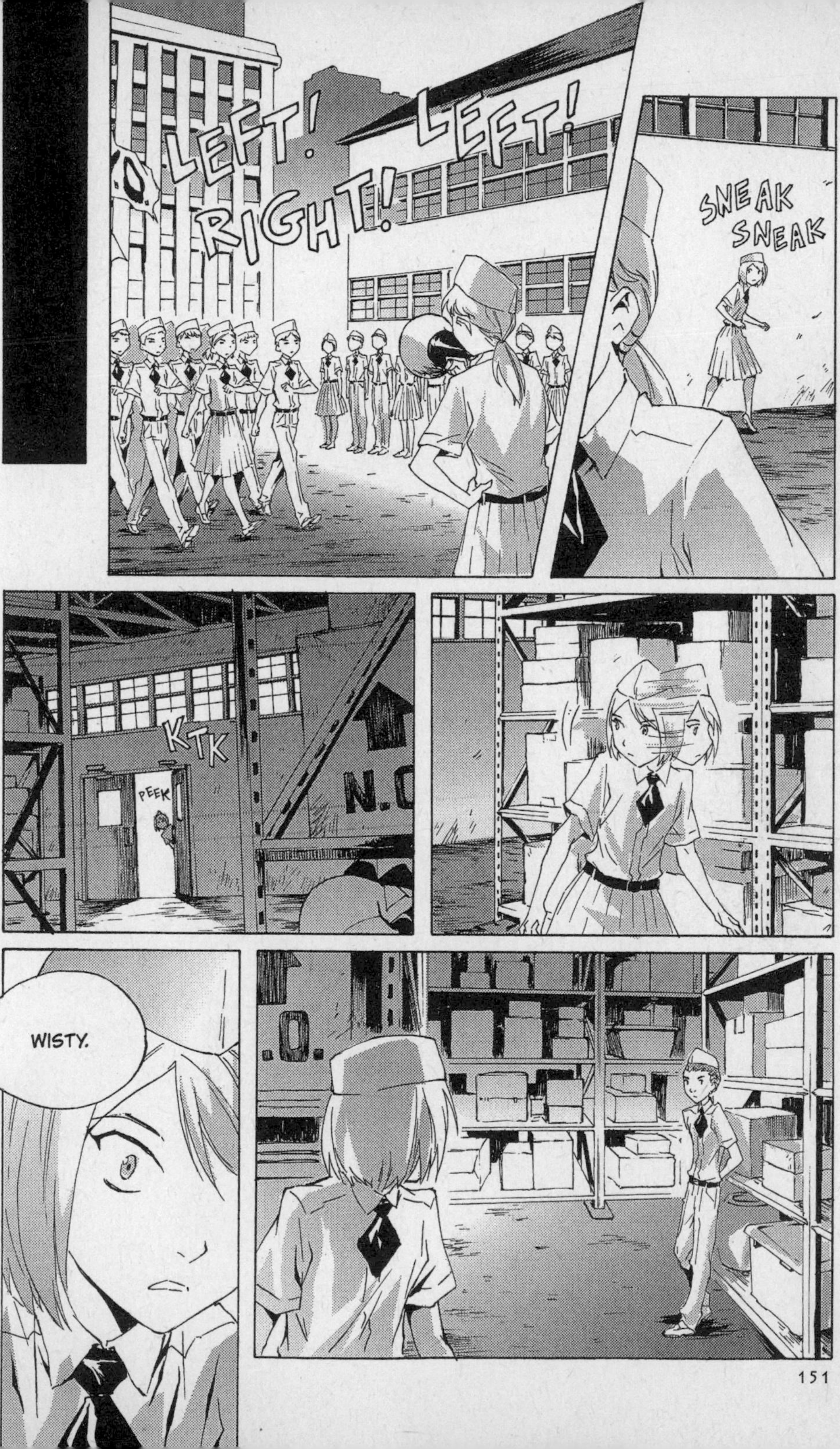
LEFT! RIGHT! LEFT!
SNEAK SNEAK
KTK
PEEK
WISTY.

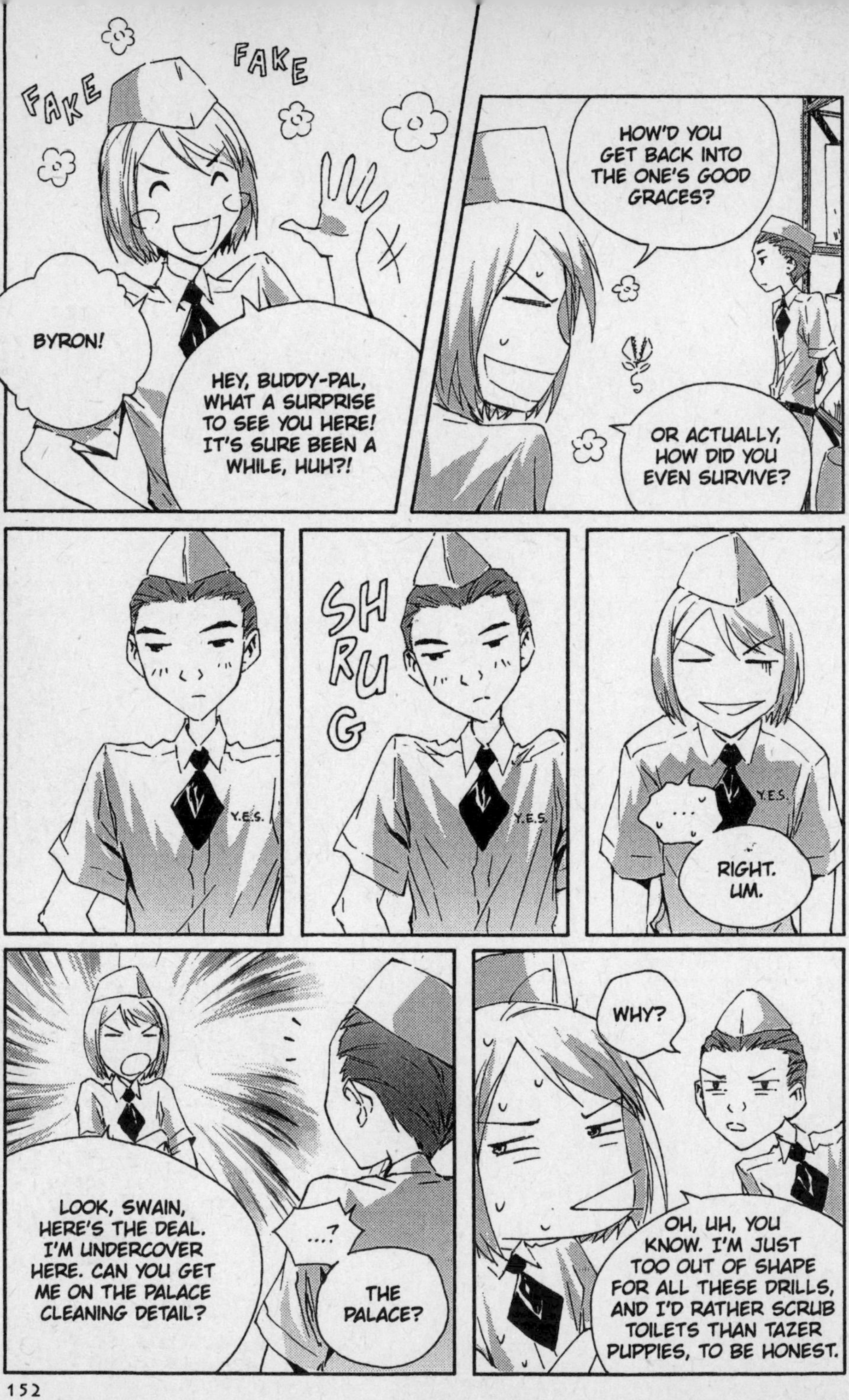
FAKE
FAKE
BYRON!
HEY, BUDDY-PAL, WHAT A SURPRISE TO SEE YOU HERE! IT'S SURE BEEN A WHILE, HUH?!
HOW'D YOU GET BACK INTO THE ONE'S GOOD GRACES?
OR ACTUALLY, HOW DID YOU EVEN SURVIVE?
Y.E.S.
SHRUG
Y.E.S.
Y.E.S.
...
RIGHT. UM.
LOOK, SWAIN, HERE'S THE DEAL. I'M UNDERCOVER HERE. CAN YOU GET ME ON THE PALACE CLEANING DETAIL?
...?
THE PALACE?
WHY?
OH, UH, YOU KNOW. I'M JUST TOO OUT OF SHAPE FOR ALL THESE DRILLS, AND I'D RATHER SCRUB TOILETS THAN TAZER PUPPIES, TO BE HONEST.

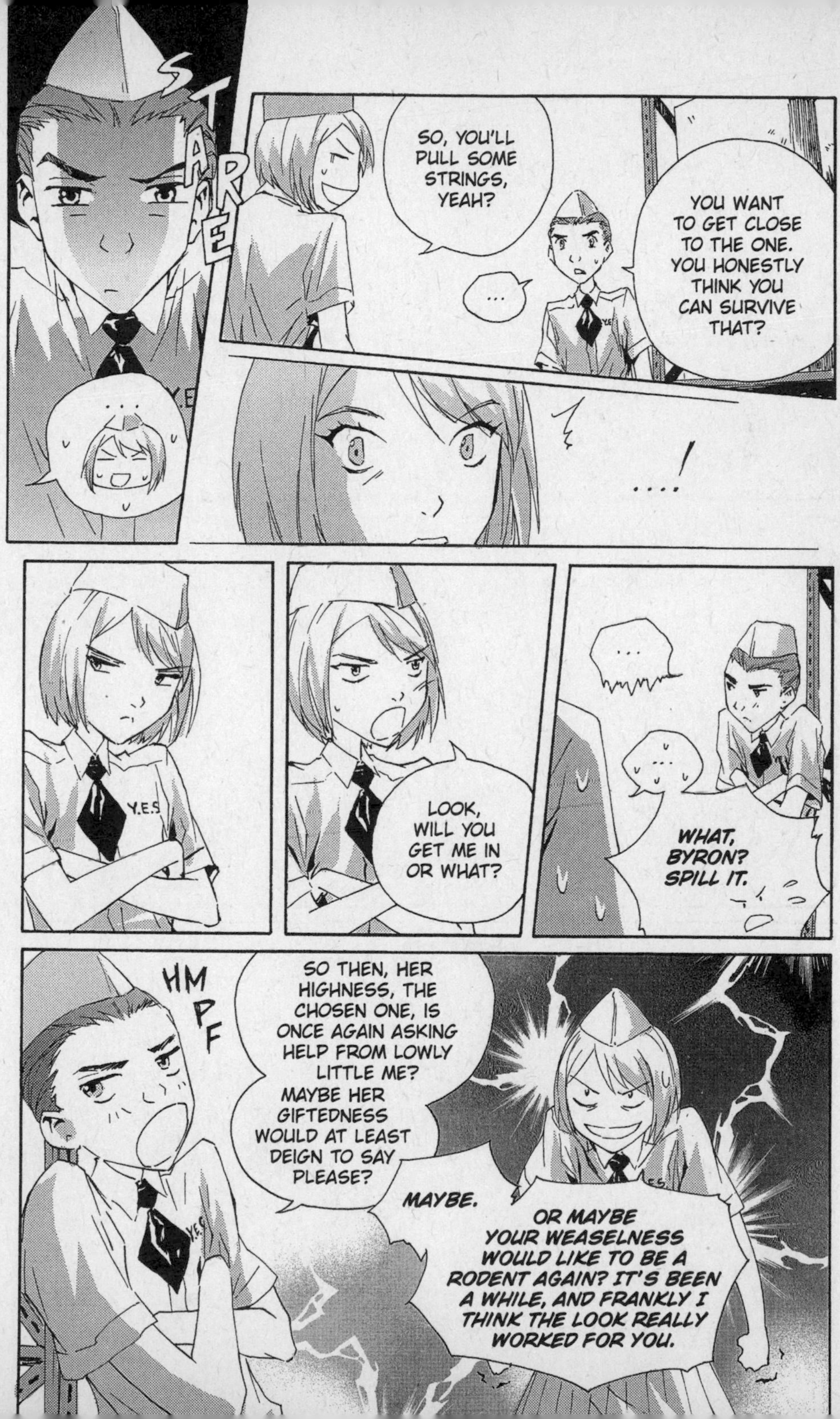

STARE
SO, YOU'LL PULL SOME STRINGS, YEAH?
...
YOU WANT TO GET CLOSE TO THE ONE. YOU HONESTLY THINK YOU CAN SURVIVE THAT?
...
....!
LOOK, WILL YOU GET ME IN OR WHAT?
...
...
WHAT, BYRON? SPILL IT.
HMPF
SO THEN, HER HIGHNESS, THE CHOSEN ONE, IS ONCE AGAIN ASKING HELP FROM LOWLY LITTLE ME? MAYBE HER GIFTEDNESS WOULD AT LEAST DEIGN TO SAY PLEASE?
MAYBE.
OR MAYBE YOUR WEASELNESS WOULD LIKE TO BE A RODENT AGAIN? IT'S BEEN A WHILE, AND FRANKLY I THINK THE LOOK REALLY WORKED FOR YOU.

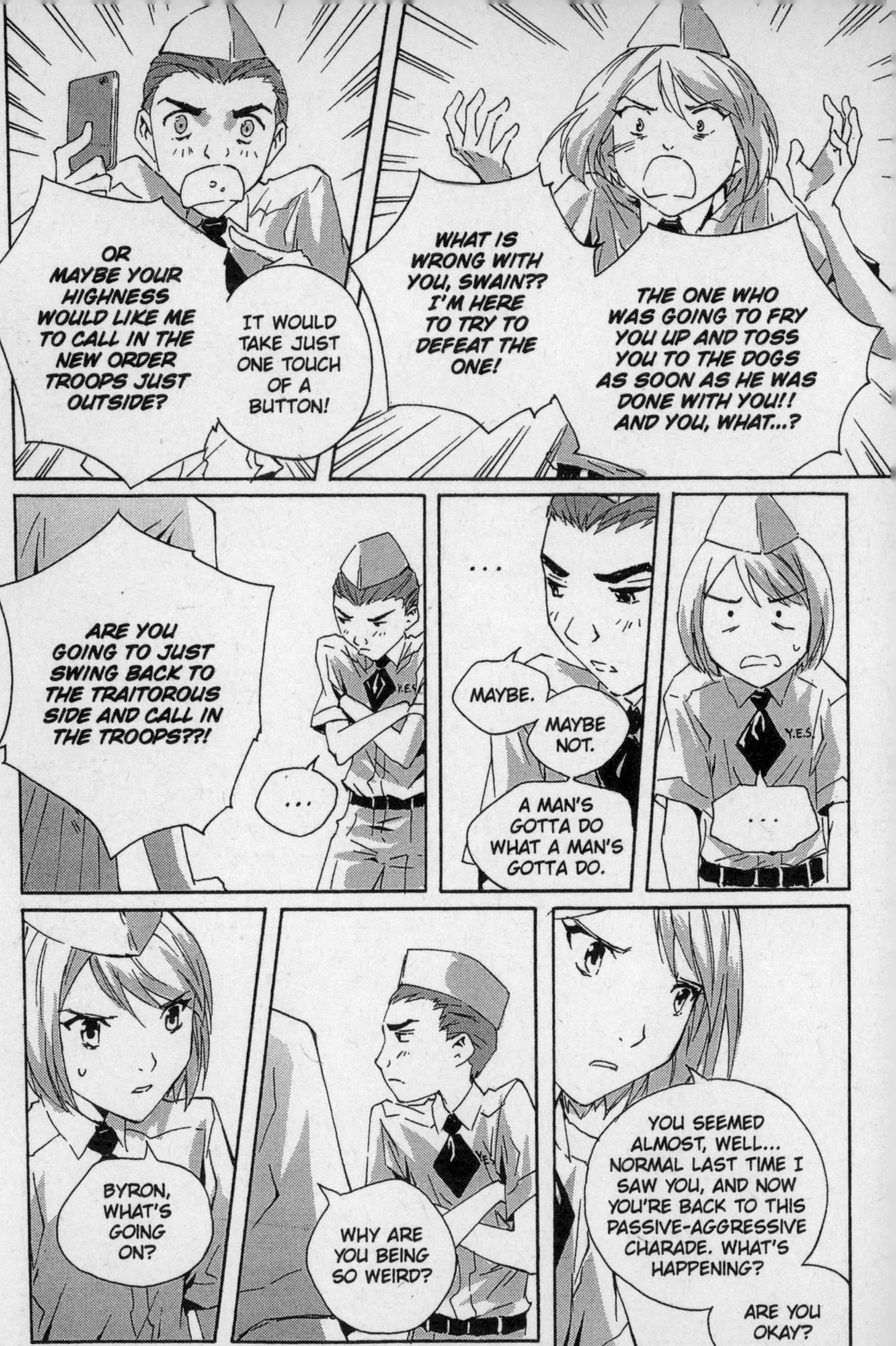
OR MAYBE YOUR HIGHNESS WOULD LIKE ME TO CALL IN THE NEW ORDER TROOPS JUST OUTSIDE?
IT WOULD TAKE JUST ONE TOUCH OF A BUTTON!
WHAT IS WRONG WITH YOU, SWAIN?? I'M HERE TO TRY TO DEFEAT THE ONE!
THE ONE WHO WAS GOING TO FRY YOU UP AND TOSS YOU TO THE DOGS AS SOON AS HE WAS DONE WITH YOU!! AND YOU, WHAT...?
ARE YOU GOING TO JUST SWING BACK TO THE TRAITOROUS SIDE AND CALL IN THE TROOPS??!
...
...
MAYBE.
MAYBE NOT.
A MAN'S GOTTA DO WHAT A MAN'S GOTTA DO.
...
BYRON, WHAT'S GOING ON?
WHY ARE YOU BEING SO WEIRD?
YOU SEEMED ALMOST, WELL... NORMAL LAST TIME I SAW YOU, AND NOW YOU'RE BACK TO THIS PASSIVE-AGGRESSIVE CHARADE. WHAT'S HAPPENING?
ARE YOU OKAY?

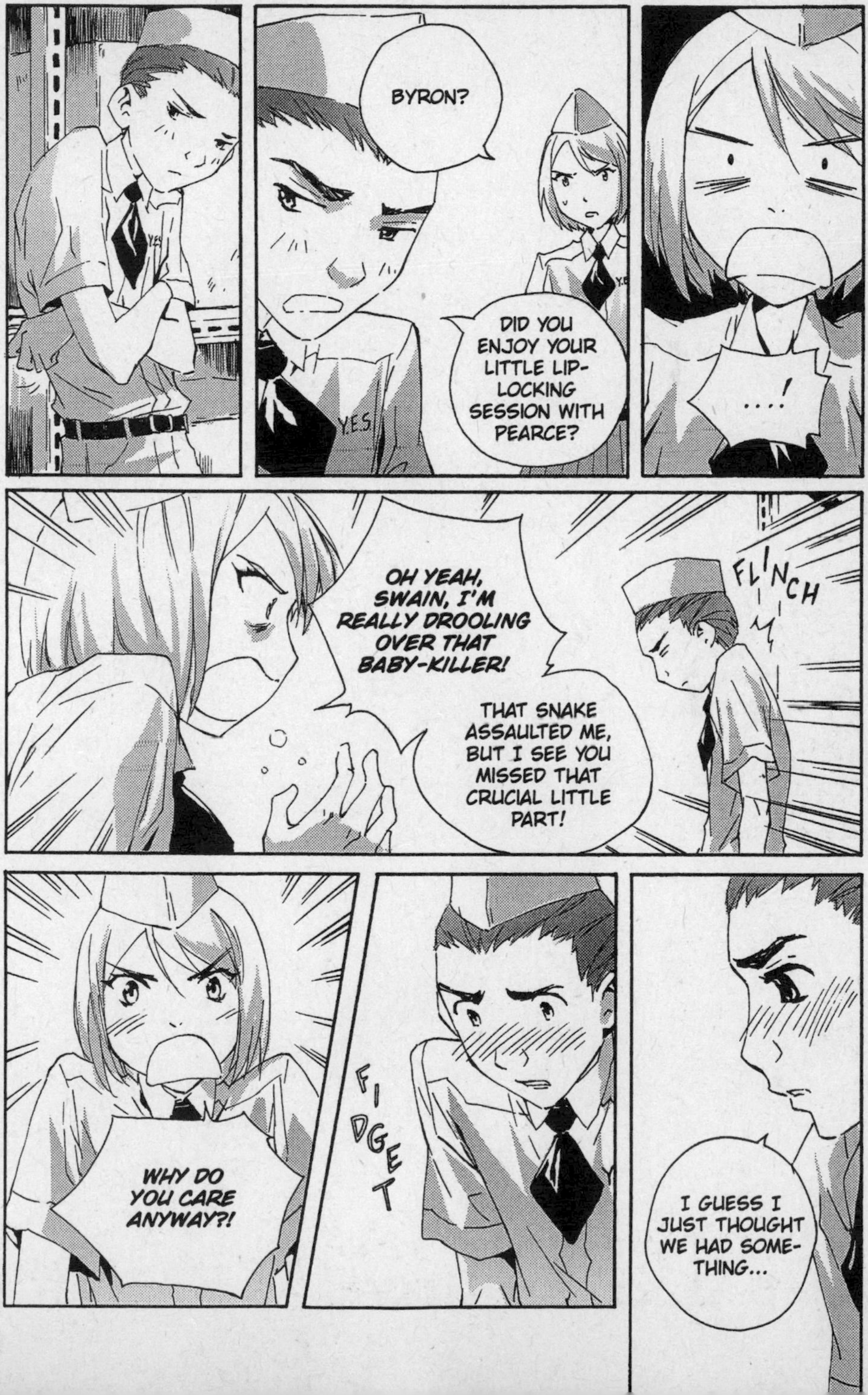
BYRON?
DID YOU ENJOY YOUR LITTLE LIP-LOCKING SESSION WITH PEARCE?
....!
OH YEAH, SWAIN, I'M REALLY DROOLING OVER THAT BABY-KILLER!
THAT SNAKE ASSAULTED ME, BUT I SEE YOU MISSED THAT CRUCIAL LITTLE PART!
FLINCH
WHY DO YOU CARE ANYWAY?!
FIDGET
I GUESS I JUST THOUGHT WE HAD SOME-THING...

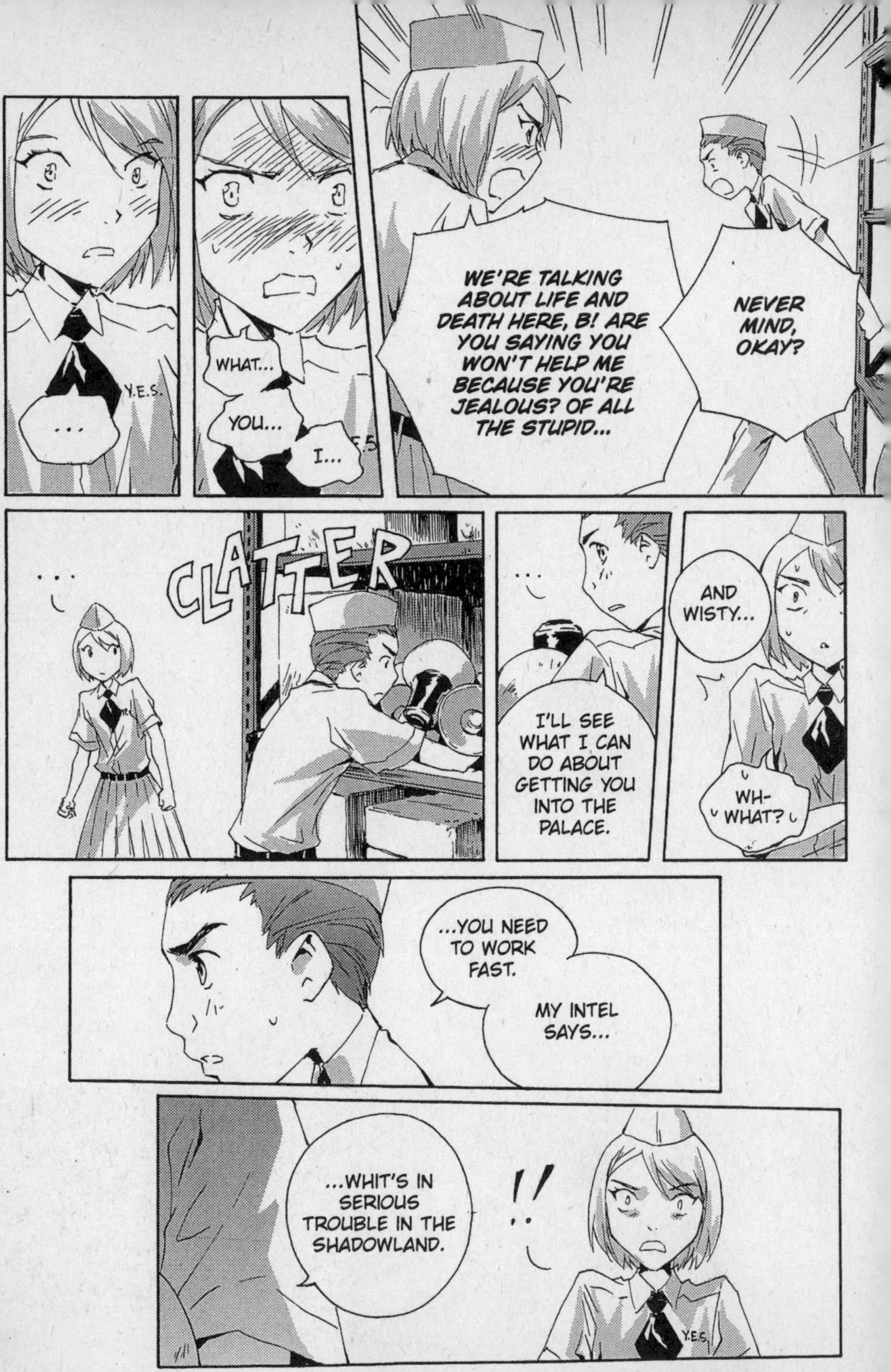

Y.E.S.
...
WHAT...
YOU...
I...
WE'RE TALKING ABOUT LIFE AND DEATH HERE, B! ARE YOU SAYING YOU WON'T HELP ME BECAUSE YOU'RE JEALOUS? OF ALL THE STUPID...
NEVER MIND, OKAY?
...
CLATTER
...
I'LL SEE WHAT I CAN DO ABOUT GETTING YOU INTO THE PALACE.
AND WISTY...
WH- WHAT?
...YOU NEED TO WORK FAST.
MY INTEL SAYS...
...WHIT'S IN SERIOUS TROUBLE IN THE SHADOWLAND.
!!
Y.E.S.

WITCH & WIZARD

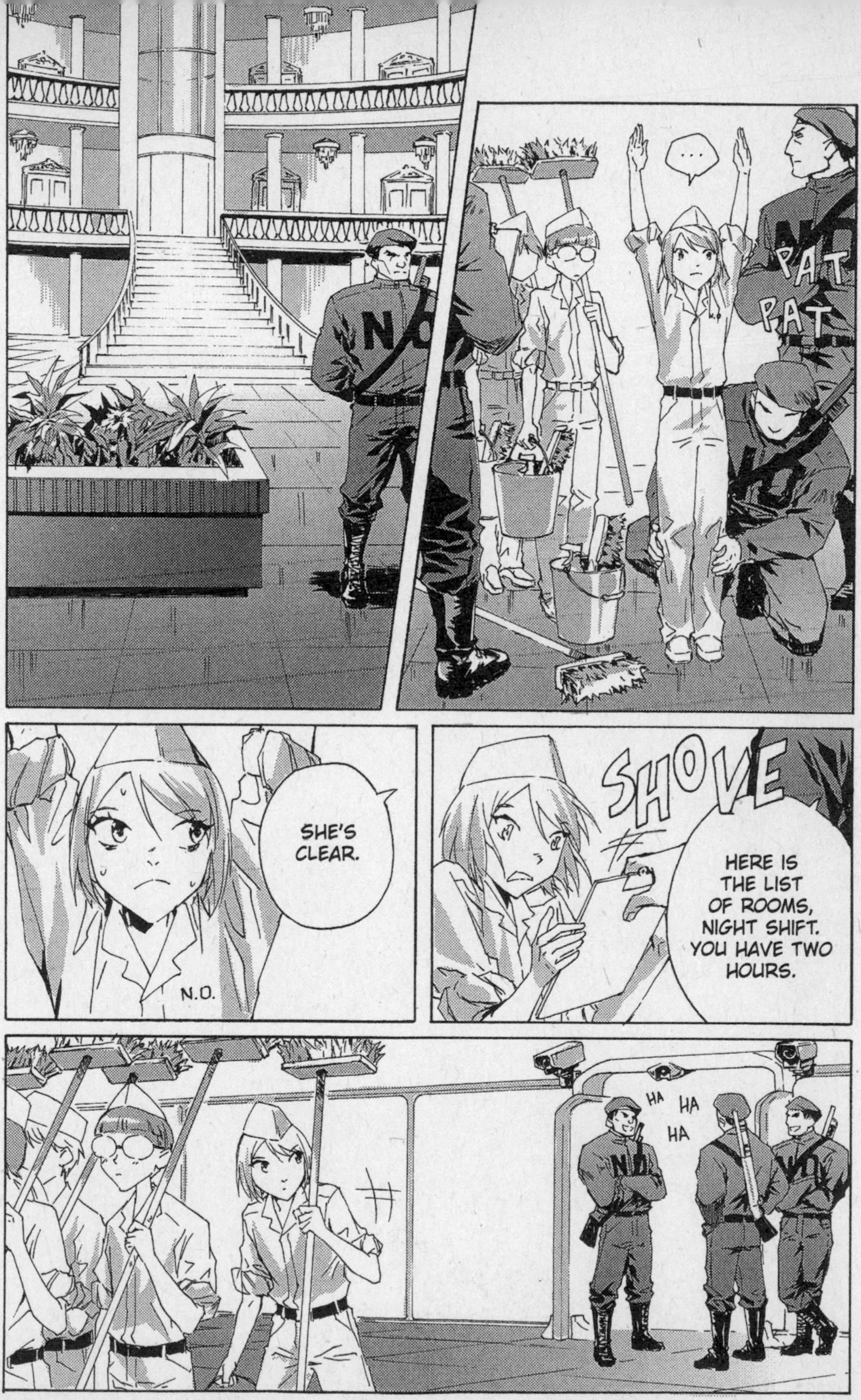
N.O.
...
PAT PAT
N.O.
SHE'S CLEAR.
N.O.
SHOVE
HERE IS THE LIST OF ROOMS, NIGHT SHIFT. YOU HAVE TWO HOURS.
HA HA HA
N.O.

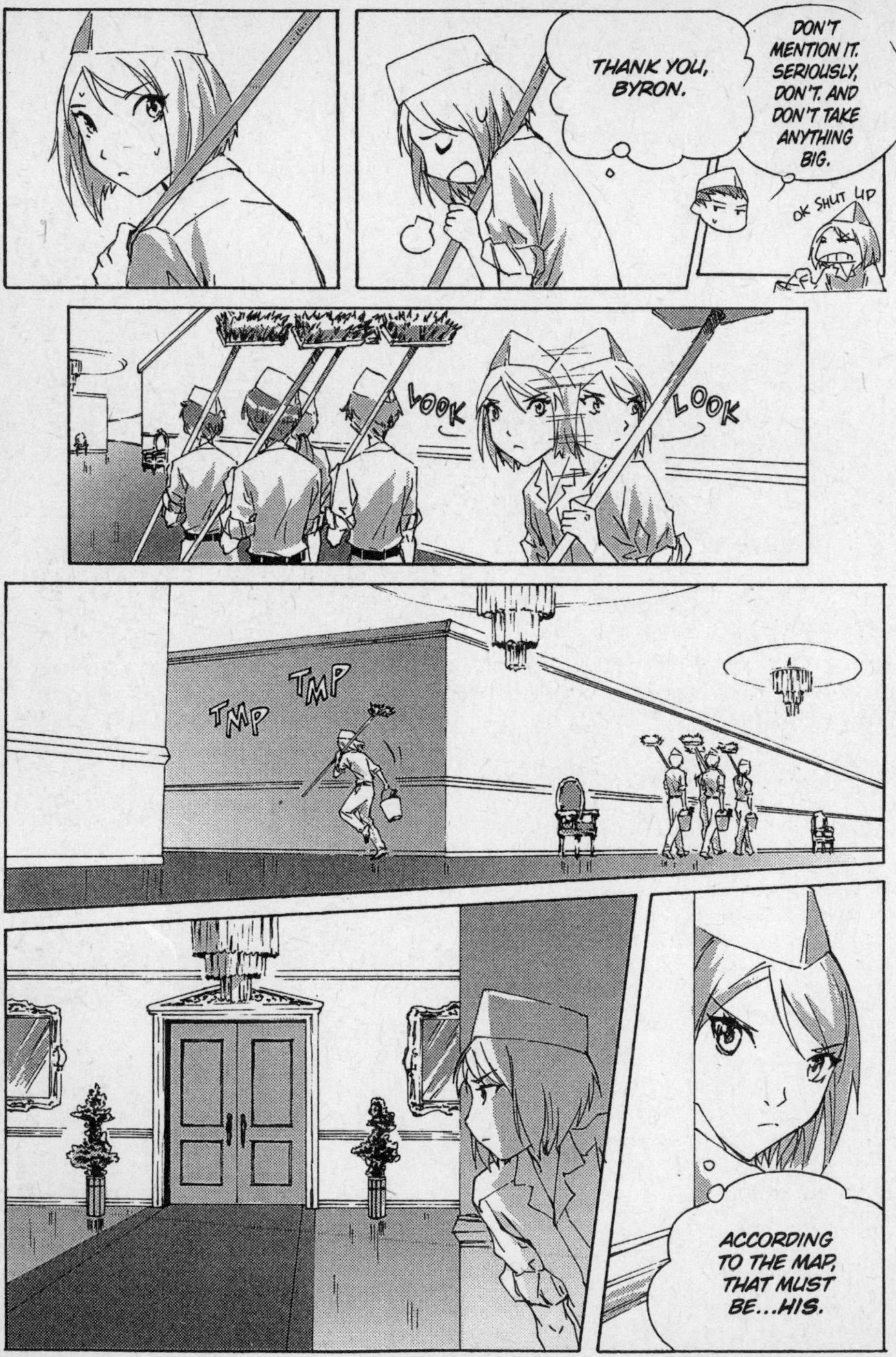
THANK YOU, BYRON.
DON'T MENTION IT. SERIOUSLY, DON'T. AND DON'T TAKE ANYTHING BIG.
OK SHUT UP
LOOK
LOOK
TMP
TMP
ACCORDING TO THE MAP, THAT MUST BE...HIS.

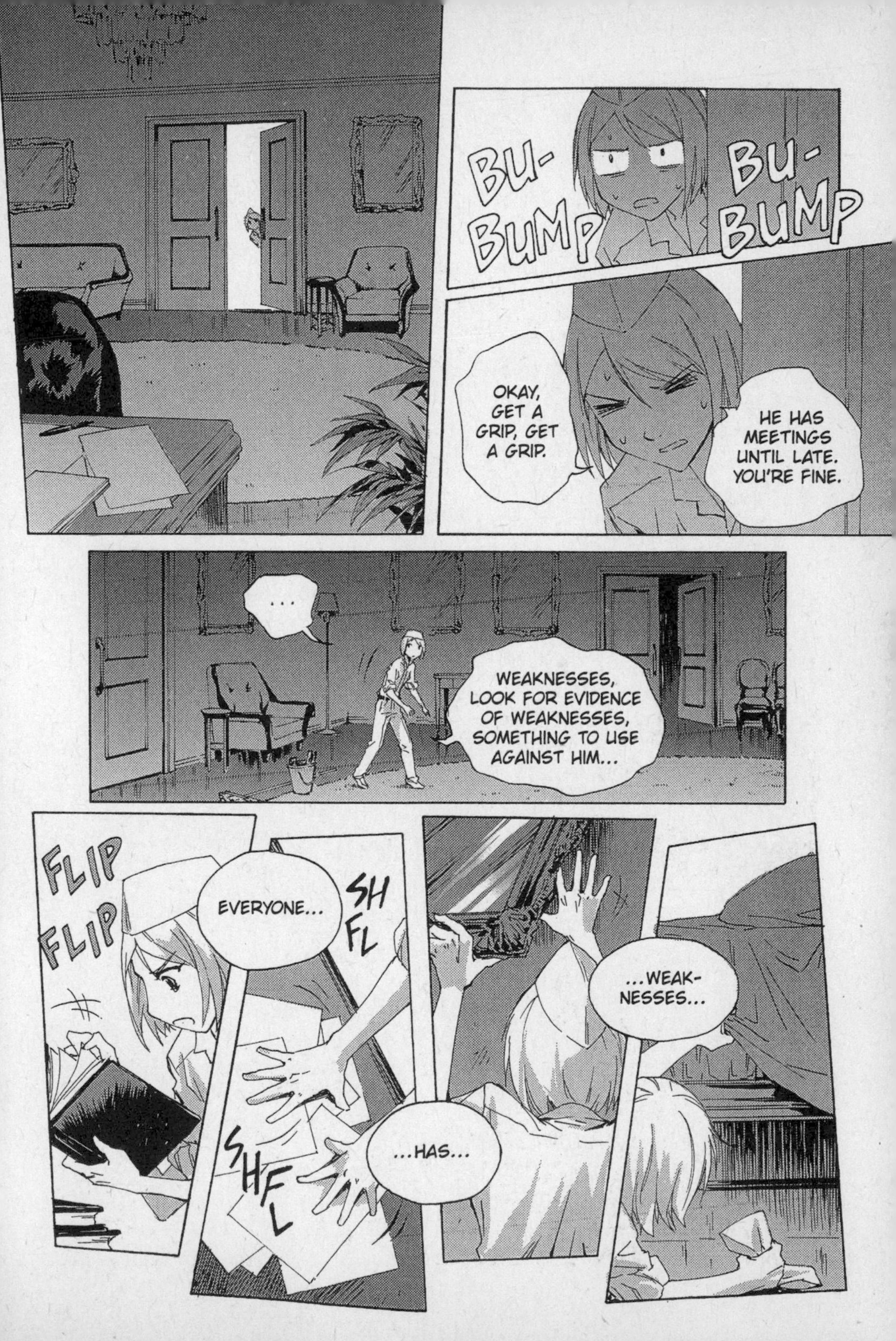
BU-BUMP
BU-BUMP
OKAY, GET A GRIP, GET A GRIP.
HE HAS MEETINGS UNTIL LATE. YOU'RE FINE.
...
WEAKNESSES, LOOK FOR EVIDENCE OF WEAKNESSES, SOMETHING TO USE AGAINST HIM...
FLIP FLIP
EVERYONE...
SHFL
...HAS...
SHFL
...WEAK-NESSES...

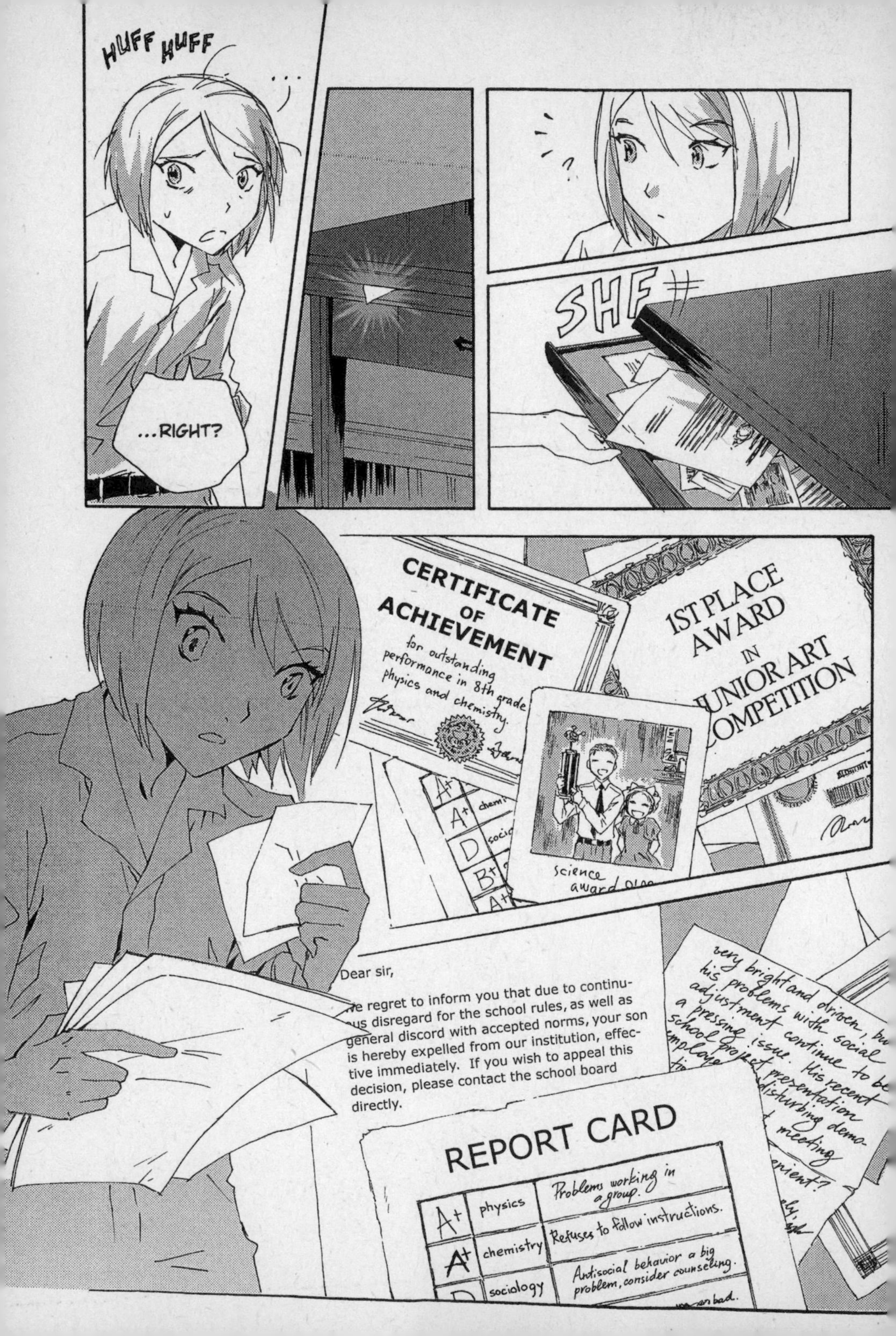
HUFF HUFF
...
...RIGHT?
?
SHF
CERTIFICATE OF ACHIEVEMENT
for outstanding performance in 8th grade physics and chemistry.
1ST PLACE AWARD IN JUNIOR ART COMPETITION
science award
Dear sir,
We regret to inform you that due to continuous disregard for the school rules, as well as general discord with accepted norms, your son is hereby expelled from our institution, effective immediately. If you wish to appeal this decision, please contact the school board directly.
very bright and driven, but his problems with social adjustment continue to be a pressing issue. His recent school project presentation disturbing demo
REPORT CARD
A+ physics Problems working in a group.
A+ chemistry Refuses to follow instructions.
sociology Antisocial behavior a big problem, consider counseling.

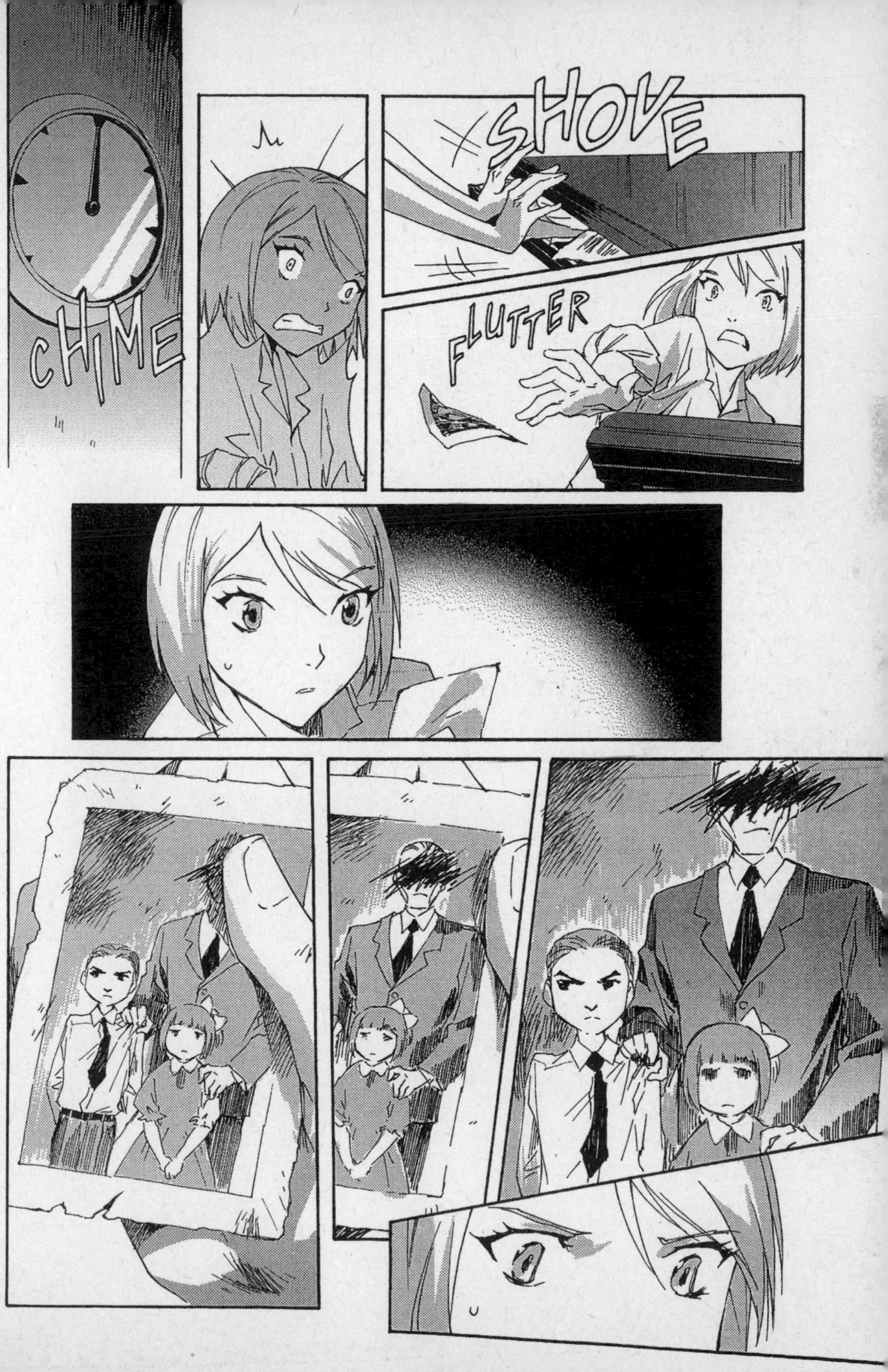
CHIME
SHOVE
FLUTTER

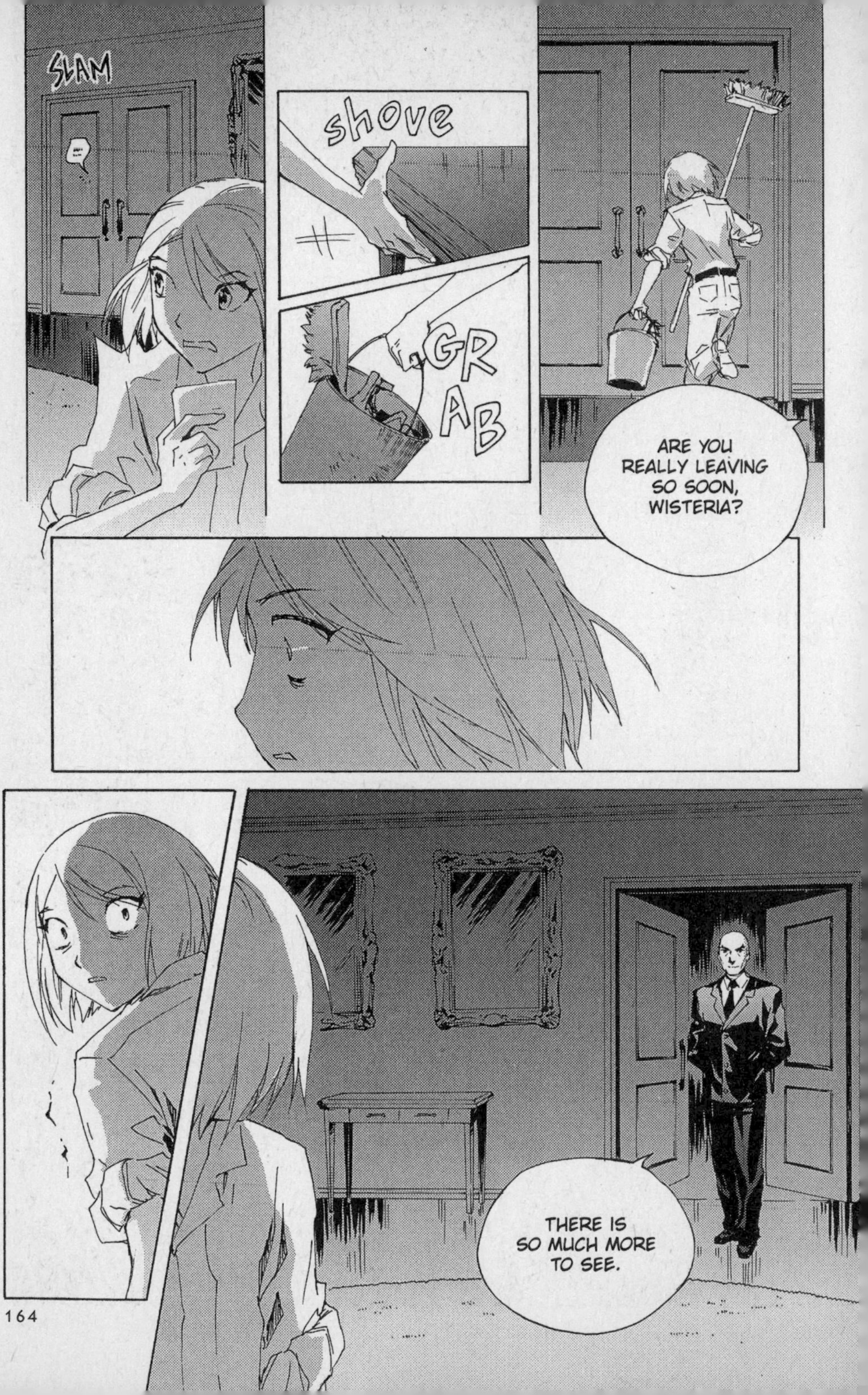
SLAM
shove
GRAB
ARE YOU REALLY LEAVING SO SOON, WISTERIA?
THERE IS SO MUCH MORE TO SEE.

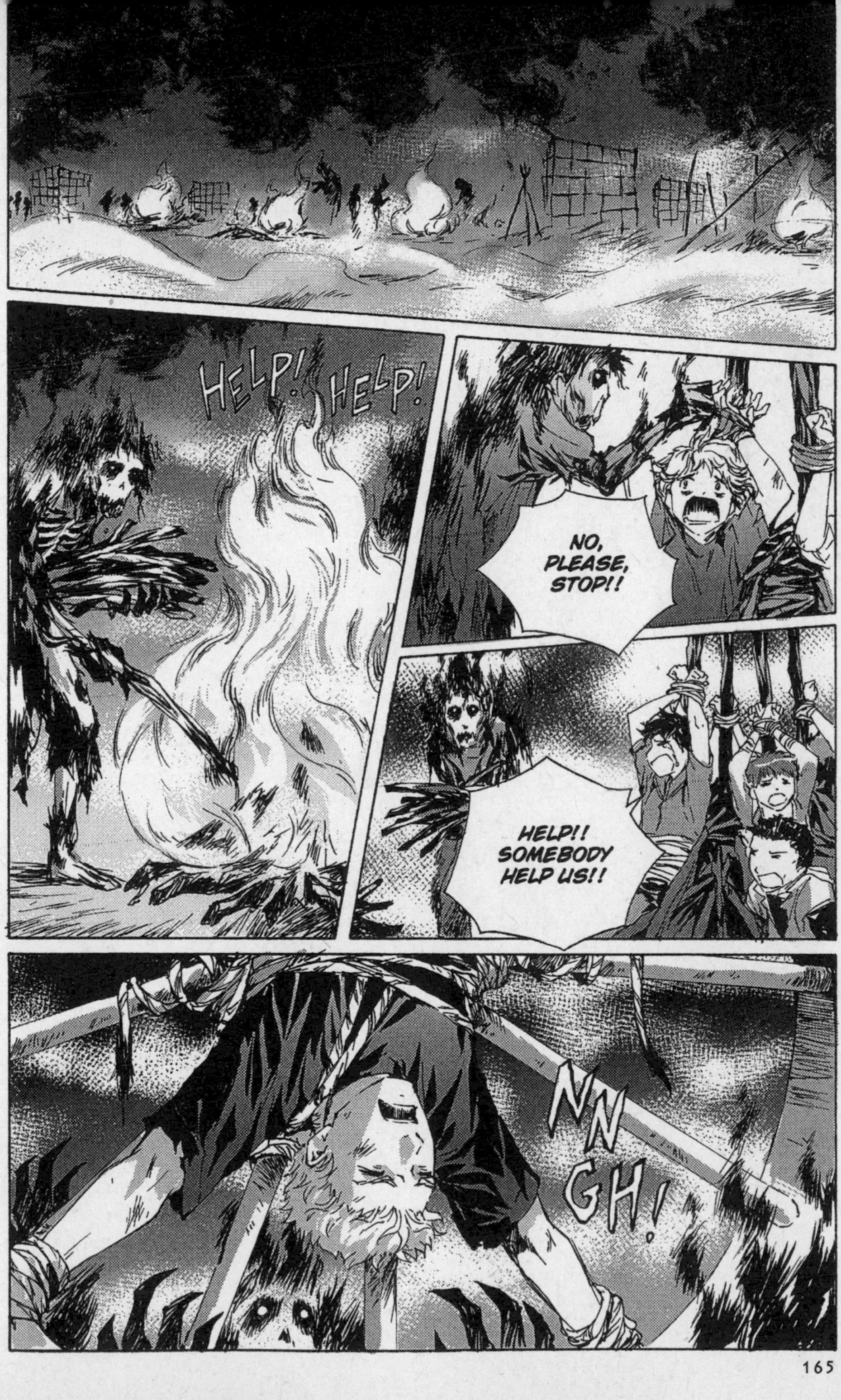
HELP! HELP!
NO, PLEASE, STOP!!
HELP!! SOMEBODY HELP US!!
NNGH!

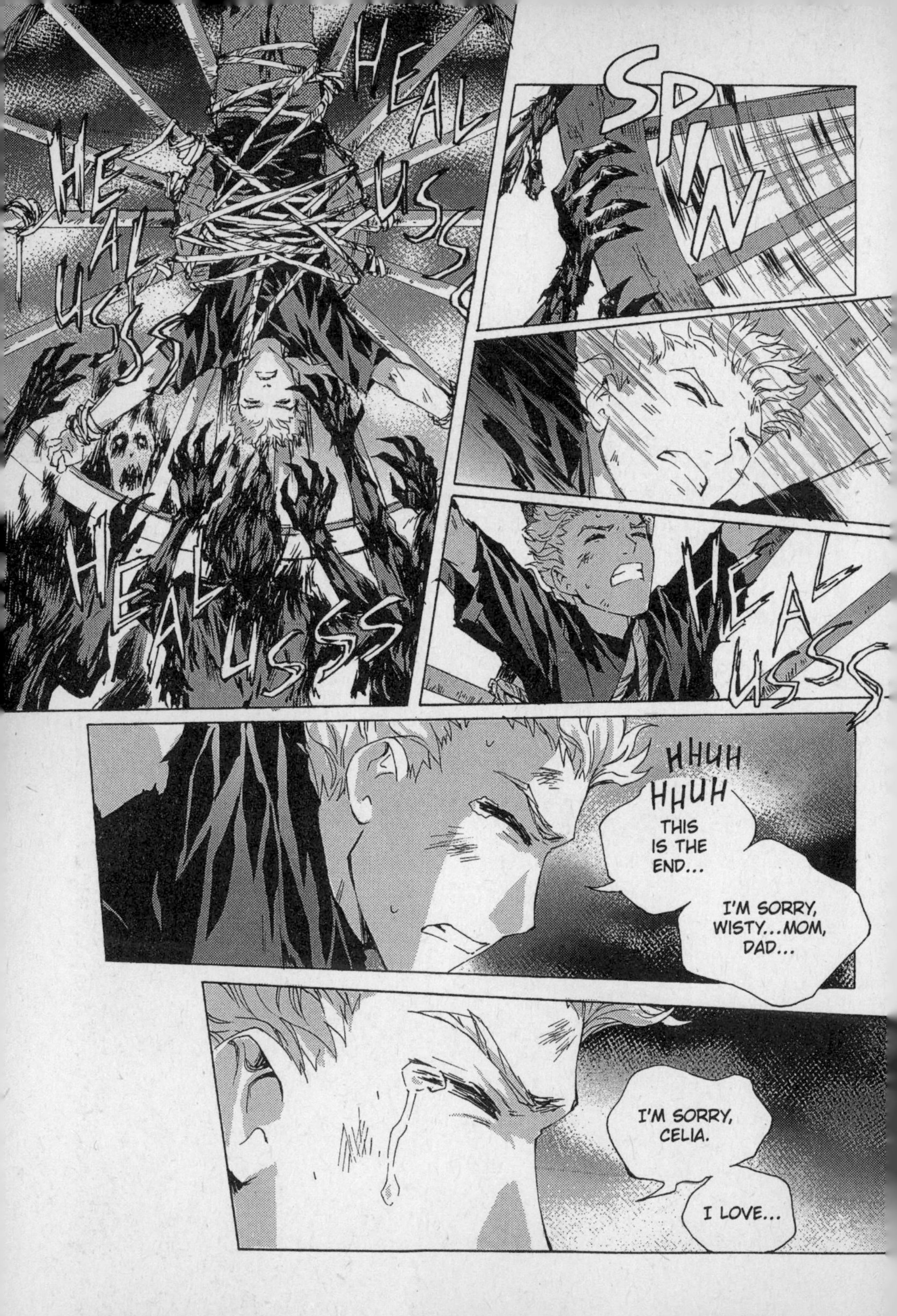
HEAL
USS
HE
AL
USSS
SPIN
HEAL
USSS
HEAL
USSS
HHUH HHUH
THIS IS THE END...
I'M SORRY, WISTY...MOM, DAD...
I'M SORRY, CELIA.
I LOVE...

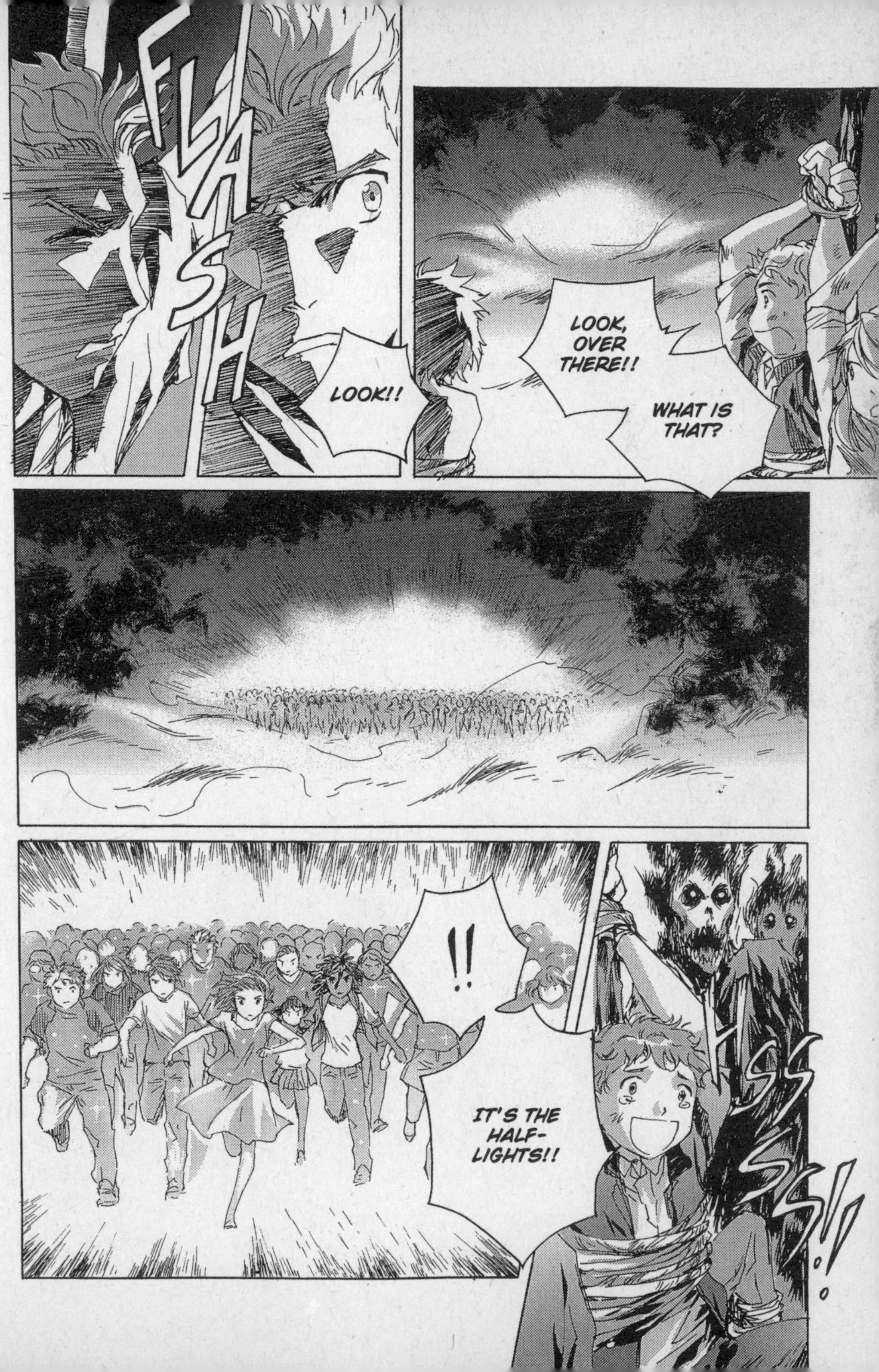
FLASH
LOOK!!
LOOK, OVER THERE!!
WHAT IS THAT?
!!
IT'S THE HALF-LIGHTS!!
HISSSS!!

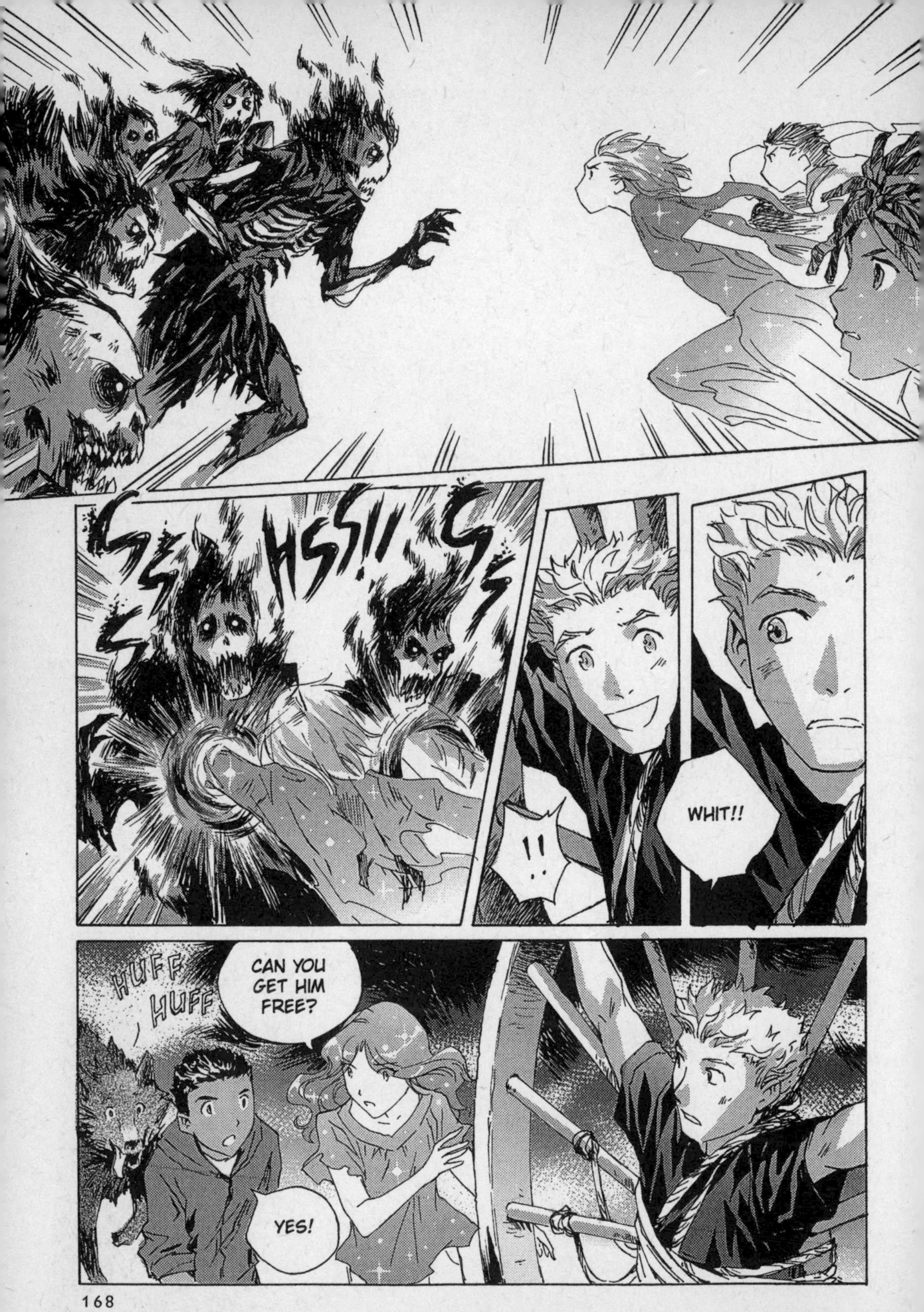
HSS!!
!!
WHIT!!
HUFF HUFF
CAN YOU GET HIM FREE?
YES!

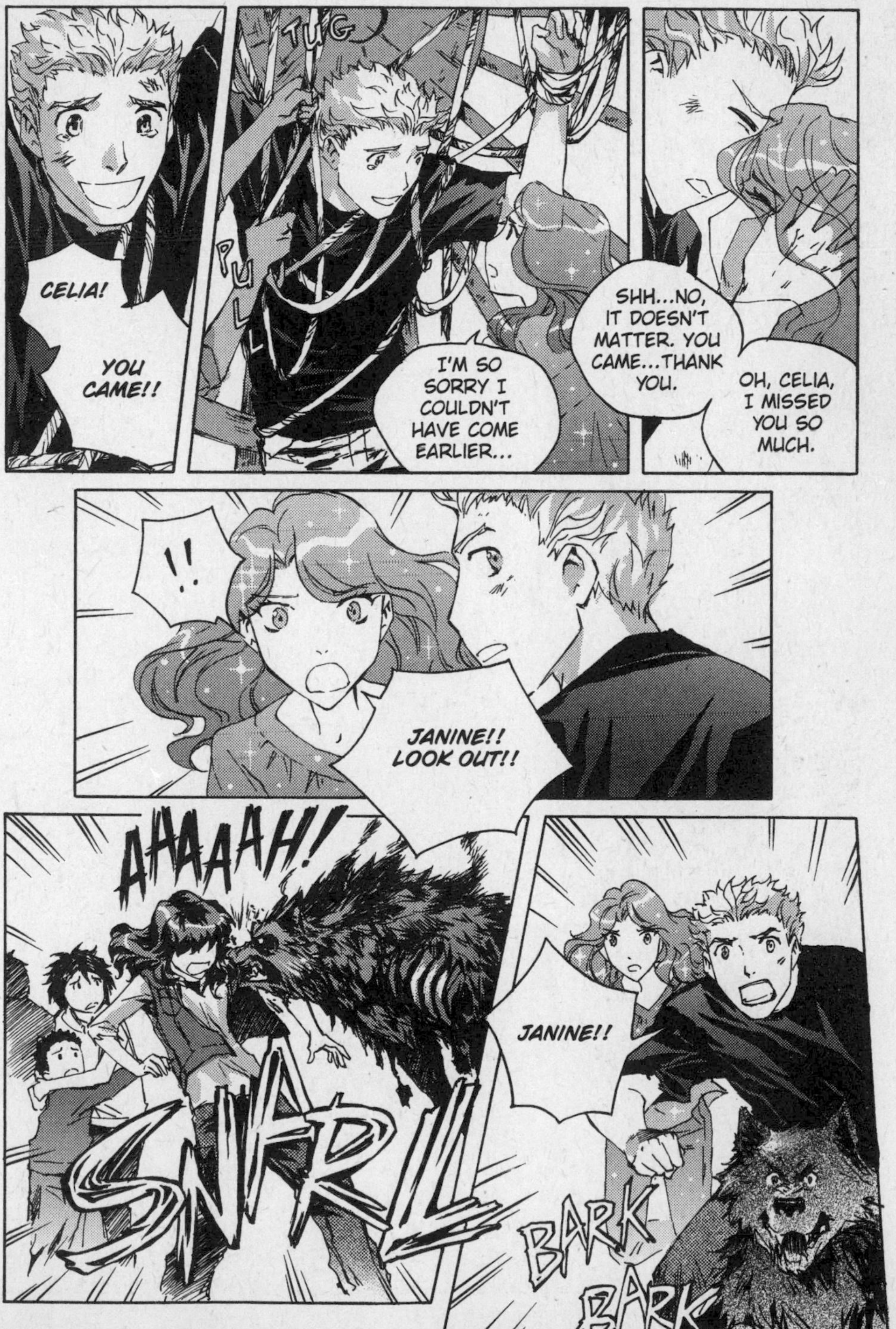
CELIA!
YOU CAME!!
TUG
PULL
I'M SO SORRY I COULDN'T HAVE COME EARLIER...
SHH...NO, IT DOESN'T MATTER. YOU CAME...THANK YOU.
OH, CELIA, I MISSED YOU SO MUCH.
!!
JANINE!! LOOK OUT!!
AHAAAH!
SNARL
JANINE!!
BARK
BARK

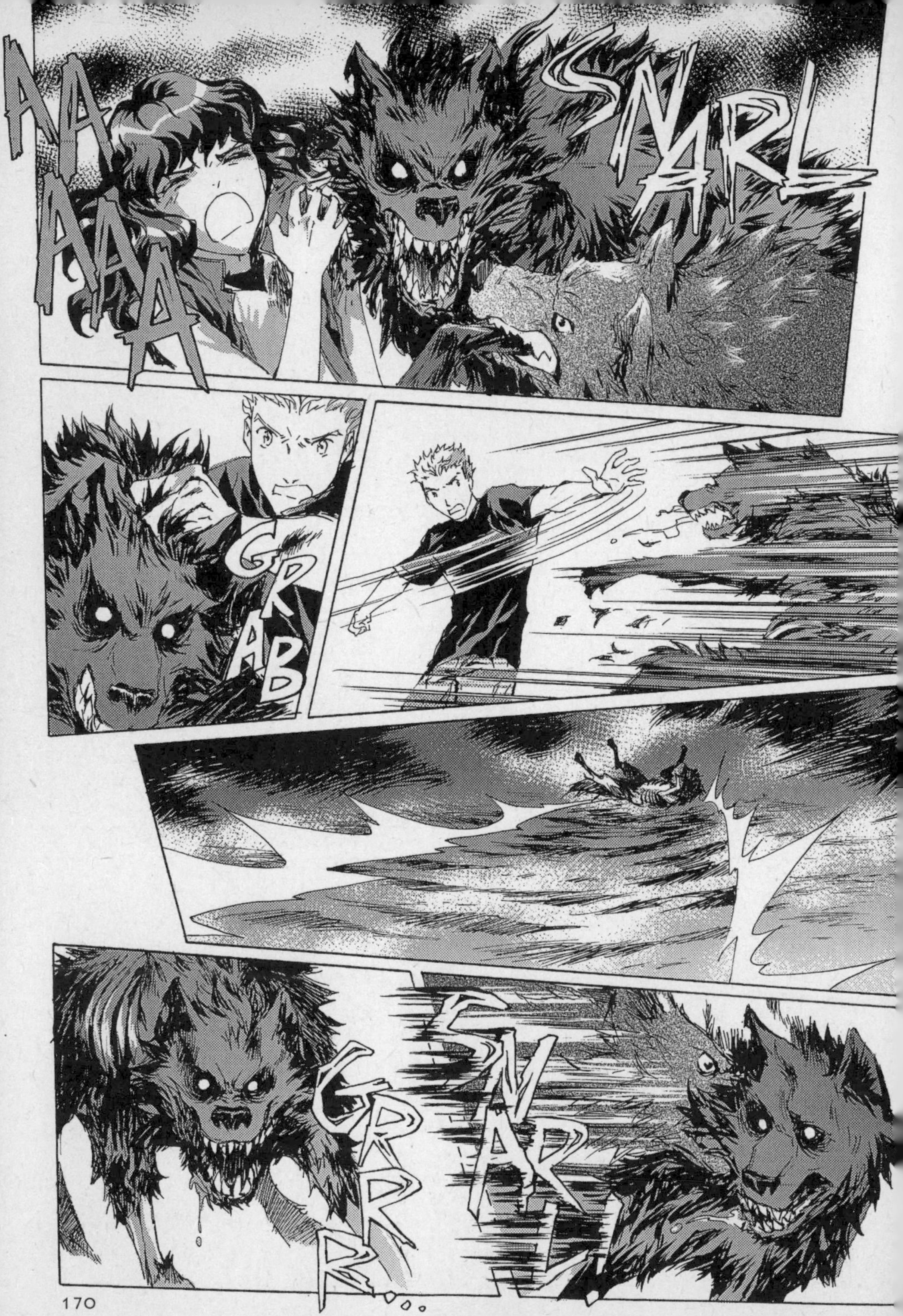
SNARL
AAAAAA
GRAB
GRRR...
SNARL

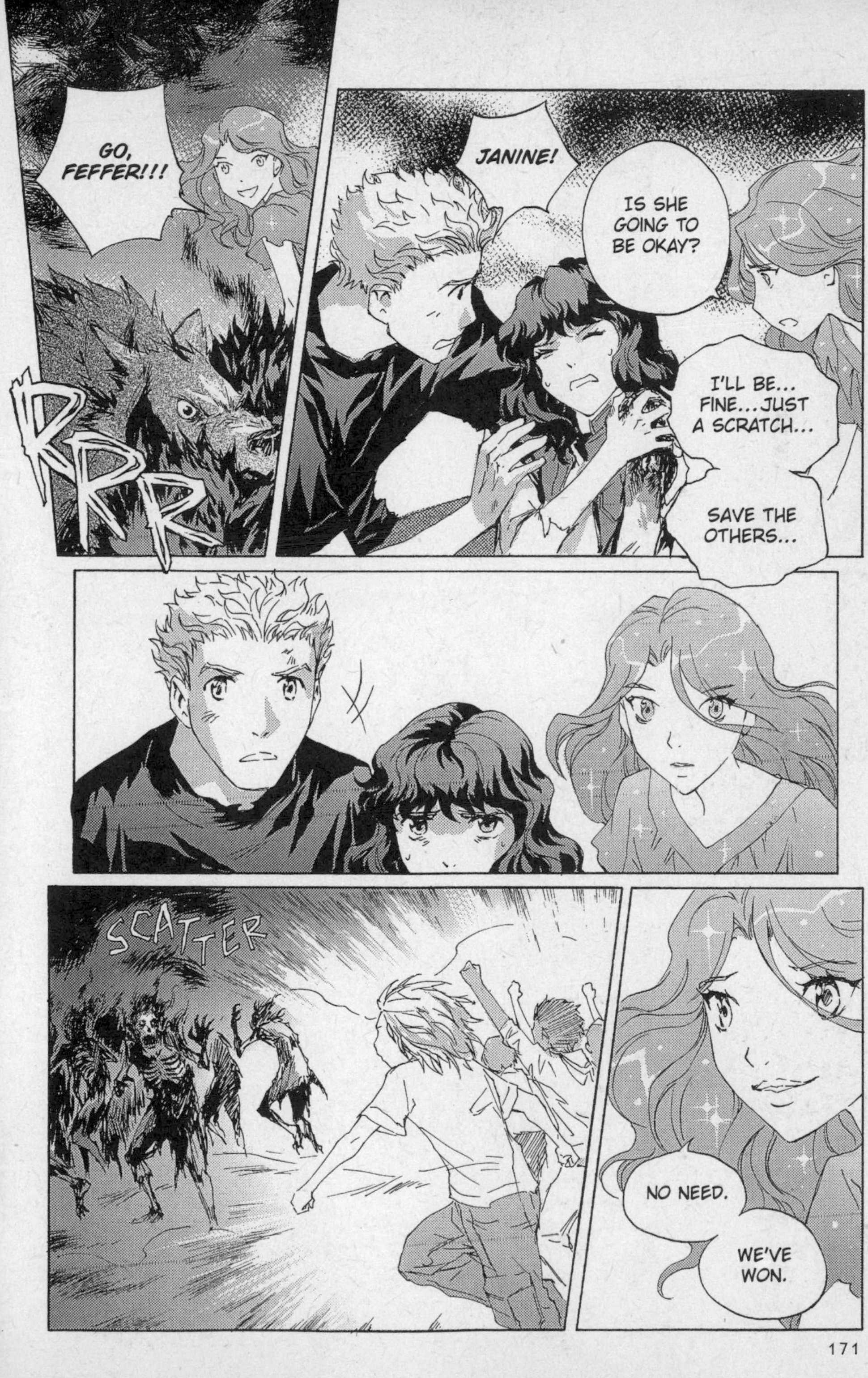
GO, FEFFER!!!
RRRR
JANINE!
IS SHE GOING TO BE OKAY?
I'LL BE... FINE... JUST A SCRATCH...
SAVE THE OTHERS...
SCATTER
NO NEED.
WE'VE WON.

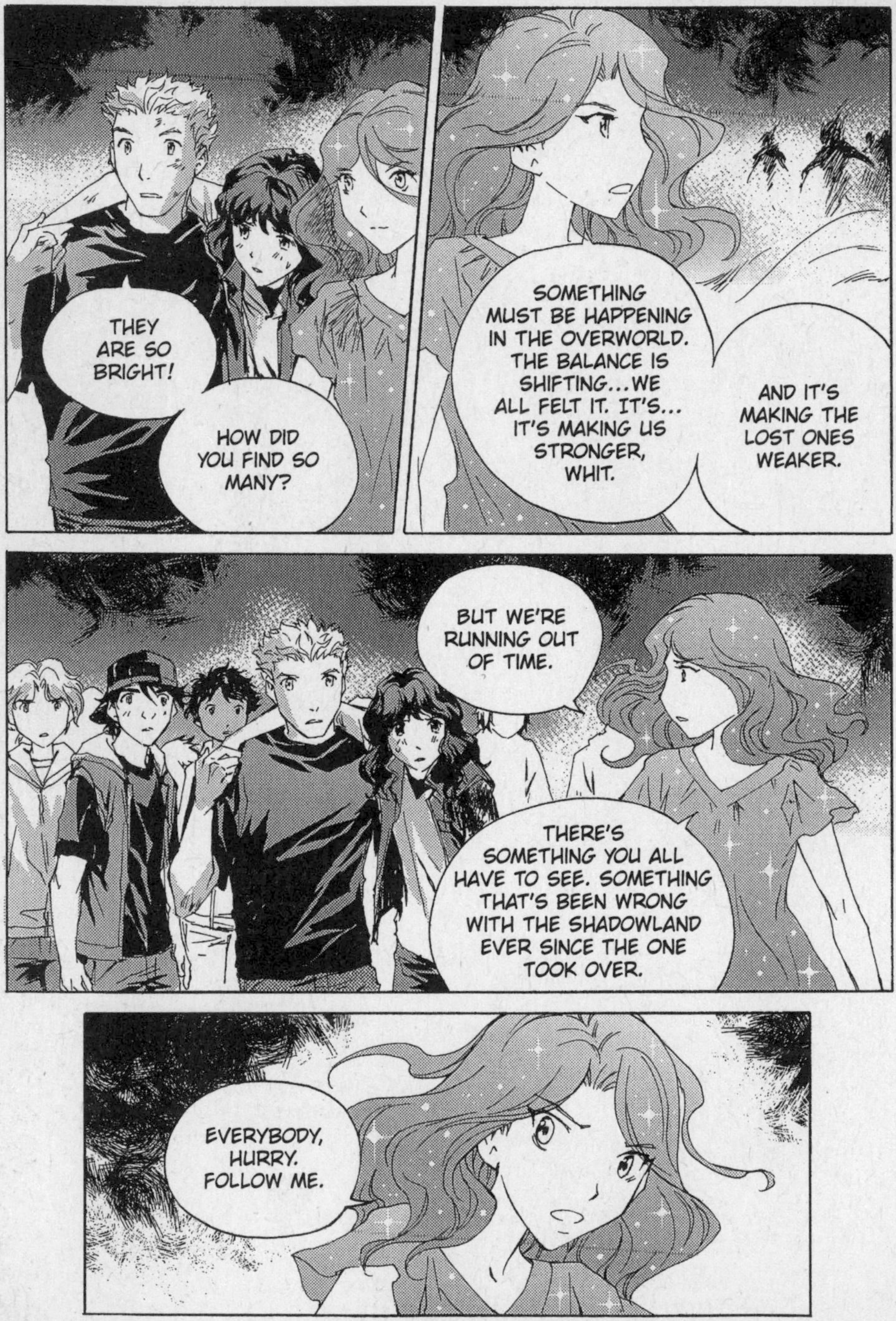
THEY ARE SO BRIGHT!
HOW DID YOU FIND SO MANY?
SOMETHING MUST BE HAPPENING IN THE OVERWORLD. THE BALANCE IS SHIFTING...WE ALL FELT IT. IT'S... IT'S MAKING US STRONGER, WHIT.
AND IT'S MAKING THE LOST ONES WEAKER.
BUT WE'RE RUNNING OUT OF TIME.
THERE'S SOMETHING YOU ALL HAVE TO SEE. SOMETHING THAT'S BEEN WRONG WITH THE SHADOWLAND EVER SINCE THE ONE TOOK OVER.
EVERYBODY, HURRY. FOLLOW ME.

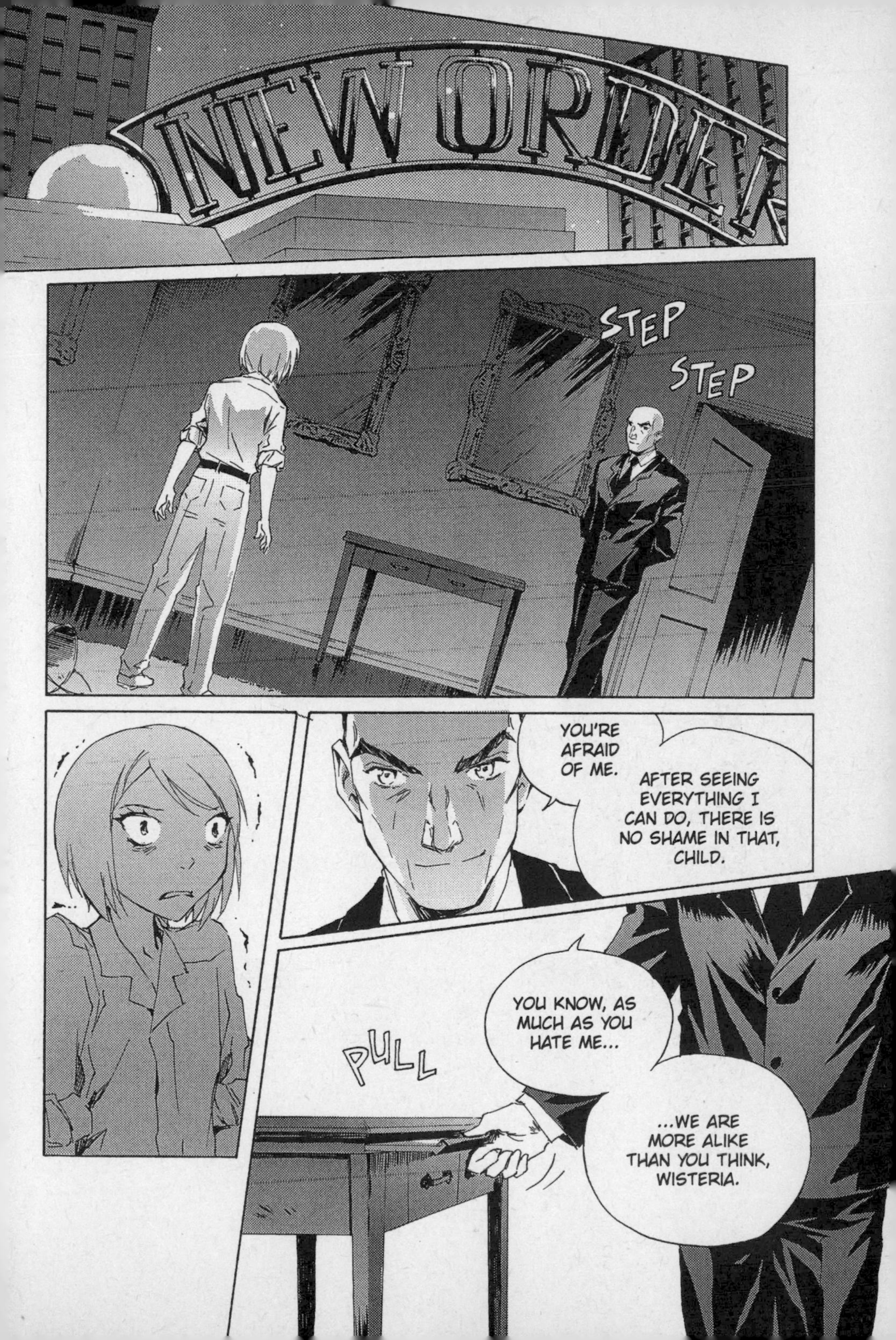
NEW ORDER
STEP
STEP
YOU'RE AFRAID OF ME.
AFTER SEEING EVERYTHING I CAN DO, THERE IS NO SHAME IN THAT, CHILD.
YOU KNOW, AS MUCH AS YOU HATE ME...
PULL
...WE ARE MORE ALIKE THAN YOU THINK, WISTERIA.

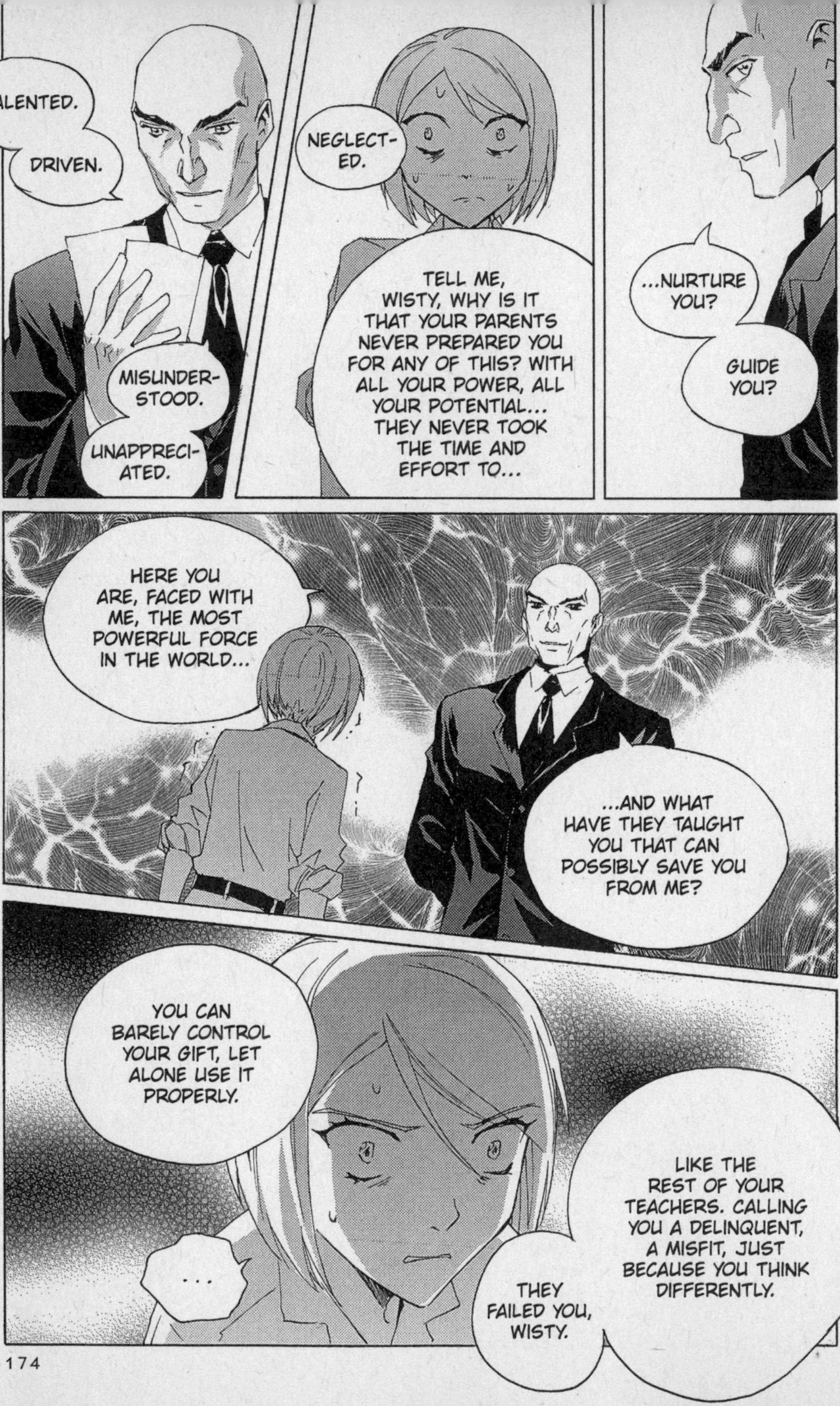
TALENTED.
DRIVEN.
MISUNDER-STOOD.
UNAPPRECI-ATED.
NEGLECT-ED.
TELL ME, WISTY, WHY IS IT THAT YOUR PARENTS NEVER PREPARED YOU FOR ANY OF THIS? WITH ALL YOUR POWER, ALL YOUR POTENTIAL... THEY NEVER TOOK THE TIME AND EFFORT TO...
...NURTURE YOU?
GUIDE YOU?
HERE YOU ARE, FACED WITH ME, THE MOST POWERFUL FORCE IN THE WORLD...
...AND WHAT HAVE THEY TAUGHT YOU THAT CAN POSSIBLY SAVE YOU FROM ME?
YOU CAN BARELY CONTROL YOUR GIFT, LET ALONE USE IT PROPERLY.
LIKE THE REST OF YOUR TEACHERS. CALLING YOU A DELINQUENT, A MISFIT, JUST BECAUSE YOU THINK DIFFERENTLY.
THEY FAILED YOU, WISTY.
...

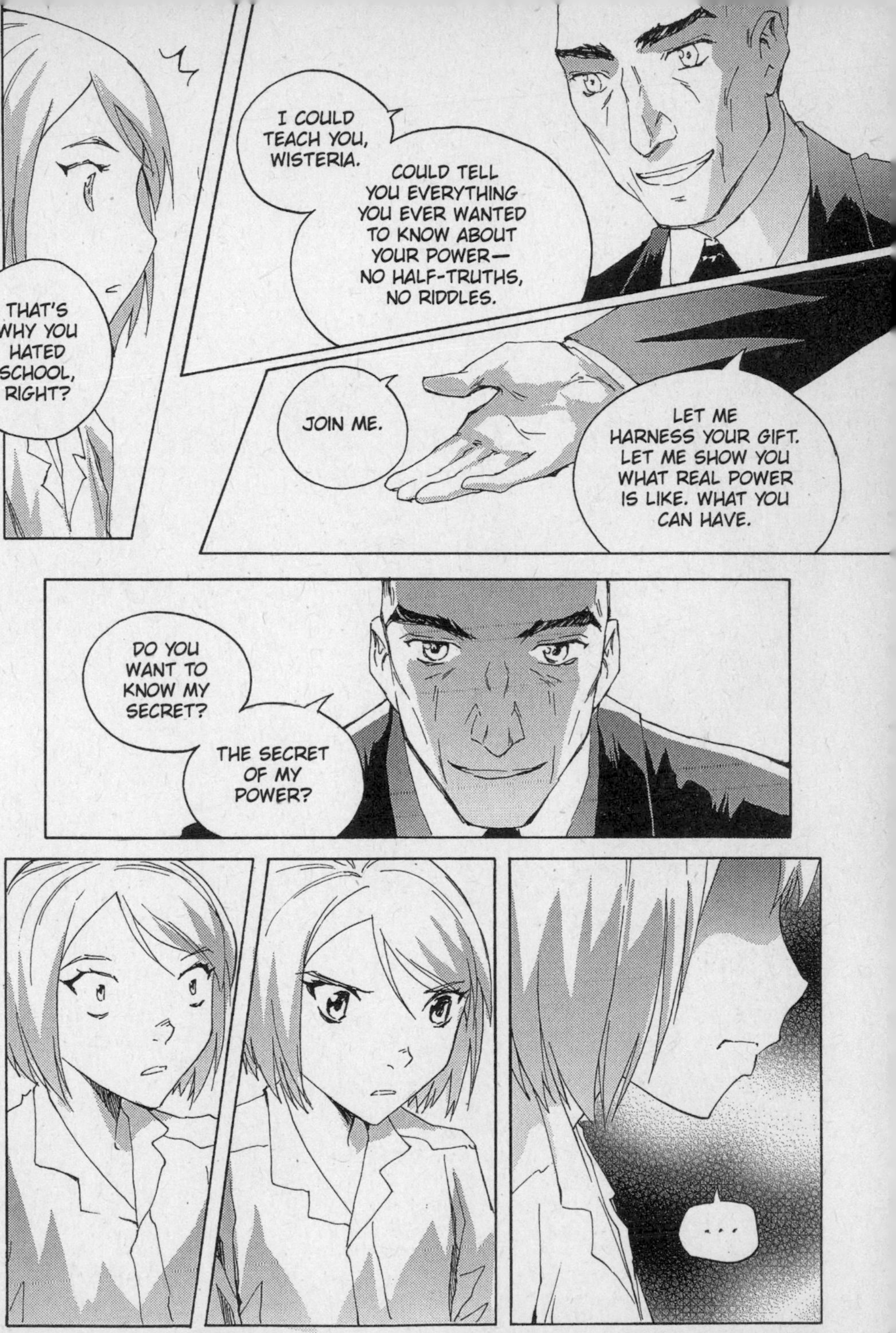
THAT'S WHY YOU HATED SCHOOL, RIGHT?
I COULD TEACH YOU, WISTERIA.
COULD TELL YOU EVERYTHING YOU EVER WANTED TO KNOW ABOUT YOUR POWER—NO HALF-TRUTHS, NO RIDDLES.
JOIN ME.
LET ME HARNESS YOUR GIFT. LET ME SHOW YOU WHAT REAL POWER IS LIKE. WHAT YOU CAN HAVE.
DO YOU WANT TO KNOW MY SECRET?
THE SECRET OF MY POWER?
...

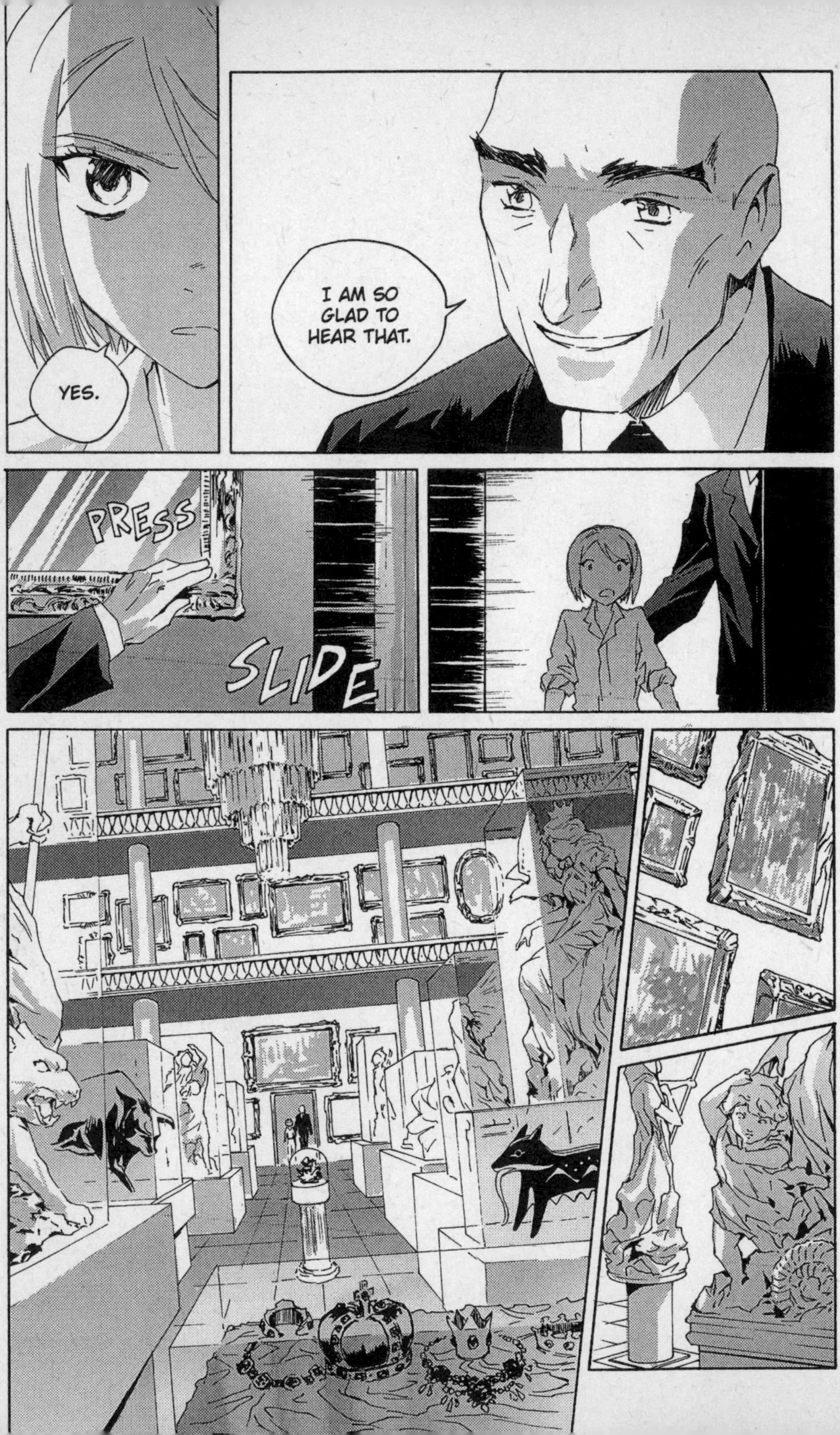
YES.
I AM SO GLAD TO HEAR THAT.
PRESS
SLIDE

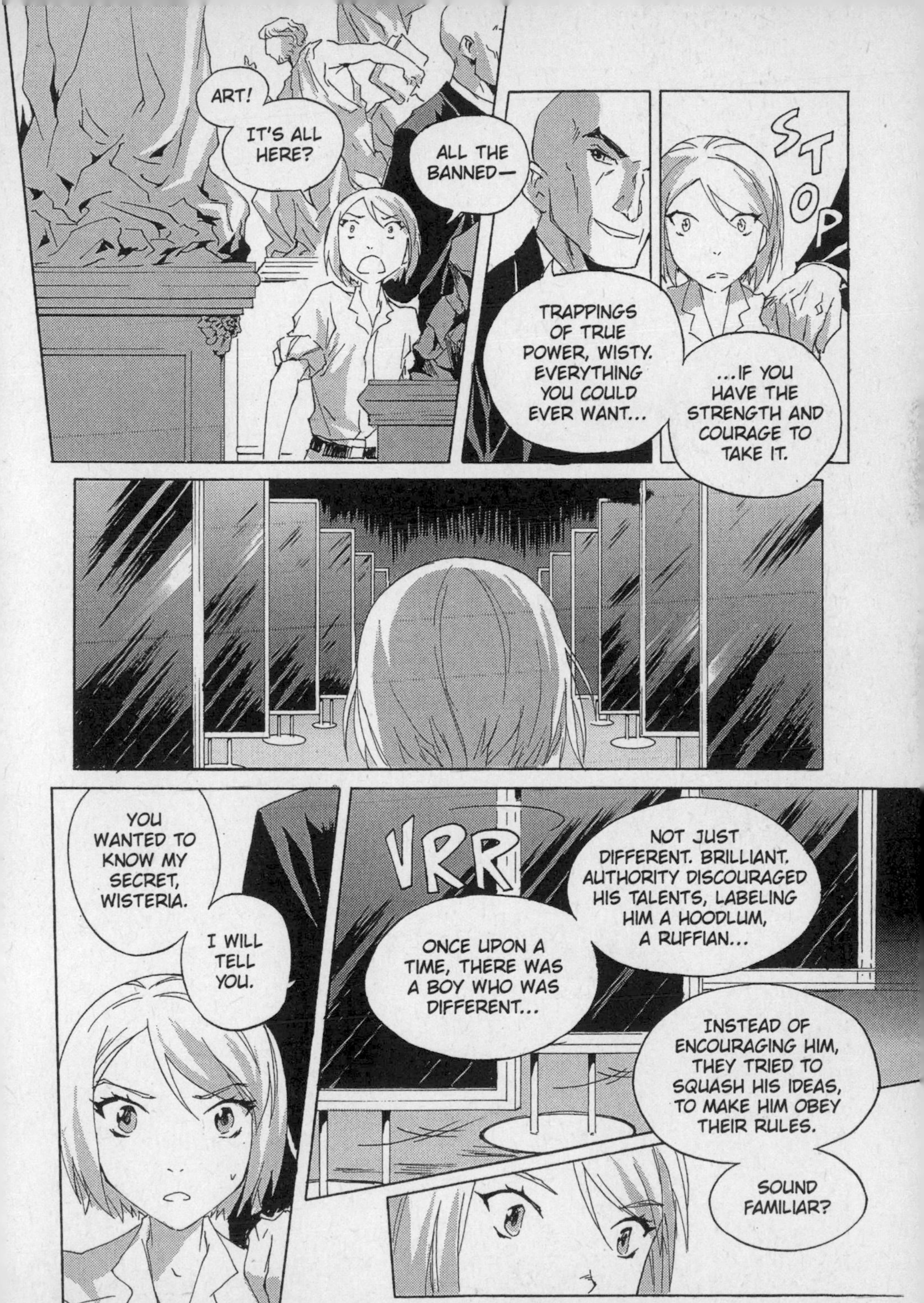
ART!
IT'S ALL HERE?
ALL THE BANNED—
TRAPPINGS OF TRUE POWER, WISTY. EVERYTHING YOU COULD EVER WANT...
STOP
...IF YOU HAVE THE STRENGTH AND COURAGE TO TAKE IT.
YOU WANTED TO KNOW MY SECRET, WISTERIA.
I WILL TELL YOU.
VRR
ONCE UPON A TIME, THERE WAS A BOY WHO WAS DIFFERENT...
NOT JUST DIFFERENT. BRILLIANT. AUTHORITY DISCOURAGED HIS TALENTS, LABELING HIM A HOODLUM, A RUFFIAN...
INSTEAD OF ENCOURAGING HIM, THEY TRIED TO SQUASH HIS IDEAS, TO MAKE HIM OBEY THEIR RULES.
SOUND FAMILIAR?

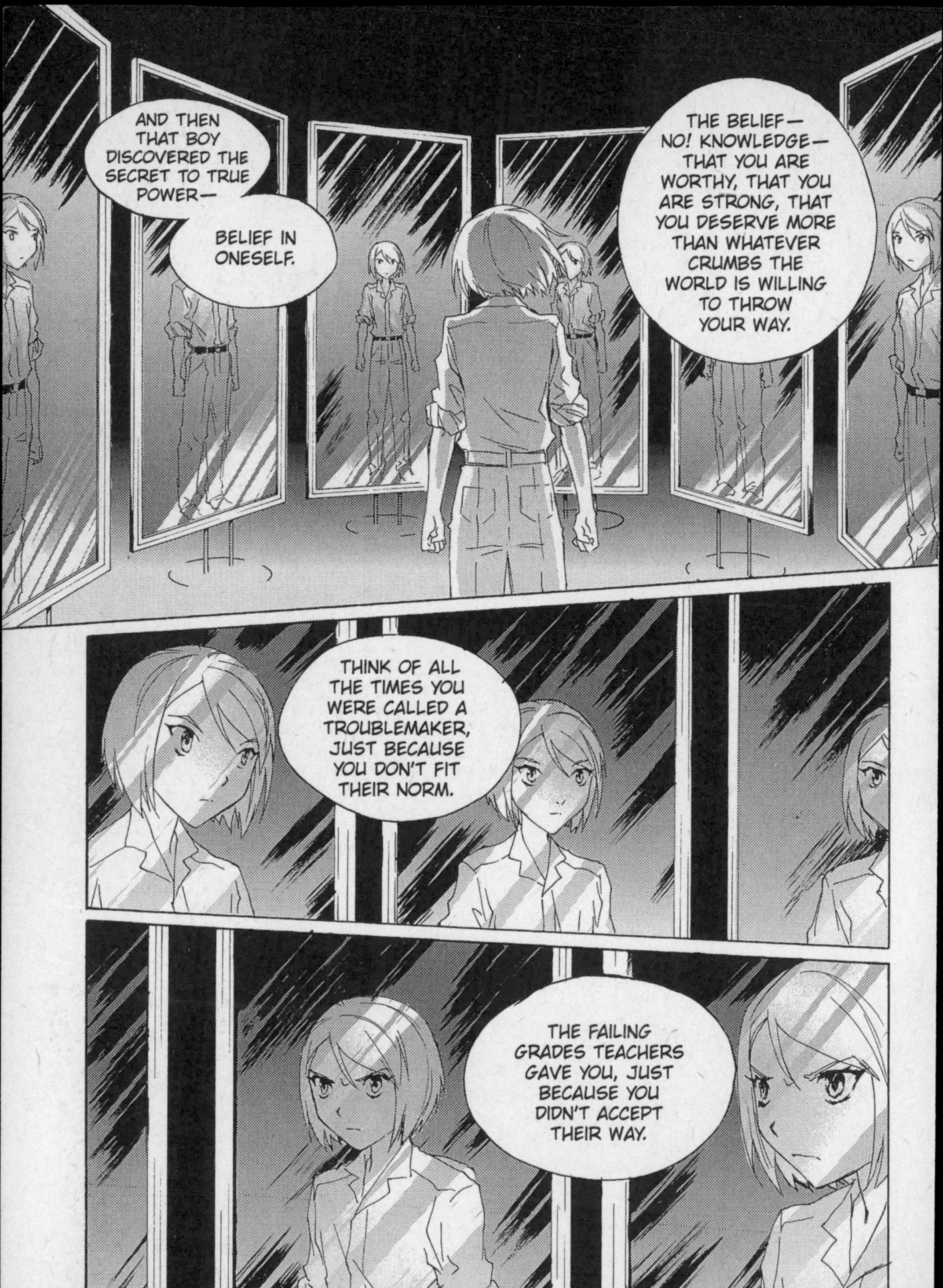
AND THEN THAT BOY DISCOVERED THE SECRET TO TRUE POWER—
BELIEF IN ONESELF.
THE BELIEF—NO! KNOWLEDGE—THAT YOU ARE WORTHY, THAT YOU ARE STRONG, THAT YOU DESERVE MORE THAN WHATEVER CRUMBS THE WORLD IS WILLING TO THROW YOUR WAY.
THINK OF ALL THE TIMES YOU WERE CALLED A TROUBLEMAKER, JUST BECAUSE YOU DON'T FIT THEIR NORM.
THE FAILING GRADES TEACHERS GAVE YOU, JUST BECAUSE YOU DIDN'T ACCEPT THEIR WAY.

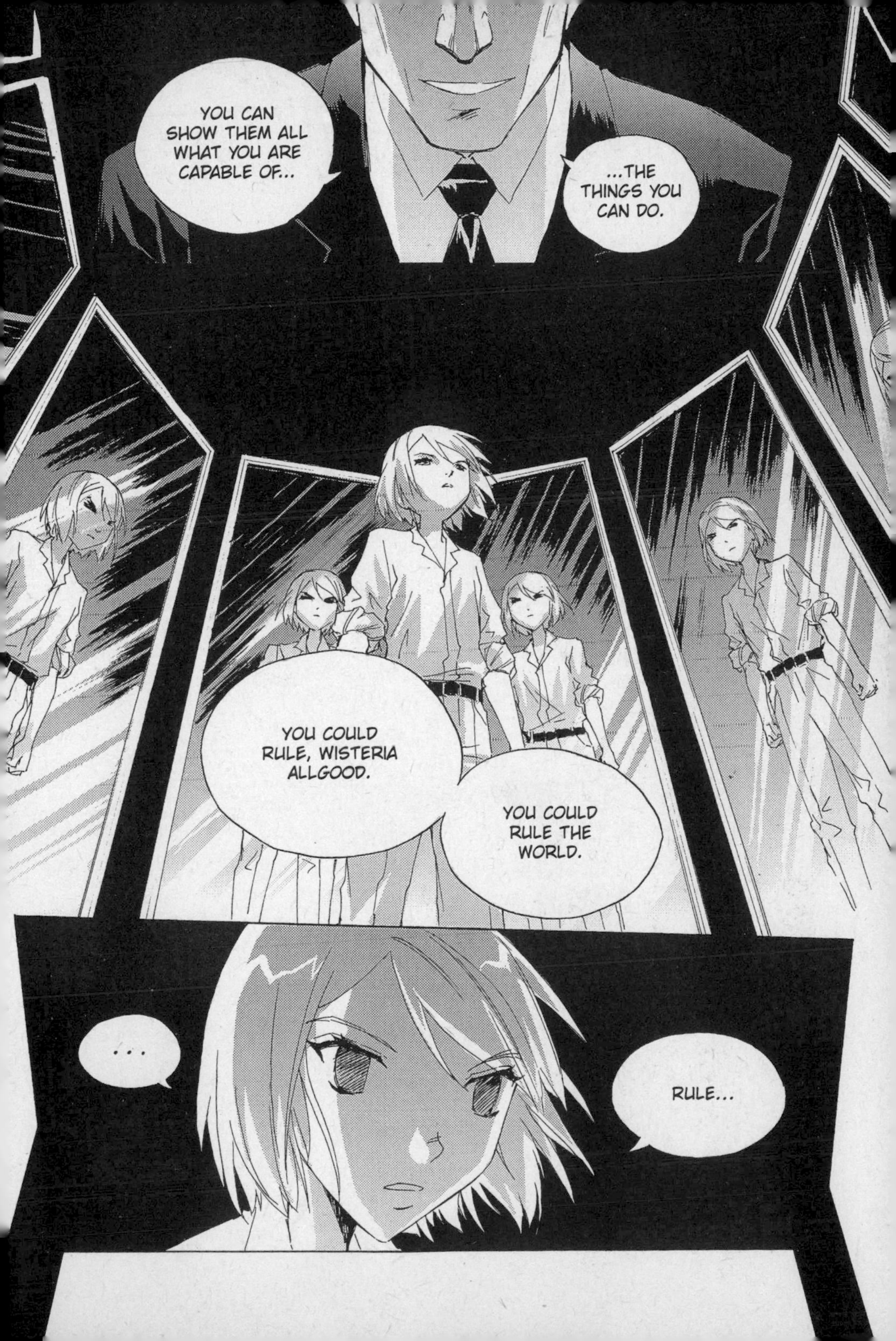
YOU CAN SHOW THEM ALL WHAT YOU ARE CAPABLE OF...
...THE THINGS YOU CAN DO.
YOU COULD RULE, WISTERIA ALLGOOD.
YOU COULD RULE THE WORLD.
...
RULE...

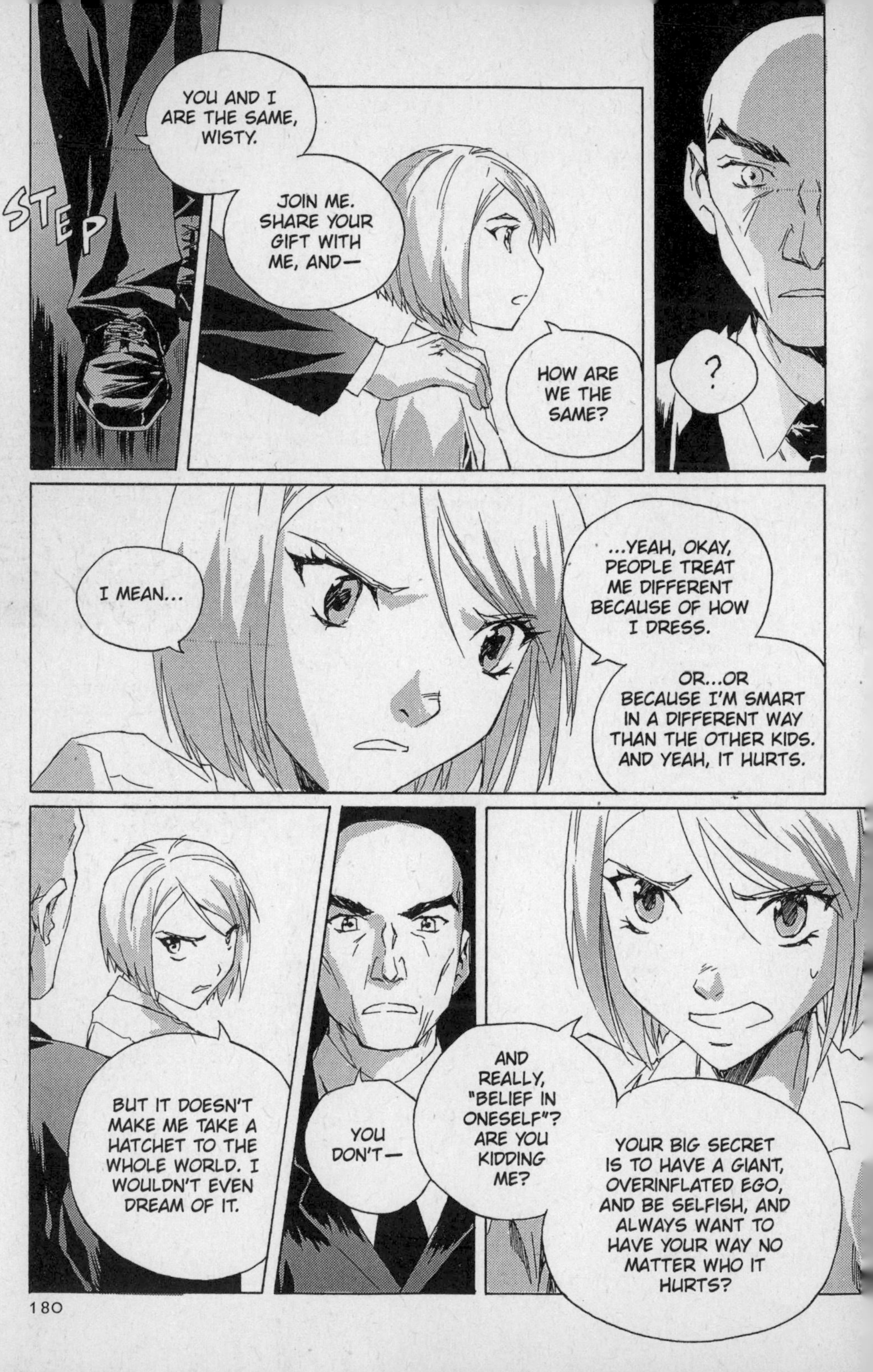
YOU AND I ARE THE SAME, WISTY.
STEP
JOIN ME. SHARE YOUR GIFT WITH ME, AND—
HOW ARE WE THE SAME?
?
I MEAN...
...YEAH, OKAY, PEOPLE TREAT ME DIFFERENT BECAUSE OF HOW I DRESS.
OR...OR BECAUSE I'M SMART IN A DIFFERENT WAY THAN THE OTHER KIDS. AND YEAH, IT HURTS.
BUT IT DOESN'T MAKE ME TAKE A HATCHET TO THE WHOLE WORLD. I WOULDN'T EVEN DREAM OF IT.
YOU DON'T—
AND REALLY, "BELIEF IN ONESELF"? ARE YOU KIDDING ME?
YOUR BIG SECRET IS TO HAVE A GIANT, OVERINFLATED EGO, AND BE SELFISH, AND ALWAYS WANT TO HAVE YOUR WAY NO MATTER WHO IT HURTS?

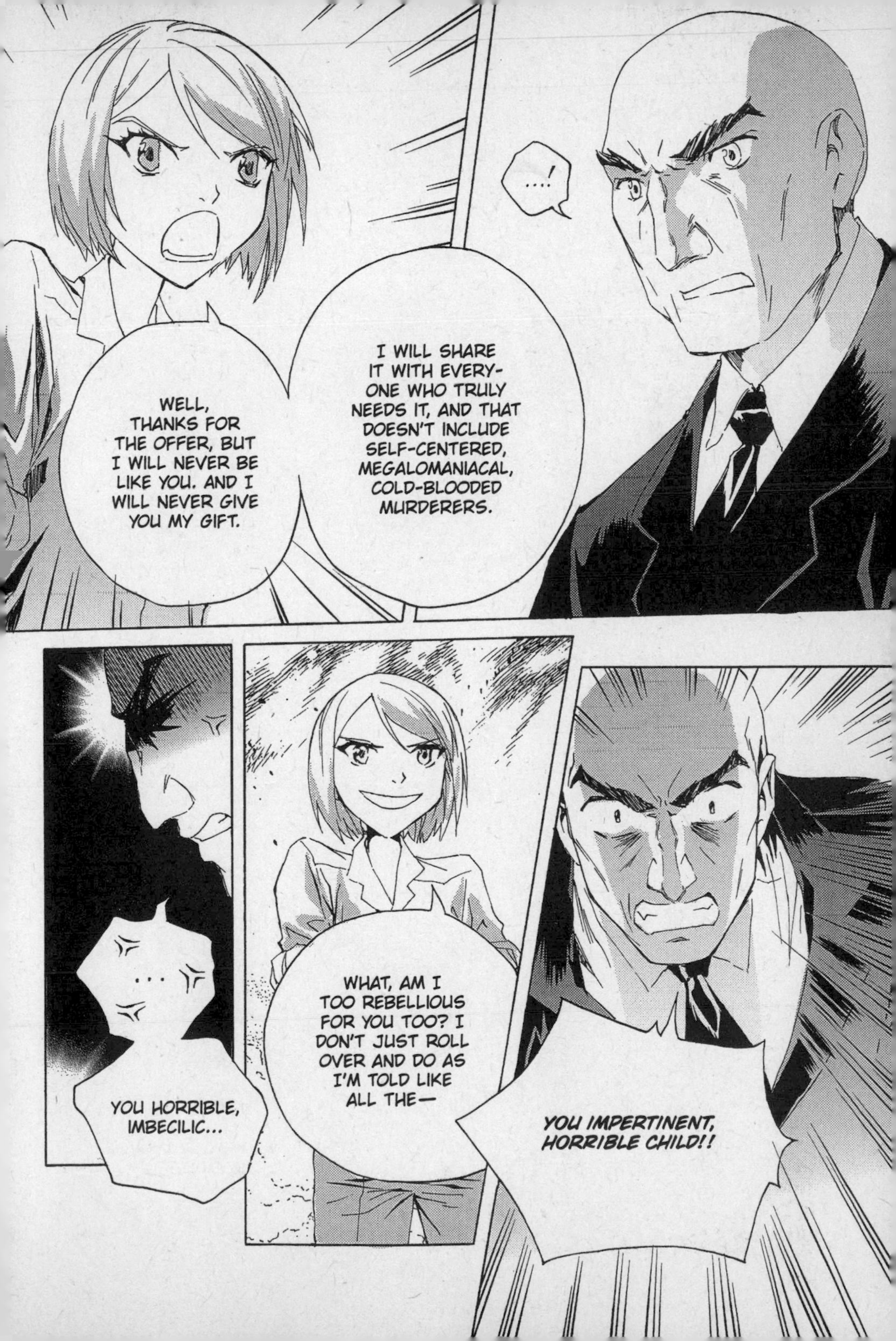
....!
WELL, THANKS FOR THE OFFER, BUT I WILL NEVER BE LIKE YOU. AND I WILL NEVER GIVE YOU MY GIFT.
I WILL SHARE IT WITH EVERY-ONE WHO TRULY NEEDS IT, AND THAT DOESN'T INCLUDE SELF-CENTERED, MEGALOMANIACAL, COLD-BLOODED MURDERERS.
...
YOU HORRIBLE, IMBECILIC...
WHAT, AM I TOO REBELLIOUS FOR YOU TOO? I DON'T JUST ROLL OVER AND DO AS I'M TOLD LIKE ALL THE—
YOU IMPERTINENT, HORRIBLE CHILD!!

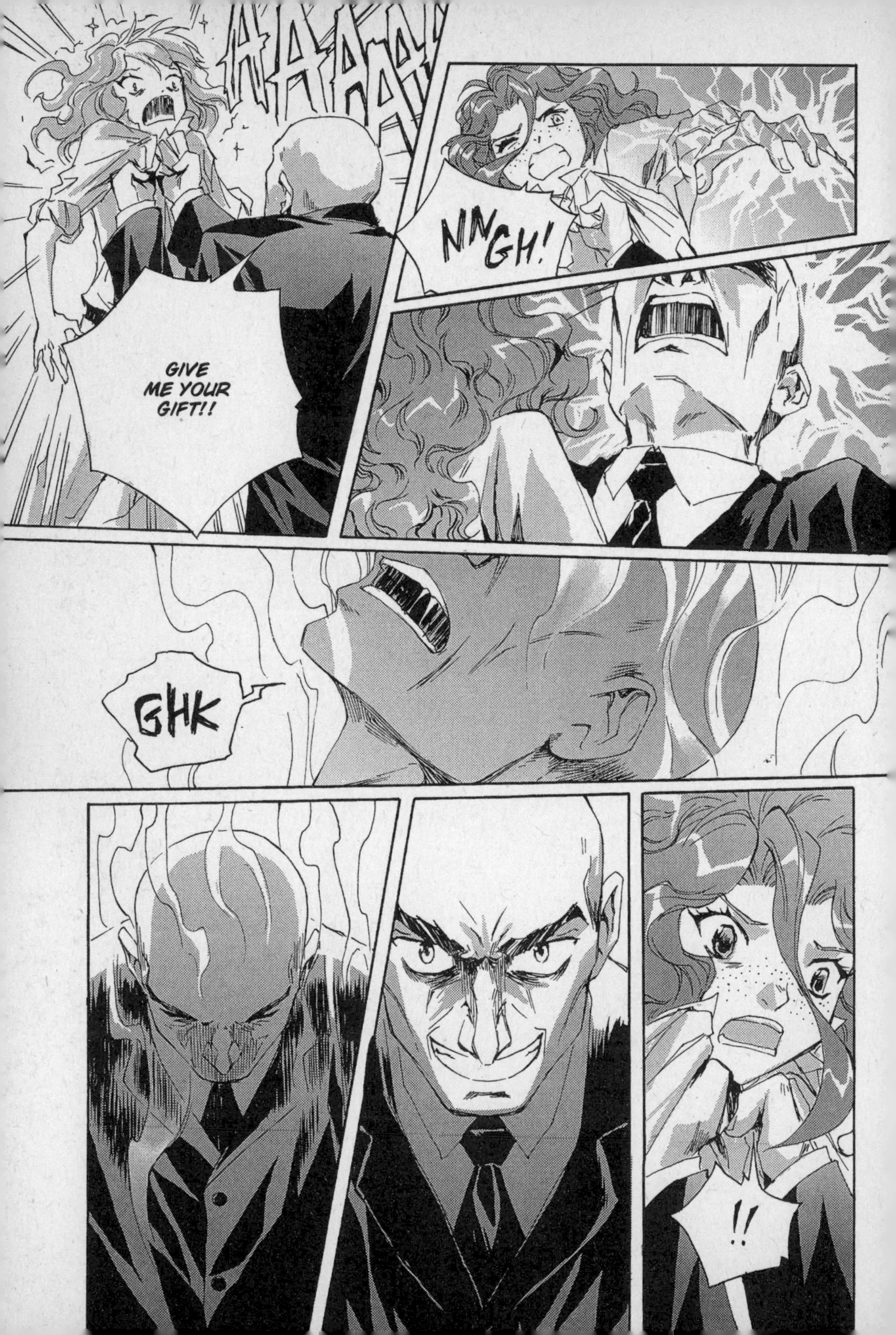
GIVE ME YOUR GIFT!!
NNGH!
GHK
!!

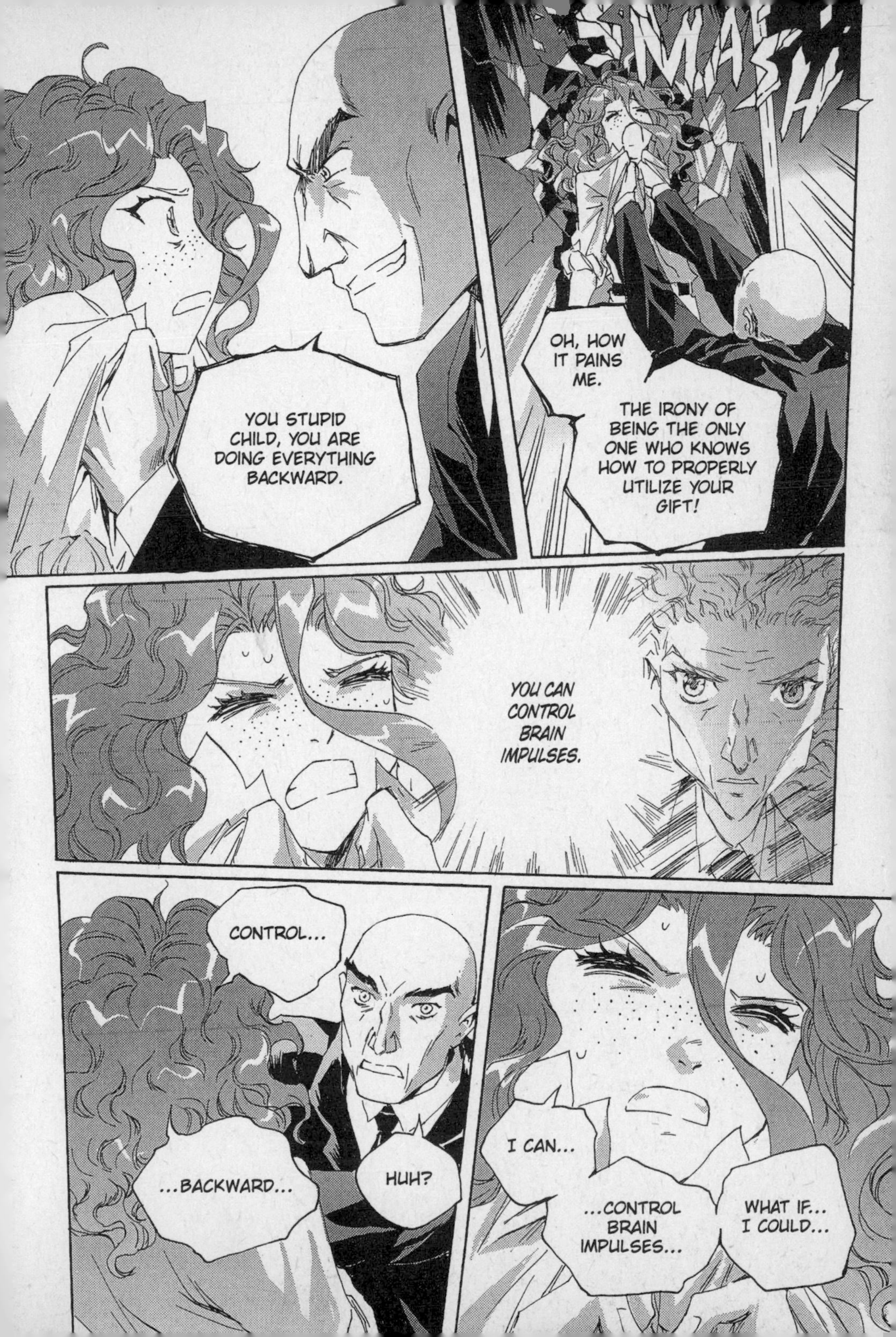
YOU STUPID CHILD, YOU ARE DOING EVERYTHING BACKWARD.
SMASH!
OH, HOW IT PAINS ME.
THE IRONY OF BEING THE ONLY ONE WHO KNOWS HOW TO PROPERLY UTILIZE YOUR GIFT!
YOU CAN CONTROL BRAIN IMPULSES.
CONTROL...
...BACKWARD...
HUH?
I CAN...
...CONTROL BRAIN IMPULSES...
WHAT IF... I COULD...

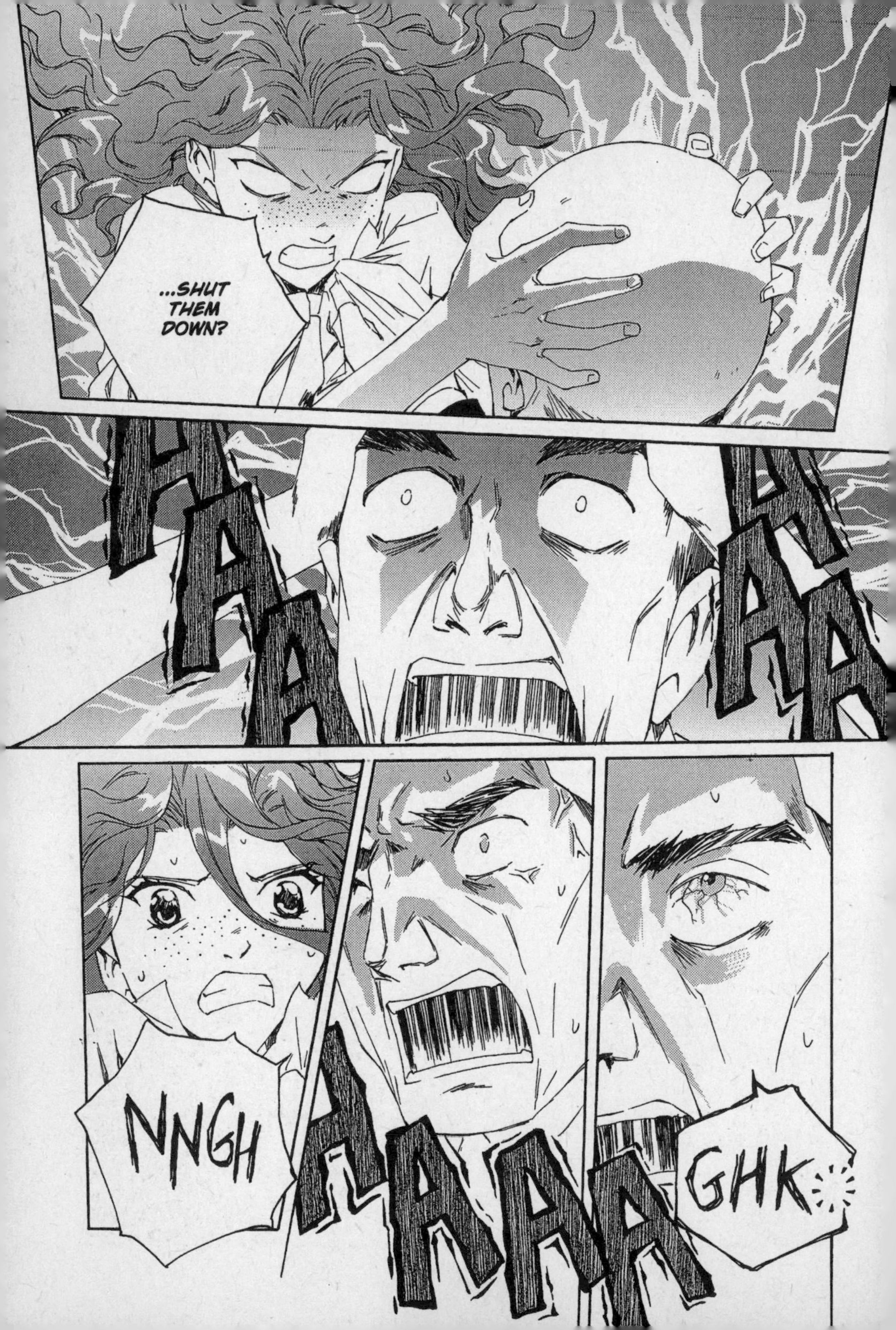
...SHUT THEM DOWN?
HAAAA
AAAA
NNGH
AAAA
GHK

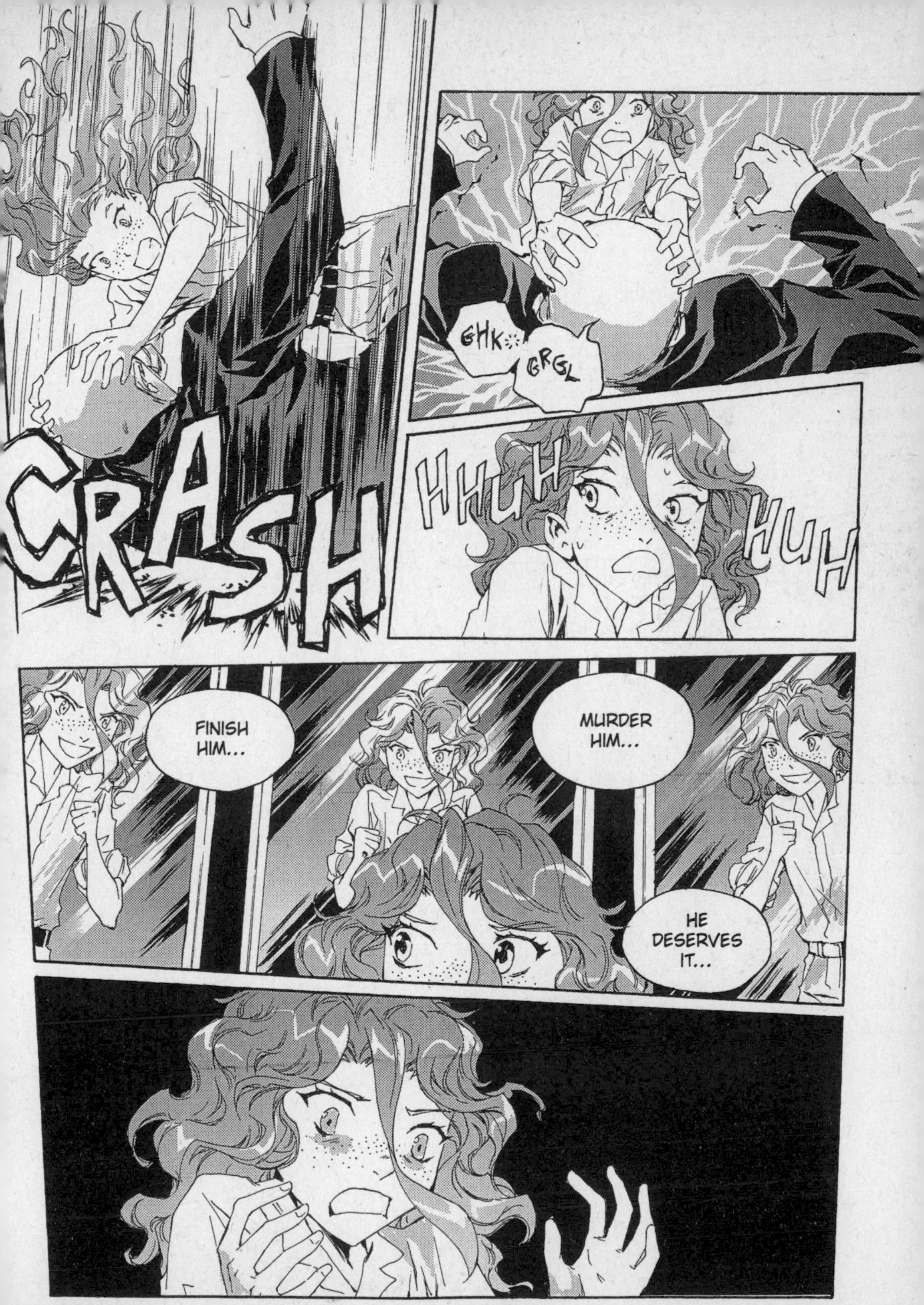
CRASH
GHK
GRGL
HHUH
HUH
FINISH HIM...
MURDER HIM...
HE DESERVES IT...

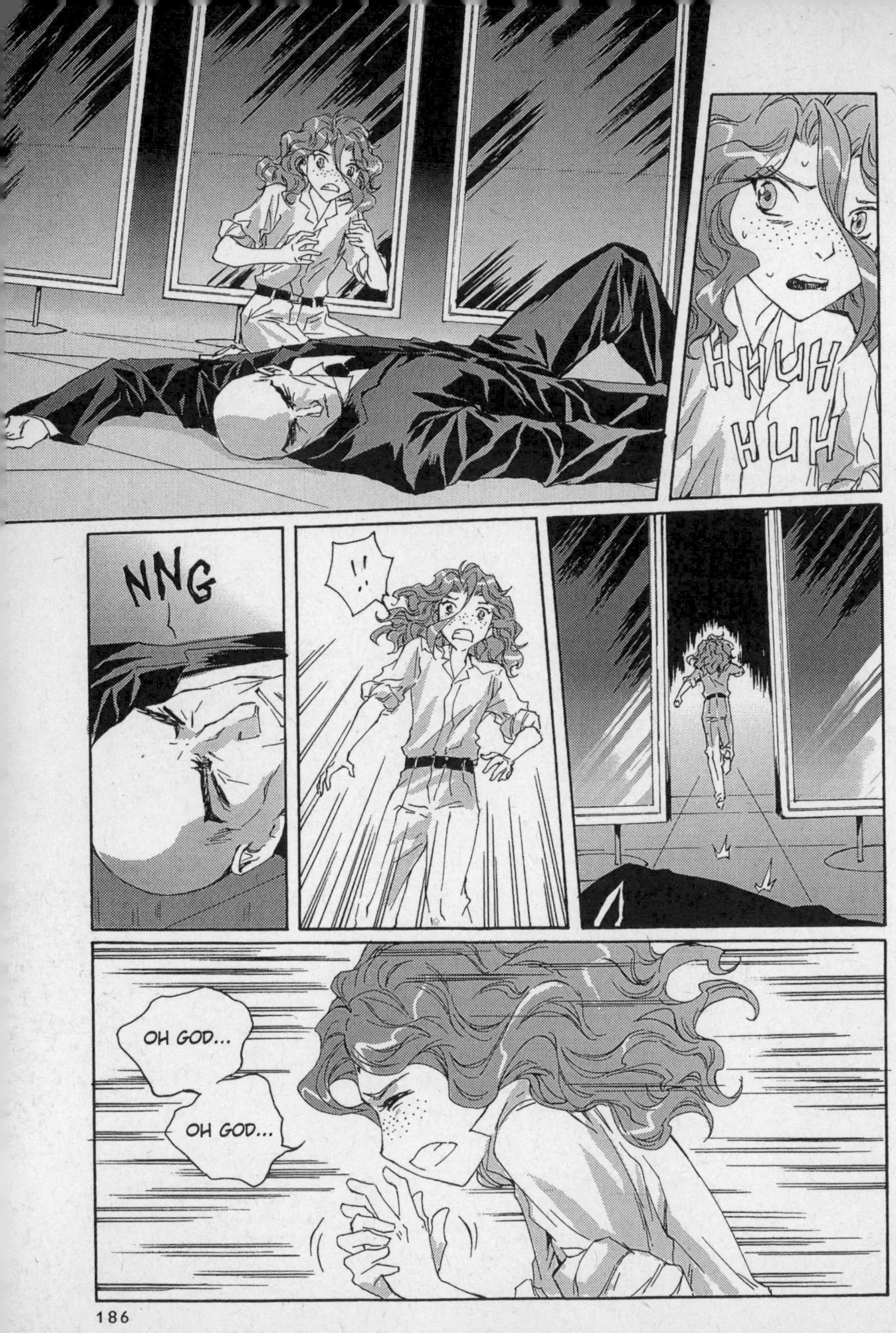
HHUH
HUH
NNG
!!
OH GOD...
OH GOD...

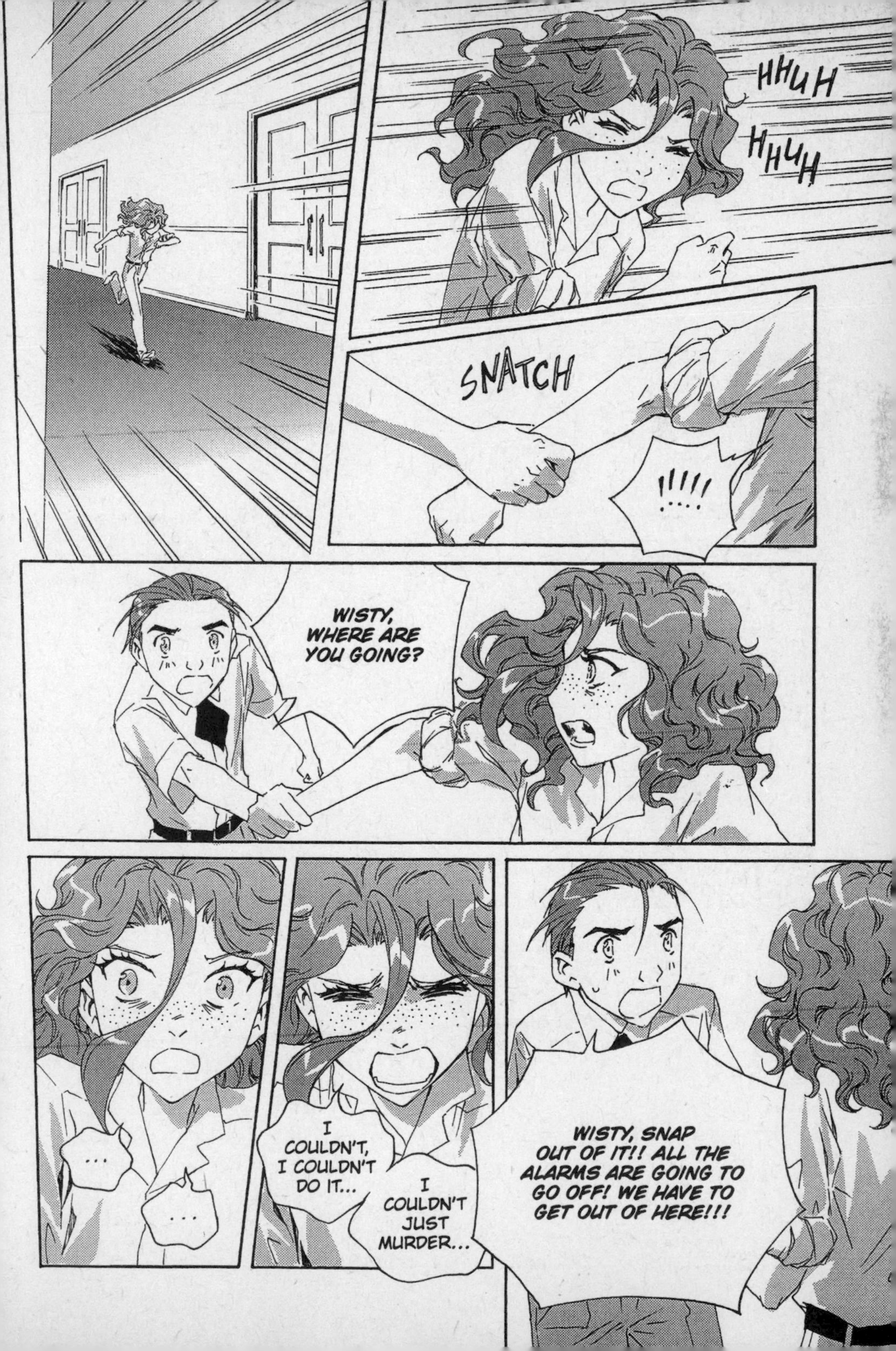
HHUH
HHUH
SNATCH
!!!!
WISTY, WHERE ARE YOU GOING?
...
...
I COULDN'T, I COULDN'T DO IT...
I COULDN'T JUST MURDER...
WISTY, SNAP OUT OF IT!! ALL THE ALARMS ARE GOING TO GO OFF! WE HAVE TO GET OUT OF HERE!!!

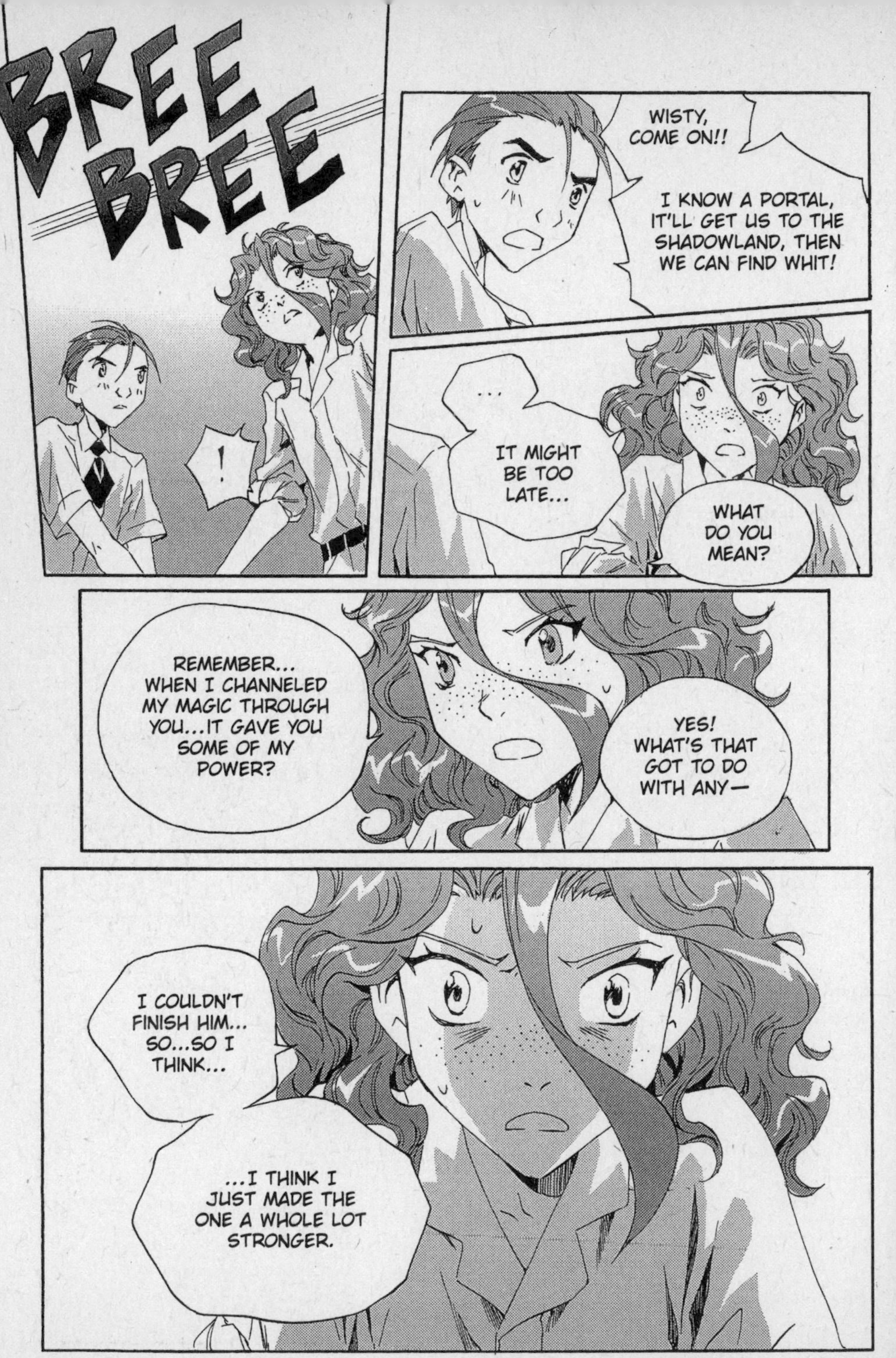
BREE BREE
!
WISTY, COME ON!!
I KNOW A PORTAL, IT'LL GET US TO THE SHADOWLAND, THEN WE CAN FIND WHIT!
...
IT MIGHT BE TOO LATE...
WHAT DO YOU MEAN?
REMEMBER... WHEN I CHANNELED MY MAGIC THROUGH YOU...IT GAVE YOU SOME OF MY POWER?
YES! WHAT'S THAT GOT TO DO WITH ANY—
I COULDN'T FINISH HIM... SO...SO I THINK...
...I THINK I JUST MADE THE ONE A WHOLE LOT STRONGER.

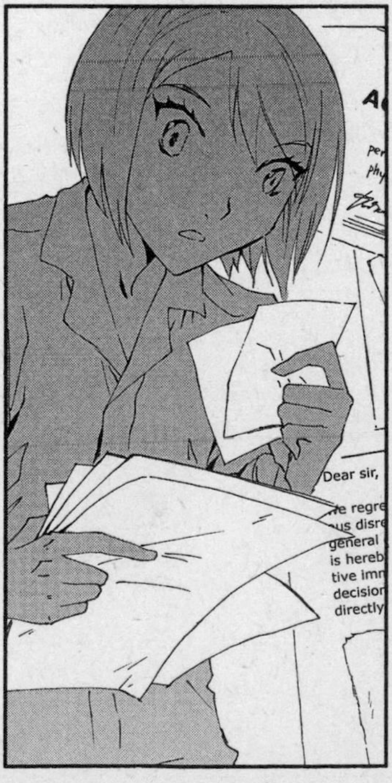
Dear sir,

WITCH
&
WIZARD

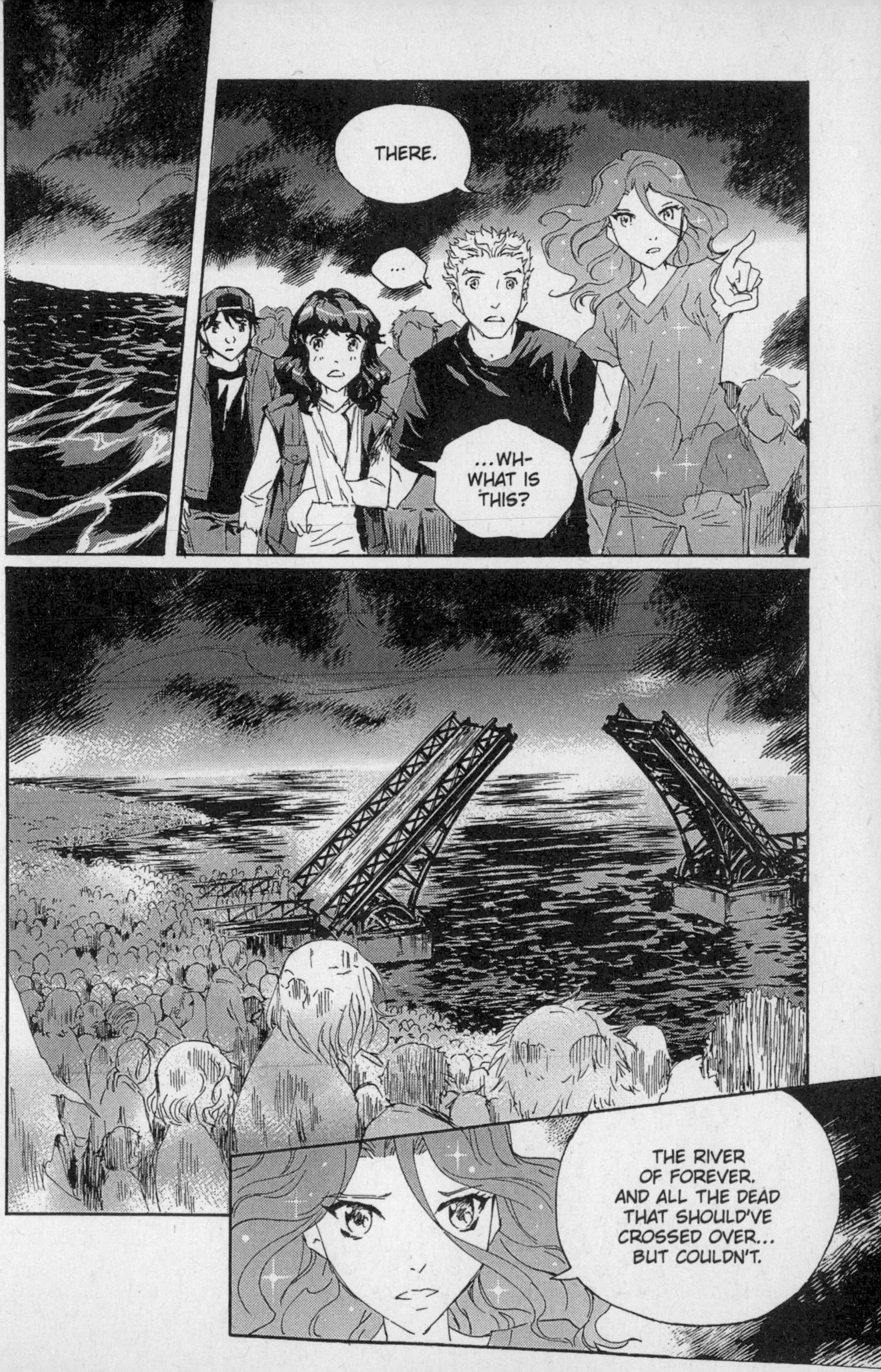
THERE.
...
...WH- WHAT IS THIS?
THE RIVER OF FOREVER. AND ALL THE DEAD THAT SHOULD'VE CROSSED OVER... BUT COULDN'T.

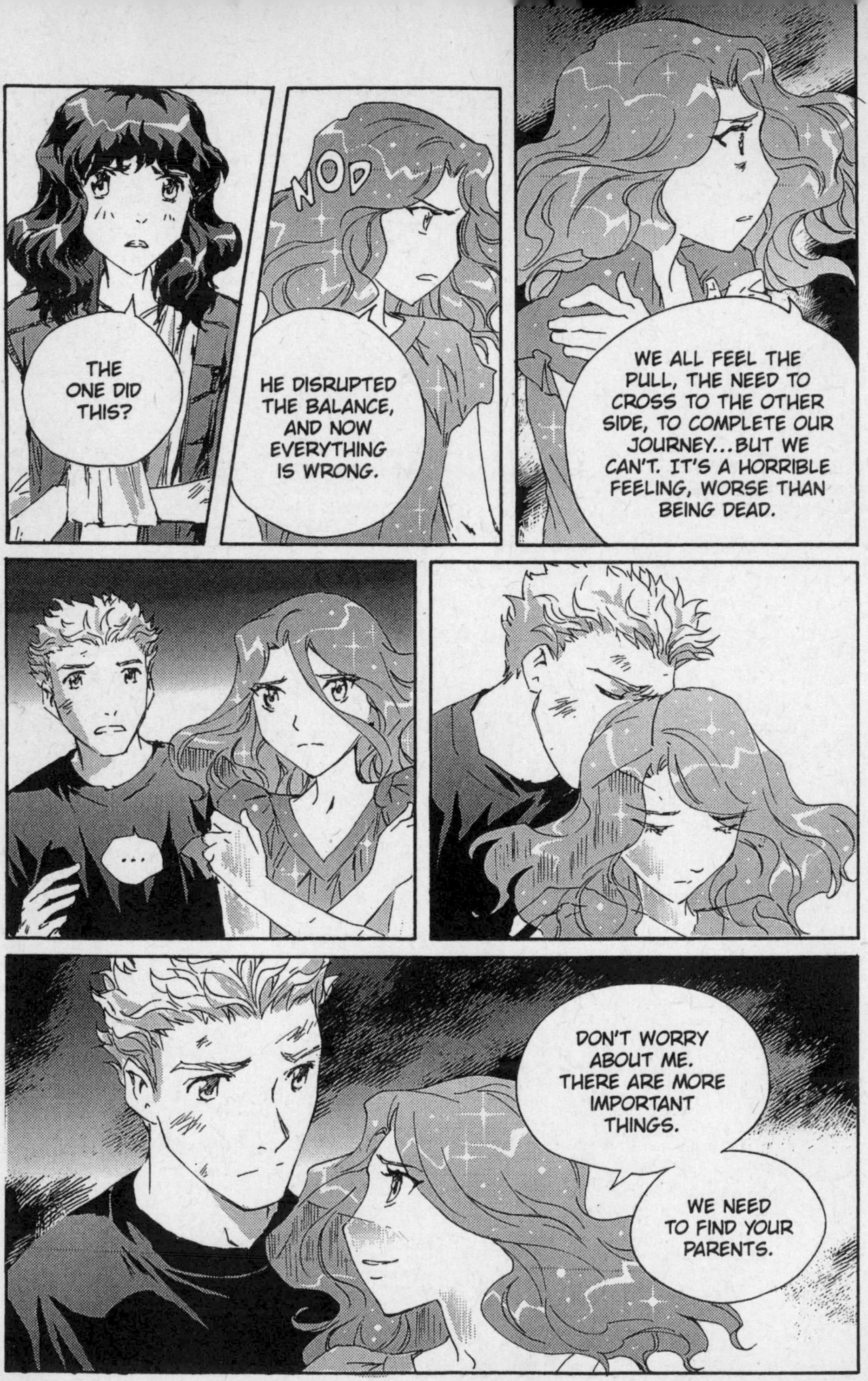
THE ONE DID THIS?
NOD
HE DISRUPTED THE BALANCE, AND NOW EVERYTHING IS WRONG.
WE ALL FEEL THE PULL, THE NEED TO CROSS TO THE OTHER SIDE, TO COMPLETE OUR JOURNEY...BUT WE CAN'T. IT'S A HORRIBLE FEELING, WORSE THAN BEING DEAD.
...
DON'T WORRY ABOUT ME. THERE ARE MORE IMPORTANT THINGS.
WE NEED TO FIND YOUR PARENTS.

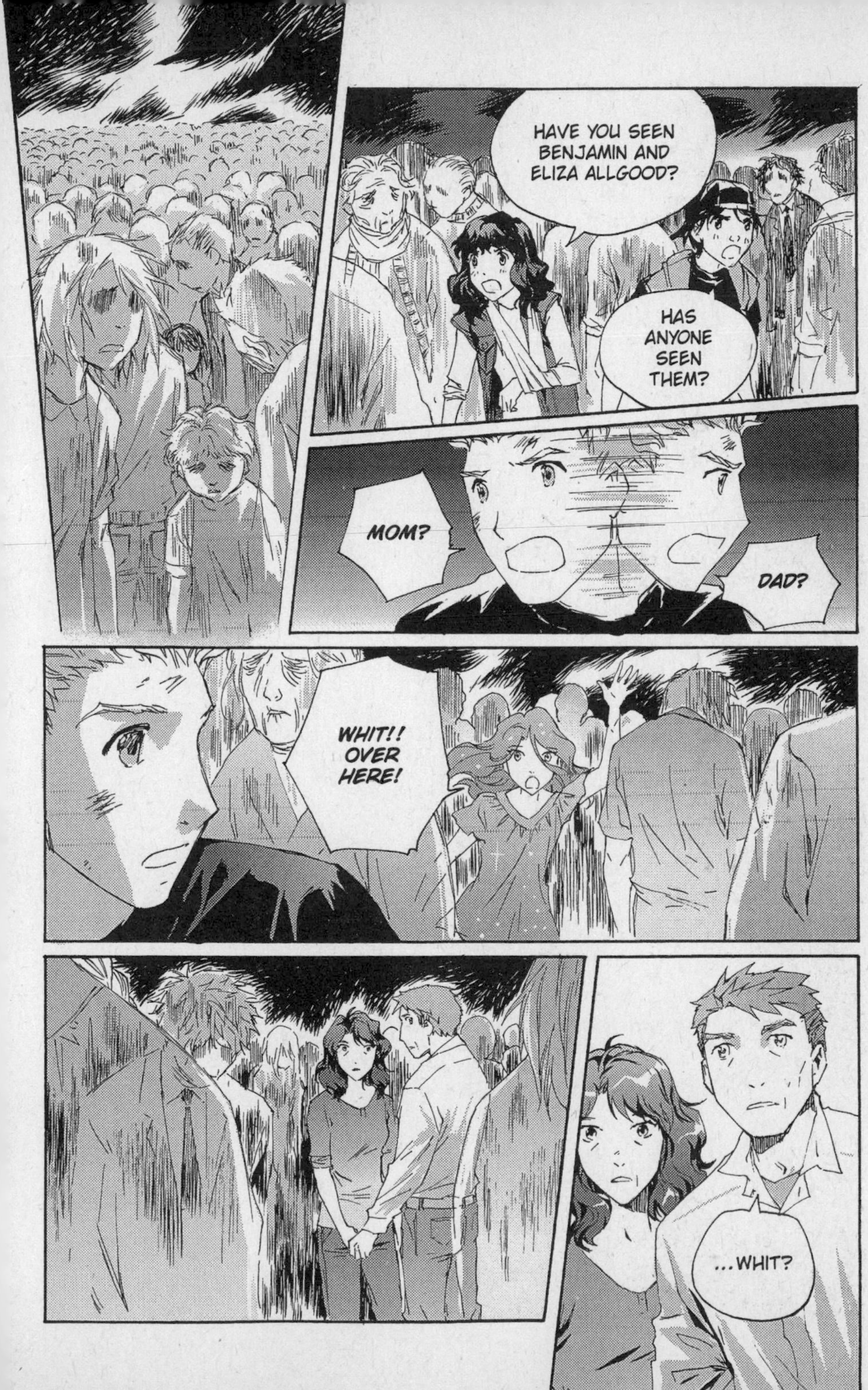
HAVE YOU SEEN BENJAMIN AND ELIZA ALLGOOD?
HAS ANYONE SEEN THEM?
MOM?
DAD?
WHIT!! OVER HERE!
...WHIT?

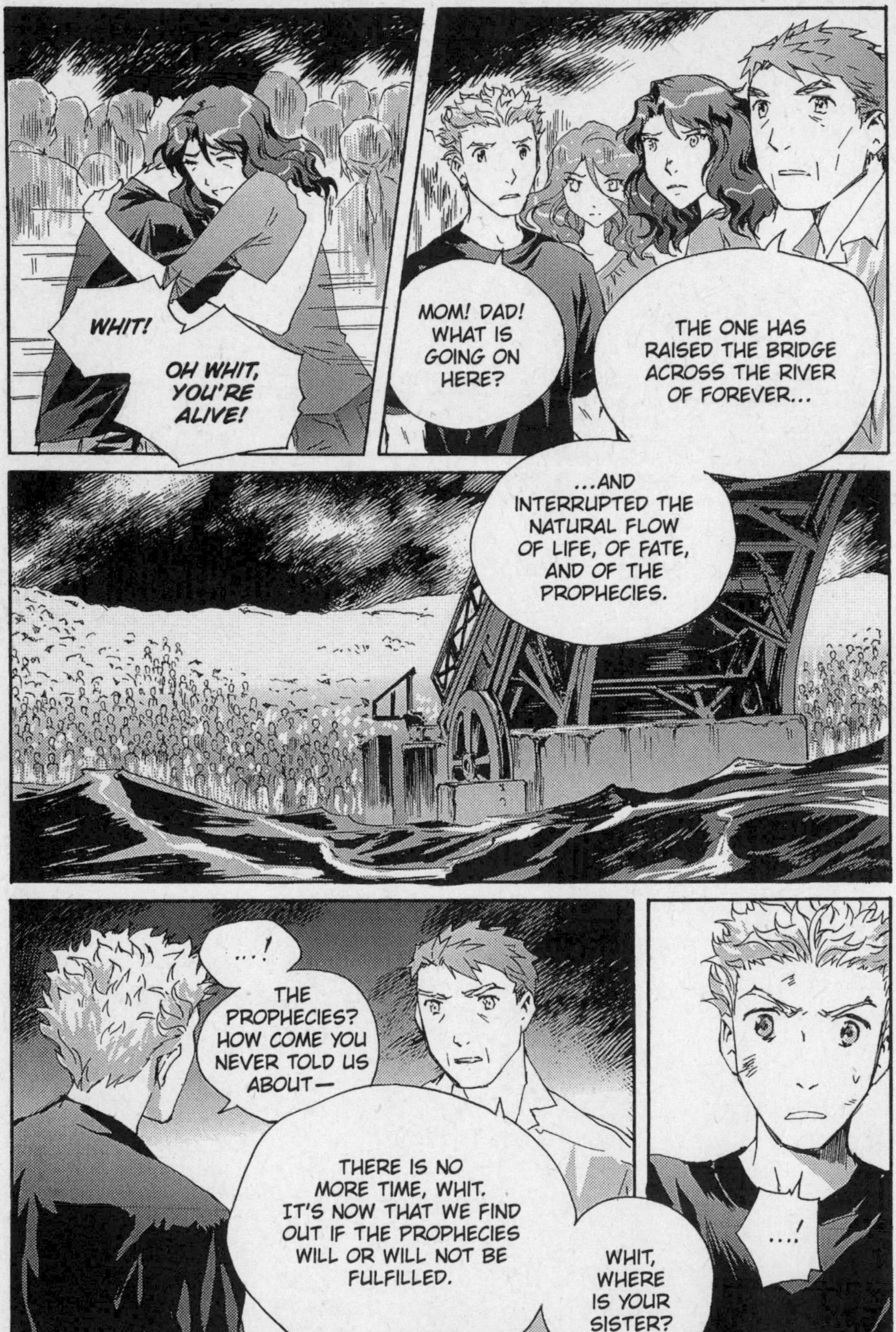
WHIT!
OH WHIT, YOU'RE ALIVE!
MOM! DAD! WHAT IS GOING ON HERE?
THE ONE HAS RAISED THE BRIDGE ACROSS THE RIVER OF FOREVER...
...AND INTERRUPTED THE NATURAL FLOW OF LIFE, OF FATE, AND OF THE PROPHECIES.
...!
THE PROPHECIES? HOW COME YOU NEVER TOLD US ABOUT—
THERE IS NO MORE TIME, WHIT. IT'S NOW THAT WE FIND OUT IF THE PROPHECIES WILL OR WILL NOT BE FULFILLED.
WHIT, WHERE IS YOUR SISTER?
...!

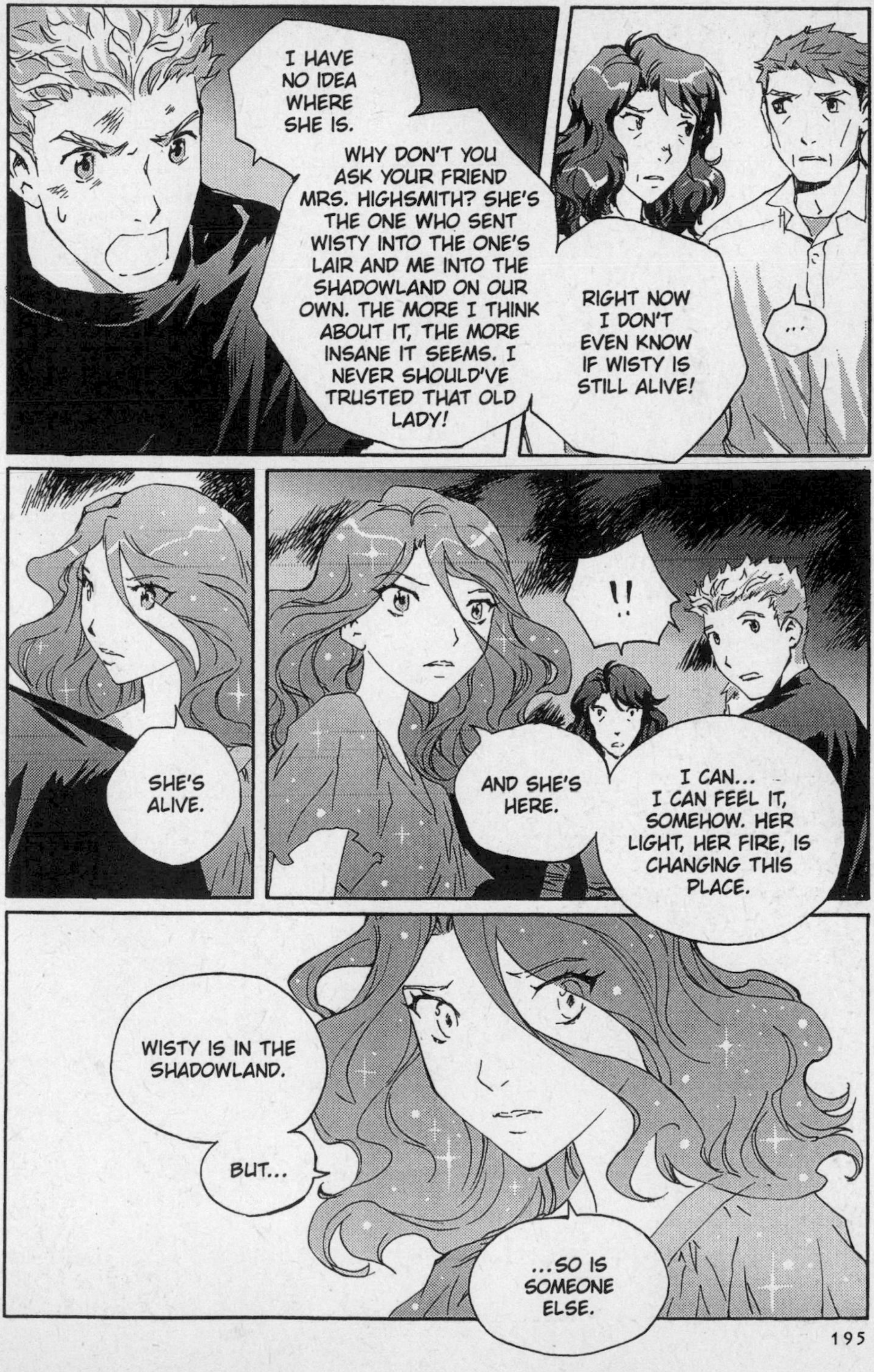
I HAVE NO IDEA WHERE SHE IS.
WHY DON'T YOU ASK YOUR FRIEND MRS. HIGHSMITH? SHE'S THE ONE WHO SENT WISTY INTO THE ONE'S LAIR AND ME INTO THE SHADOWLAND ON OUR OWN. THE MORE I THINK ABOUT IT, THE MORE INSANE IT SEEMS. I NEVER SHOULD'VE TRUSTED THAT OLD LADY!
RIGHT NOW I DON'T EVEN KNOW IF WISTY IS STILL ALIVE!
...
SHE'S ALIVE.
!!
AND SHE'S HERE.
I CAN... I CAN FEEL IT, SOMEHOW. HER LIGHT, HER FIRE, IS CHANGING THIS PLACE.
WISTY IS IN THE SHADOWLAND.
BUT...
...SO IS SOMEONE ELSE.

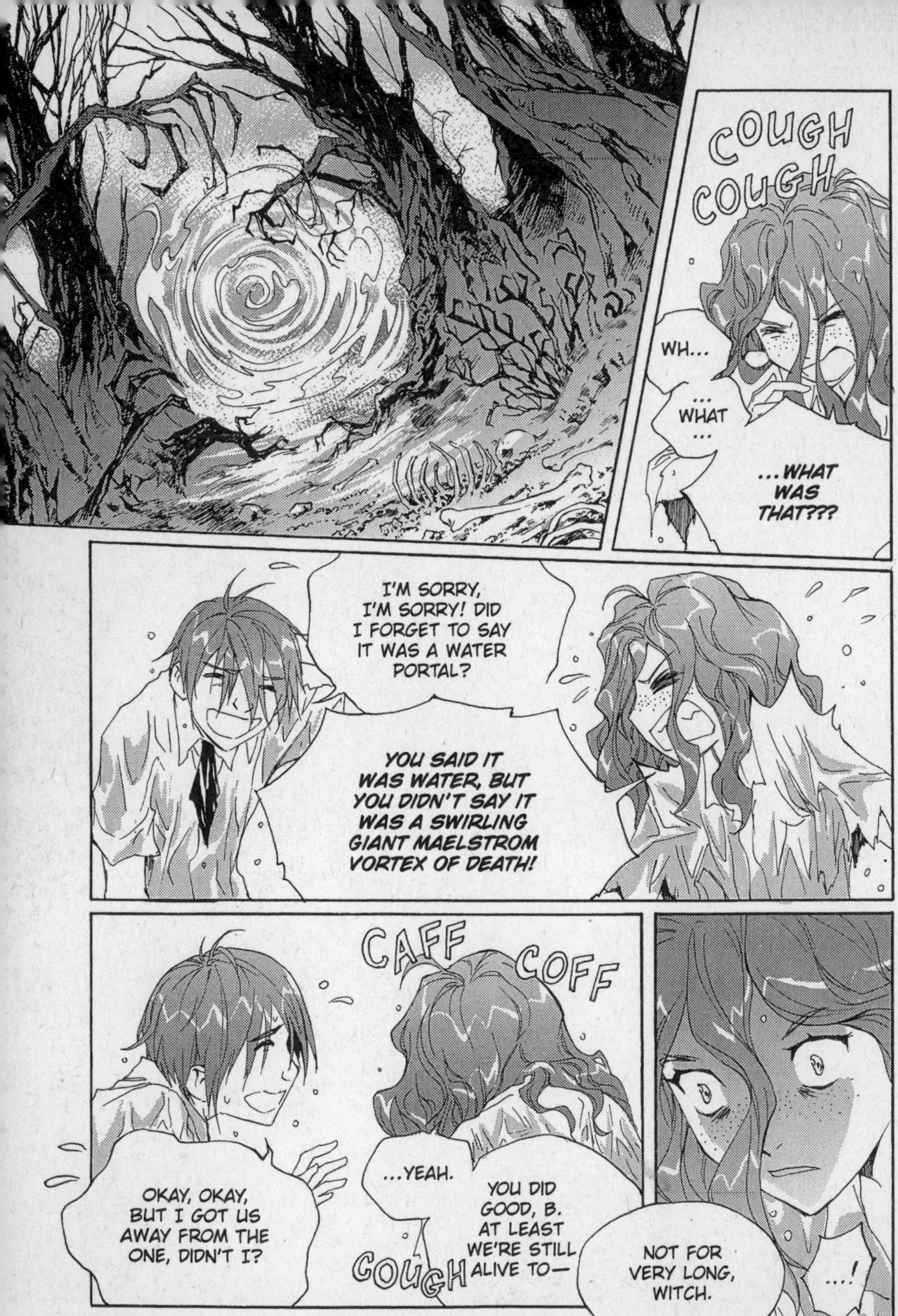
COUGH COUGH
WH...
... WHAT ...
...WHAT WAS THAT???
I'M SORRY, I'M SORRY! DID I FORGET TO SAY IT WAS A WATER PORTAL?
YOU SAID IT WAS WATER, BUT YOU DIDN'T SAY IT WAS A SWIRLING GIANT MAELSTROM VORTEX OF DEATH!
CAFF COFF
OKAY, OKAY, BUT I GOT US AWAY FROM THE ONE, DIDN'T I?
...YEAH.
YOU DID GOOD, B. AT LEAST WE'RE STILL ALIVE TO—
COUGH
NOT FOR VERY LONG, WITCH.
...!

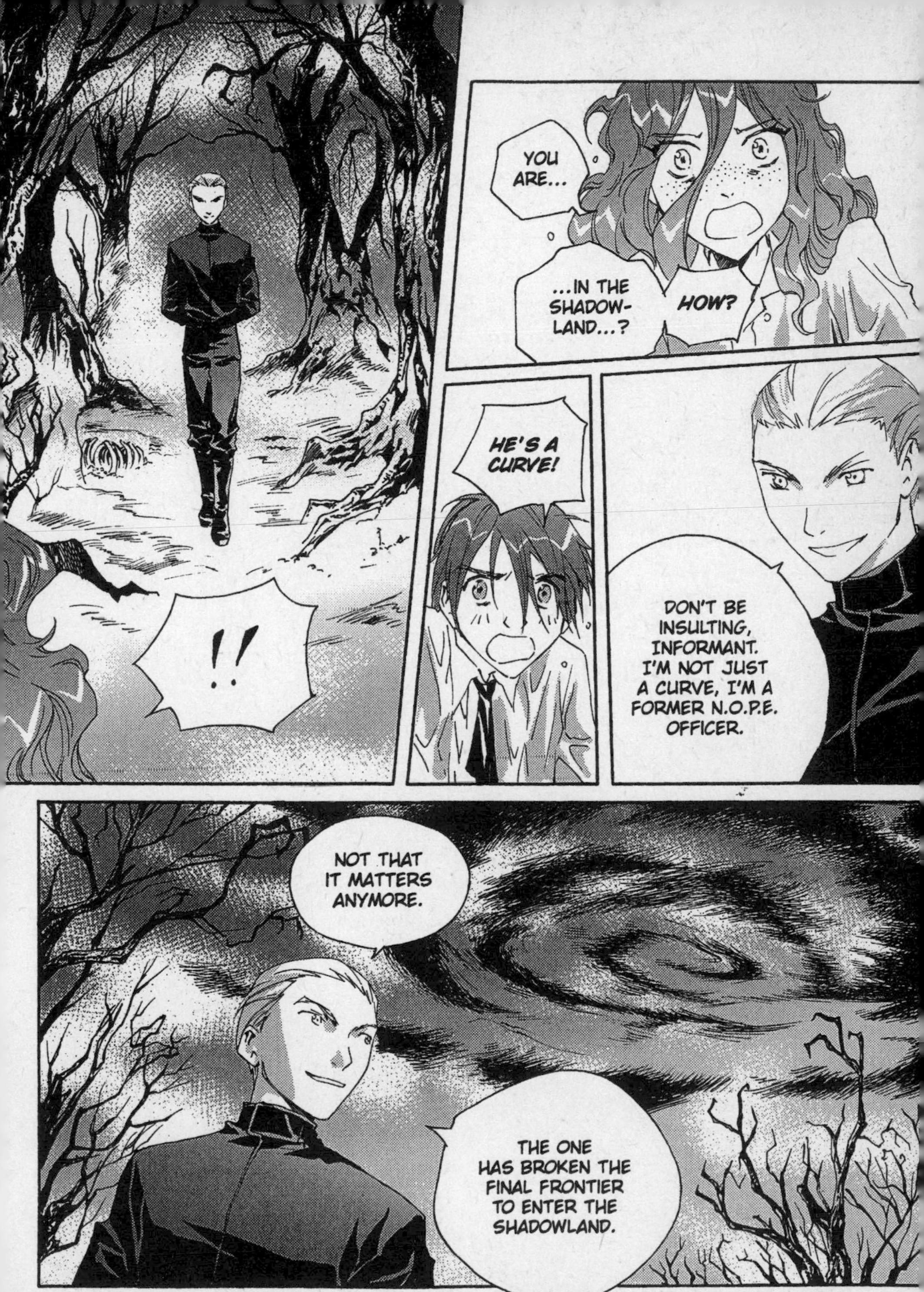

!!
YOU ARE...
...IN THE SHADOWLAND...?
HOW?
HE'S A CURVE!
DON'T BE INSULTING, INFORMANT. I'M NOT JUST A CURVE, I'M A FORMER N.O.P.E. OFFICER.
NOT THAT IT MATTERS ANYMORE.
THE ONE HAS BROKEN THE FINAL FRONTIER TO ENTER THE SHADOWLAND.

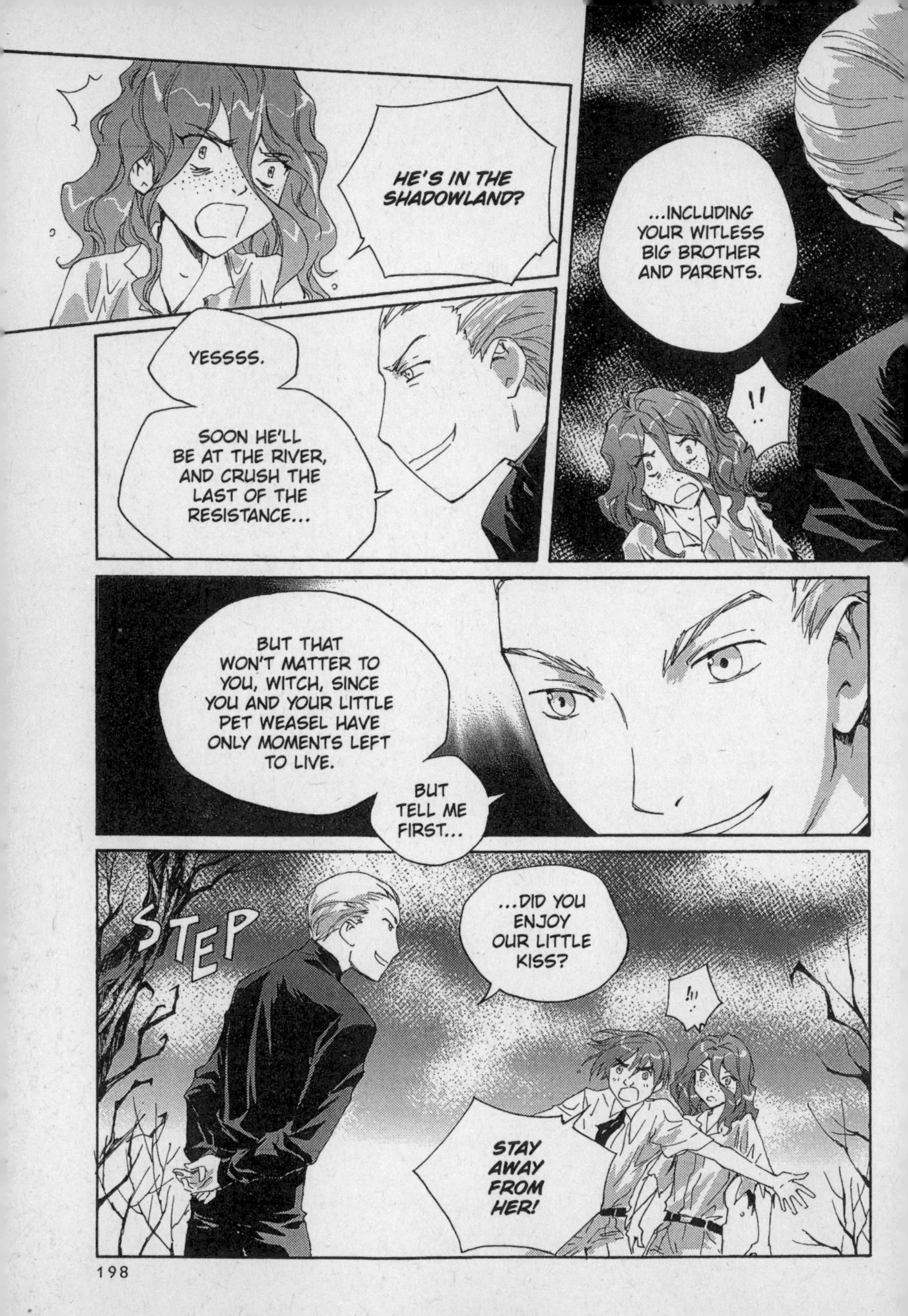
HE'S IN THE SHADOWLAND?
YESSSS.
SOON HE'LL BE AT THE RIVER, AND CRUSH THE LAST OF THE RESISTANCE...
...INCLUDING YOUR WITLESS BIG BROTHER AND PARENTS.
!!
BUT THAT WON'T MATTER TO YOU, WITCH, SINCE YOU AND YOUR LITTLE PET WEASEL HAVE ONLY MOMENTS LEFT TO LIVE.
BUT TELL ME FIRST...
STEP
...DID YOU ENJOY OUR LITTLE KISS?
!!!
STAY AWAY FROM HER!

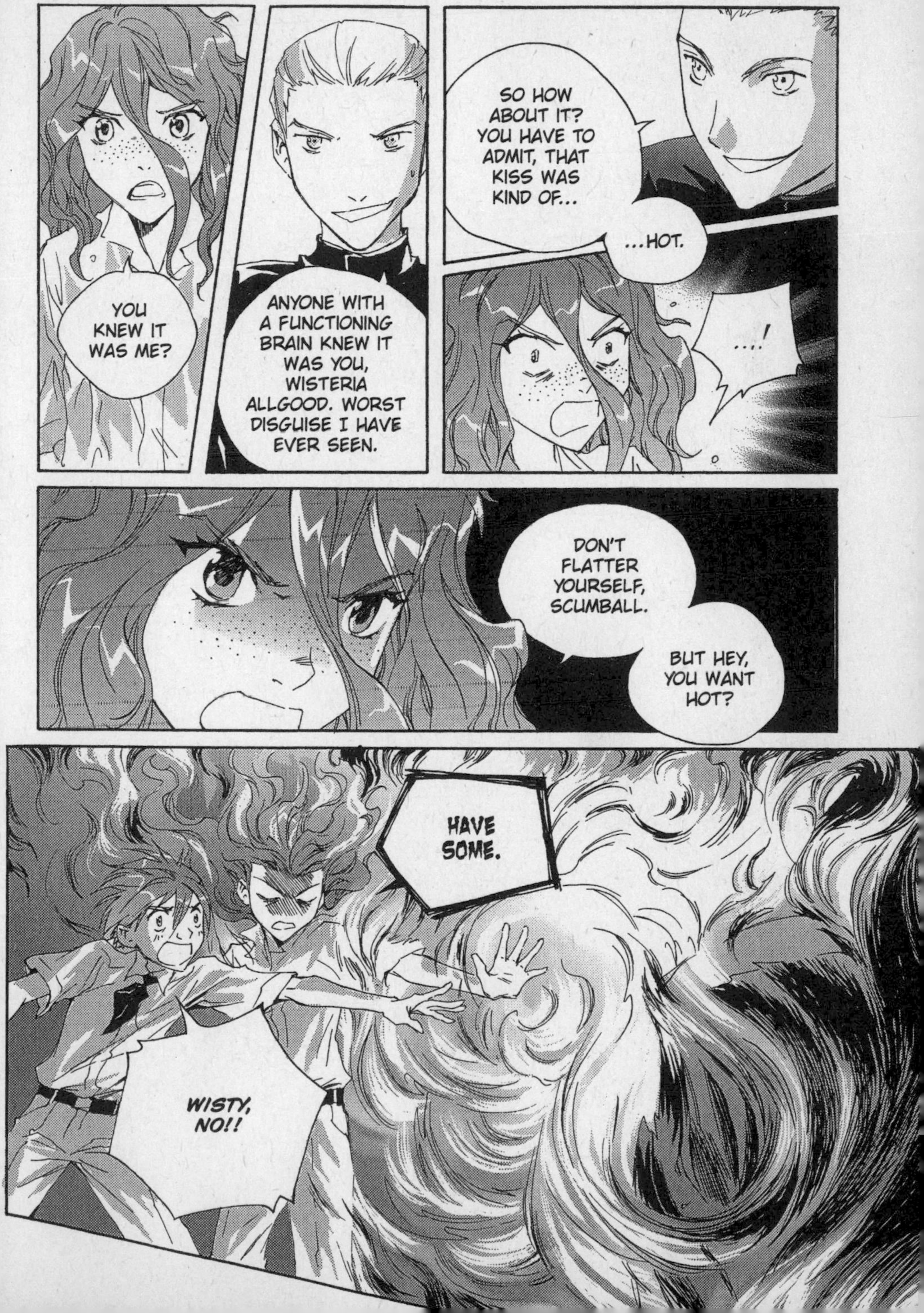
YOU KNEW IT WAS ME?
ANYONE WITH A FUNCTIONING BRAIN KNEW IT WAS YOU, WISTERIA ALLGOOD. WORST DISGUISE I HAVE EVER SEEN.
SO HOW ABOUT IT? YOU HAVE TO ADMIT, THAT KISS WAS KIND OF...
...HOT.
...!
DON'T FLATTER YOURSELF, SCUMBALL.
BUT HEY, YOU WANT HOT?
HAVE SOME.
WISTY, NO!!

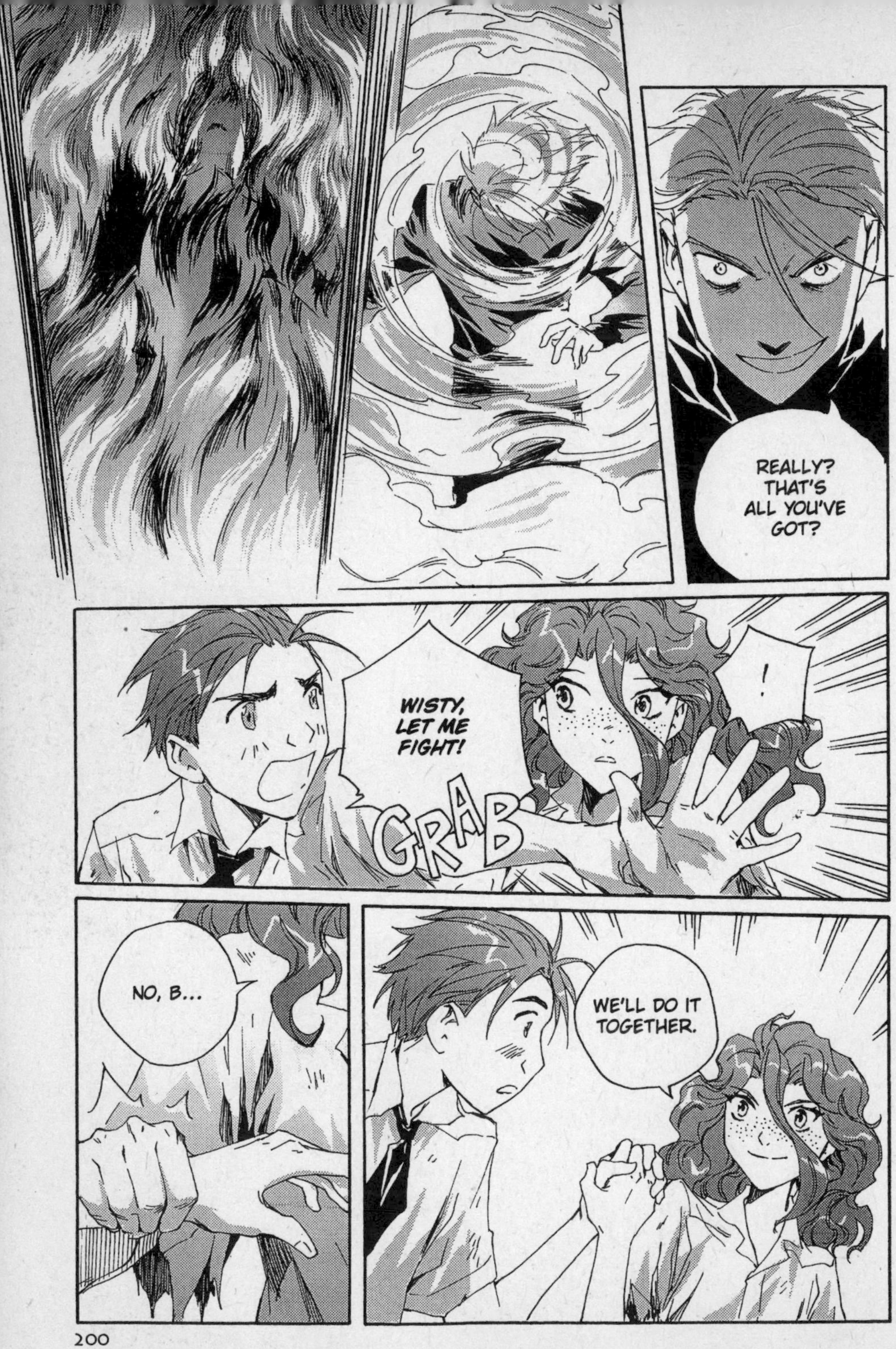
REALLY? THAT'S ALL YOU'VE GOT?
WISTY, LET ME FIGHT!
!
GRAB
NO, B...
WE'LL DO IT TOGETHER.

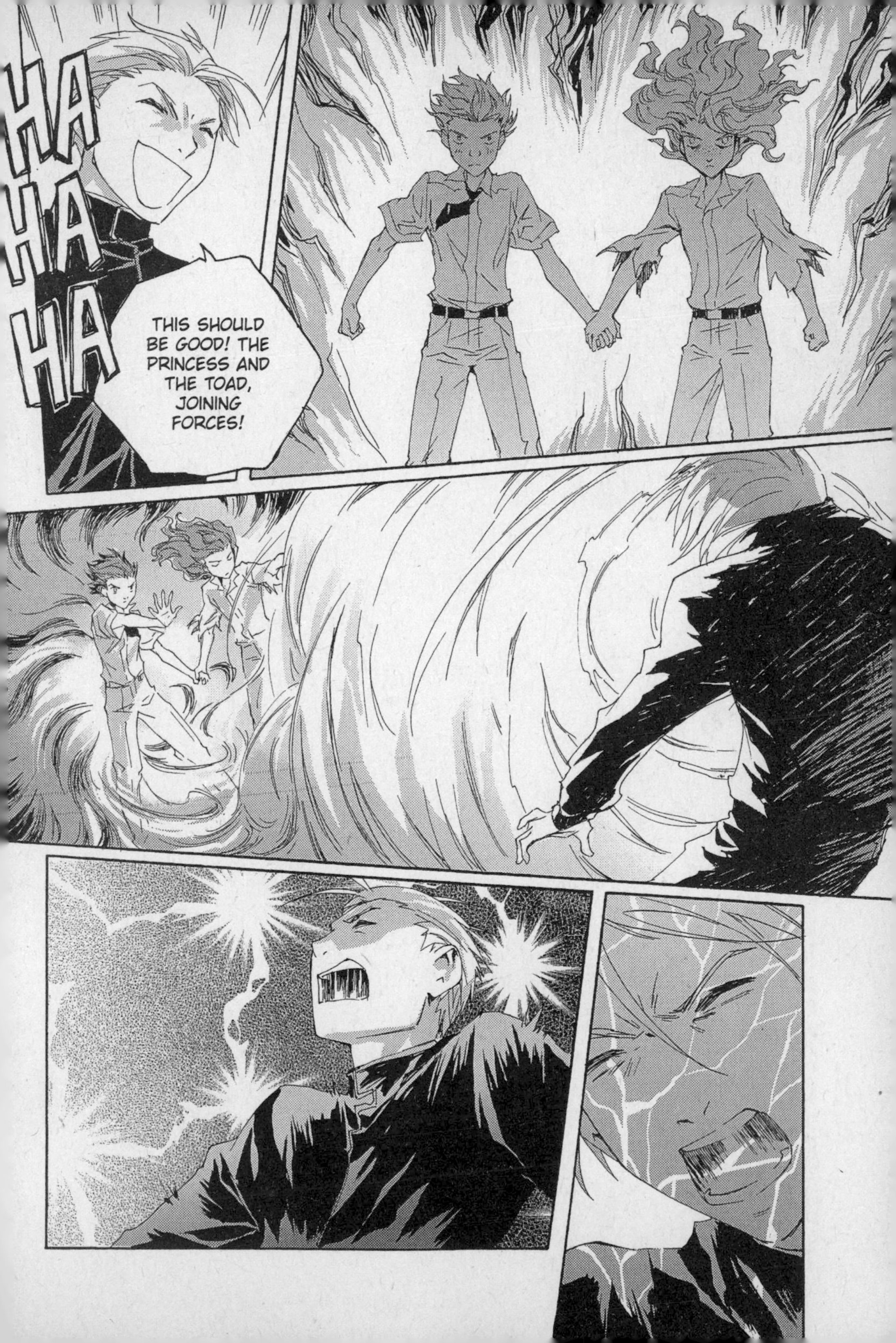
HA HA HA HA
THIS SHOULD BE GOOD! THE PRINCESS AND THE TOAD, JOINING FORCES!

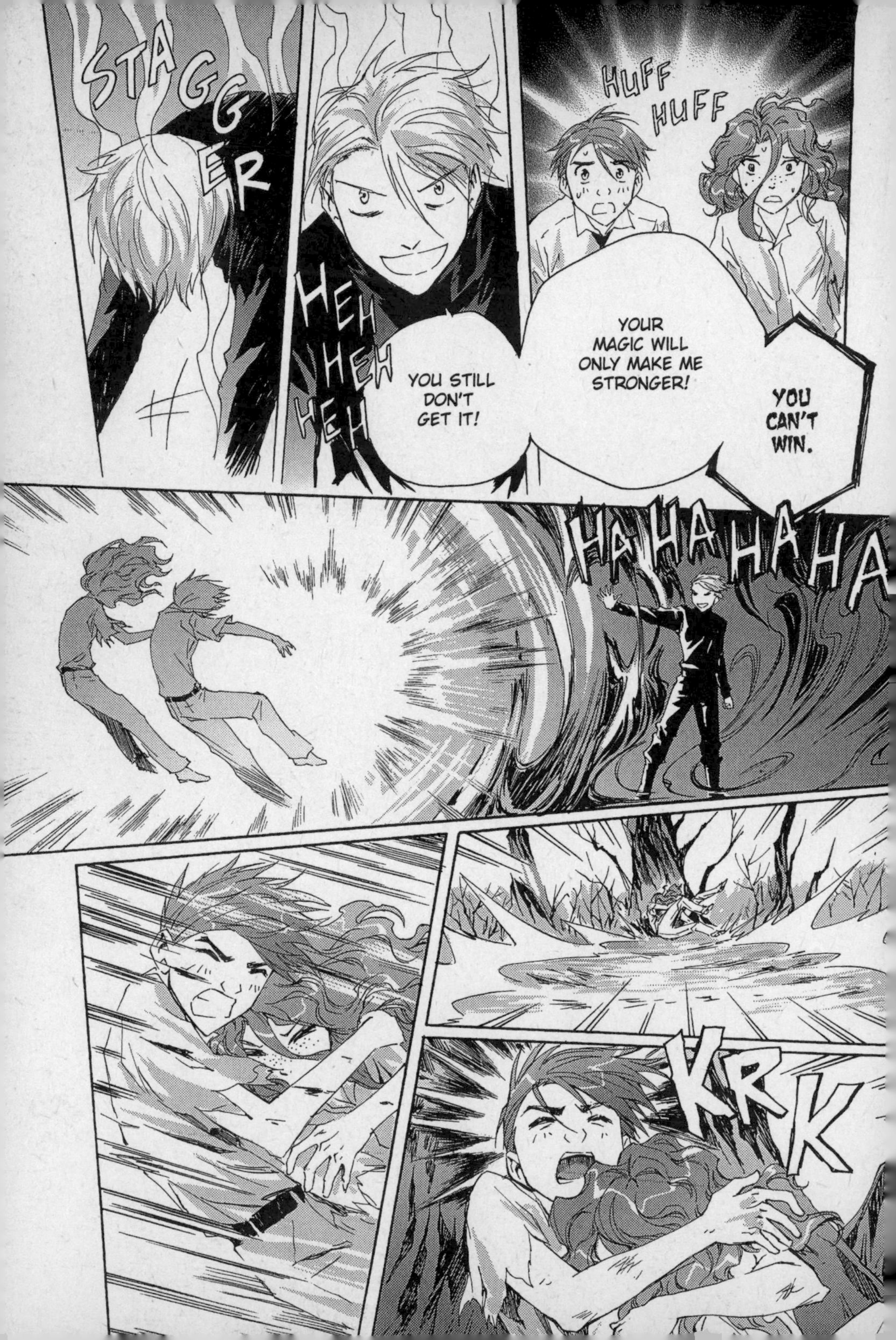
STAGGER
HEH HEH HEH
HUFF HUFF
YOU STILL DON'T GET IT!
YOUR MAGIC WILL ONLY MAKE ME STRONGER!
YOU CAN'T WIN.
HAHAHAHAHA
KRK

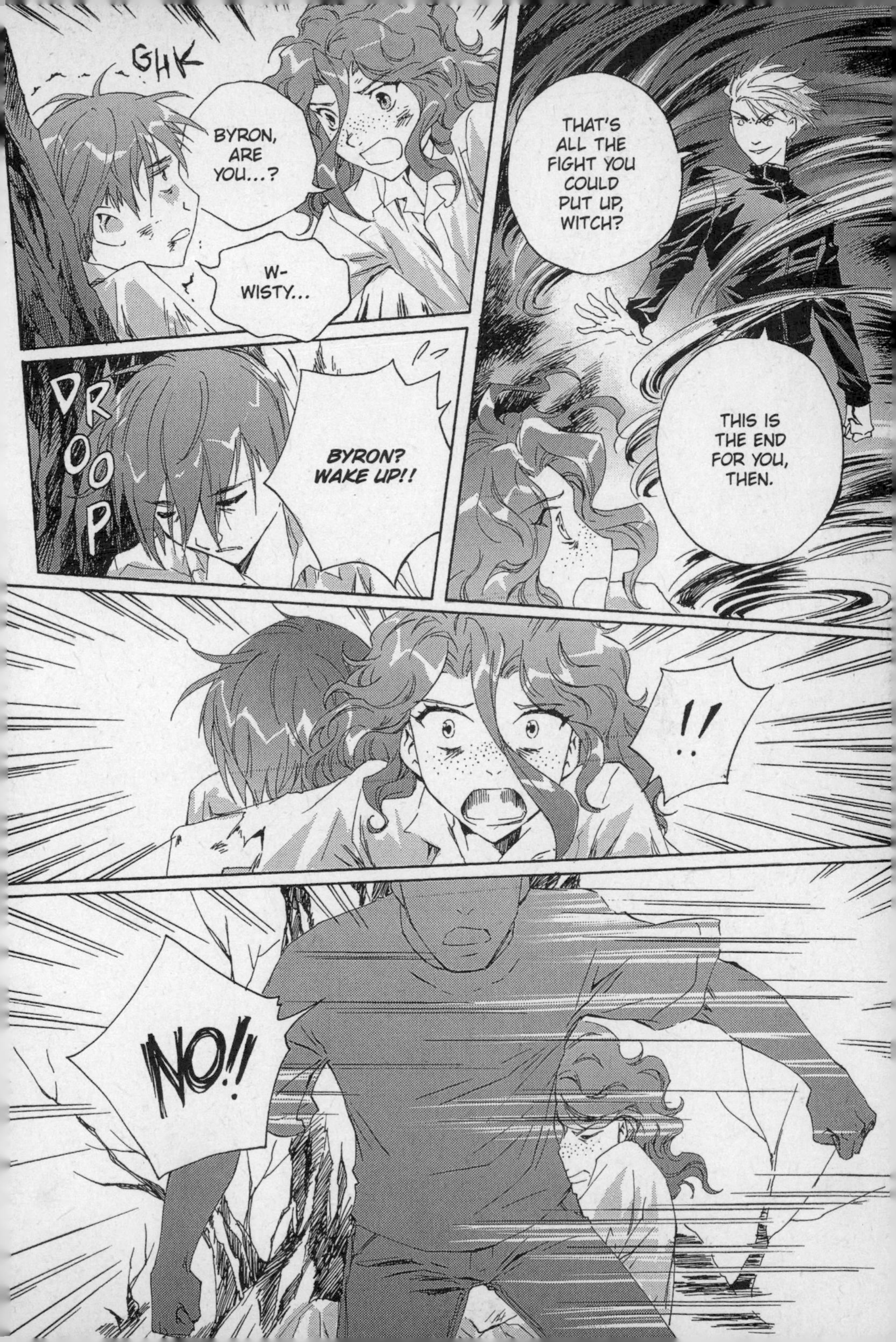
GHK
BYRON, ARE YOU...?
W- WISTY...
THAT'S ALL THE FIGHT YOU COULD PUT UP, WITCH?
THIS IS THE END FOR YOU, THEN.
DROOP
BYRON? WAKE UP!!
!!
NO!!

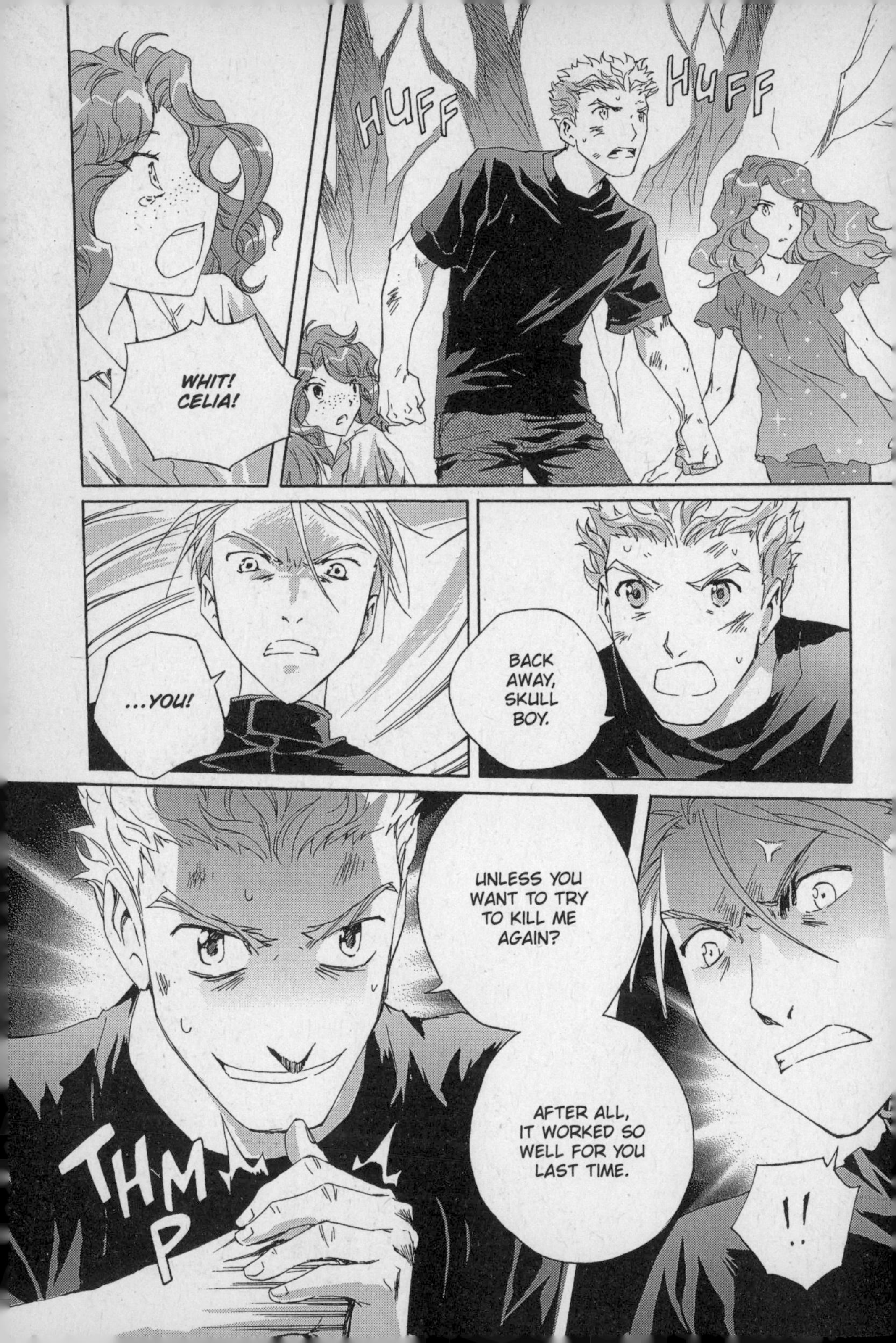
WHIT!
CELIA!
HUFF
HUFF
...YOU!
BACK AWAY, SKULL BOY.
UNLESS YOU WANT TO TRY TO KILL ME AGAIN?
AFTER ALL, IT WORKED SO WELL FOR YOU LAST TIME.
THMP
!!

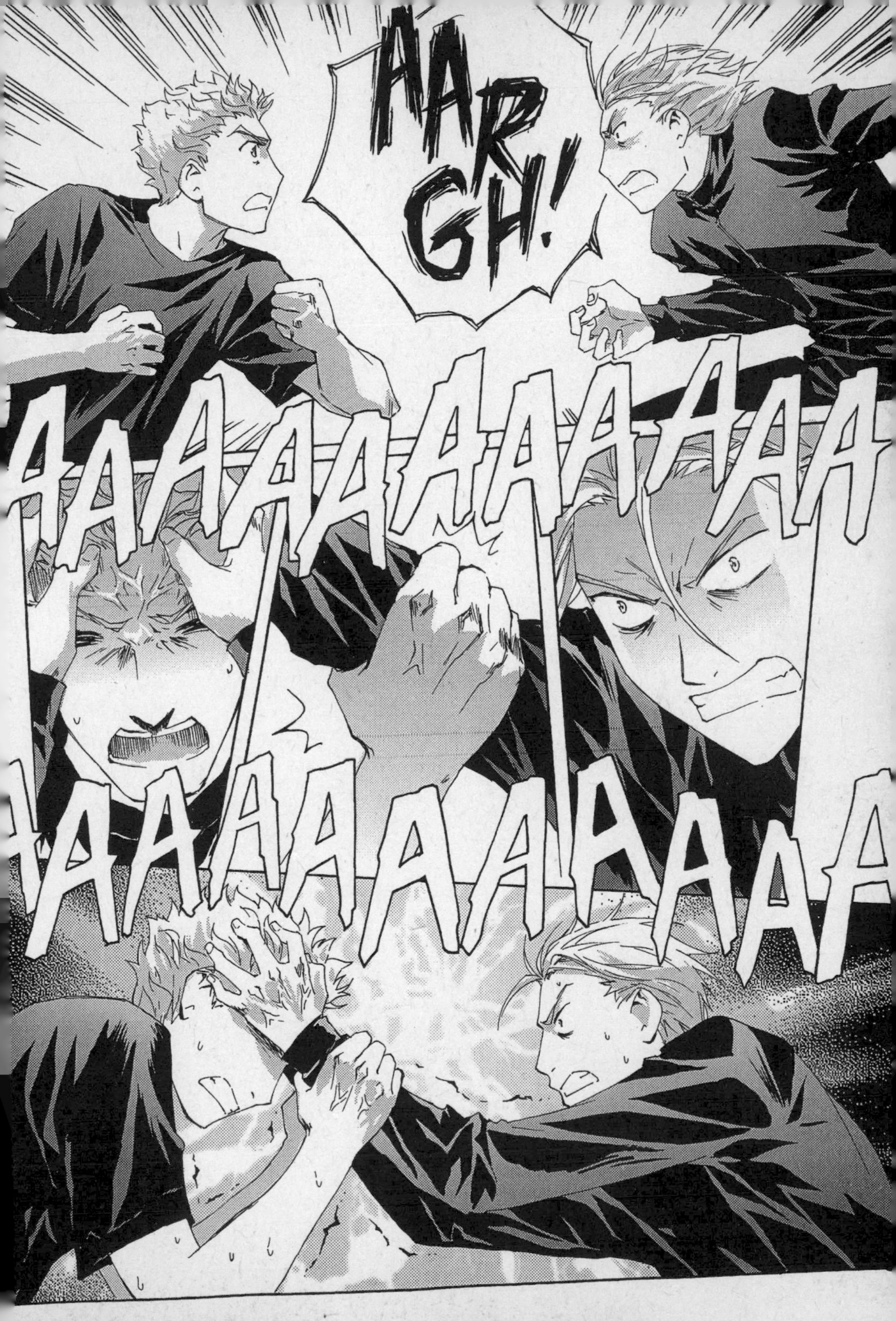
AARGH!
AAAAAAAAAAAA
AAAAAAAAAAAA

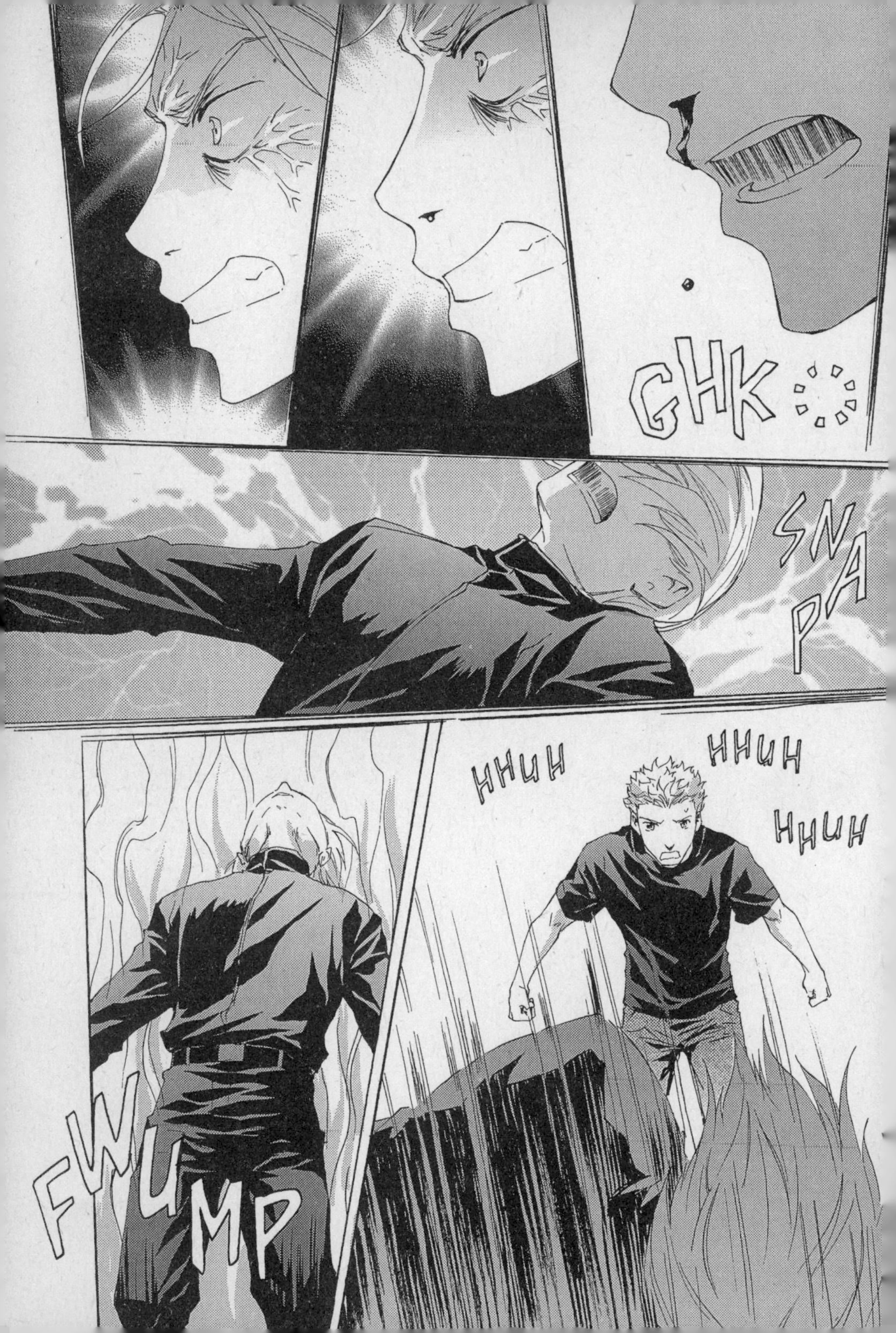
GHK…
SNAPA
HHUH
HHUH
HHUH
FWUMP

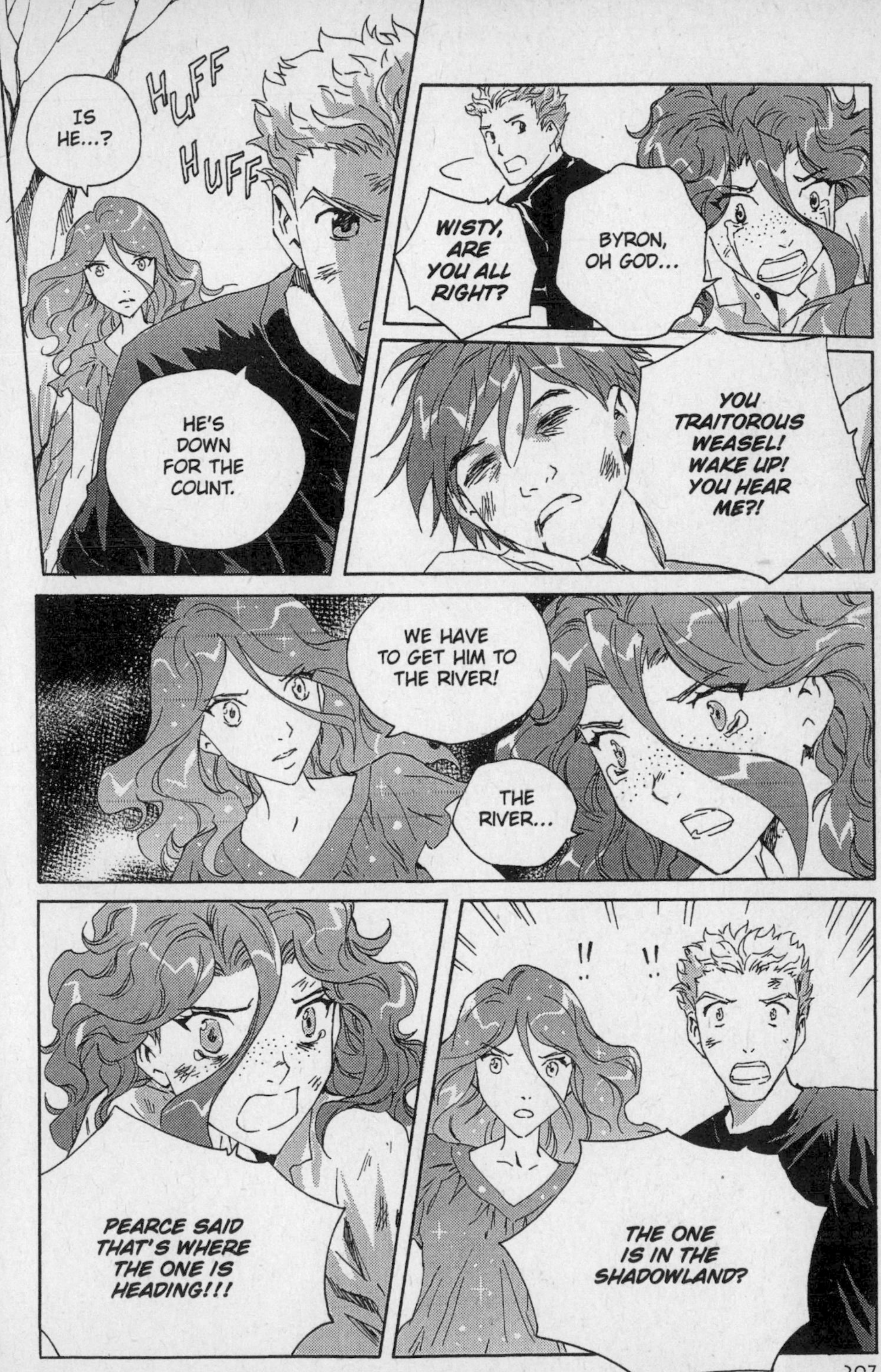
IS HE...?
HUFF HUFF
HE'S DOWN FOR THE COUNT.
WISTY, ARE YOU ALL RIGHT?
BYRON, OH GOD...
YOU TRAITOROUS WEASEL! WAKE UP! YOU HEAR ME?!
WE HAVE TO GET HIM TO THE RIVER!
THE RIVER...
PEARCE SAID THAT'S WHERE THE ONE IS HEADING!!!
!! !!
THE ONE IS IN THE SHADOWLAND?

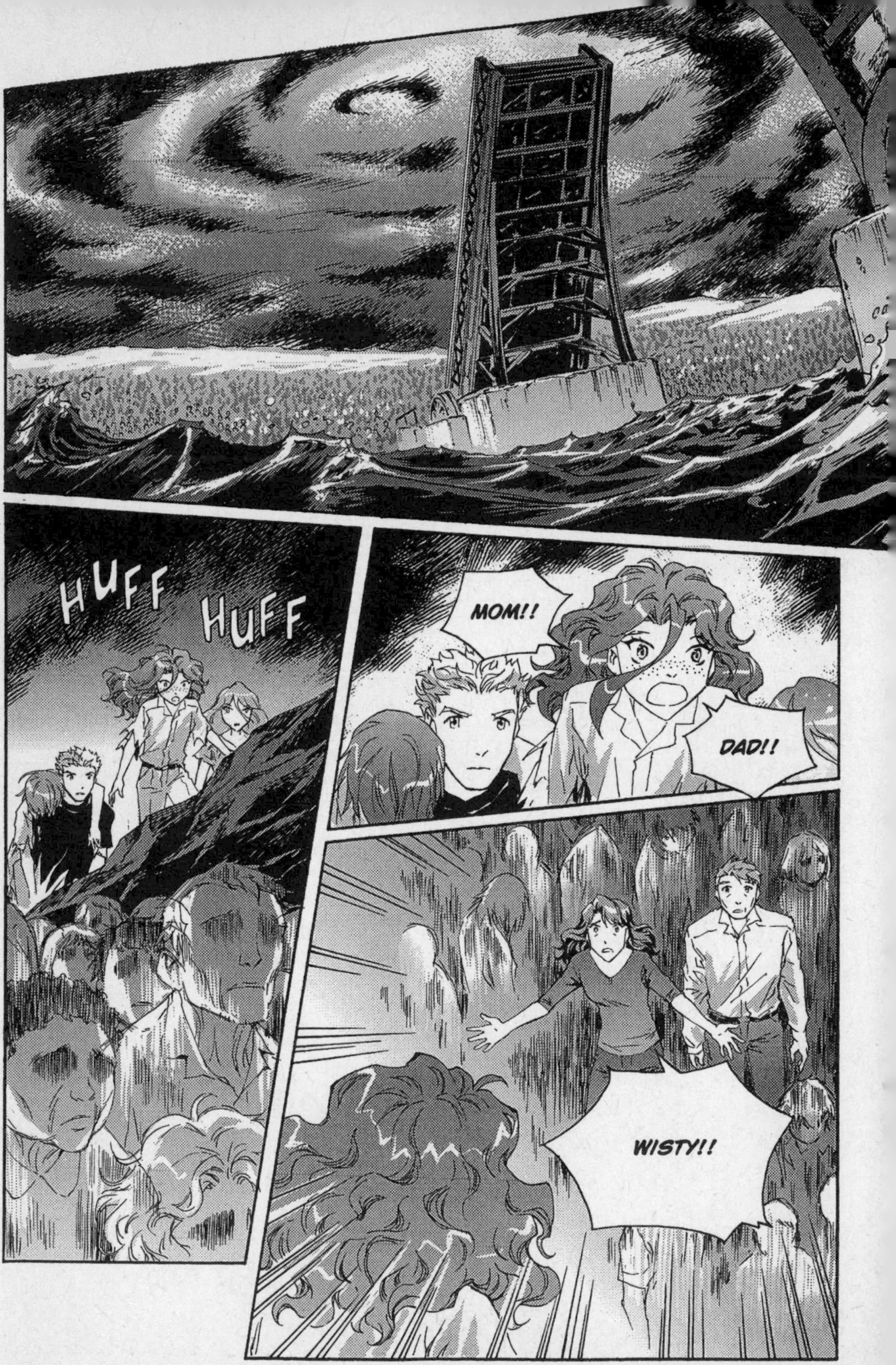
HUFF HUFF
MOM!!
DAD!!
WISTY!!

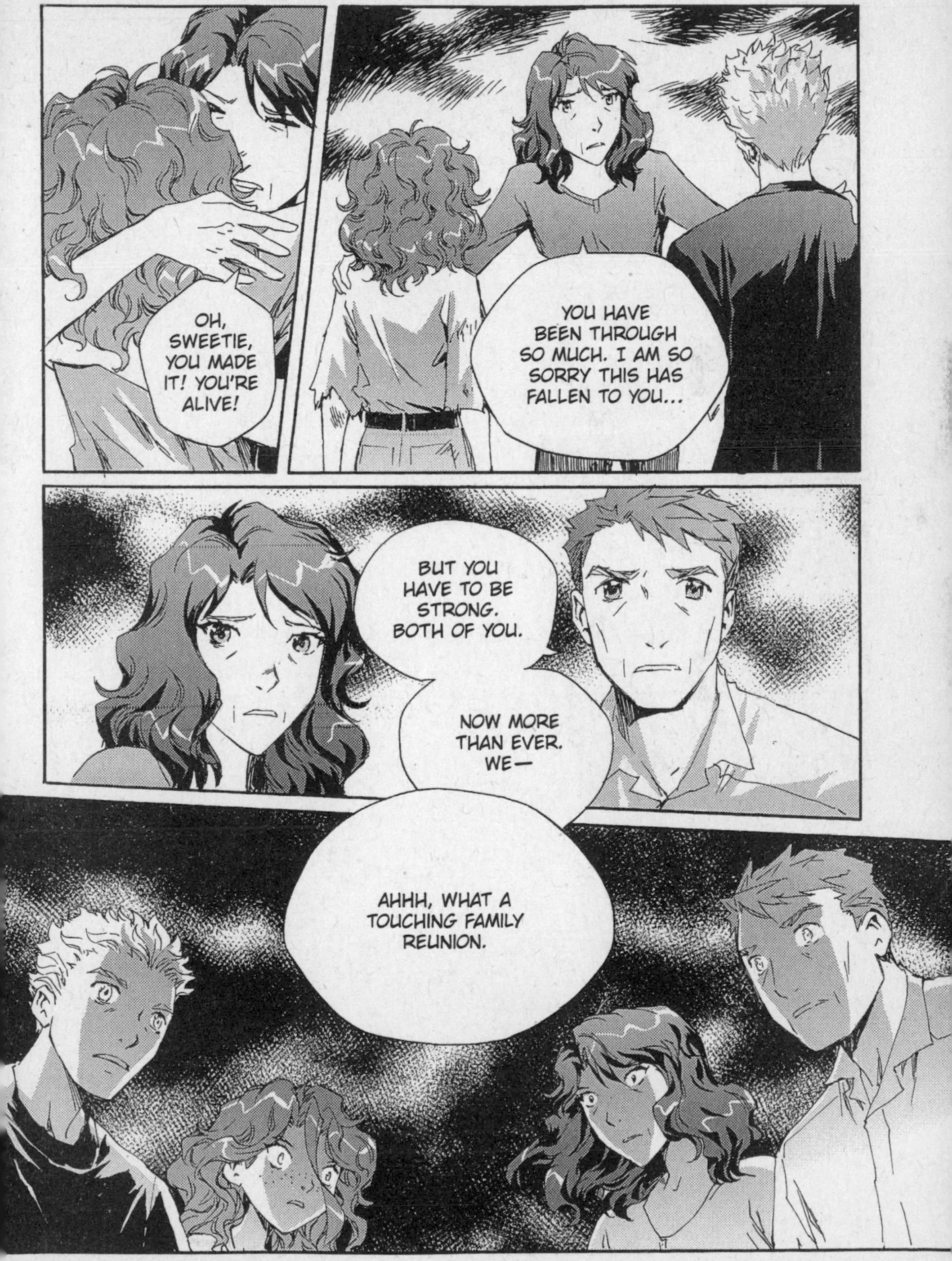
OH, SWEETIE, YOU MADE IT! YOU'RE ALIVE!
YOU HAVE BEEN THROUGH SO MUCH. I AM SO SORRY THIS HAS FALLEN TO YOU...
BUT YOU HAVE TO BE STRONG. BOTH OF YOU.
NOW MORE THAN EVER. WE—
AHHH, WHAT A TOUCHING FAMILY REUNION.

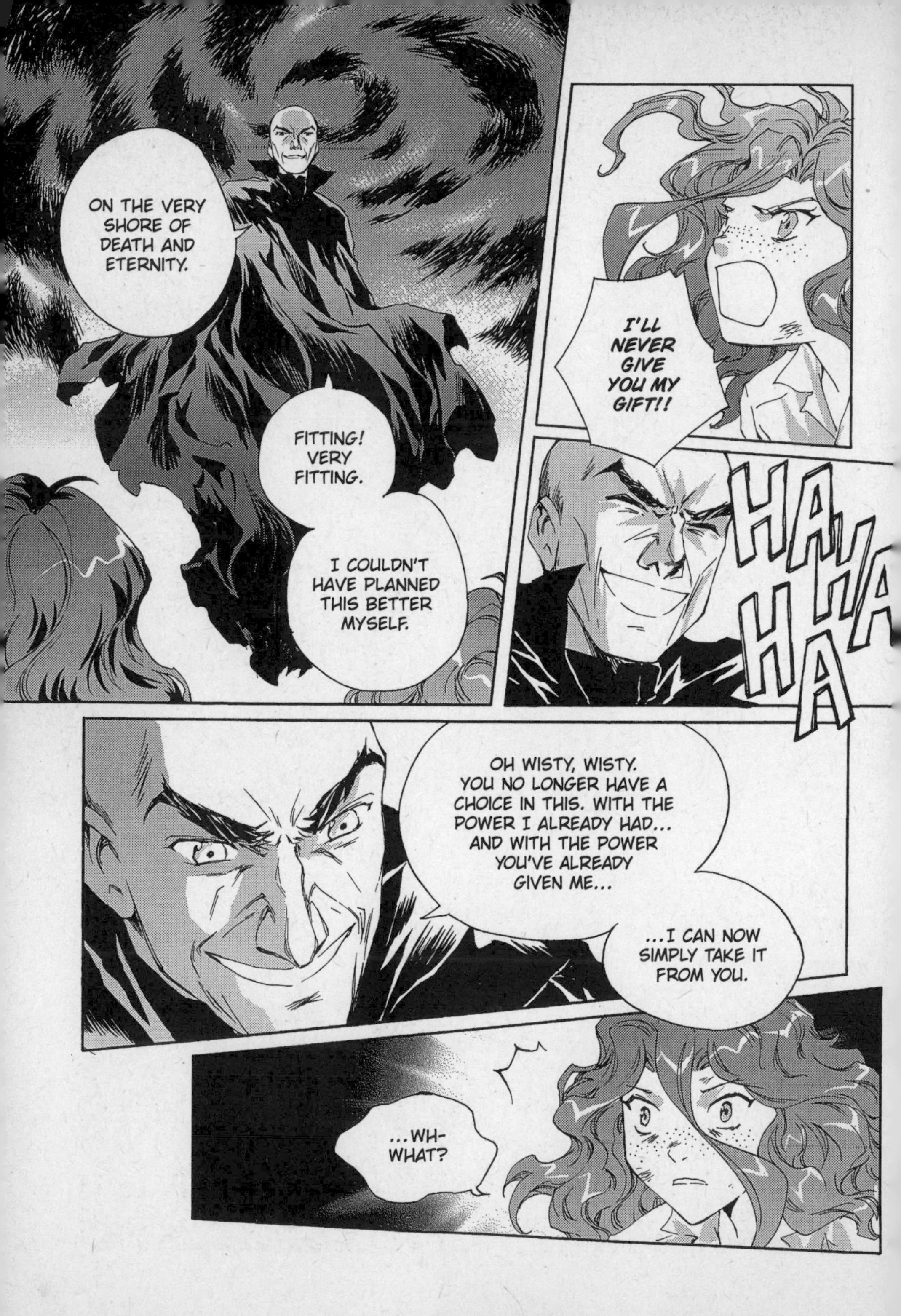
ON THE VERY SHORE OF DEATH AND ETERNITY.
FITTING! VERY FITTING.
I COULDN'T HAVE PLANNED THIS BETTER MYSELF.
I'LL NEVER GIVE YOU MY GIFT!!
HA HA HA HA HA
OH WISTY, WISTY. YOU NO LONGER HAVE A CHOICE IN THIS. WITH THE POWER I ALREADY HAD... AND WITH THE POWER YOU'VE ALREADY GIVEN ME...
...I CAN NOW SIMPLY TAKE IT FROM YOU.
...WH-WHAT?

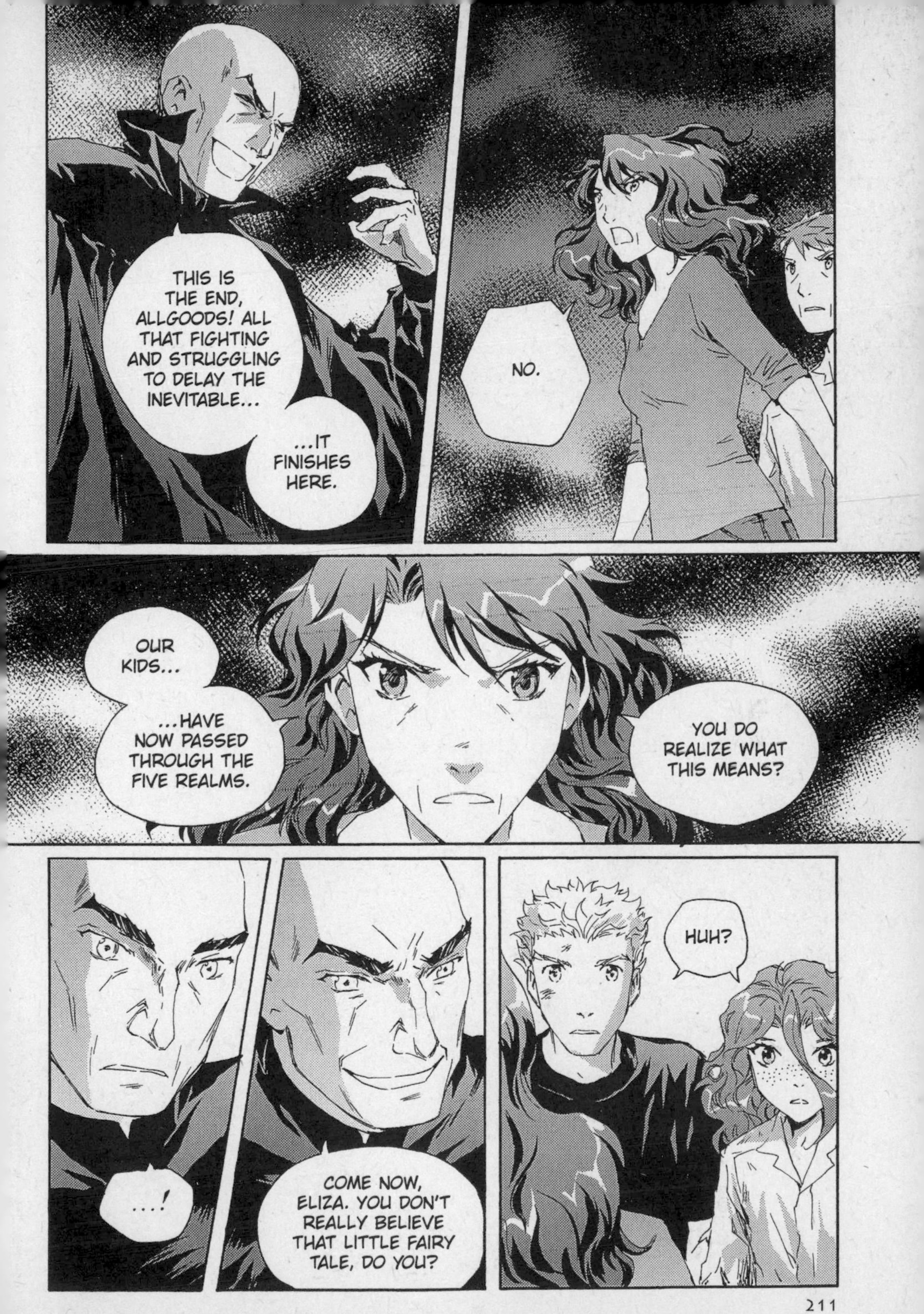
THIS IS THE END, ALLGOODS! ALL THAT FIGHTING AND STRUGGLING TO DELAY THE INEVITABLE...
...IT FINISHES HERE.
NO.
OUR KIDS...
...HAVE NOW PASSED THROUGH THE FIVE REALMS.
YOU DO REALIZE WHAT THIS MEANS?
...!
COME NOW, ELIZA. YOU DON'T REALLY BELIEVE THAT LITTLE FAIRY TALE, DO YOU?
HUH?

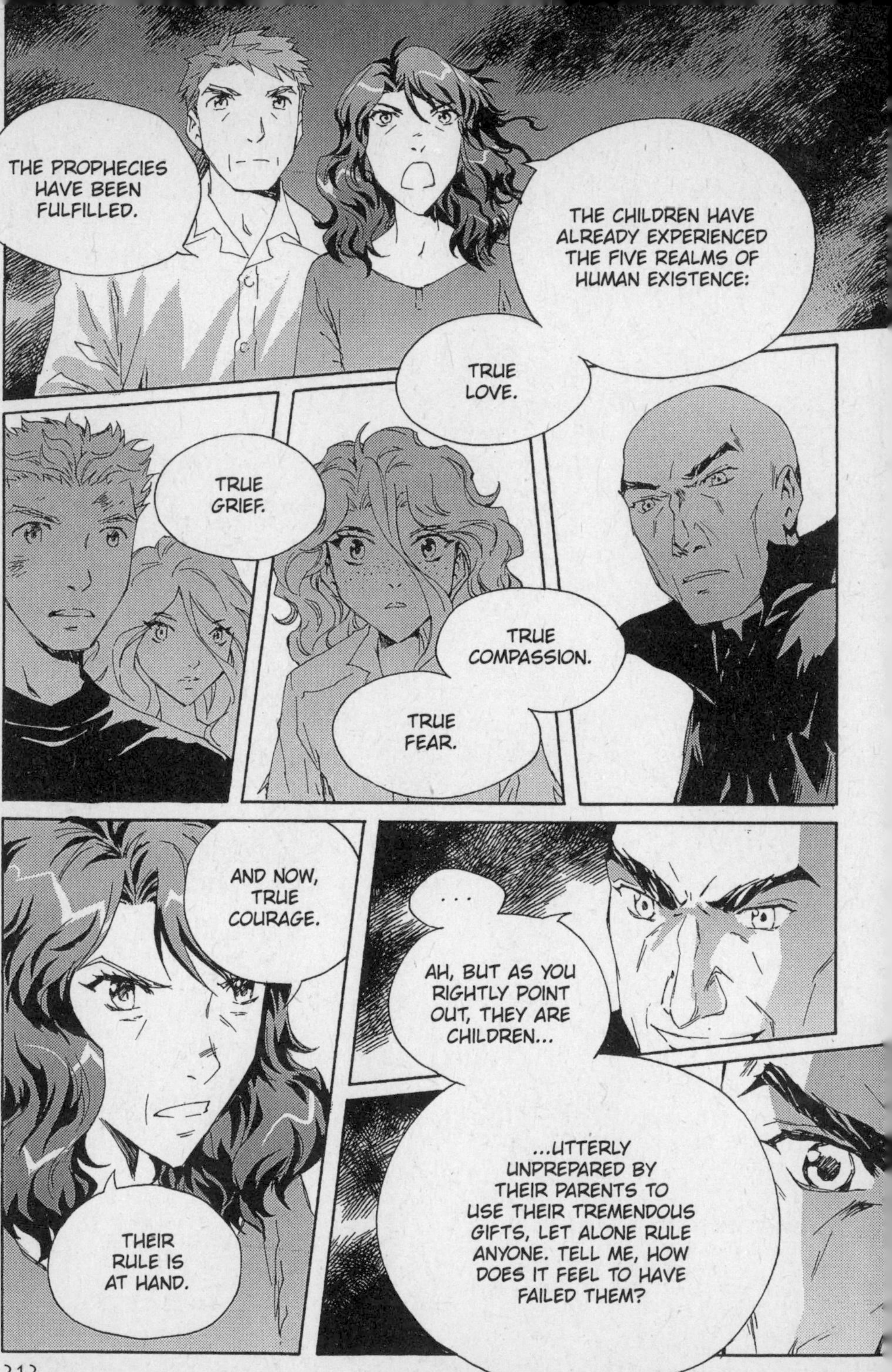
THE PROPHECIES HAVE BEEN FULFILLED.
THE CHILDREN HAVE ALREADY EXPERIENCED THE FIVE REALMS OF HUMAN EXISTENCE:
TRUE LOVE.
TRUE GRIEF.
TRUE COMPASSION.
TRUE FEAR.
AND NOW, TRUE COURAGE.
THEIR RULE IS AT HAND.
. . .
AH, BUT AS YOU RIGHTLY POINT OUT, THEY ARE CHILDREN...
...UTTERLY UNPREPARED BY THEIR PARENTS TO USE THEIR TREMENDOUS GIFTS, LET ALONE RULE ANYONE. TELL ME, HOW DOES IT FEEL TO HAVE FAILED THEM?

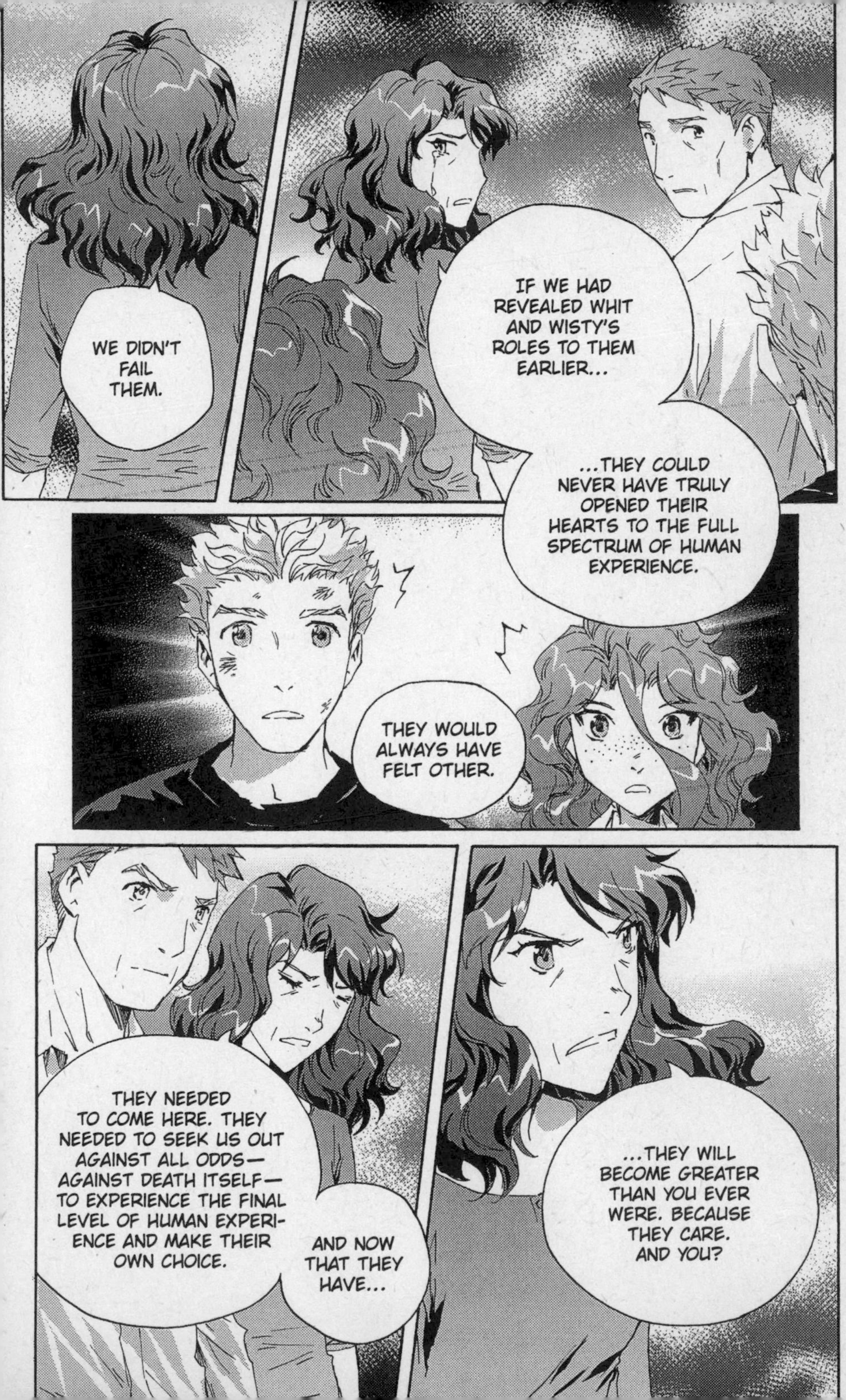
WE DIDN'T FAIL THEM.
IF WE HAD REVEALED WHIT AND WISTY'S ROLES TO THEM EARLIER...
...THEY COULD NEVER HAVE TRULY OPENED THEIR HEARTS TO THE FULL SPECTRUM OF HUMAN EXPERIENCE.
THEY WOULD ALWAYS HAVE FELT OTHER.
THEY NEEDED TO COME HERE. THEY NEEDED TO SEEK US OUT AGAINST ALL ODDS— AGAINST DEATH ITSELF— TO EXPERIENCE THE FINAL LEVEL OF HUMAN EXPERI- ENCE AND MAKE THEIR OWN CHOICE.
AND NOW THAT THEY HAVE...
...THEY WILL BECOME GREATER THAN YOU EVER WERE. BECAUSE THEY CARE. AND YOU?

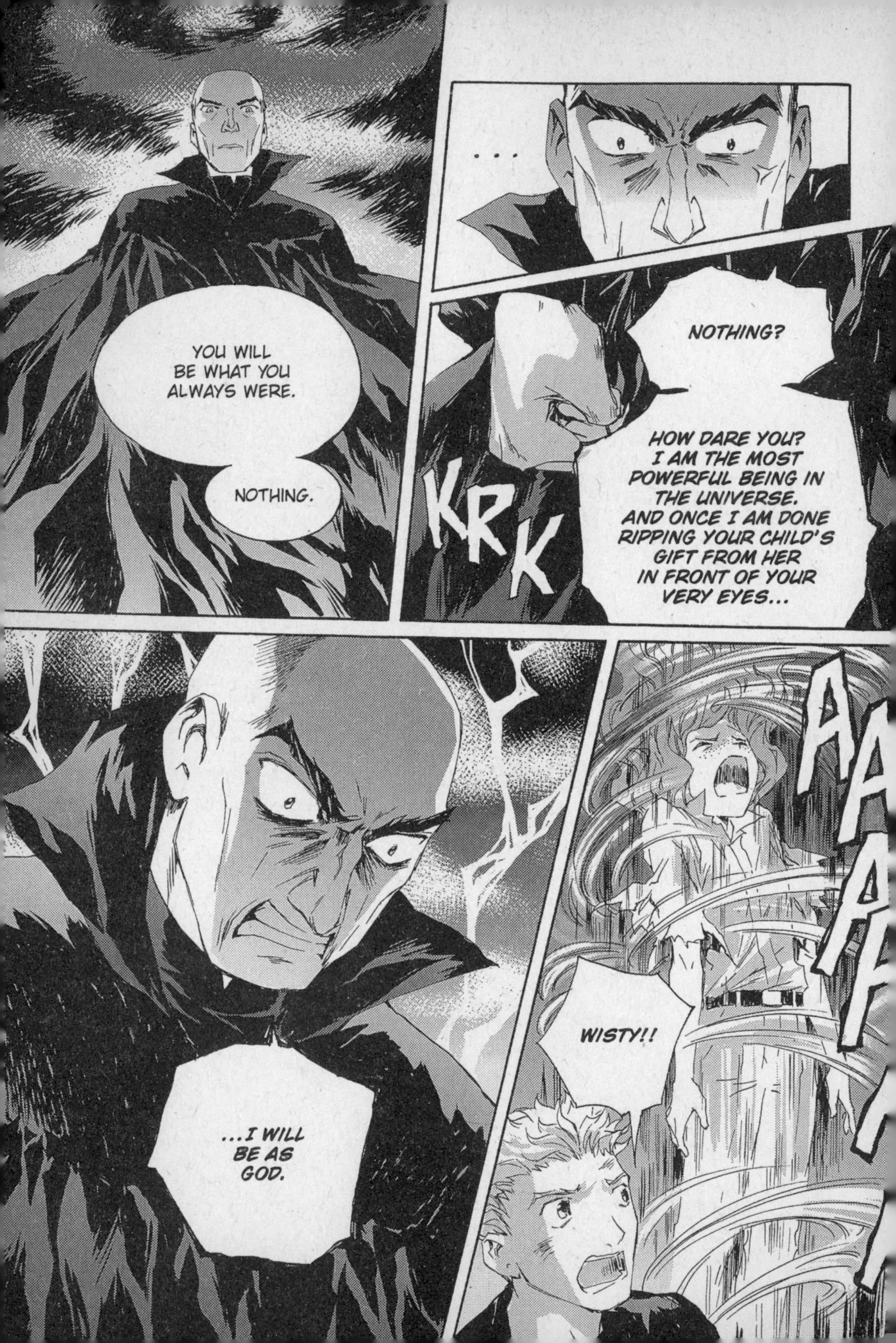
YOU WILL BE WHAT YOU ALWAYS WERE.
NOTHING.
...
NOTHING?
KRK
HOW DARE YOU? I AM THE MOST POWERFUL BEING IN THE UNIVERSE. AND ONCE I AM DONE RIPPING YOUR CHILD'S GIFT FROM HER IN FRONT OF YOUR VERY EYES...
...I WILL BE AS GOD.
WISTY!!

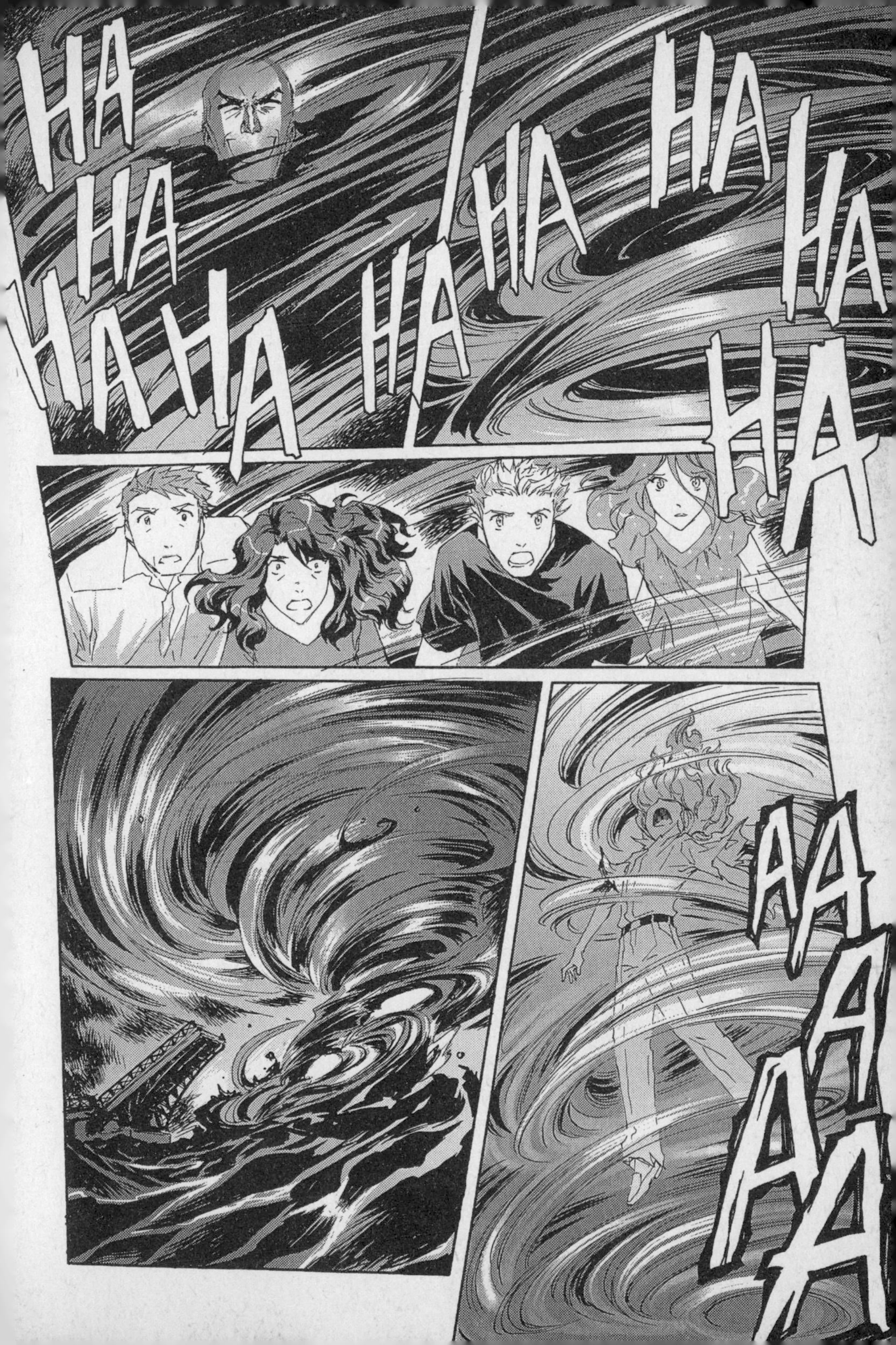
HA HA HA HA HA HA HA HA HA HA HA HA
AAAAAAAA

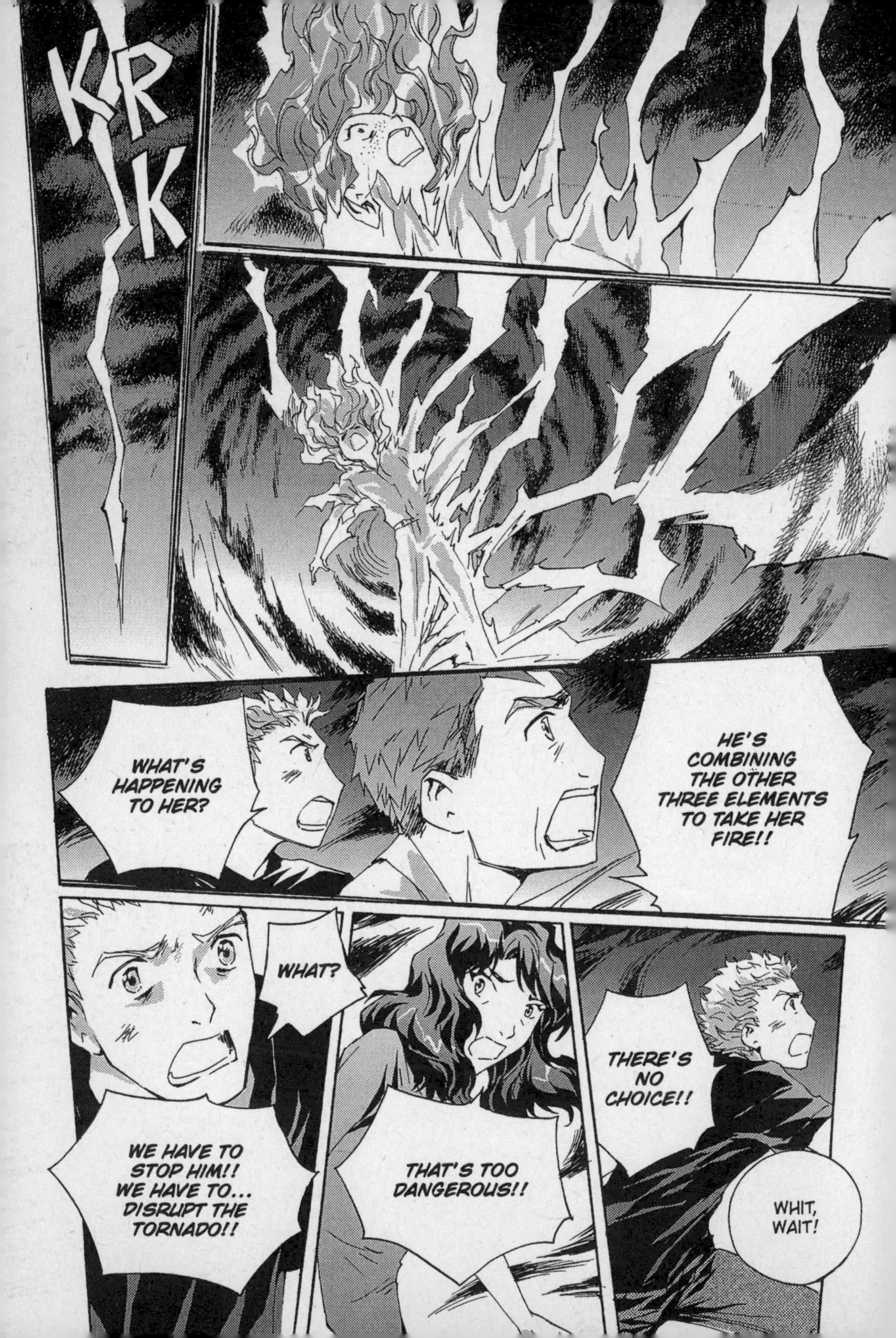
KRK
WHAT'S HAPPENING TO HER?
HE'S COMBINING THE OTHER THREE ELEMENTS TO TAKE HER FIRE!!
WHAT?
WE HAVE TO STOP HIM!! WE HAVE TO... DISRUPT THE TORNADO!!
THAT'S TOO DANGEROUS!!
THERE'S NO CHOICE!!
WHIT, WAIT!

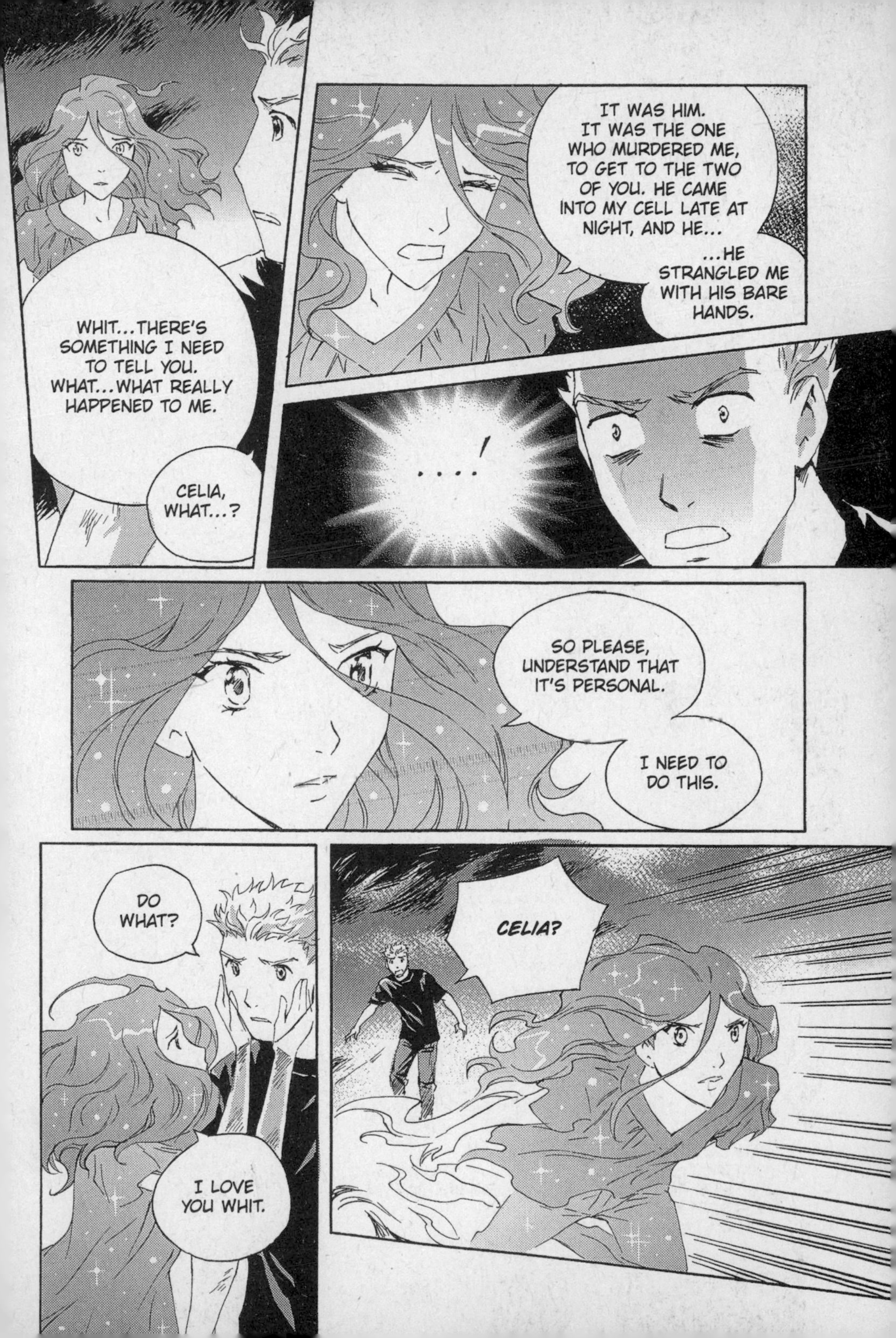
WHIT...THERE'S SOMETHING I NEED TO TELL YOU. WHAT...WHAT REALLY HAPPENED TO ME.
CELIA, WHAT...?
IT WAS HIM. IT WAS THE ONE WHO MURDERED ME, TO GET TO THE TWO OF YOU. HE CAME INTO MY CELL LATE AT NIGHT, AND HE...
...HE STRANGLED ME WITH HIS BARE HANDS.
....!
SO PLEASE, UNDERSTAND THAT IT'S PERSONAL.
I NEED TO DO THIS.
DO WHAT?
I LOVE YOU WHIT.
CELIA?

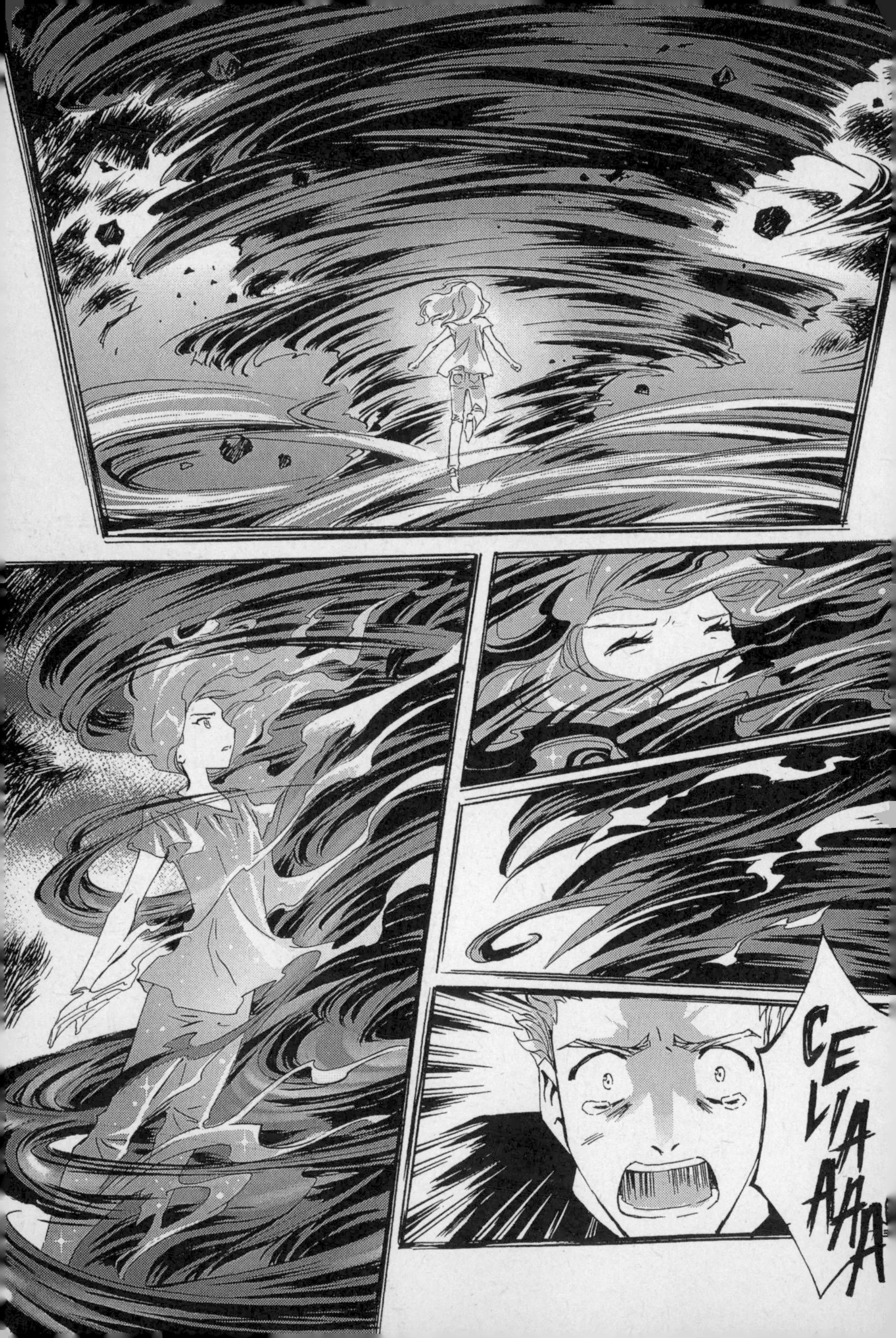
CELIAAAAA

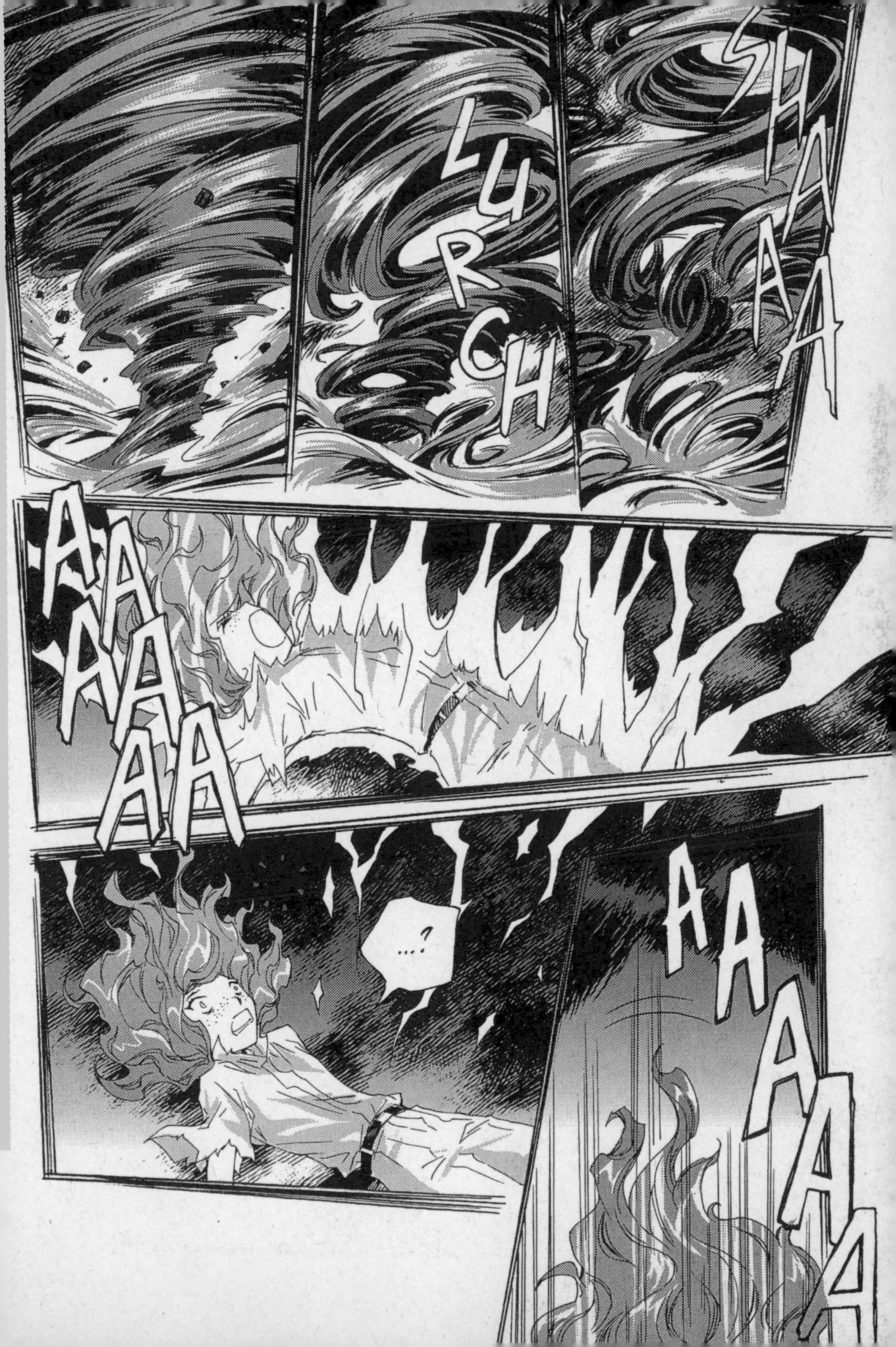
SHAAAA
LURCH
AAAAAAA
...?
AAAAAA

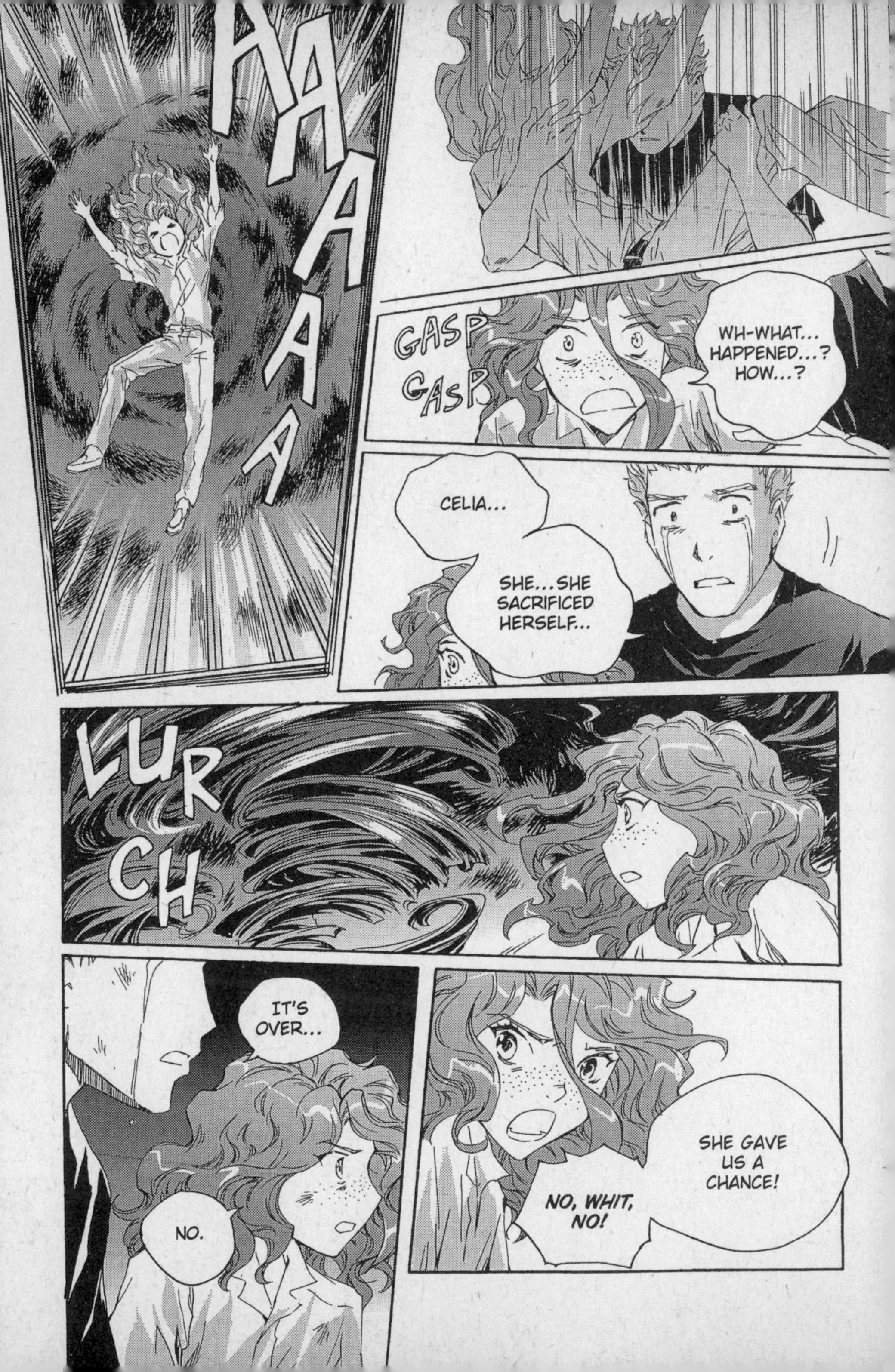
AAAAAAA
GASP GASP
WH-WHAT... HAPPENED...? HOW...?
CELIA...
SHE...SHE SACRIFICED HERSELF...
LURCH
IT'S OVER...
NO.
SHE GAVE US A CHANCE!
NO, WHIT, NO!

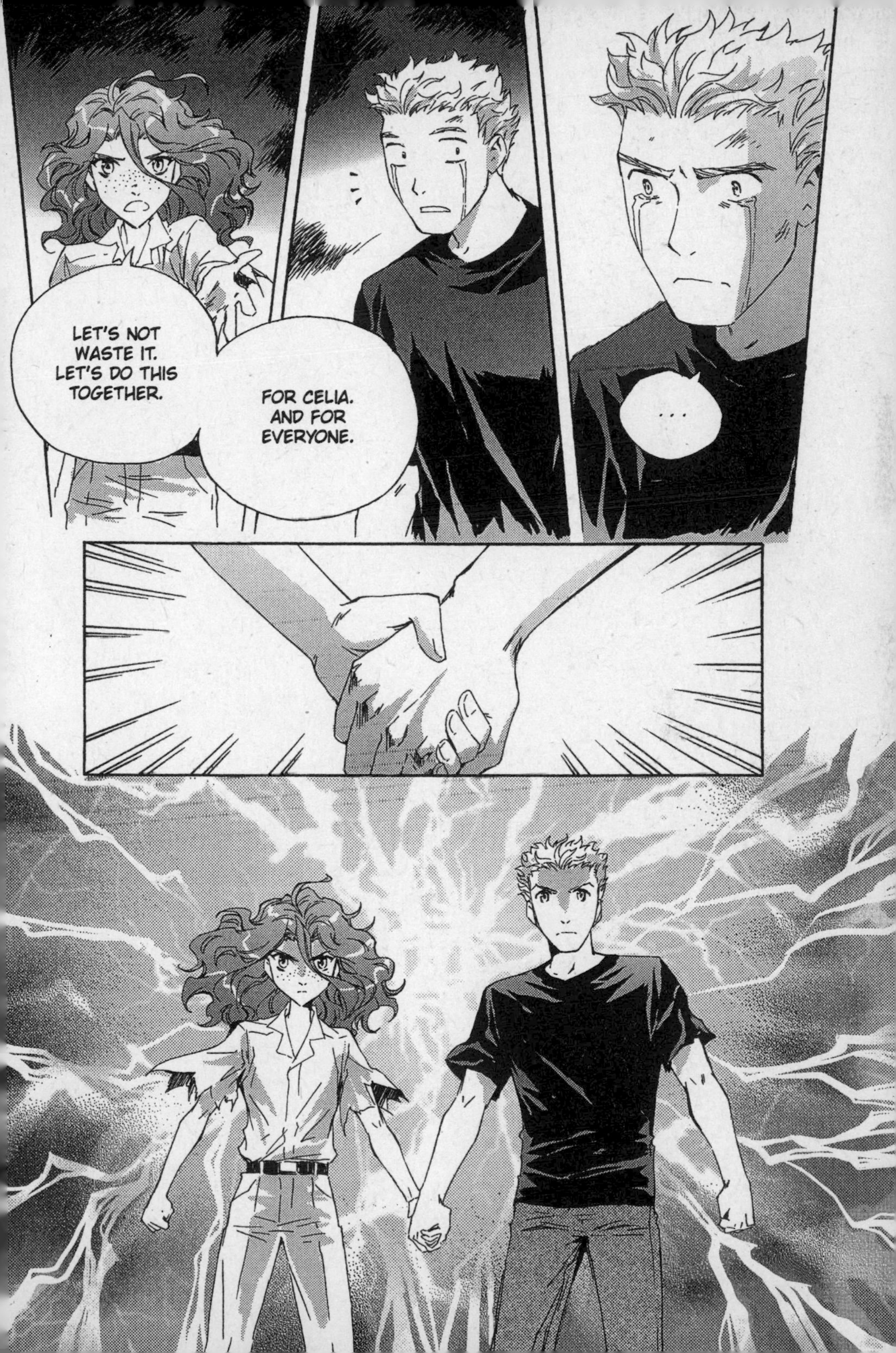
LET'S NOT WASTE IT. LET'S DO THIS TOGETHER.
FOR CELIA. AND FOR EVERYONE.
...

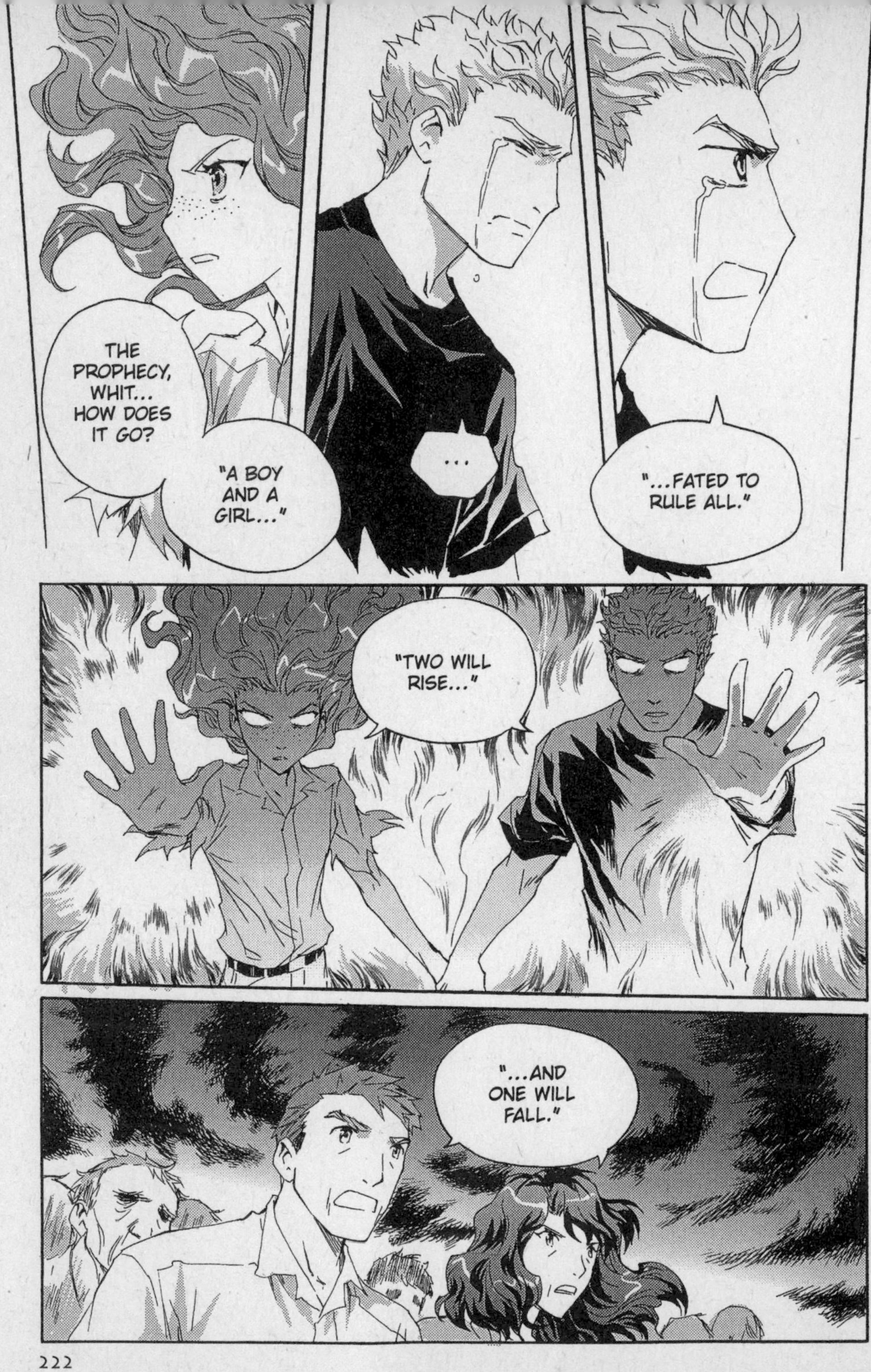
THE PROPHECY, WHIT... HOW DOES IT GO?
"A BOY AND A GIRL..."
...
"...FATED TO RULE ALL."
"TWO WILL RISE..."
"...AND ONE WILL FALL."

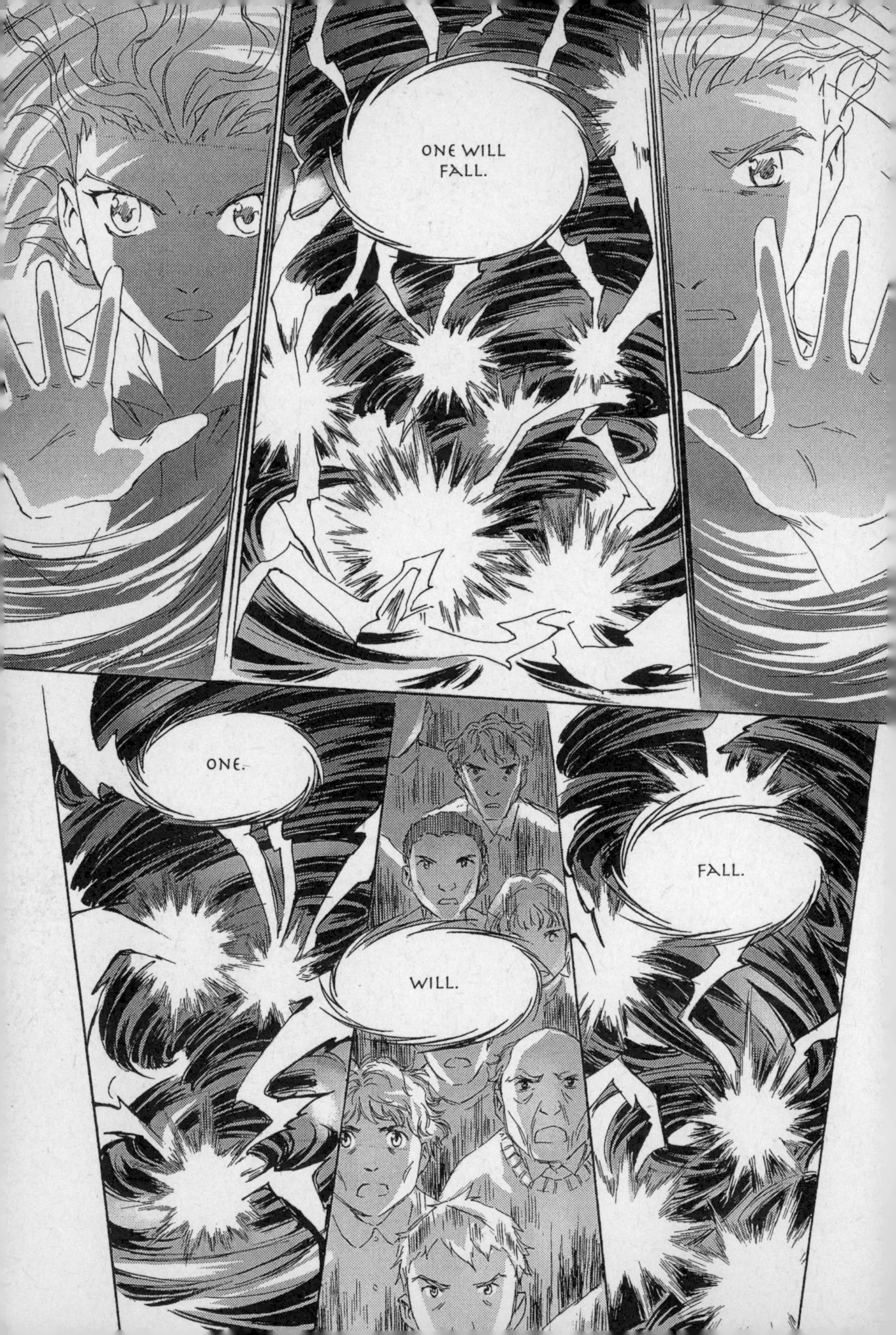
ONE WILL FALL.
ONE.
WILL.
FALL.

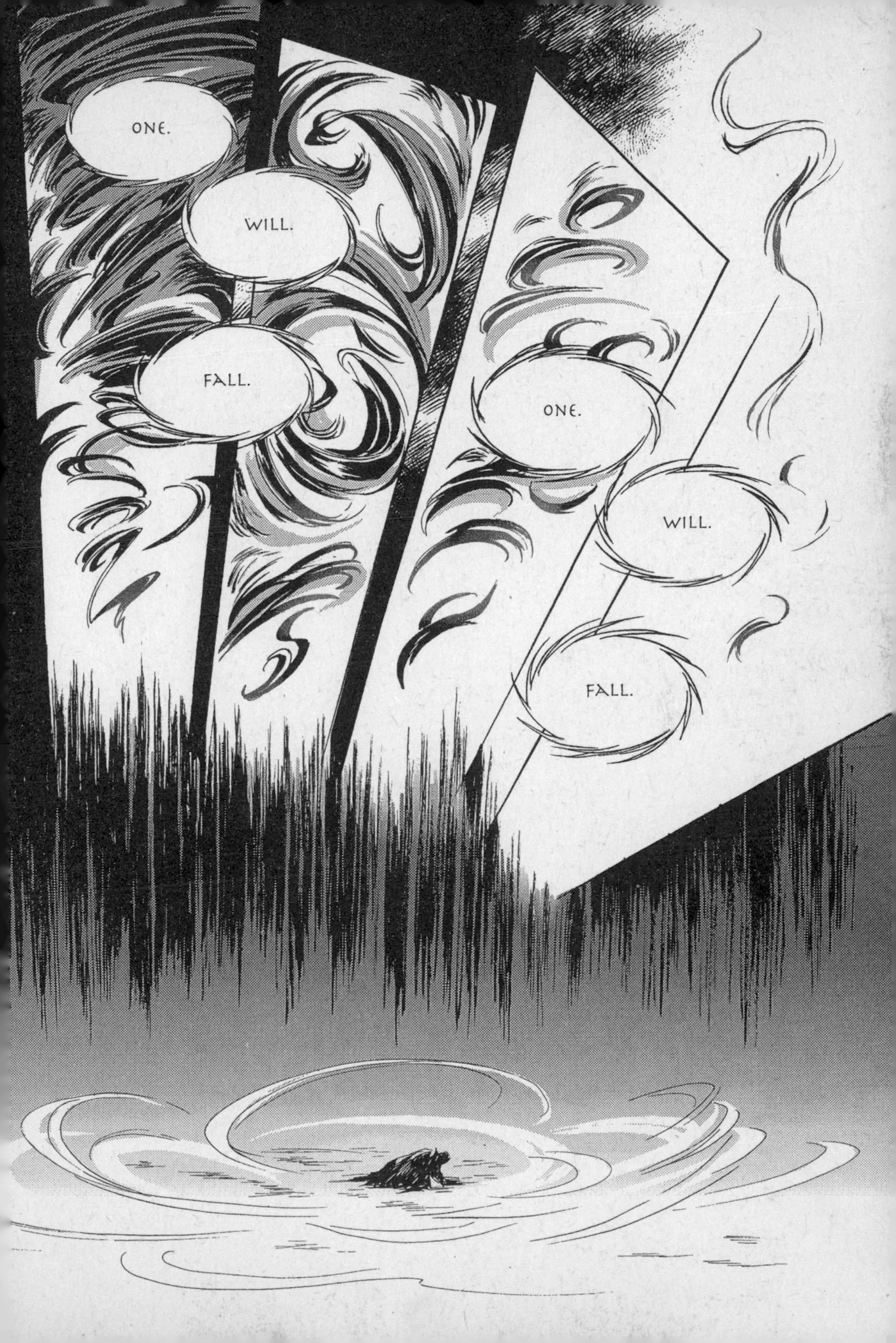
ONE.
WILL.
FALL.
ONE.
WILL.
FALL.

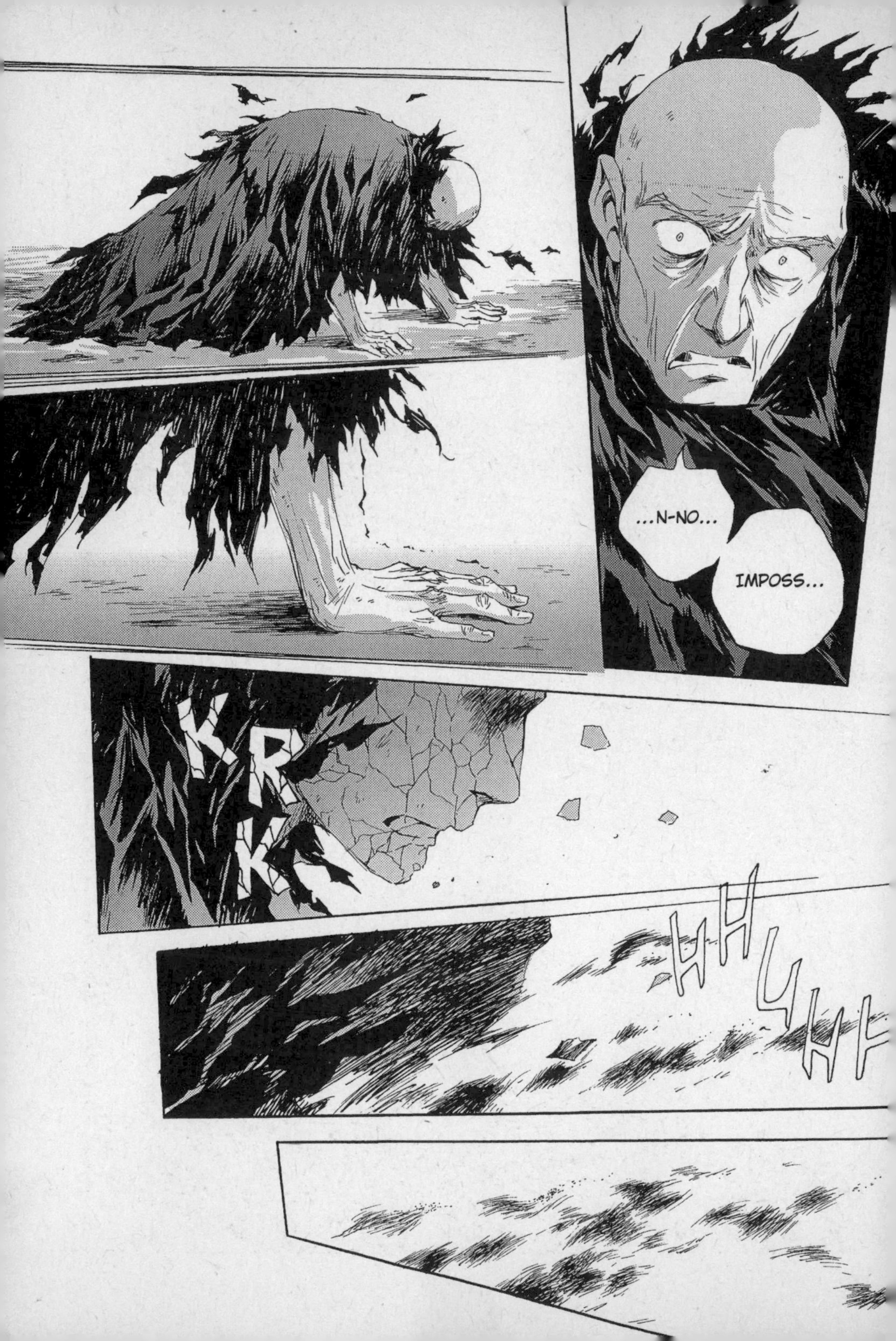
...N-NO...
IMPOSS...
KRK
WHUHH

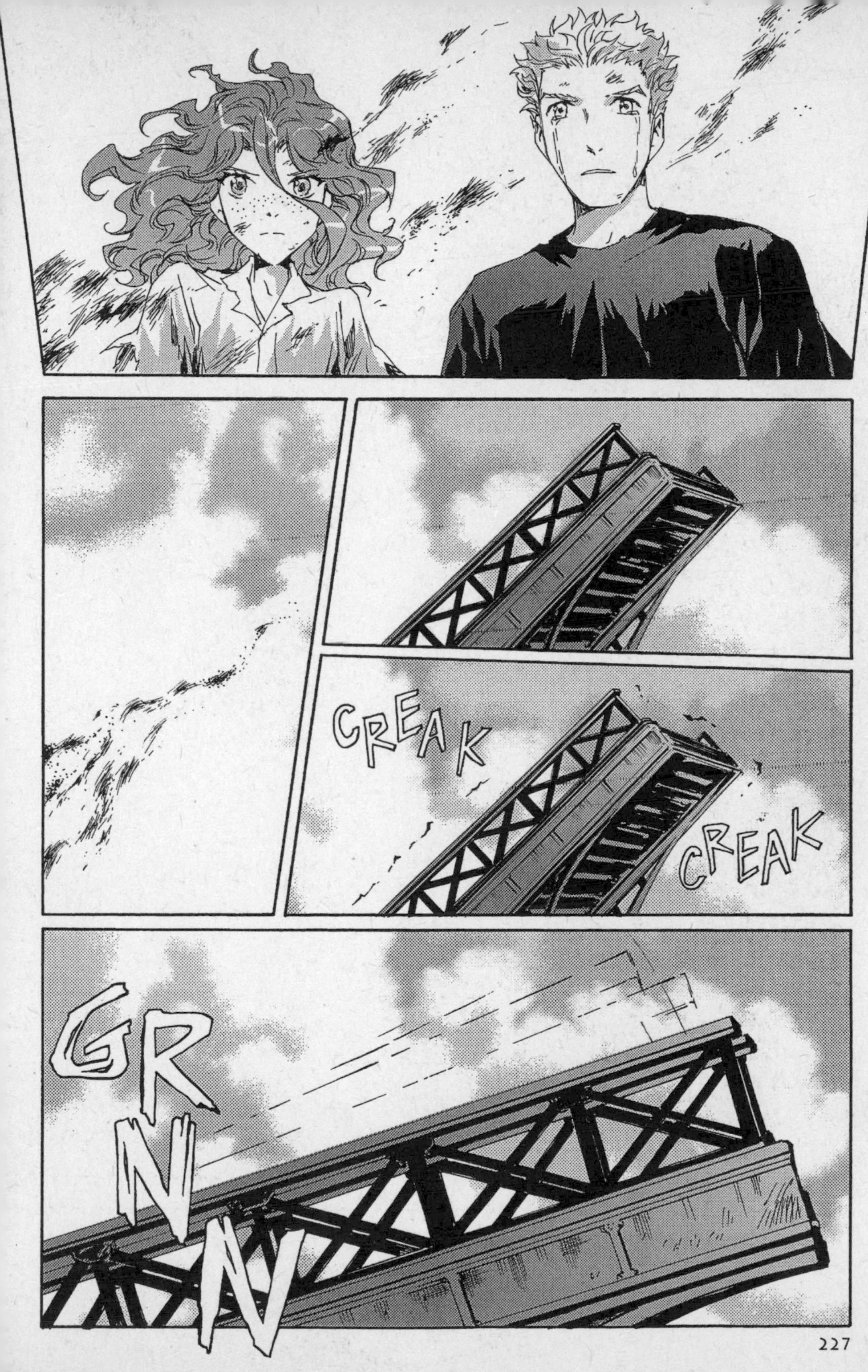
CREAK
CREAK
GRNN

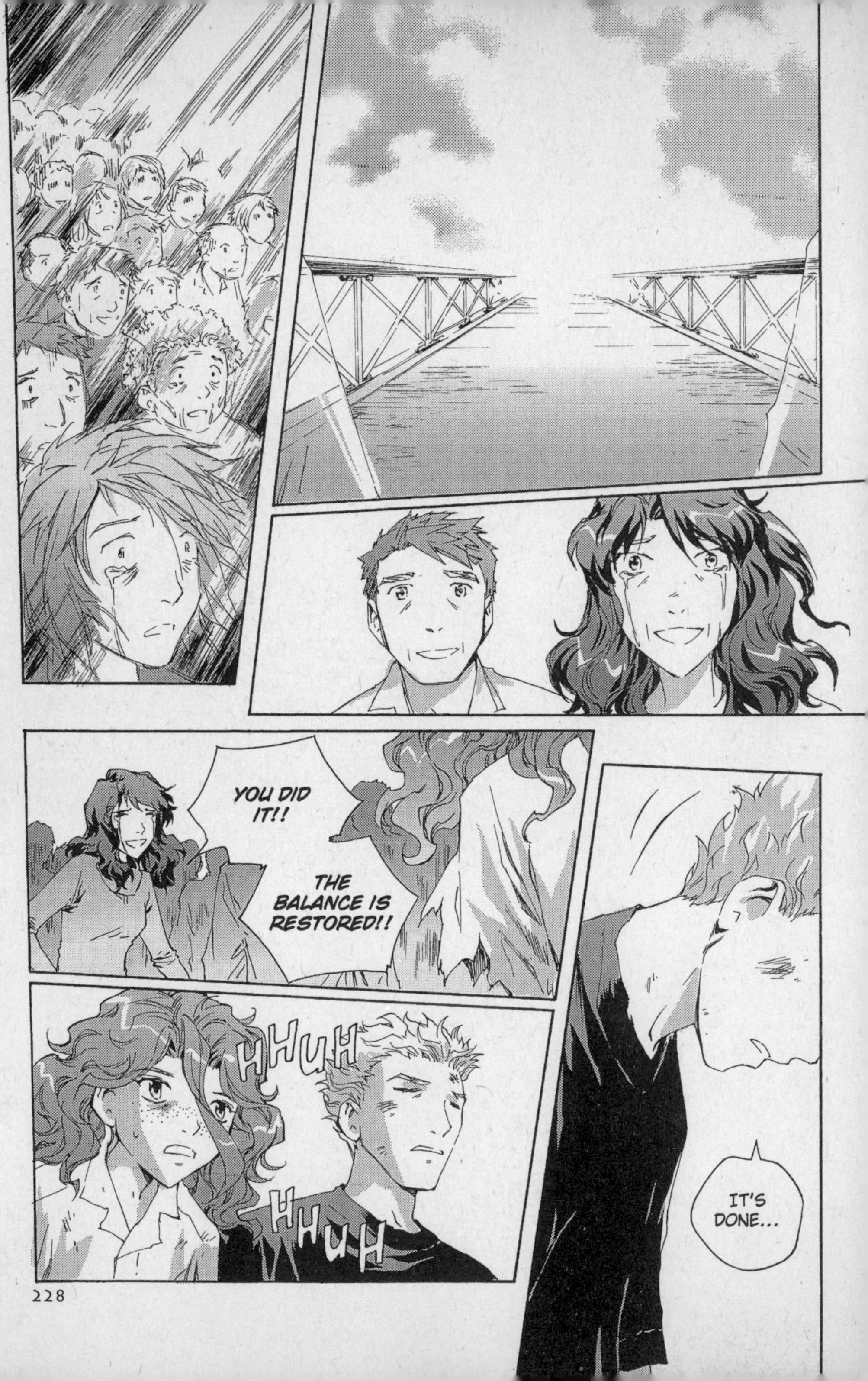
YOU DID IT!!
THE BALANCE IS RESTORED!!
HHUH
HHUH
IT'S DONE...

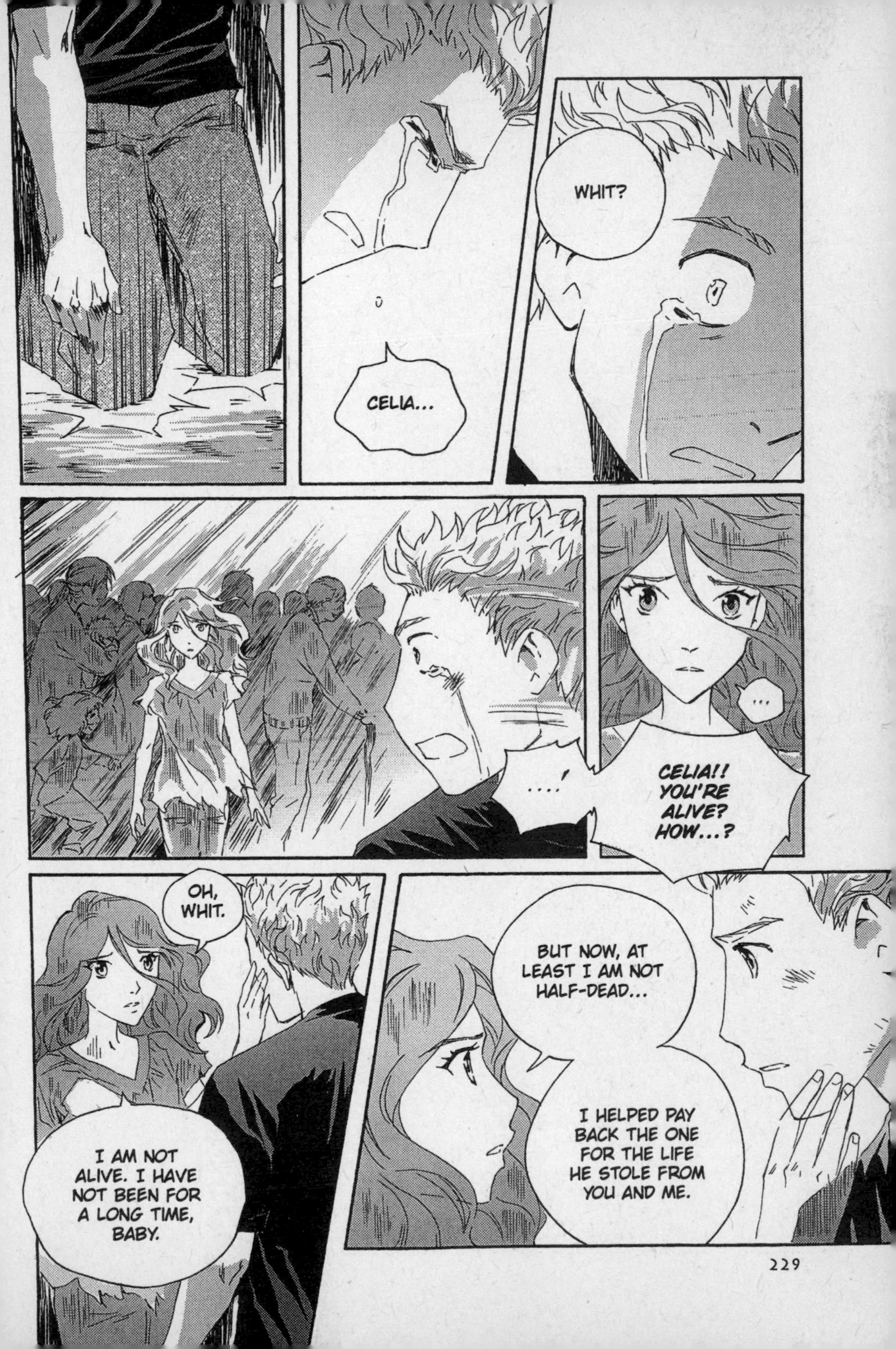
CELIA...
WHIT?
CELIA!! YOU'RE ALIVE? HOW...?
...!
...
OH, WHIT.
I AM NOT ALIVE. I HAVE NOT BEEN FOR A LONG TIME, BABY.
BUT NOW, AT LEAST I AM NOT HALF-DEAD...
I HELPED PAY BACK THE ONE FOR THE LIFE HE STOLE FROM YOU AND ME.

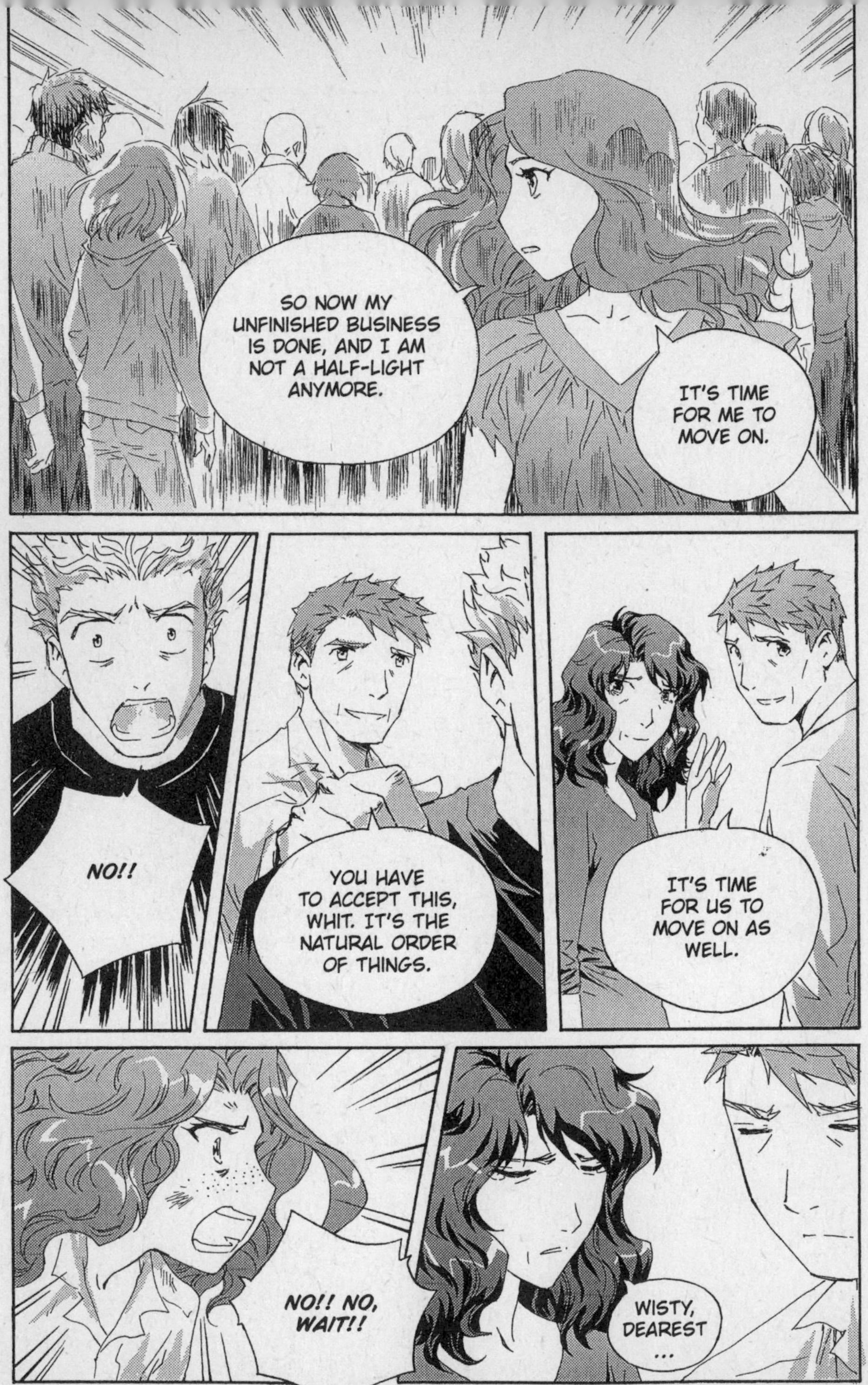
SO NOW MY UNFINISHED BUSINESS IS DONE, AND I AM NOT A HALF-LIGHT ANYMORE.
IT'S TIME FOR ME TO MOVE ON.
NO!!
YOU HAVE TO ACCEPT THIS, WHIT. IT'S THE NATURAL ORDER OF THINGS.
IT'S TIME FOR US TO MOVE ON AS WELL.
NO!! NO, WAIT!!
WISTY, DEAREST ...

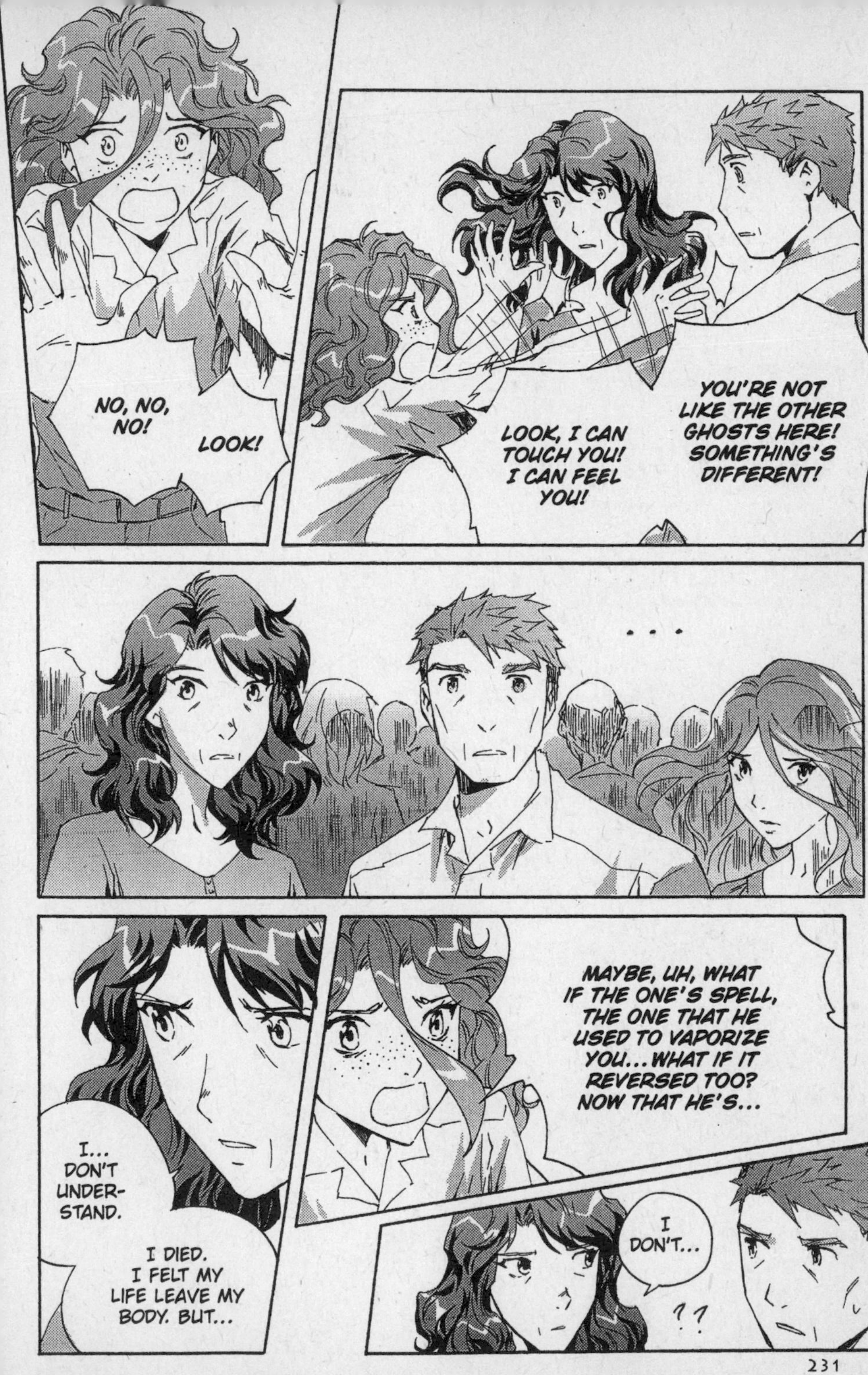
NO, NO, NO!
LOOK!
LOOK, I CAN TOUCH YOU! I CAN FEEL YOU!
YOU'RE NOT LIKE THE OTHER GHOSTS HERE! SOMETHING'S DIFFERENT!
. . .
MAYBE, UH, WHAT IF THE ONE'S SPELL, THE ONE THAT HE USED TO VAPORIZE YOU...WHAT IF IT REVERSED TOO? NOW THAT HE'S...
I... DON'T UNDER-STAND.
I DIED. I FELT MY LIFE LEAVE MY BODY. BUT...
I DON'T...
??

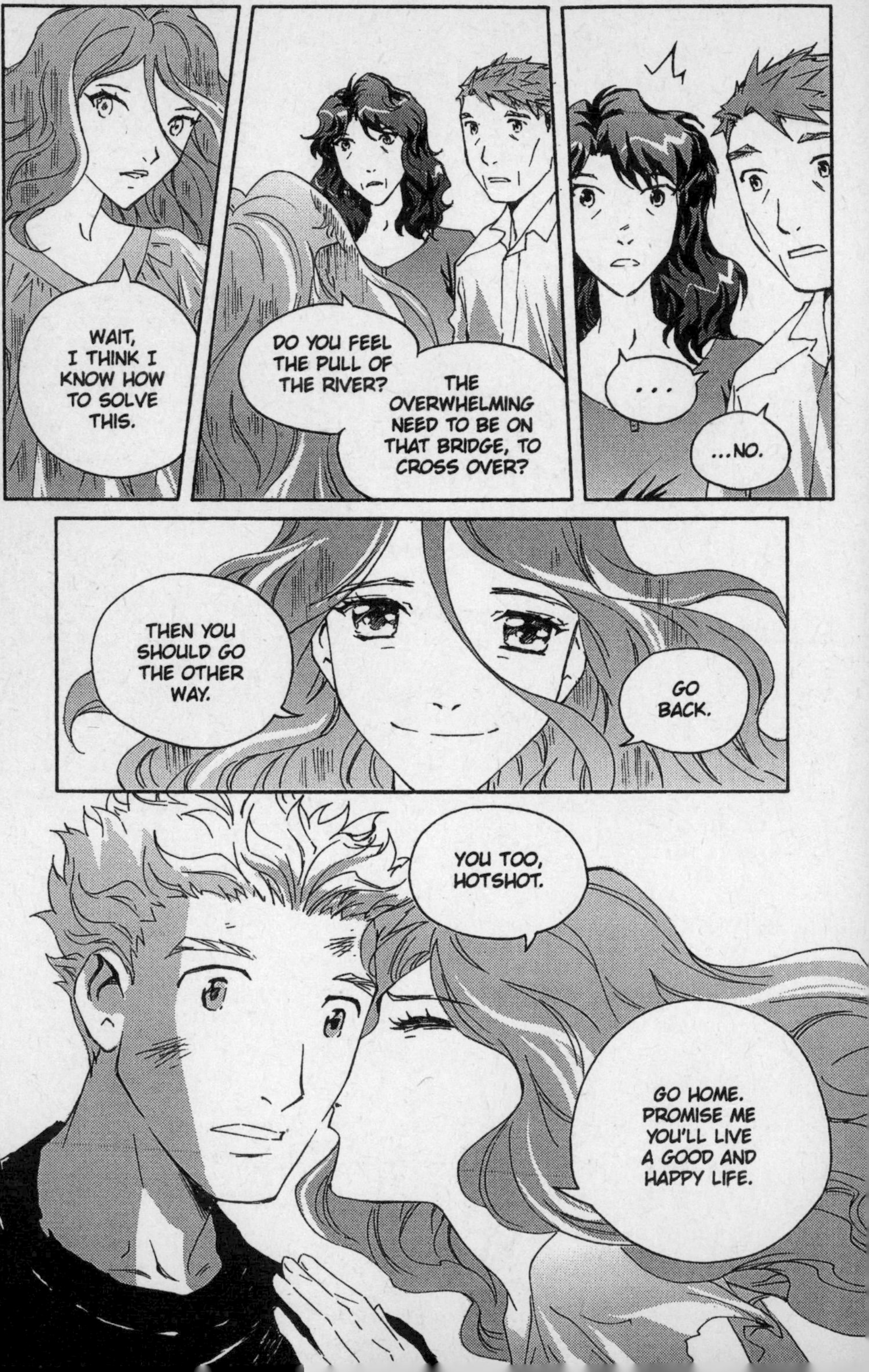
WAIT, I THINK I KNOW HOW TO SOLVE THIS.
DO YOU FEEL THE PULL OF THE RIVER?
THE OVERWHELMING NEED TO BE ON THAT BRIDGE, TO CROSS OVER?
...
...NO.
THEN YOU SHOULD GO THE OTHER WAY.
GO BACK.
YOU TOO, HOTSHOT.
GO HOME. PROMISE ME YOU'LL LIVE A GOOD AND HAPPY LIFE.

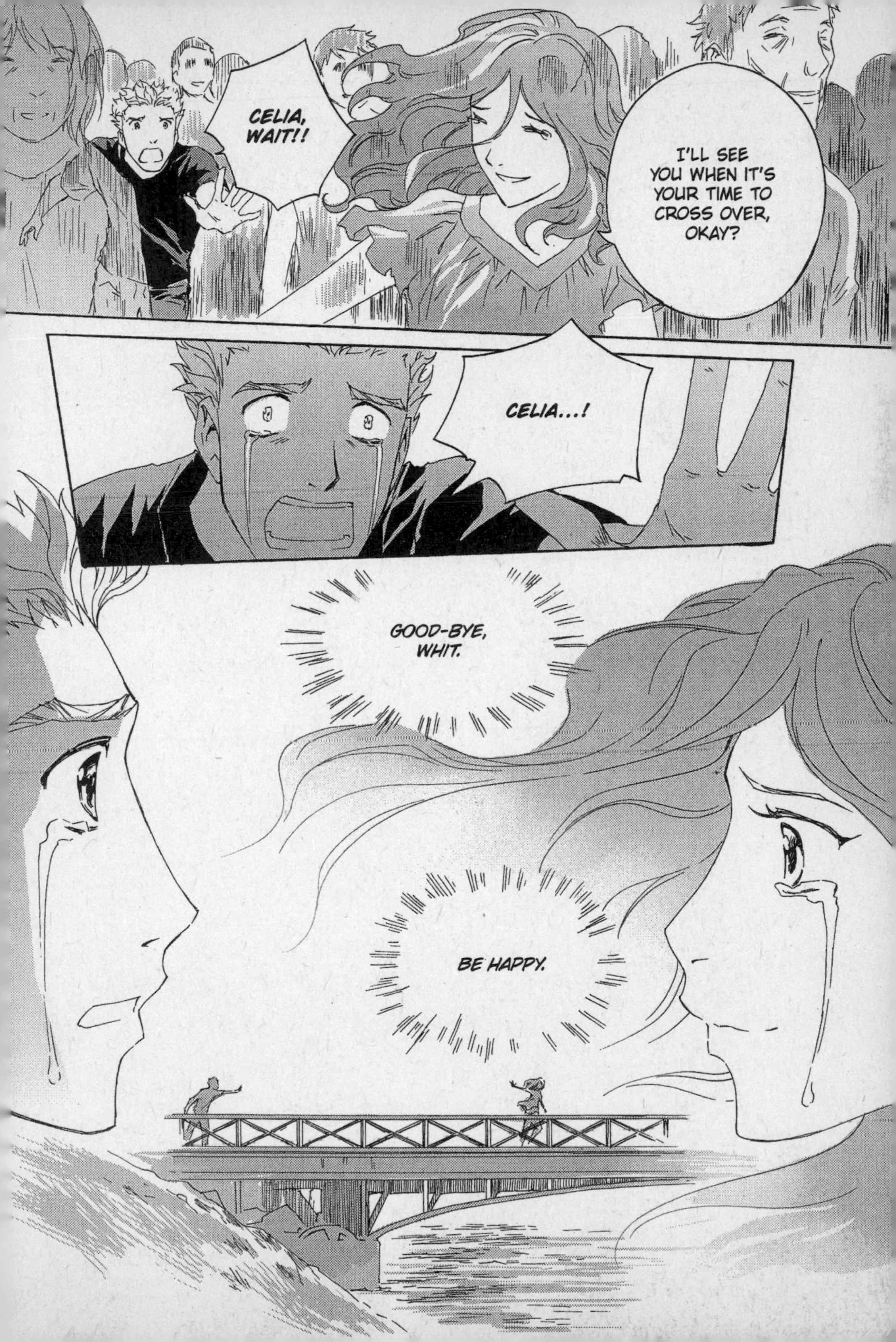
CELIA, WAIT!!
I'LL SEE YOU WHEN IT'S YOUR TIME TO CROSS OVER, OKAY?
CELIA...!
GOOD-BYE, WHIT.
BE HAPPY.

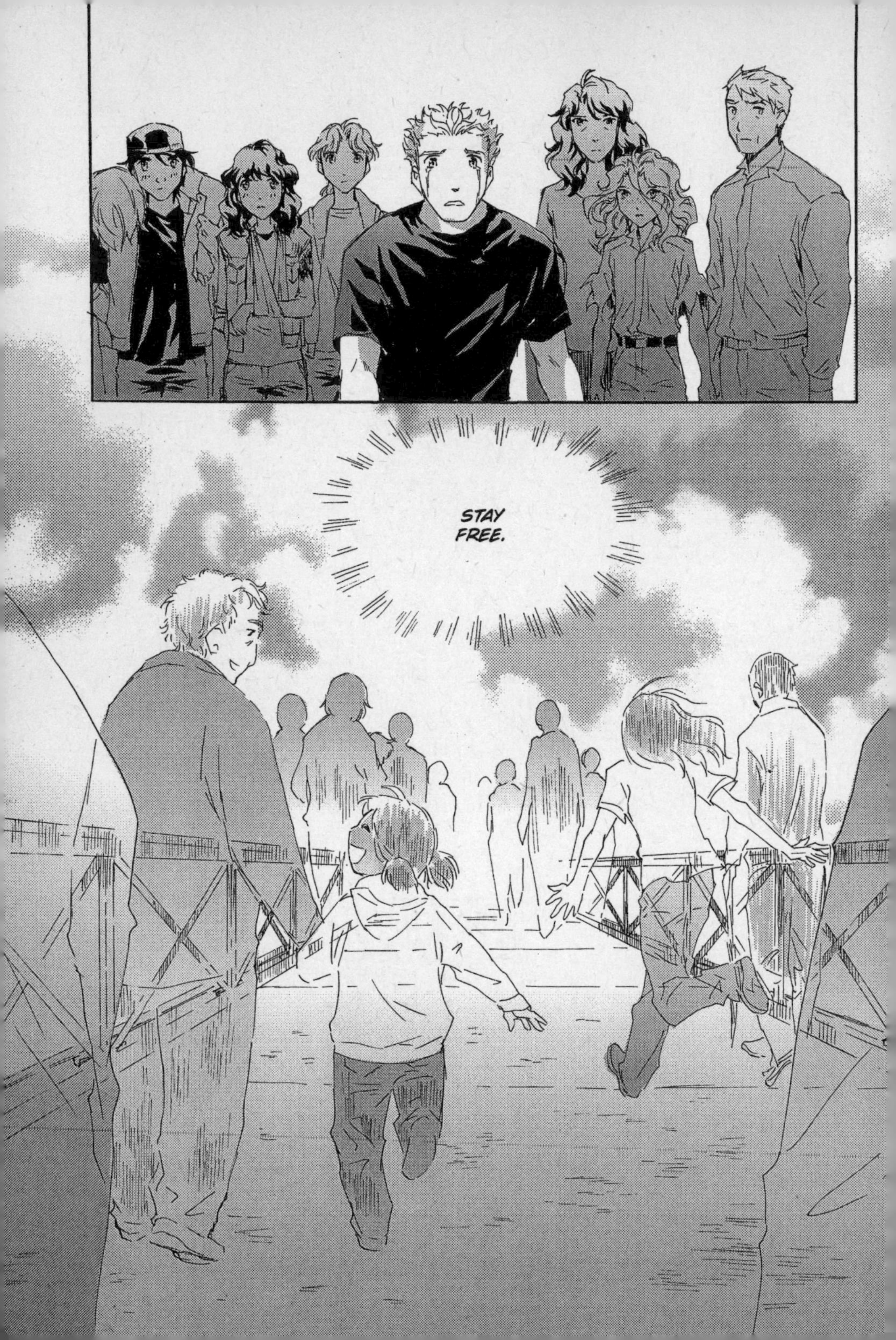
STAY FREE.

WITCH & WIZARD

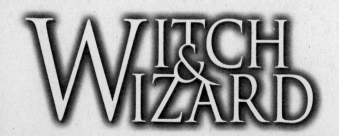

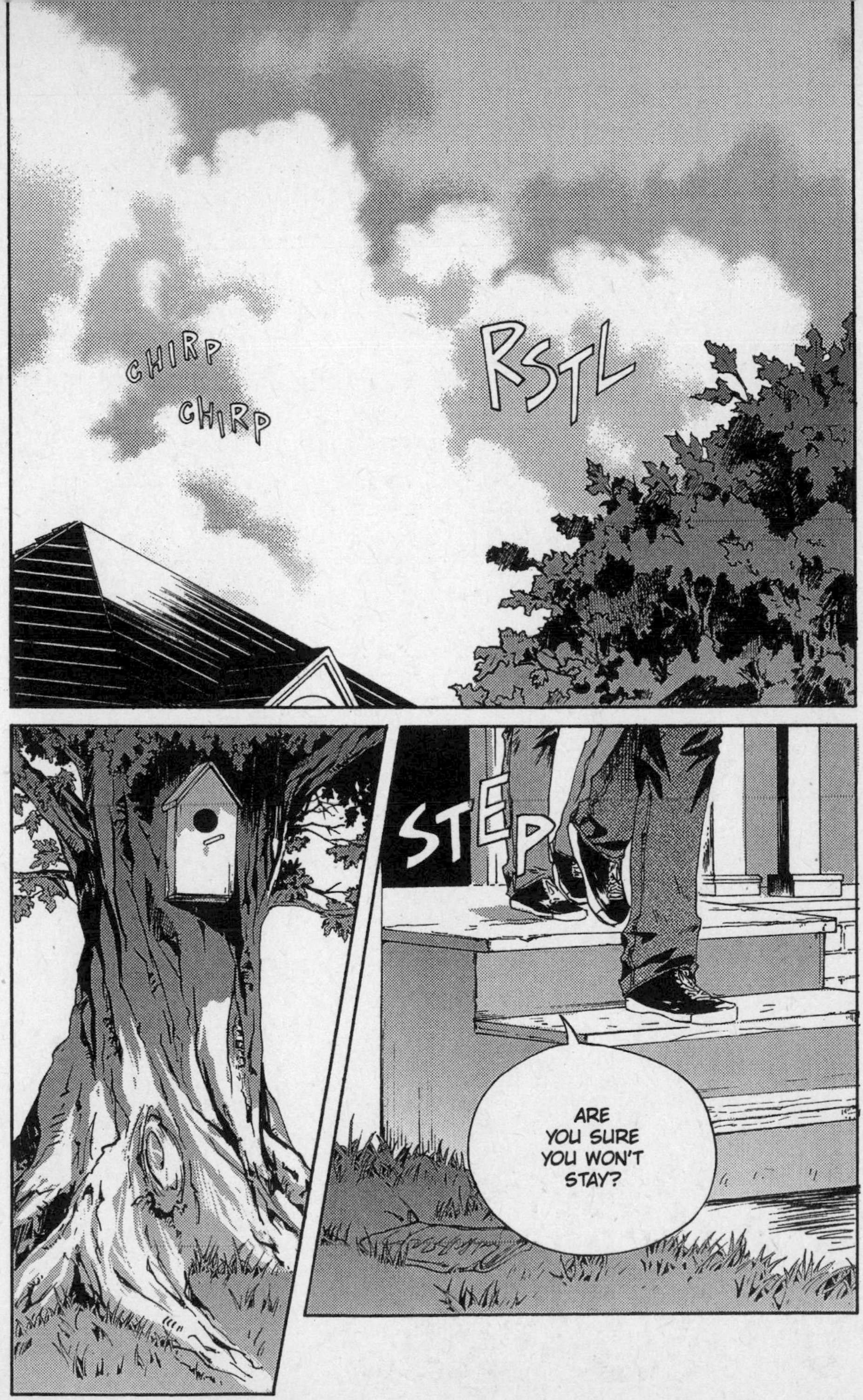
CHIRP
CHIRP
RSTL
STEP
ARE YOU SURE YOU WON'T STAY?

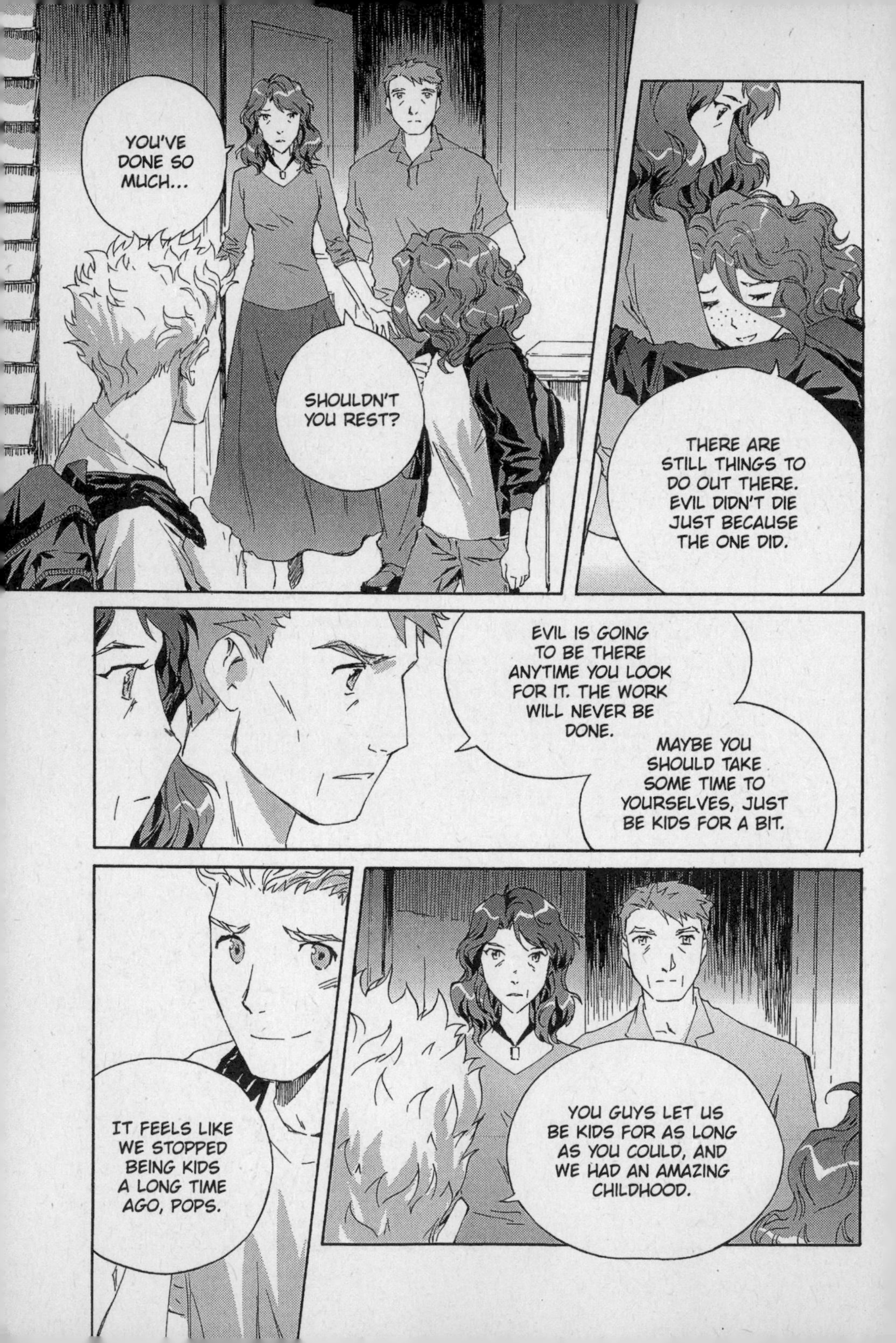
YOU'VE DONE SO MUCH...
SHOULDN'T YOU REST?
THERE ARE STILL THINGS TO DO OUT THERE. EVIL DIDN'T DIE JUST BECAUSE THE ONE DID.
EVIL IS GOING TO BE THERE ANYTIME YOU LOOK FOR IT. THE WORK WILL NEVER BE DONE.
MAYBE YOU SHOULD TAKE SOME TIME TO YOURSELVES, JUST BE KIDS FOR A BIT.
IT FEELS LIKE WE STOPPED BEING KIDS A LONG TIME AGO, POPS.
YOU GUYS LET US BE KIDS FOR AS LONG AS YOU COULD, AND WE HAD AN AMAZING CHILDHOOD.

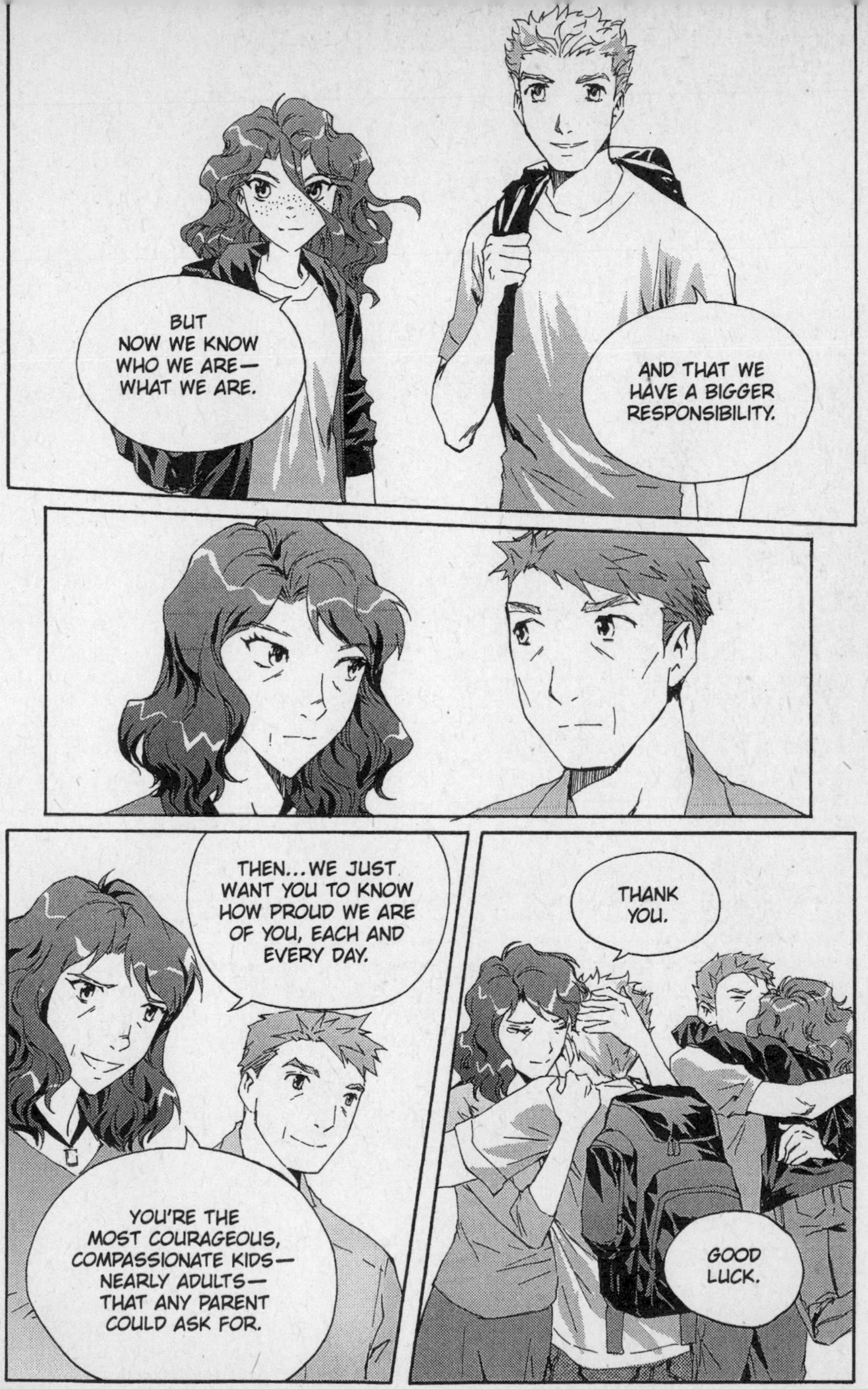
BUT NOW WE KNOW WHO WE ARE— WHAT WE ARE.
AND THAT WE HAVE A BIGGER RESPONSIBILITY.
THEN...WE JUST WANT YOU TO KNOW HOW PROUD WE ARE OF YOU, EACH AND EVERY DAY.
YOU'RE THE MOST COURAGEOUS, COMPASSIONATE KIDS— NEARLY ADULTS— THAT ANY PARENT COULD ASK FOR.
THANK YOU.
GOOD LUCK.

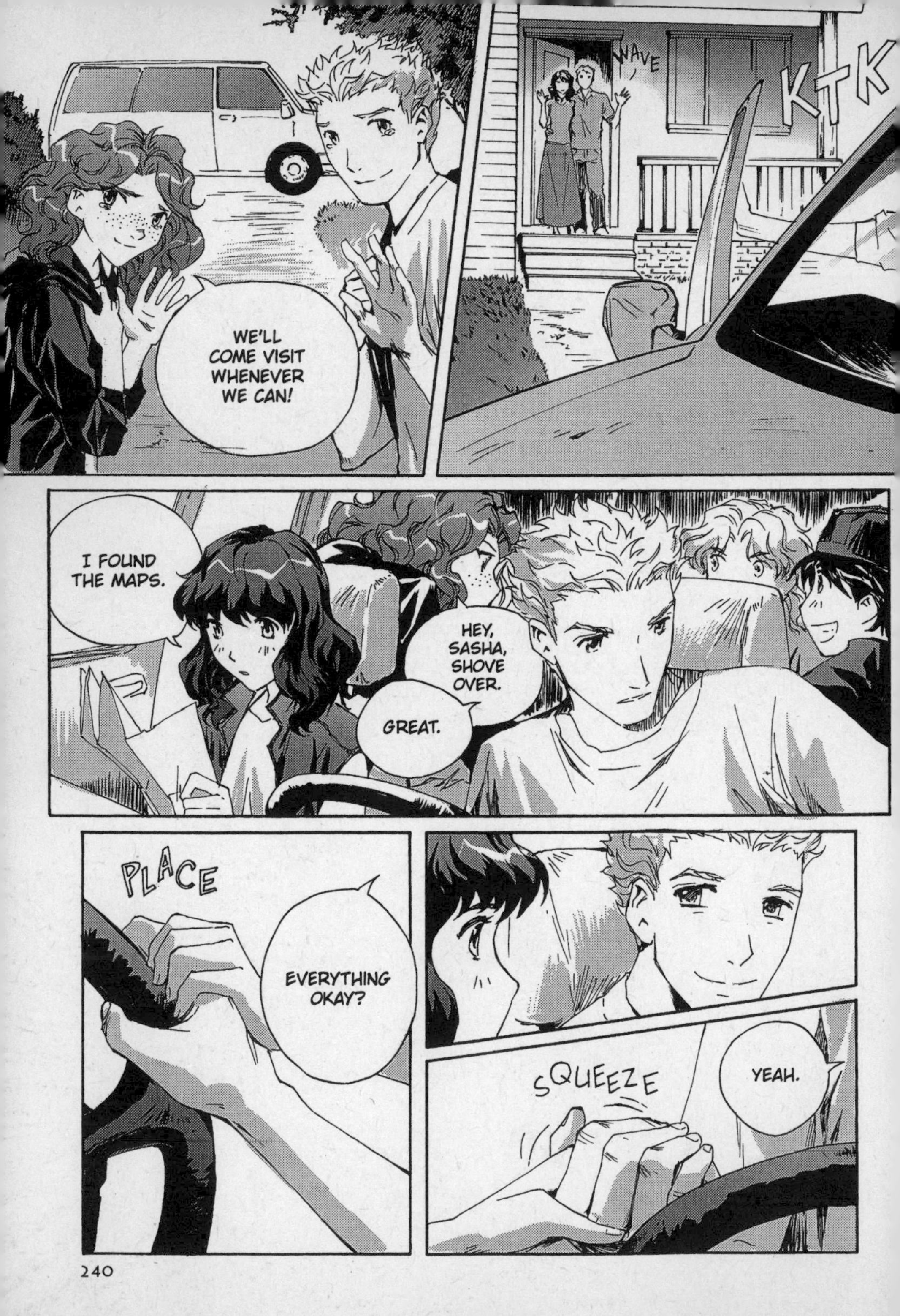
WE'LL COME VISIT WHENEVER WE CAN!
WAVE
KTK
I FOUND THE MAPS.
HEY, SASHA, SHOVE OVER.
GREAT.
PLACE
EVERYTHING OKAY?
SQUEEZE
YEAH.

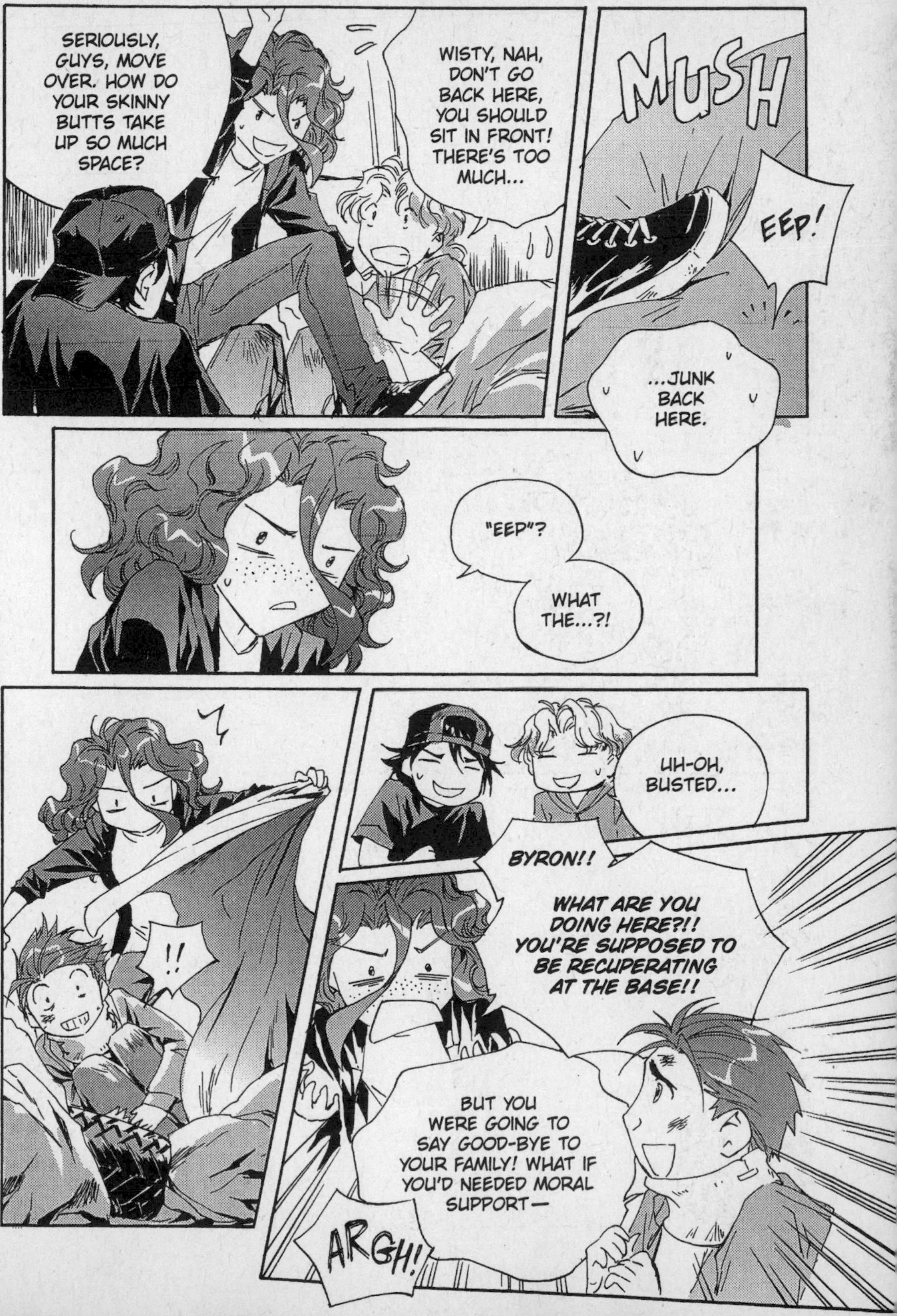
SERIOUSLY, GUYS, MOVE OVER. HOW DO YOUR SKINNY BUTTS TAKE UP SO MUCH SPACE?
WISTY, NAH, DON'T GO BACK HERE, YOU SHOULD SIT IN FRONT! THERE'S TOO MUCH...
MUSH
EEP!
...JUNK BACK HERE.
"EEP"?
WHAT THE...?!
!!
UH-OH, BUSTED...
BYRON!!
WHAT ARE YOU DOING HERE?!! YOU'RE SUPPOSED TO BE RECUPERATING AT THE BASE!!
BUT YOU WERE GOING TO SAY GOOD-BYE TO YOUR FAMILY! WHAT IF YOU'D NEEDED MORAL SUPPORT—
ARGH!

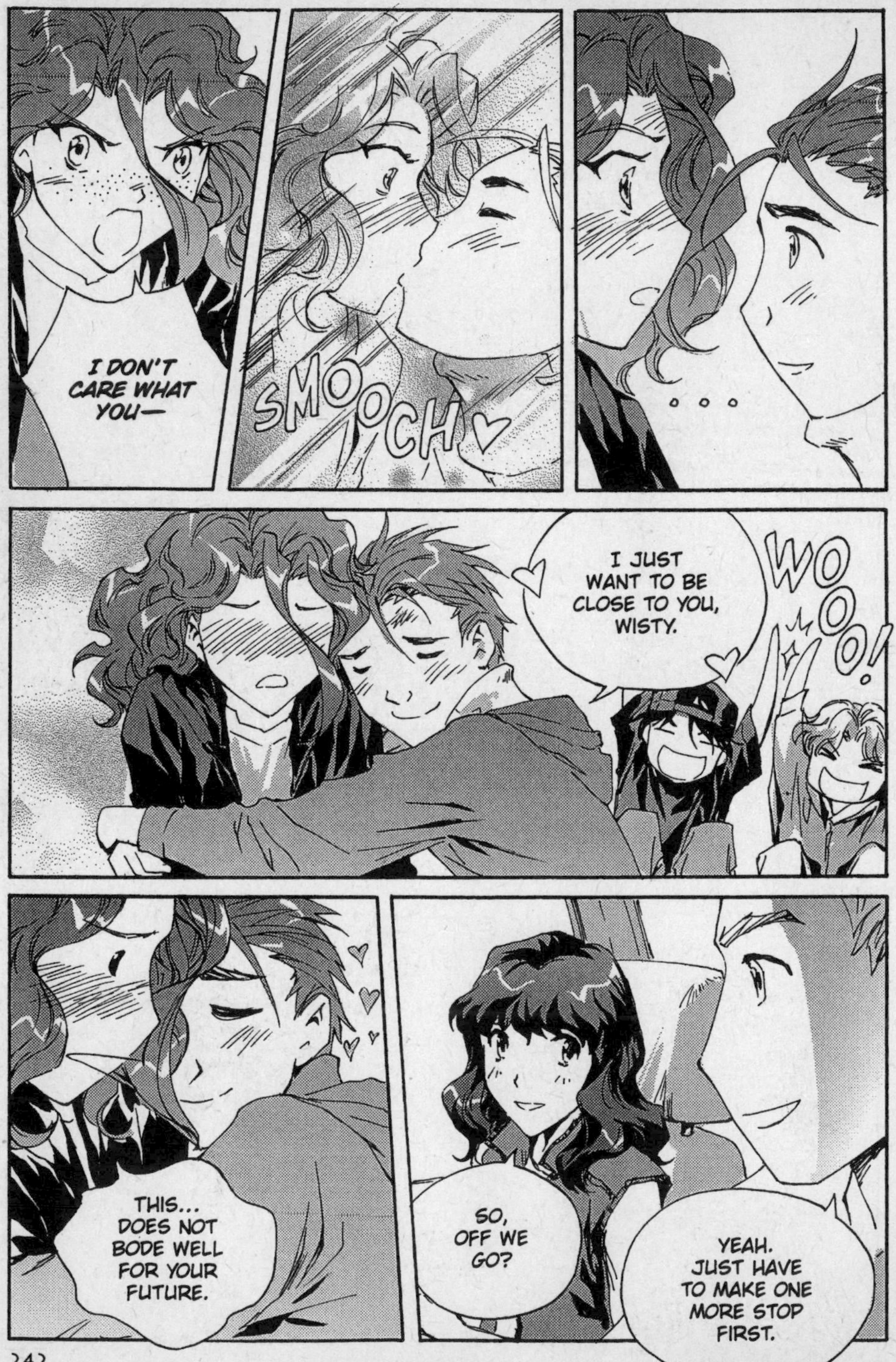
I DON'T CARE WHAT YOU—
SMOOCH ♥
. . .
I JUST WANT TO BE CLOSE TO YOU, WISTY.
WOOOO!
THIS... DOES NOT BODE WELL FOR YOUR FUTURE.
SO, OFF WE GO?
YEAH. JUST HAVE TO MAKE ONE MORE STOP FIRST.

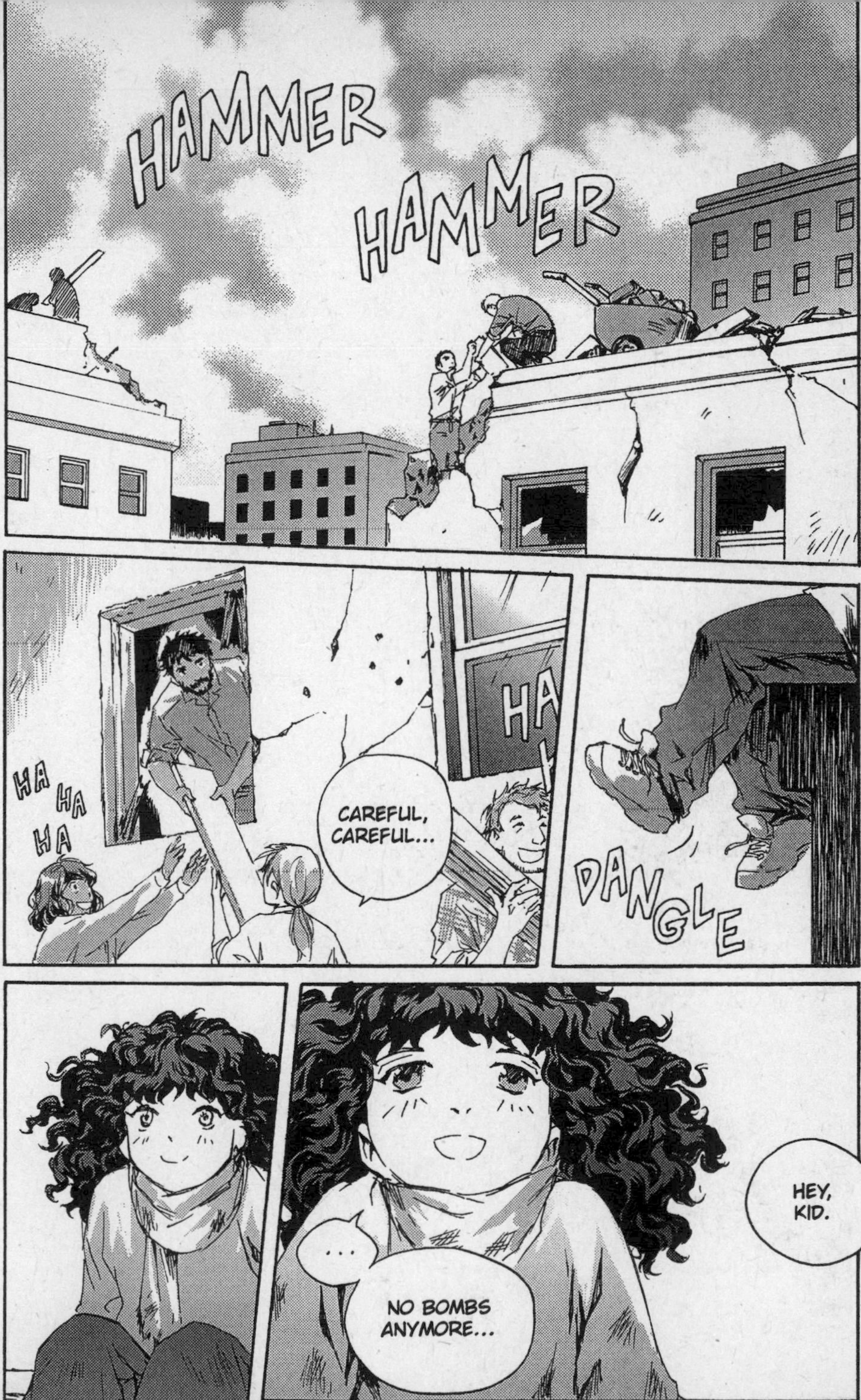
HAMMER
HAMMER
DANGLE
HA
CAREFUL, CAREFUL...
HA HA HA
HEY, KID.
...
NO BOMBS ANYMORE...

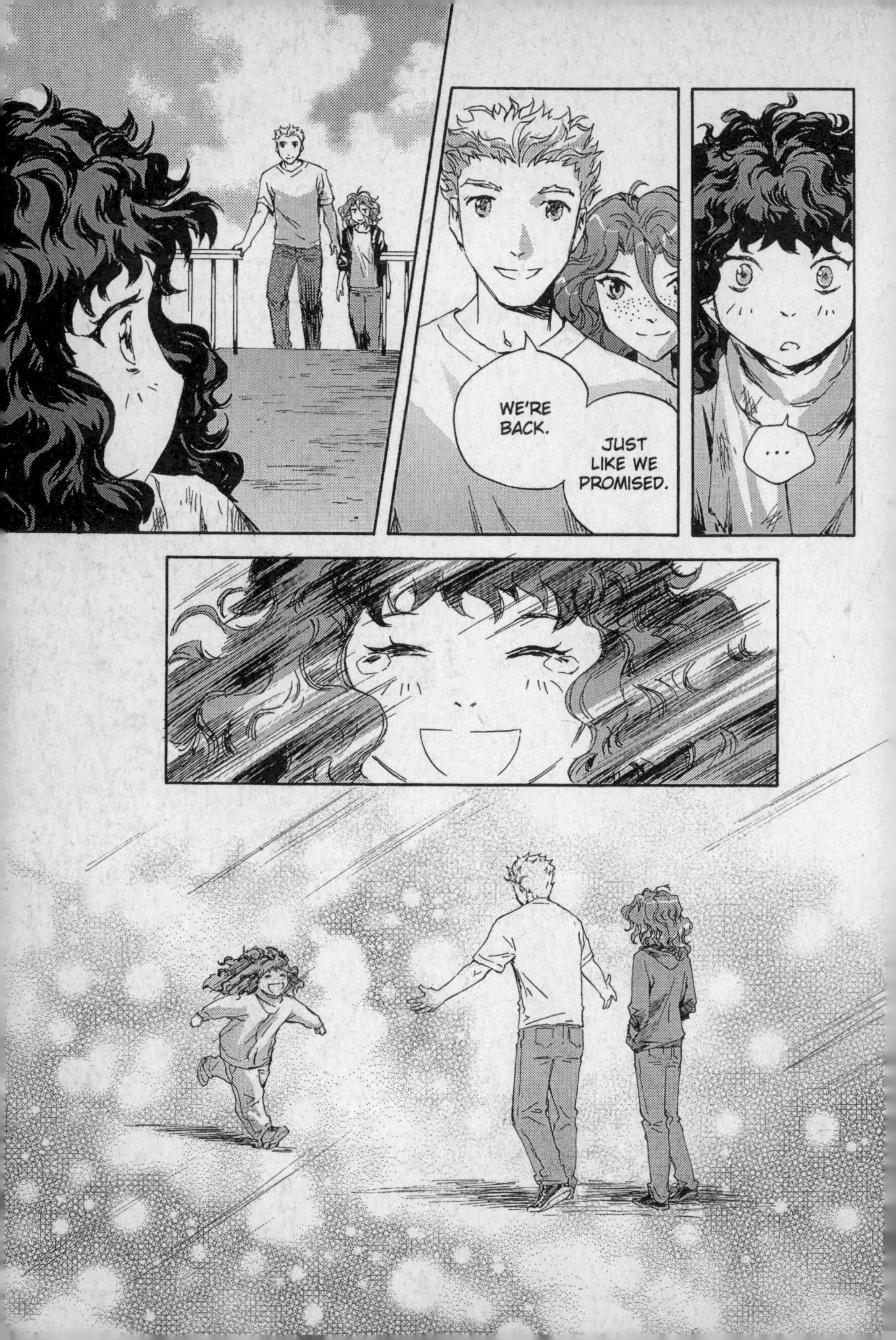
WE'RE BACK.
JUST LIKE WE PROMISED.
...